BASEBALL
MEAT MARKET

BASEBALL MEAT MARKET

THE STORIES BEHIND THE BEST AND WORST TRADES IN HISTORY

SHAWN KREST

PAGE STREET
PUBLISHING CO.

PAGE STREET
PUBLISHING CO.

Copyright © 2017 Shawn Krest

First published in 2017 by
Page Street Publishing Co.
27 Congress Street, Suite 105
Salem, MA 01970
www.pagestreetpublishing.com

Distributed by Macmillan, sales in Canada by The Canadian Manda Group.

20 19 18 17   1 2 3 4

ISBN-13: 978-1-62414-238-3   **33614080199218**
ISBN-10: 1-62414-238-9

Library of Congress Control Number: 2016951738

Cover and book design by Page Street Publishing Co.

Printed and bound in the United States

Page Street is proud to be a member of 1% for the Planet. Members donate one percent of their sales to one or more of the over 1,500 environmental and sustainability charities across the globe who participate in this program.

First book goes to Dad.
But my girls also get a mention—Kayla, Gayle,
Lauren, Kimmy and Krissy

CONTENTS

Introduction   *9*

What Is WAR?   *13*

FIRE SALE!   14
THE STORY BEHIND THE MIKE PIAZZA TRADE

A shameful dismantling of a champion hits its low point.

GUESS WHO'S COMING TO THANKSGIVING DINNER   25
THE STORY BEHIND THE CURT SCHILLING TRADE

A holiday road trip and strong stomachs produce a memorable trade.

AU REVOIR, MONTREAL   35
THE STORY BEHIND THE BARTOLO COLÓN TRADE

A city's last stand deserved a better trade.

TO HAVE AND HAVE NOT   46
THE STORY BEHIND THE QUARTER-BILLION-DOLLAR TRADE

The rare salary dump that produces a good trade.

A TRADE ABOUT NOTHING   56
THE STORY BEHIND THE JAY BUHNER TRADE

When comedians use your trade for material, you've made a bad trade.

THE 180-DEGREE RIP-OFF   66
THE STORY BEHIND THE JOHN SMOLTZ TRADE

Both teams get exactly what they wanted and then some, the definition of a good deal.

THE WHITE FLAG TRADE   75
THE STORY BEHIND THE WILSON ÁLVAREZ TRADE

A team pulls the plug too soon with a deplorable deal.

THE THROW-IN   84
THE STORY BEHIND THE RYNE SANDBERG TRADE

A second-thought throw in turns out to be a winning lottery ticket in this top-shelf trade.

NOTHING TO CELEBRATE   95
THE STORY BEHIND THE MIGUEL CABRERA TRADE

A once-in-a-generation talent, traded away for a forgettable package of prospects.

FOR SALE TO THE SECOND-HIGHEST BIDDER   107
THE STORY BEHIND THE ALEX RODRIGUEZ TRADE

A bad free-agent contract leads to months of offseason melodrama that frustrated everyone except producers of sports chat shows.

WHO IS RICK SUTCLIFFE?   118
THE STORY BEHIND THE RICK SUTCLIFFE TRADE

Perhaps the best midseason pickup in history leads the Cubs to the postseason.

541
THE STORY BEHIND THE VON HAYES TRADE   127

Paying a big price for a poor fit leads to a much-mocked trade.

A GIFT FROM GOD   137
THE STORY BEHIND THE DAVID WELLS TRADE

Choosing the wrong package of prospects leads to years of regret.

"I'M THE DECIDER, AND I DECIDE WHAT'S BEST"   147
THE STORY BEHIND THE SAMMY SOSA TRADE

The trade bad enough to help win an election.

THE RENT IS TOO DARN HIGH   158
THE STORY BEHIND THE MARK TEIXEIRA TRADE

The Braves get held up in a failed attempt to prolong their dynasty.

WHITE RAT RUN AMOK   170
THE STORY BEHIND THE 1980 WINTER MEETINGS

It's the Whitey Herzog show as a series of shrewd deals helps build dynasties.

THE BLEEPING TRADE   182
THE STORY BEHIND THE BUCKY DENT TRADE

A prospect-for-veteran trade works to perfection.

JUST SEVENTEEN   192
THE STORY BEHIND THE BIGGEST TRADE IN HISTORY

The more the merrier as the Yankees and Orioles put together a gem.

THE NO-SHOWS   201
THE STORY BEHIND THE CURT FLOOD TRADE

A trade that helped reshape the face of baseball.

THE BLOCKBUSTER   210
THE STORY BEHIND THE ROBERTO ALOMAR TRADE

A good old-fashioned baseball trade.

Conclusion   *221*
Acknowledgments   *223*
About the Author   *225*
Index   *226*

— INTRODUCTION —

They call it a bunker because "staff meeting" just doesn't have the same ring to it.

It may shatter the image fans have of Major League Baseball's trade deadline, but much of the work surrounding the giant midseason swap meet that makes and breaks the fortunes of contenders and helps build future dynasties is the same thing that people do in office cubicles around the country every day.

"You have to evaluate where you are as an organization," said former Texas Rangers general manager Tom Grieve—who once traded Sammy Sosa. "What are your needs?"

"You get reports from everyone in the organization," adds Tampa Bay Rays farm director Mitch Lukevics—who was a member of the Yankees' front office when they were debating whether to deal prospects Derek Jeter and Mariano Rivera for immediate pitching help. "Then you put together projections."

And then?

"Then you go into the bunker," Lukevics said.

Then it's deal-making time. Most fans envision a scene similar to the stock market floor, with people frantically shouting into phones as they try to put deals together. Again, they're in for a disappointment.

"You look at the other organizations and try to anticipate what they'll identify as their needs," Grieve explained. "Then you identify teams who match up well with you—where you can meet their needs and they have players that can meet yours."

"You don't just call everyone," Grieve added, shattering another myth. "You focus on the teams where you think you can help each other."

And once the phones start to ring, then it's time to wheel and deal. Bluffs and smoke screens are thrown up, ultimatums issued, as GMs try to wring as much as they can from their trading partner.

Right?

"I mean, I guess it's better if they call you than if you call them," Grieve said. "I guess that gives you a slight advantage in the negotiation. But really you just want to find someone whose projections for your prospects are slightly better than yours."

Yes, by all reports, the day-to-day of the MLB trade deadline is far more humdrum than people would think. Chances are, a fan's most recent fantasy team trade contained more drama than the majority of the midseason blockbusters last July.

But unlike fantasy baseball, where trades are made because one team needs more stolen bases and has an extra reliever to deal, real trades aren't so cut-and-dry. There are dozens of factors behind every deal, proposed or consummated. It's why trades can sometimes look awful on paper, years after the fact. And there is the human dimension to it all.

Evaluating the players swapped for each other in a trade is a little like judging a waltz by watching one step. The players directly involved in the deal are a small piece within dozens of interwoven decisions.

At 1995's July 31 trade deadline, the Detroit Tigers traded left-hander David Wells to the Reds. Wells was a workhorse starter, although he hadn't yet developed into the top-of-the-rotation pitcher he would eventually become. Out of shape and a bit of a head case, Wells was dealt for more reliable players, including lefty C.J. Nitkowski, who would start 19 games for the Tigers over the next two years, and infielder Mark Lewis, who would become Detroit's starting second baseman in 1996. Wells finished the season with the Reds, then wore out his welcome there and was dealt to the Baltimore Orioles. He became a free agent after that season.

All in all, the deal doesn't seem significant: an unreliable player with potential was swapped for a few pieces that fit the Tigers' roster. Widening the focus a bit, the New York Yankees pulled off a blockbuster three days earlier, sending three minor leaguers to Toronto for ace righty David Cone. The deal was a coup for the Yankees, who added a pitcher who was coming off a Cy Young–winning season in 1994 and would finish fourth in the award voting in '95. Cone would spend the next five years as a key component on New York's World Series teams. He was the Yankees' second choice at the deadline, however. New York pulled off the Cone trade only after they couldn't finalize a deal for their first target: David Wells. The Yankees were close to landing Wells, and they were offering a minor league starting pitcher who wasn't a lock to crack the starting rotation anytime soon—a guy named Mariano Rivera.

The Tigers could have traded the headache of David Wells for the man who would become the best closer in MLB history. It kind of takes the luster off of C.J. Nitkowski and Mark Lewis a bit.

Despite all the near misses on the trading block, deals are completed all the time. In the last four years, there have been an average of 88 trades a season involving 247 players. That means that, on average, one-third of all major league players get traded each year.

That includes players at the highest level of the sport. There have been 205 trades involving players that eventually were enshrined in the Baseball Hall of Fame, and 121 different Hall of Famers were traded at least once in their careers. Considering there are only 215 MLB players in the Hall (as of 2015), that's a high percentage of all-time greats who were dealt to other teams at some time during their career. Pitcher Burleigh Grimes was traded six times. Three Hall of Famers—Gaylord Perry, Hoyt Wilhelm and Bert Blyleven—were dealt five times each.

Forty-one Most Valuable Player awards have been earned by players after they'd been traded at least once. That includes Frank Robinson, also a future Hall of Famer, who was considered "an old 30" by the Reds, just five years after winning an MVP award for Cincinnati. Ten months after the Reds traded him to the Orioles in December 1965, Robinson added the American League MVP, a Triple Crown and a World Series championship to his trophy case. Forty-nine Cy Young Awards have been given to players who had been traded. That doesn't include Cy Young himself, who was traded in February 1909 for pitchers Jack Ryan and Charlie Chech. It does include Rick Sutcliffe, who was traded to the Chicago Cubs in June 1984. He went 16–1 the rest of the season and led the Cubs to the playoffs for the first time in a generation. It could be argued, however, that the Indians didn't fare too badly in that deal, getting outfielders Joe Carter and Mel Hall in exchange.

Every trade is a single thread in a complex tapestry connected to two dozen teams and hundreds of players. That makes it tough to determine which trades are the best and worst in the history of the sport. It won't stop us from trying, however.

Normally, a ranking of baseball trades focuses on the mismatches: the Boston Red Sox sending Babe Ruth to the New York Yankees, for instance—although technically, that was a player sale, not a trade. There's Lou Brock for Ernie Broglio, Jeff Bagwell for Larry Andersen, Mark McGwire for some potpourri. A lopsided trade can be fun to review, but unless you're a fan of one of the teams involved, the fact that a trade went heavily in favor of one team or the other doesn't necessarily make it one of the best, or the worst.

That means that some significant trades won't get included, leaving angry readers shouting, "Where's Lou Brock?" and "What about Bagwell?" That's also partly due to the highly subjective concept of Best Trade Ever and Worst Trade Ever. The Jeff Bagwell trade was one of the best in Astros history . . . and one of the worst from a Red Sox perspective. So which is it?

Instead of the first-round knockouts, we'll take a look at the twelve-round title fights of baseball trades. A great trade is one that not only helps both teams involved but pays more benefit than any of the other options available to the teams at the time. We'll discuss some fleecings, of course, but a bad trade is often one that may not look like a mismatch on paper. It's only when the opportunity cost of the deal is taken into account that the trade's impact can be seen.

We'll also play the role of baseball commissioner a bit. Sometimes, a trade isn't good or bad for the teams involved, but it's included here because of how it helped to serve the "best interests of baseball."

The best trades helped build two organizations, often winning a pennant in the short term for one while building the foundation of another. These trades altered the history of a sport. The worst trades didn't only get a general manager fired; they cost a city its team. They were mocked a decade after the fact by a top-rated sitcom.

From hot-stove rumors to the players-to-be-named-later, trades are an integral part of the fabric of baseball. Done right, they are a fast way to build a franchise. Done poorly, they're an even faster way to ruin one. With the sheer number of players on the block at any one time and the number of offers a GM has to juggle, it's amazing that deals ever get consummated, let alone every four days or so, all year long.

To fully understand a trade, we must peek inside the front office, listen to the phone calls and read the texts and emails. We must look at the scouting reports and see who's thought to be losing a step and who might be able to extend his career if we move him to the bullpen. We need to check the locker room for cancers. Then we need to make a choice—the unproven prospect or the known, but perhaps unpredictable, major leaguer.

Evaluating one trade, on its own, outside of any context is like evaluating a pitch in the same way. A pitcher throws a curveball in the dirt. In isolation, that's clearly a bad pitch. However, White Sox pitcher Philip Humber finished a perfect game with exactly that pitch. The count, game situation, scouting report on the batter and pitch sequence up to that point—both in the at bat and the game—all play a role in determining whether that pitch was a good one or a poor one.

General managers face a much tougher job than the owners of fantasy teams, and, best or worst, the trades in this book were not driven by stat-line numbers, nor were they meant to be evaluated in a "we got–they got" vacuum. Teams have to consider a mindboggling array of factors when negotiating a trade. Finances are, and always have been, a factor. Personalities are a factor.

Plus, there's a butterfly effect that, even in a book-length analysis, is impossible to fully capture. Fred Stanley makes an error in the 1976 World Series, and an arbitrator rules in favor of Andy Messersmith. All of a sudden, Reggie Jackson is a Yankee, and LaMarr Hoyt wins the 1983 Cy Young Award. As Tom Grieve said, "The best trades are the ones where you can shake hands with the other general manager involved, and both of you are happy with what you got. And, when you see that general manager five years later, you can both shake hands again and still be happy."

Included here are ten times when it was done better than anyone else, and ten times that someone wishes he could take it back, along with his job.

— WHAT IS WAR? —

While much more goes into a trade decision than just on-field performance, statistics provide an easy way for fans to evaluate a trade over the long term.

The statistic used to compare the trades in this book is WAR, short for Wins Above Replacement. It was developed by sabermetricians as a comprehensive measure of a player's value to his team.

Essentially, a player's WAR measures how many more games a team wins by having him on the roster. Pitching, hitting, base running and fielding contributions are combined to come up with an expected number of wins that they would add to an average team. That's then compared to the production of a "replacement-level player"—someone a team could sign from the waiver wire or call up from Triple A.

Unlike batting average or ERA, WAR isn't something that a fan can quickly calculate in the margin of his or her scorecard. It involves complex algorithms. This book uses the calculations provided by BaseballReference.com.

For comparison purposes, a WAR of 8 is the equivalent of an MVP-caliber season. A WAR of 5 or higher would land a player on an All-Star team. If a player wants to keep his spot in the starting lineup, he needs a WAR of 2 or greater. A WAR between 0 and 2 would likely be a utility player, mop-up reliever or other type of backup. A WAR of 0 means that a player is equally as good as any of the replacements available in the minors or on the street.

Barry Bonds' 73-home-run season of 2001 had a WAR of 11.9. In 1968, Bob Gibson produced one of the most dominant pitching seasons in history, which was good for a WAR of 11.2.

Mario Mendoza, a middle infielder whose futility at the plate inspired the term "Mendoza Line" for a .200 batting average, played nine years in the majors. His year-by-year WAR numbers were -0.1, -0.3, -0.1, -0.4, 0.3, -1.6, -0.6, 1.0 and -0.7. (Negative WAR means that he was actually *worse* than what would have been available at Triple A during those seasons.)

Why include WAR at all, especially considering that many of the trades discussed were completed long before the statistic was invented? It's a way of keeping score. In many of the trades discussed, front offices had to choose from a mind-boggling array of trade partners and players. How well did they choose? WAR provides a quick and easy way to compare what might have been to what actually occurred.

CHAPTER 1

— FIRE SALE! —

THE STORY BEHIND THE MIKE PIAZZA TRADE

A shameful dismantling of a champion hits its low point.

Seven months after winning the 1997 World Series, the Florida Marlins decided to dismantle the team and swung one of the biggest-name, lowest-impact trades in memory. Mike Piazza went from the Dodgers to Miami—for eight days—before he was flipped to the New York Mets. Gary Sheffield, Bobby Bonilla and Charles Johnson all went to LA, where they showed their best days were behind them.

Washington, D.C., is a city that understands the impact of budget cuts, so President Bill Clinton probably didn't take it as an insult when 11 of the 25 invited players didn't show up at the White House on February 17, 1998.

It was four months after the Florida Marlins won the World Series. As is customary, Clinton invited the champions to be honored at the White House. A total of 19 members of the Marlins organization showed up, and that included the manager, Jim Leyland, and members of his coaching staff.

Bobby Bonilla made excuses for the missing members of the championship team, telling the president, "They're all working on the '98 budget cuts."

Later, Bonilla told the media, "I wish everyone could have been here to meet the president. It's a thrill, but it's also a sweet-and-sour type of thing."

Robb Nen couldn't make it. The Marlins closer had saved two of the team's four World Series wins and then was traded to the San Francisco Giants on November 18, twenty-three days after the Marlins won Game Seven. He spent the day of the White House visit working out at the Giants' spring training camp in Scottsdale, Arizona. "There's no use going to Washington," he said. "It's not worth it to meet the president. If I was still with those guys, maybe. But now, I'm dedicated to this team. My goal now is to get ready for March thirty-first [Opening Day]."

Al Leiter couldn't make it. He'd started two games in the Series, including Game Seven, and struck out a total of 10 batters. Eleven days before the visit, he'd been traded to the Mets. He wasn't about to make the trip from the team's camp site at Port St. Lucie, Florida, to Washington by himself. "Other than to get a picture with the President, it just seemed like a pretty hectic day," he said.

Pitcher Kevin Brown also started two Series games. He also wasn't at the White House. Brown was in Peoria, Arizona, reporting to the San Diego Padres' spring training, after getting traded in December. "I think we all felt like we got blindsided with the dismantling of the team," he said. "But after the trade came about, reality kind of sank in and you kind of move on."

Two players who were no longer on the Marlins did make the trip. Jeff Conine, an original Marlin from the team's first season in 1993, had been sent to the Kansas City Royals shortly after the World Series. "Obviously it would have been nice to have everyone here," he said of the White House visit, "because we won it as a team."

Pitcher Tony Saunders, who had moved on to the Tampa Bay Devil Rays after spending his rookie season with the champion Marlins, said, "When we won, that was one of the first things I thought of, 'I get to go to the White House now.' It's exciting."

The excitement had been diminished by the events of the previous four months. All told, 13 of the 25 members of the Marlins roster that won the World Series were no longer with the team by the time they visited Washington. Clinton, who endured two government shutdowns in his first term, found himself at the center of another budget crisis.

Marlins owner Wayne Huizenga also didn't make the trip to the White House with his team. He was trying to sell the franchise, and, in baseball, low payroll makes for a more enticing purchase than do championship rings. The term "fire sale" was first thrown around on November 7, less than two weeks after the World Series ended.

The Marlins wanted to slash their payroll, from $53 million in 1997 to between $22 and $25 million the following year. They would accomplish this by getting rid of the core players that had led the franchise to a championship in its fifth year of existence.

"It's definitely going to be ugly, if that's what they're talking about doing," Leiter said.

"It's going to be different," GM Dave Dombrowski said. "We're not going to be putting a world championship caliber team on the field." Dombrowski had built the 1997 champions, signing a half dozen free agents to contracts totaling $89 million the year before. All of them would be headed for the door, as Dombrowski set about tearing it all down.

"We've already talked to a couple of them, and they're not happy. But they are happy about getting the ring."

Dombrowski traded players. He released players. He let free agents walk and gave up players in the expansion draft. At the start of spring training, the Marlins had gotten rid of the players who had produced 40 percent of the team's at bats, hits and runs; half of the home runs; and nearly half of the RBI. They'd also dealt away the pitchers who had made five of the team's seven World Series starts, pitched more than half of the innings and produced nearly two-thirds of the strikeouts.

Make no mistake: this wasn't a youth movement, dumping high salaries to build for the future. This was an outright fire sale. Of the 18 players the Marlins received in the offseason trades, 10 never made it to the major leagues. Five combined to play a total of 70 games for the Marlins. The other three prospects the Marlins received were, in fact, building blocks for the future—outfielder Derrek Lee, reliever Jesus Sanchez and starter A. J. Burnett—but they hardly balanced out the talent that departed. (Lee would later be a part of the Marlins' fire sale following the team's 2003 World Series victory.)

At the end of the White House ceremony, Bonilla presented Clinton with a teal-and-white Marlins jersey.

"It may not be the precise same Marlin team that played the Indians last year that takes the field on opening day," Clinton told the surviving members of the champion squad. "But if the players keep the same spirit, they'll be sure to be in the hunt again when the season comes to a close."

Like many promises made by politicians, this one didn't have a chance of coming to pass.

Meanwhile, at the Dodgers camp in Vero Beach, Florida, on the same day, catcher Mike Piazza spoke to the media about his contract situation.

Piazza was the most popular player on the team. Although he was born near Philadelphia, he seemed to have grown up in Dodger blue. His father, Vince, was childhood friends with Tommy Lasorda, the Hall of Fame Dodger manager. Lasorda was the godfather of Piazza's younger brother, also named Tommy. As a child, when the Dodgers played in Philadelphia, Piazza served as batboy for the visiting team.

The Dodgers selected Piazza in the 62nd round of the 1988 draft, when no other team seemed interested, and the favor to Lasorda paid off handsomely. Piazza eventually developed into the best hitting catcher in baseball.

As spring training opened in 1998, he was looking for a contract that rewarded him as such.

"Obviously, I'm a little disappointed," he said about not receiving a comparable offer from the team. "But I've dealt with it. I'm fine as far as my state of mind. I'm ready to play this year. That's it."

Piazza was on a team that was about to have an even more dysfunctional year than the Marlins.

On January 5, 1997, back when the Marlins were being criticized for their offseason spending spree, Dodgers general manager Fred Claire and his wife arrived home from dinner to find two messages on the answering machine, both from owner Peter O'Malley.

"In 30 years with the organization, I could never remember Peter leaving TWO messages to return a call," Claire wrote in his memoir.

O'Malley's father, Walter, had been involved with the Dodgers organization since 1933. He bought 25 percent of the team in 1944 and became primary owner in 1950. Peter took over as president in 1970. For six and a half decades, the O'Malley family had played a major role in the operation of the team. For nearly half a century, an O'Malley had been in charge. Over that time, the Dodgers had won six World Series and revolutionized baseball twice—breaking the color barrier in 1947 and moving to the West Coast in 1958.

"I've been talking to my family for some time, and we've decided to sell the team," Peter O'Malley told Claire that January evening in 1997. "We've crossed the emotional barriers, and we know it's time to sell."

At a press conference the next day, O'Malley said, "Family ownership of sports today is a dying breed. It's a high-risk business. You need a broader base than an individual family to carry you through the storms. Groups or corporations are probably the wave of the future."

By May, Rupert Murdoch's News Corp, which owns the Fox television network, among other properties worldwide, emerged as a bidder. By September, O'Malley had agreed to sell the team to the Fox Group for $311 million, then a record in professional sports.

Owners ratified the deal in March 1998 by a 27–2 vote, although there were concerns raised over a potential conflict of interest. Fox had a national TV contract with MLB and had full or partial local broadcast rights with 22 of the 30 teams.

"They answered our questions about having financial interests in 21 other clubs," Giants owner Peter Magowan said. "That was our biggest concern."

The Fox people promised there would be a "wall" between the television side of the business and the baseball side. Claire later claimed that the wall had large holes in it from the very beginning.

"The first thing one needs to understand about Fox's purchase of the Dodgers is that it was an investment triggered by the company's desire to establish a regional sports network in Southern California," he wrote. In order to beat out Disney, which owned the newly renamed Anaheim Angels (as well as major interests in ABC and ESPN), Fox needed a product for the network to air on summer nights. Dodger games would be a perfect solution to the new network's programming problem.

While the sale of the Dodgers was being finalized, Mike Piazza and his agent, Dan Lozano, were choosing the worst possible time to push for a new contract.

Following the 1996 season, the White Sox had signed outfielder Albert Belle to a five-year, $55 million contract, making him the first $10 million a year player and the first to sign a $50 million deal. Dave Dombrowski helped Gary Sheffield break the $60 million barrier five months later, on a six-year deal with Florida, and, in December 1997, Pedro Martínez signed with the Boston Red Sox for six years, $75 million.

Piazza was ready to become baseball's first $100 million player. He was already making $8 million a year, and his contract had one year remaining, as the 1998 season dawned. He wanted to renegotiate and sign the first nine-figure deal.

If there was going to be a $100 million player, Piazza certainly had a good case to be the man. He was the best hitting catcher in baseball and had been an All-Star and in the top 10 of MVP voting every year of his career. In 1997, Piazza had 40 home runs, 124 RBI, and a .362 average, setting all-time records for catchers for most homers in a season and highest batting average.

Immediately after the season, Piazza and Lozano began negotiating a contract extension. They asked for seven years, $105 million. With the franchise in the process of being sold, no one in the organization was going to agree to such a massive contract. The Dodgers offered a six-year, $80 million deal, which still would have made Piazza the highest-paid player in baseball. He turned them down.

In an attempt to spur things on, Piazza issued an ultimatum. If he didn't have an extension by February 15, he would cut off talks with the Dodgers and pursue free agency after the season. The logic was that Fox, who knew the value of a star, wouldn't want to risk losing him in their first year owning the team.

Unfortunately for Piazza, the sale of the team was still a month away from being finalized. The slow progress had the side effect of allowing the team to call Piazza's bluff, leaving him and his negotiating team scrambling to save face.

"We were very comfortable with our position," Lozano said, explaining that they weren't backing down from the ultimatum as much as giving the Dodgers a chance to work out their ownership issue. "Considering the Dodgers' efforts, and because of the change in ownership, we felt we owed it to them and the fans to see how much the Dodgers really want to keep Mike here."

In a spring training interview with legendary Dodgers broadcaster Vin Scully, Piazza said, "Those things get misconstrued in the papers and come out a little aggressive."

Scully responded by saying, "Ultimatum is a heavy word. You know, that's the kind of thing, 'If you don't do this, we bomb you.'"

"That wasn't the intention at all," Piazza replied.

In other words, "We'll still take that extension."

The franchise sale was finalized in mid-March, and Lozano made a follow-up contract offer a few days later: eight years, $144 million. In addition to an average annual salary of $18 million, the deal included a hotel suite for road trips and a luxury box at Dodger Stadium. Not a luxury box in the outfield, either. It had to be overlooking the infield, "between the bases."

"It was the type of offer you just write down, because there is no verbal response that makes sense," Claire recalled. "There was a lot of work to be done to even get to the area of a reasonable deal."

The team's new president, Bob Graziano, made statements to the media saying there was no urgency to meet with Piazza, since the catcher was already under contract. Graziano also said that the completion of the sale didn't mean that the team would move any faster on an extension.

Piazza, already frustrated by the slow progress of the negotiations, made a tactical mistake. He assumed that since Dodger fans loved him, they'd take his side. Almost immediately, however, he went from hero to spoiled brat in their eyes. While fans love their star player, they love their team more. Any indication that a player will choose money over the team nearly always results in a backlash.

On opening day of the 1998 season, Piazza blew up in an interview with *Los Angeles Times* beat writer Jason Reid. "I'm not going to lie and say I'm not concerned about this, that I'm not confused and disappointed by the whole thing, because I am," Piazza said. "I'm mad that this has dragged into the season, and that it now has the potential to become a distraction. I'm not going to use this as an excuse if things aren't going well, because that wouldn't be fair to the fans, my teammates or [team management]. But how can I not think about this?"

"If they say they have the intent to sign me, then sign me," he added. "But if they don't have the intent to sign me, then just let me know. Just let me know, so at least I'll be able to start to think about having a future somewhere else after the season. But what they're doing now, the way this is going, I just don't get it."

When asked about the lukewarm public response from Graziano, Piazza dug himself even deeper into a hole. "When I see something like that from Mr. Graziano, I don't know what to think," Piazza said. "Are they trying to smoke us out, trying to get us to reveal something to help their negotiating position? If that's the case, they really don't have to do that. We've been upfront from the beginning, and it's not like we're holding a gun to anyone's head."

"I understand that this is business, and we're trying to handle this the way we feel we have to," he said. "But if they're going to force our hand, I'll play the season out and see what other teams out there want me."

The fans had heard enough. Piazza was going to make $8 million that season and turned down $80 million from the team, a contract that would have been the richest in baseball history. Those numbers make it tough to win public sympathy, and his threat to leave in free agency, even as conditional and nuanced as it was worded, turned the public against him.

"It was a terrible mistake by Mike," Claire wrote, years later.

When Jason Reid called him for a reaction, Graziano played it perfectly. "I'm surprised by this," he said. "I have to believe that if they're committed to winning, Mike Piazza has to be a big part of that. But right now, the ball is in their court, and we don't have any idea what they're doing."

A few days later, the Dodgers released a statement that helped their public relations case, making it clear that they wanted to keep Piazza, and pay him well, but they just couldn't come to an agreement as to his value. "Unfortunately, to date, we have not been able to bridge the wide gap that exists between our respective positions, primarily because, at this point in the negotiations, there is no good way for either side to accurately assess the level of compensation that a player of Mike's caliber can command in today's market."

A furious Piazza met with Claire prior to that day's game. He accused the team of "lowballing" him and twice told Claire to get the contract done or "get me out of here."

The Dodgers had opened the season on the road, first in St. Louis and then in Cincinnati. When the team returned home to host the Diamondbacks, Lozano and the team exchanged their final, best offers. They were still more than $20 million apart.

The Dodgers' hometown fans, who had watched the drama unfold, first in Florida during spring training and then in other National League ballparks, finally had their chance to express an opinion. Piazza was booed every time he came to bat.

"They really booed when Mike Piazza stepped up to bat," one game story reported. "Yes, Mike Piazza, the pride of the organization that selected him in the 62nd round of the 1988 amateur draft as a favor for family friend Tommy Lasorda. An All-Star catcher who has been arguably the most popular Dodger in years. Booed extensively in the city where it doesn't matter what you know, but who you know, because of his contract demands."

"It was really surprising, because people love him," said former Dodger outfielder Karim Garcia, then with Arizona. "Everybody cheers for Piazza all the time."

Piazza, who considered himself a lifelong Dodger, was clearly hurt by the treatment, even as he tried to downplay it in the media.

"I try not to be sensitive to that," he said. "They're entitled to their opinions. There were a lot of people out there who were supportive, too. . . . It's part of baseball. Whether you like it or not, it's part of baseball, and I definitely won't be the last guy [booed]."

He released a statement. "I have instructed my agent, Dan Lozano, to shut down contract negotiations with the Dodgers. I let the talks become a distraction, and for that, I apologize to my teammates and our fans. For the rest of the season, I will focus completely on bringing a championship to Los Angeles and will not discuss my contract status with anyone until the season ends."

It was too little, too late. Piazza had burned bridges with the fans and, more importantly, with the team's new ownership group.

On May 14, the visiting Phillies were leading, 2–0, at Dodger Stadium. The Dodgers got a runner on and, with one out, infielder José Vizcaíno came to the plate representing the tying run. At that moment, Claire's phone rang. Graziano was calling from the Dominican Republic, where the team had a training complex.

"Fred, we have made a trade that needs to be announced tonight," Graziano told him. This came as a surprise to Claire, since general managers are usually heavily involved in trade talks.

Claire had received a call from the Marlins' Dombrowski the previous month, two days after the start of the season, when the Piazza situation had reached the boiling point.

Dombrowski asked if Claire would be interested in trading Piazza and a minor league pitcher for catcher Charles Johnson and outfielders Gary Sheffield and Jim Eisenreich. Claire told him that the Dodgers would be interested in pursuing a deal for Sheffield, but the team was hoping to re-sign Piazza instead of trading him.

That was the last Claire heard from Dombrowski. Claire didn't know that the Marlins and Dodgers ownership groups had continued to pursue the deal. (Dombrowski swore that he didn't go over Claire's head to continue the talks.)

At the time the deal was announced, Claire was busy planning for a meeting he and Graziano had scheduled with Fox executive Peter Chernin two days later. "I was developing a strategy and list of teams I felt might be interested in Piazza if Fox gave the order to trade Mike," Claire wrote in his memoir. "We had a couple months before the trading deadline . . . to evaluate our chances for postseason play and to quietly explore the market for Mike without triggering wild rumors."

"The deal . . . was struck without even the courtesy of informing me, the Dodger general manager," he wrote. "Instead, incredibly, it was orchestrated by Fox television executive Chase Carey, as part of his pursuit of a regional sports channel in Florida. Carey wanted the Marlins to be part of that venture. It's true. This seven-player trade was, first and foremost, a television deal."

The business concerns of the Dodgers, Marlins and Fox had all come together in a perfect storm that brought down the walls between the baseball and TV sides of Murdoch's enterprise. Carey called Marlins president Don Smiley, who was in the process of buying the team from Wayne Huizenga. He asked about SportsChannel Florida, another Huizenga property that he was trying to sell. Carey was hoping to acquire the channel for Fox and add it to the large group of MLB team broadcast rights the company controlled.

Adding a star player like Piazza, someone to get fans to tune in, would certainly help the Marlins' ratings on the new channel. Furthermore, the Dodgers' assistance in the Marlins' continuing salary dump wouldn't hurt Fox's chances of being the ones to land the rights to the channel.

The deal, as it was explained that night, sent Piazza to the Marlins, along with third baseman Todd Zeile. In exchange, the Marlins sent Sheffield, Eisenreich, Johnson and third baseman Bobby Bonilla to Los Angeles.

The four players Florida traded away were scheduled to make $25.5 million in 1998 and $91.6 million over the life of their contracts. With the departure of those four, pitcher Liván Hernández ($1.475 million) was the only Marlins player due to earn more than a million dollars. That didn't include Piazza and Zeile, of course, but neither of them would be long for the team.

After learning of the trade, Claire waited for the end of the game and took Piazza and Zeile into the team doctor's office to tell them the news.

Piazza responded with, "Who are we going to? The Marlins aren't going to keep us."

Claire didn't have the answer to that question, and he couldn't answer Piazza's next question either: Who were we traded for?

Sheffield had a no-trade clause in his Marlins contract, and he needed to be convinced to waive it, for some type of compensation, before the deal could become official. It's the type of detail that general managers make sure is taken care of—when they're consulted on trades.

Zeile just stood in stunned silence, while Piazza grew frustrated at the lack of information.

Later, the two ex-Dodgers shared a house during their brief time in Florida. "I'm going to go into his bedroom and scream at him every morning at 4 a.m.," Zeile joked later. "The only reason I ended up in Florida is because he didn't sign."

Sheffield arrived in Los Angeles with his agent the day after the trade was announced. Before going to Dodger Stadium, the limo rented by the team took him to meet the executives at Fox Studios. The executives brushed aside the risk that the no-trade clause entailed, but it was not a trivial issue for Sheffield. He was going from a state that had no income tax to California, which has one of the heavier state taxes in the union.

When met by reporters at LAX, Sheffield was asked what he would need in order to waive his no-trade. "I don't know yet," he said. "We have to sit down and talk about it. No decisions have been made. We have a lot in the contract that has to be discussed, there are a lot of arrangements that need to be made. There are the issues of my living arrangements, my option year . . . but I want to come here, and I'm excited about the possibility of coming here."

Meanwhile, Dombrowski was doing his best on the other end to learn more about the details of the trade. He called Claire to explain that the Marlins were also expected to throw in a pitching prospect to the Dodgers in the deal. There was a list of five pitchers, and the Marlins got to choose which one they were willing to give up.

"Dave told me he had not been aware of this aspect of the deal, and that he didn't really want to part with any of these five pitchers," Claire recalled. "He asked if I would consider another player. I told him I also knew nothing about this part of the deal."

Finally, it was decided that the Marlins would give up right-hander Manuel Barrios, whom the team had just acquired in November when they dealt Moises Alou to Houston.

At the start of the Dodgers' game that night, Sheffield and his agent met Fred Claire. The first thing the player said was, "I want to either get this done or get back to the Marlins. This isn't fair to the other players involved, my teammates, and Mike and Todd."

Sheffield eventually agreed to take a payment of $5.5 million, $3 million from the Dodgers and $2.5 million from the Marlins, to consent to the trade.

At a press conference introducing Sheffield, Claire opened with the complete truth. "I want to be perfectly clear and accurate about this," he said. "I got a call from Bob Graziano, and he informed me that the trade had been made."

Graziano took responsibility for the trade. "The trade came about because of a broader discussion between the people at Fox and the Florida Marlins, but I recommended the deal to people at Fox," he said. "I think this helps improve our chemistry, helps improve our hitting and helps improve our defense. I think the team is markedly improved."

Of Claire's noninvolvement, he said, "I had many discussions with Fred about the trade. But this was an unusual deal, and it involved an unusual number of players. In making the deal, I didn't view Fred's input as any less significant."

Claire attempted to resign the night he was told about the trade, but Graziano talked him into staying. Five weeks after the press conference, the team fired him, as well as the team's manager, Bill Russell.

With the trade, the Marlins had rid themselves of the players responsible for three-quarters of the at bats from the previous October's World Series, as well as more than three-quarters of the runs, hits and RBI. No player that hit a World Series home run remained with the team.

There was only one player left on the roster who had played in all seven World Series games—Édgar Rentería—and he would be traded after the season. By the end of 1998, no one who had played in more than three games in the 1997 Series remained with Florida.

Mike Piazza would play five games and come to bat 19 times in a Florida Marlins uniform. A National Leaguer for most of his career, Piazza played more games at DH (49, mostly in interleague games) than he did as a Marlin. The slow-footed catcher would play more games (six) as a leadoff hitter. He played more regular season games at Hiram Bithorn Stadium in San Juan, Puerto Rico (six) than he did for the Marlins. He had more at bats in World Series and the All-Star games (22 and 25, respectively) than he did in a Marlins uniform.

A week after being traded to the Marlins, Mike Piazza was dealt to the Mets.

"I can't describe it," Piazza said after hearing of the second trade. "I mean, I was with one organization for ten years, major and minor leagues, and then to get traded twice in one week is just—I don't know what to think. I'm just trying to collect myself here. It's been very strange."

"It was a series of bizarre events that led him to New York," said agent Dan Lozano. "His head is still spinning."

The Marlins held onto Todd Zeile ten times as long as they did Piazza, but he too was in a different uniform before the end of the season. Florida dealt him to the Texas Rangers at the July 31 trade deadline, after 66 games with the team. Of the five players the Marlins received from the Mets and Rangers, three never made it to the major leagues. Another, Ed Yarnall, never made it to the majors with the Marlins. All the Marlins had to show for Gary Sheffield, Charles Johnson, Jim Eisenreich, Bobby Bonilla, Mike Piazza, Todd Zeile and Manuel Barrios was outfielder Preston Wilson, who played five years with the team before he too was traded away.

While Piazza was becoming the toast of New York, the Marlins set an MLB record for most losses by a defending world champion, going 54–108 in 1998, a record 34 games worse than the previous year.

Shortly after acquiring Piazza, Marlins president Don Smiley said that he planned to further cut the team payroll for the following season, to between $10 and $16 million.

Alex Fernandez, a Marlins pitcher who was on the disabled list, said, "It sucks. It's embarrassing. There's nothing good about it. Whenever I decide I want to get traded, that's when I'll pitch. I was lied to, and so was everyone else. We were told we were going to be competitive for a certain number of years, and obviously that's not going to happen. I know one thing now—I know they're going to trade me. And that's unfortunate, because I want to remain a Marlin. If I didn't want to play here for five years, I wouldn't have signed here for five years."

Fernandez ended up playing out his contract with the Marlins, during which time the team went 194–292. Nevertheless, Fernandez posted a winning record (28–24) in his three seasons with Florida.

The sale of the Marlins franchise was completed in 1999, to a group headed by John Henry. In 2001, he turned the team over to Jeffrey Loria, while he took control of the Red Sox, in a complicated deal brokered by MLB. Loria's Marlins won the 2003 World Series—and then he set about dismantling the team in a cost-cutting fire sale the following year.

Fox's ownership of the Dodgers lasted about four decades less than the O'Malley family's. The network sold the team in 2004, after the team failed to reach the playoffs during its ownership. Fox was also foiled in its bid to acquire SportsChannel, which Huizenga eventually sold to Cablevision in late 1999.

On October 25, 1998, Mike Piazza signed a seven-year deal with the Mets for $91 million, earning him the title of highest-paid player in baseball, with the richest contract in history.

He held the title for 48 days, until free agent pitcher Kevin Brown became the first baseball player to sign a $100 million contract. Brown signed—with the Fox-owned Los Angeles Dodgers—for seven years, $105 million. The contract included perks like eight premium season tickets and twelve private jet trips for his family to visit him during the season.

Sandy Alderson, from the MLB Commissioner's office, ripped the deal, which had been made in the face of the commissioner's repeated efforts to preach fiscal sanity among owners. "The commissioner is certainly frustrated," Alderson said. "We held a meeting last week in Chicago that wasn't even attended by these people who made this deal today."

On the day his signing became official, Brown praised his new team's dedication to building a championship club. "From the first moment we visited with the Dodgers in Los Angeles, we knew that they were not only committed to us but committed to winning," Brown said. "Everyone we met made it clear to us that getting the Dodgers back to the level they were at in the past was the priority."

WAR COMPARISON

The 1997 World Champion Florida Marlins had a team WAR of 37.1 wins over replacement. By the start of the 1998 season, Florida had traded away players responsible for 24.5 wins over replacement. The Mike Piazza deal alone rid the team of 9.2 WAR.

For their troubles, and the fourteen contributors they dealt away in the offseason purge, the Marlins acquired a grand total of three prospects that would eventually produce starter-quality numbers.

MARLINS RECEIVED	WAR PRE-TRADE	WAR POST-TRADE
Mike Piazza	31.9	-0.1
Todd Zeile	2.5	1.1
DODGERS RECEIVED	WAR PRE-TRADE	WAR POST-TRADE
Gary Sheffield	13.1	17
Charles Johnson	9.3	0.6
Bobby Bonilla	2.2	-1.2
Jim Eisenreich	0.3	-1
Manuel Barrios	0.1	0.0

(continued)

METS RECEIVED	WAR PRE-TRADE	WAR POST-TRADE
Mike Piazza	-0.1	24.5
MARLINS RECEIVED	WAR PRE-TRADE	WAR POST-TRADE
Preston Wilson	-0.1	6.1
Ed Yarnall	0.0	0.0
Geoff Goetz	0.0	0.0
MARLINS FIRE SALE: TRADED AWAY NOV/DEC 1997	WAR PRE-TRADE	WAR POST-TRADE
Al Leiter	1.3	28
Robb Nen	5	10.4
Jeff Conine	11	0.1
Devon White	4.5	3.7
Moises Alou	3.5	11.7
Kevin Brown	15	8.6
Dennis Cook	0.5	2.8
Ed Vosberg	-0.1	-0.7
Kurt Abbott	2	-0.4
MARLINS FIRE SALE ACQUISITIONS	WAR PRE-TRADE	WAR POST-TRADE
AJ Burnett	0.0	12
Derrek Lee	0.3	9.8
6 others that played for Florida	-0.8	-2.6
10 players were acquired that never made it to the Majors with Florida		

CHAPTER 2

GUESS WHO'S COMING TO THANKSGIVING — DINNER —

THE STORY BEHIND THE CURT SCHILLING TRADE

A holiday road trip and strong stomachs produce a memorable trade.

After the 2003 season, the Boston Red Sox needed one piece to break their 85-year curse. General manager Theo Epstein was convinced that piece was pitcher Curt Schilling. Epstein spent Thanksgiving Day meeting with Schilling and his wife at their home, and by the end of Black Friday, Epstein had his man.

The story of the Boston Red Sox's first World Series championship since 1918 had its roots in a dirty sock.

No, not that sock. True, Schilling bled through a sock while pitching the Red Sox to victory following a between-start ankle procedure during Boston's comeback in the 2004 ALCS, but it was another sock, soaked in bodily fluids, that helped put the events into motion 10 months earlier.

"I think I had to change my socks," assistant general manager Jed Hoyer said of his 2003 Thanksgiving, spent in Phoenix, Arizona. "I think I puked on my socks. Larry [Lucchino, Red Sox CEO] gave me a pair of his socks." It was just another Thanksgiving with the Schillings.

Curt Schilling and his wife, Shonda Brewer, first met thirteen years earlier, in 1990, long before he was the most sought-after player on the trading block. Schilling was in his first full season with the Orioles, pitching out of the bullpen. Brewer was an associate producer for Home Team Sports, the cable network that carried Orioles games.

The couple didn't meet at the ballpark, however. They claim that they met at the mall. Schilling was shopping, and Brewer was working at Foot Locker to keep a flow of income in between baseball and hockey seasons. The pair fell in love, but the budding relationship seemed doomed when, in January, Schilling was traded to the Astros, along with Pete Harnisch and Steve Finley, for Glenn Davis.

"As Curt said the words, I burst into tears," Shonda wrote in a memoir. "Just when I'd felt comfortable enough to let my guard down and enjoy our relationship, he'd been traded, and to a team halfway across the country. It was my first taste of just how difficult it was to be in love with a baseball player."

Schilling begged her to come with him, but she was hesitant to give up her job. Finally, she agreed to move to Houston in April. Curt went to spring training, and Shonda spent five weeks taking care of the move from Baltimore to Texas—packing, cleaning the houses they were vacating and finding a place in Houston—"my first taste of my 'job' for the next 20 years or so, always packing and moving and arranging," she wrote.

The couple slept on the floor on Opening Day, waiting for the furniture to be delivered. They soon settled in and prepared for year two. They went to spring training in Florida together and, as Shonda was driving from Orlando to Houston for the start of the season, she heard on the radio that Curt had been traded to Philadelphia.

She reached Curt on the phone and the two spoke briefly before he left to meet the Phillies in Miami. Shonda continued to Houston and began packing and planning another move. "I wouldn't even get a chance to say good-bye to anyone," she wrote.

By the time Schilling was traded next, in 2000, from Philadelphia to Arizona, Curt and Shonda had been married for eight years and had three children. (A fourth would come along in 2002.)

By then, both of them were more experienced in the way things worked in MLB. Curt orchestrated the trade, demanding that the Phillies trade him to a contender and providing a list of teams for whom he'd waive his no-trade clause.

Shonda was busy running not only the growing family, but also the couple's charity efforts. Both Schillings were active with the ALS Association and, after undergoing melanoma surgery in 2001, Shonda started the SHADE Foundation to promote sun-safety awareness.

The year 2001 was also when Curt Schilling helped lead the Diamondbacks to a World Series title, teaming up with Hall of Fame pitcher Randy Johnson to beat the Yankees in a wild seven-game Series. The two aces were co-winners of the Series MVP award. Schilling, never afraid to say what's on his mind, rallied his team after a pair of heartbreaking late-game losses in Games 4 and 5. When asked about the Yankees' October mystique and the aura around the team, Schilling said, "Mystique and Aura? Those are dancers in a night club. Those are not things we concern ourselves with on the ball field."

In addition to the dirty sock, the story of the Boston Red Sox's first World Series championship since 1918 also had its roots in a holiday meal.

No, not that holiday meal. Although Thanksgiving 2003 would be a key moment, the first meal that set the dominoes in motion for the Red Sox took place on Christmas Eve 2001 and involved an altogether different pitcher.

The defending champion Diamondbacks were about to add another elite pitcher to a staff that already included the best one-two punch in baseball in Schilling and Johnson. In late December, the team had a verbal agreement with 38-year-old free agent left-hander David Wells to sign a two-year contract for $1 million per year, with performance incentives pushing the potential value of the deal up to as much as $4 million.

Wells had pitched for the Yankees in 1997 and 1998, before being traded to Toronto for Roger Clemens. Wells was a lifelong fan of Babe Ruth, who shared a similar body type, and he once wore one of Ruth's old caps, purchased at auction for $35,000, out to the mound. Wells won 35 games in two years for the Yankees and pitched a perfect game.

Wells had made no secret of his desire to return to the club, but the interest didn't appear to be mutual. Wells had lunch with Yankees owner George Steinbrenner in early December and said he'd like to return to the team, to no avail.

So, when the Diamondbacks came through with their offer, Wells flew to Arizona on December 20 and shook hands with Diamondbacks owner Jerry Colangelo. He needed to pass a physical and be given a clean bill of health before any contract could be signed. Due to the holidays, however, the Diamondbacks' team doctor wouldn't be back in the office until January 4. So Wells left town with promises to return and finalize things after the new year.

"The offer they gave me was very appealing at that point in time," Wells said. "But I never signed anything."

Steinbrenner had been telling his baseball people all month that he believed Wells had something left. The fact that another team—the team that had just beaten his in the World Series—agreed with him spurred Steinbrenner into action.

Steinbrenner and Wells, both Tampa residents, met for Christmas Eve lunch at Pete & Shorty's Tavern. After about an hour, they had finished their plates of mini "shorty burgers," and Steinbrenner pulled out a holiday gift for the pitcher.

"He pulled out some paper and said, 'This is what I think that we can do,'" Wells recalled.

"I want to bring you back," Steinbrenner told Wells. "I want you to retire as a Yankee."

Steinbrenner was holding a Yankee contract for Wells, and the owner quickly ran him through the high points. It would be a two-year deal, with an option for a third. Wells would get at least $7 million for the two years, plus another $7 million if the club exercised the option for 2004. He could also earn up to $4 million in incentives each year of the contract, based on the number of games he started and innings he pitched.

After listening to the details, which blew the Arizona deal out of the water, Wells said, "Well, I don't want to be traded on July 15." Steinbrenner added a full no-trade clause to the deal.

"The baseball gods were at Pete & Shorty's that day," Wells said. "I couldn't believe what he was saying. . . . I said, 'Why didn't you say anything earlier? Why wasn't this brought up? You know, you could have done it at any time and you know what I would have said.' I guess he made me sweat. I don't know. Maybe it was just me going out there and showing a lot of interest in Arizona."

Wells hadn't told his agent, Gregg Clifton, of his lunch plans, and now he had to inform the representative that he'd agreed to a new deal with a new team.

"In my 16 years of doing this, I've never been involved in negotiations like these," Clifton said. "It's a weird situation, but it's one that makes everyone happy."

Not quite everyone.

Colangelo said that, in all his time negotiating with athletes, he'd never had a player go back on a verbal agreement.

"Whether it was a zillion dollars or 10 cents, once you shake hands on a deal, it's a deal," he said.

Of Steinbrenner, Colangelo said, "Was it unethical? Yes. I think what Steinbrenner did was not appropriate. . . . A partner in our own business encourages a player to break a commitment. You talk about what's wrong with the game. That's wrong."

Diamondbacks general manager Joe Garagiola Jr. also ripped Wells, saying, "The guy gave his word, or so we thought. Jerry specifically asked him, 'Look, this isn't about you taking this deal and going shopping to another team, is it?' And Wells said, 'No, absolutely not.'"

"I can understand that," Wells said of Garagiola's displeasure. "But he's got to look at it sort of like a business thing."

That June, the Diamondbacks played an interleague series at Yankee Stadium. With Colangelo watching from a box seat along first base, Wells retired 15 of the first 16 batters he faced, en route to a win. Afterward, Colangelo called it "water over the dam," but his true feelings soon came out.

"He knows and I know what took place and what transpired," he said, "and everybody has to live with the decisions they make."

Steinbrenner took one last parting shot, saying, "It's a free country. If he wants to bring charges up, that's up to him. I'm not going to get in the middle of this."

A seething Colangelo then left town.

Sixteen months later, Curt Schilling completed the second-to-last year on his Diamondbacks contract. At age 37, he hoped to pitch four more seasons. The Diamondbacks made it clear that they wouldn't give him a contract extension to let him retire with the team he had led to the championship. In fact, the team was looking to cut $14 million from their payroll, and Schilling was scheduled to make $12 million.

However, neither the team nor Schilling was willing to admit that he was likely headed elsewhere during the offseason. In September, Schilling was asked by a local newspaper if he would approve a trade. "I would say no, just offhand," he answered. "I would imagine I'll play my final year here and become a free agent."

"We're not really listening for offers," Arizona's assistant GM Sandy Johnson said on November 7. "If we're going to win, we're going to need Curt Schilling. His contract's a no-trade. A lot of clubs are targeting him, but there's no way we're going to be out shopping Curt Schilling. If something would come up in conversation, you'd probably listen. But that's going to be up to Curt if we did get something going."

At about that time, Steinbrenner was looking for someone to replace Roger Clemens, who was retiring, at the top of the Yankees pitching staff. A source close to Steinbrenner told a New York paper, "He's got the hots for Schilling."

By the time the general managers' meetings opened, a week later, it was clear that Schilling was going to be dealt, and he was willing to waive his no-trade clause for a few select teams.

"If I had to bet, I think the only thing I'd bet on is I probably won't be in a Diamondbacks uniform when the season starts," Schilling said on November 13. "I've said it before: If it's impossible for me to finish my career with them, I'd like to do it in Philadelphia, because that's home, and it's comfortable. That team has a chance to win the World Series. There's a new park. I love the fans there. The chance to pitch in that environment would be cool."

"As it stands right now, there are only two phone calls that would interest me," he continued. "One would be [Phillies general manager] Ed Wade saying, 'We have 72 hours to strike a deal.' The other would be [Yankees GM] Brian Cashman saying the same thing."

There had been reports that Schilling would consider a trade to the Red Sox, but he denied them. "I'm not going to Boston," he said. "I never said that. I never mentioned Boston. I'm a right-handed fly-ball pitcher. In Fenway Park, that's not a tremendous mix."

Meanwhile, Cashman was working the meetings, pursuing several angles to replace Clemens. He approached the Diamondbacks and was told that Schilling could be had, along with second baseman Junior Spivey, in exchange for Yankees second baseman Alfonso Soriano and first baseman Nick Johnson, one of the top prospects in their farm system. Cashman turned down the offer.

While waiting for the Diamondbacks to come back with a more palatable request, the Yankees GM met with the Dodgers three times, hoping to swing a deal for Odalis Perez. He followed that up with a call to the agent for free-agent pitcher Bartolo Colón and then went to dinner with Expos GM Omar Minaya to attempt to swing a deal for Javier Vazquez.

Cashman seemed to enjoy all the activity. "We don't have a plan in place," he said. "I'm a hunter and gatherer right now. I'm more of a gatherer. I haven't gotten to the hunting point."

Later, Cashman said, "I'm like a honeybee. I'll get all the honey and go back to the hive and have at it. There's been a lot of buzzing."

Confident that one of his discussions about power pitchers would bear fruit, Cashman told the Diamondbacks that Soriano was off the table. In the Yankees' view, the team was giving Arizona financial freedom by trading for Schilling, so they shouldn't be expected to give equal value in players.

The Diamondbacks were also interested in adding Milwaukee Brewers slugger Richie Sexson. The Yankees tried to set up a three-way trade that would send Sexson to Arizona, Nick Johnson to Milwaukee and Schilling to New York, but those discussions were short-lived.

It would be Johnson and Soriano, or Schilling wouldn't become a Yankee.

Colangelo told reporters, "Nick Johnson is a prospect. We think he's potentially a guy who could hit 30–35 home runs a year, and that would be a welcome addition. So would Soriano because of what he brings—the power, the speed, base-stealing, etc."

The comments earned a call from the commissioner's office, since technically it violated MLB's tampering rules. Executives are prohibited from talking publicly about players under contract to other teams. Despite the scolding, Colangelo had delivered his message. The requirement that both Yankee players be included in the deal was coming from him, and Steinbrenner would get no reduced price.

The Diamondbacks turned their attention to the trade that would wound Steinbrenner most deeply: they began negotiating to trade Schilling to the Red Sox.

"The initial asking price was extremely high," Cashman said years later, adding that the negotiations "didn't go very far, ultimately, because Boston swooped in. . . . That was something that was unanticipated, at least by me. When a player comes out publicly and says he won't go somewhere, I never expected Boston to come out and try to make a play and convince him otherwise."

Sunday, November 23, began one of the craziest weeks in the Schilling family's life. It was Shonda's birthday, but the party she hosted at her house in Phoenix had nothing to do with that event. After months of planning, she hosted 40 guests at a fundraising gala for her SHADE Foundation. Among the guests was Jerry Colangelo. He'd been a major donor to the foundation since Shonda created it and had introduced her to other Phoenix-area fundraising targets.

"That night at the party, something about him kept distracting me," Shonda wrote of Colangelo. "Throughout the night, he and Curt kept disappearing and talking secretly." When she confronted her husband and his boss, whispering in Schilling's office in the house, they gave her guilty looks and mischievous grins.

"I'm trading you," Colangelo said, and Curt burst out laughing.

At the end of the event, which raised more than $200,000 for SHADE, Shonda climbed onto a chair in the kitchen and thanked the dozen volunteers who remained to help clean up.

When she finished her remarks, Curt climbed onto the chair. "We're getting traded to the Red Sox," he said.

"Where the hell did that come from?" Shonda blurted out.

"Ordinarily, this kind of decision would not have been announced or decided at a charity dinner," Shonda admitted, "but Curt has never been one to do things in an ordinary kind of way. He didn't have agents, and in his contract decisions, he represented himself, with a little help from me."

After the last of the volunteers departed, Schilling dropped the next bombshell: Shonda wasn't done hosting guests for the week. Red Sox president Larry Lucchino, GM Theo Epstein and assistant GM Jed Hoyer would be coming to negotiate with Schilling, at the house, on Monday—or, as Curt put it to Shonda, "tomorrow."

Colangelo had been negotiating with Boston for several days and had the trade worked out. In exchange for Schilling, the Diamondbacks would receive four players.

Left-hander Casey Fossum, a 25-year-old pitcher, had split time between the Red Sox starting rotation and bullpen in his three years in the majors. He would be plagued by arm trouble in spring training and go 4–15 in his only year with Arizona. A 3–1 record with Detroit in 2008 would be the only winning record he posted for the rest of his career.

Right-hander Brandon Lyon had been a starter in two seasons with the Blue Jays before going to the Red Sox, who converted him to the bullpen for his one year in Boston. Lyon would have nerve transposition surgery in his right elbow during spring training and miss the entire 2004 season. He would return to fill the closer role for Arizona for part of two seasons.

Outfielder Mike Goss had hit .398 in 21 games at Class A in 2002 and stole 29 bases at Class A in 2003. The 23-year-old played one year in the Diamondbacks minor league system and was in independent leagues by 2005.

The 22-year-old left-hander Jorge De La Rosa would be a Diamondback for all of three days, before the team traded him to Milwaukee to land the coveted Sexson. Also included in the deal was Junior Spivey, the second baseman who would have been sent to the Yankees if they'd met Colangelo's price. The Sexson deal was even more lopsided than the Schilling trade. Arizona also gave up first baseman Lyle Overbay, who would lead the league with 53 doubles the next year; veteran infielder Craig Counsell, who would later manage the Brewers; pitcher Chris Capuano, who would win 18 games in 2004 and make the All-Star team in 2005; and backup catcher Chad Moeller. Sexson would play 23 games for the Diamondbacks before injuring his shoulder on a check swing in May. He'd leave as a free agent following the season.

The package of players provided by the Red Sox represented a massive reduction in Schilling's price compared to what the Yankees had been asked to pay just two weeks earlier. The Red Sox appeared to be receiving the David Wells Revenge Discount.

With the terms of the deal agreed upon, the Red Sox just needed to convince Schilling to waive his no-trade clause and agree to come to Boston. That was the goal of the contingent the team was sending to Schilling's house during Thanksgiving week.

In addition to recovering from the gala and hosting her husband's potential new employers, Shonda was also preparing to cook her first-ever Thanksgiving dinner. Her parents, her brother and his family, and Curt's cousin and his family would all be spending the holiday there—close to a dozen people, not counting the baseball front-office men.

As the Schillings prepared for their visitors from Boston, they found themselves hosting a few more unexpected guests. "We were taken aback by the TV trucks stationed outside our house, and the group of journalists waiting for an answer or comment," Shonda wrote.

The Red Sox party didn't visit the Schillings on Monday. Instead, Epstein and Hoyer dropped off a letter saying how excited they were to meet the couple.

Monday evening, Shonda's mother watched the children while Curt and Shonda went to dinner at Red Lobster to discuss the prospect of moving to Boston and to plan their negotiating strategy. Shonda had come a long way from the woman who cried after finding out on the radio that Curt had been traded. She would be helping her husband to negotiate a contract extension.

On Tuesday, just as Shonda's brother and his family arrived, so did Lucchino, Epstein, Hoyer and Lucchino's wife, Stacey. It was an example of the Red Sox underestimating Shonda. Stacey was brought along to answer any questions Schilling's wife might have, apparently not realizing that Shonda would be helping to represent her husband in the contract talks. The group managed to earn back some of the points they'd lost with Shonda by presenting a plan to help promote her ALS and SHADE Foundations.

For her part, Shonda was underestimating the youthful Epstein and Hoyer. In the years since, she has described her first impression of them as "cute" and "12 years old."

"They were so nice," Shonda says. "And so young. I felt either motherly or big-sisterly toward them."

The group didn't stay long. They presented statistical analysis showing that Schilling's pitching style was actually a better fit for Fenway Park than it was for the Diamondbacks' home stadium, Bank One Ballpark. They pointed out that Roger Clemens and Pedro Martínez were, like Schilling, right-handed fly-ball pitchers, and the pair had combined to win five Cy Young Awards while playing at Fenway Park.

On Wednesday, the negotiating began in earnest. Schilling had a no-trade clause in his contract, and, as is standard in cases where a player needs to be convinced—usually financially—to waive the clause, MLB had granted the Red Sox a negotiating window. Boston had 72 hours to sell Schilling on coming to Boston or the deal would be off. The group had until Friday at 5:00 p.m. to come to an agreement.

"Larry actually made the first offer," Schilling said. "I remember him pushing over a document, and it said 'Plan A' on it or something like that. I looked at the numbers for about five seconds, and I said, 'Oh, that's nice. Can I see Plan B?'"

Epstein and Lucchino chuckled and admitted that there really was no plan B.

"We discussed potential salary and things like that," Schilling recalled. "They made a couple offers, and they were not even remotely doable."

"Curt took the very unusual step of representing himself," Hoyer recalled. "He was well prepared and detail oriented throughout the process. Whenever we would exchange offers, Curt would take it and then disappear to his office for an hour or so before responding." The Red Sox contingent would go down to the basement to regroup and game plan.

At some point on the first day of talks, Schilling took a call from the Yankees. "I was told if I let a certain window run out, I could basically fill out a blank check," he recalled. "Which was obviously interesting. That was a nice fallback."

Wednesday passed without a deal. Schilling held a press conference on his front lawn to update the media camped out in front of the house.

The Lucchinos left, bound for Thanksgiving in San Diego, and the two young Boston executives were left to finish the negotiations.

"We'd resigned ourselves to having Thanksgiving dinner in our hotel rooms," Epstein said. "Shonda and Curt caught on to that as we were leaving and invited us to come over for dinner. At first, we tried to fall on our swords. Though we clearly weren't psyched about room-service turkey, we feigned protest."

Curt finally declared that the deal was off unless Hoyer and Epstein came to Thanksgiving dinner.

"Shonda felt sorry for them," Curt recalled. "We'd started to get to know and like them, and she wasn't going to let them eat some drive-thru dinner."

The two groups parted amicably, and then both parties went into a panic as soon as the car disappeared from the driveway.

Shonda was making turkey, sauerkraut, stuffing, mashed potatoes, corn, cranberries and cole slaw. "I said to my mom, 'For 30 years, you cook the dinner. And now my first is going to be national news. Great,'" Shonda said.

The negotiations went until after midnight. She set her alarm for 4:00 a.m.

Meanwhile, Epstein and Hoyer had some frantic work to do as well. In addition to working the phones to try to free up more money for Schilling's contract, they couldn't show up to dinner empty-handed.

"I figured we'd buy a bottle of wine," Epstein said. However, the only thing they could find that was open on Thanksgiving Day was a coffee shop.

"We ended up buying all the brownies they had. And they didn't have a box to put them in, so we bought this boxed coffee set, cleared out all the coffee stuff, and put the brownies in that, trying to make it look proper."

The family and their guests ate dinner and watched the Thanksgiving Day football games on television. Finally, late in the day, Shonda bid farewell to the various visiting relatives, while Curt took Epstein and Hoyer into his trophy room, where he had a replica of the World Series trophy, won in 2001.

"That's what you want, right?" he asked them. "I mean, that's why you want me."

The sides still couldn't come close on salary, however. After Thursday's negotiations ended, Schilling called Arizona GM Garagiola to make sure he could still return and play out his contract. "Realistically, though, I expected the Yankees to be in our house within an hour after the 72-hour deadline passed on Friday," Curt said.

Schilling also went onto the message boards at the Red Sox fan sites, Sons of Sam Horn and RedSox.com, putting up late-night posts that denied rumors about the negotiations. "I have not and will not demand a guaranteed three-year extension," he wrote. "I am not, have not and will not be asking for a guaranteed contract of 15 million dollars per season.

"About 90 percent of what you read is crap, the other 10 vaguely resembling truth," he wrote. He also confirmed that Epstein and Hoyer had Thanksgiving dinner at the house.

When fans questioned whether it was really Schilling posting and not an Internet hoax, Curt posted the names and ages of his children and dogs to help convince fans he was who he claimed to be. "And btw," he added, "it's Shonda, not Shanda, Shondra, Shandra."

In his hotel room that night, Epstein came up with a creative way to meet Schilling's salary demands. The Sox would promise Schilling an additional $2 million bonus if the team won the World Series.

Hoyer, meanwhile, was suffering through the worst case of food poisoning in his life. "I didn't want to go to the house the next day, because I felt really terrible," he recalled. "Actually, Larry Lucchino [back for the final day of negotiations] demanded that I went, because he didn't want to change the good mojo we had going."

Hoyer vomited all over the hotel room. Epstein, who was planning to check out that day, with the window expiring at 5:00 p.m., made an effort to clean up the mess, then decided to scatter $20 bills around the room as an apology to the cleaning staff.

Lucchino lent the ailing Hoyer a pair of socks, since his had been sprayed with vomit at some point. "I tell you, it sounds ridiculous," Hoyer recalls, "but one of my proudest things was sitting there for six hours and not throwing up. It was will power."

With a deal close, the Red Sox asked for a 24-hour extension to the deadline, due to the fact that the Thanksgiving holiday was smack dab in the middle of their negotiating window.

On Friday, Lucchino informed the Schillings he couldn't go above $10 million a year. That's when Shonda dropped a bombshell.

"Hey," she said. "I don't have a problem going to New York." She stood up and prepared to walk out. "We're not signing a contract for 10 million dollars."

The Yankees, who had already scheduled a time to be at the house on Saturday, were postponed, and, late Friday, a deal with Boston was finalized. Schilling would get a three-year, $37.5 million contract with a $2 million World Series bonus.

Schilling collected his bonus that fall. He led the American League with 21 wins in 2004 and finished as the runner-up in Cy Young voting. In the postseason, he earned a spot in Red Sox lore by returning to the mound after a procedure on his ankle, bleeding through his sock as he pitched the Red Sox to a win over the Yankees in the ALCS. Schilling also won a game in the World Series sweep over St. Louis, giving Boston its first baseball championship since 1918.

Schilling went on to play a part in another Red Sox championship three years later. He would finish his Red Sox career with a 53–29 record, a 6–1 record in the postseason, and 2–0 in the World Series.

Schilling gave the Red Sox everything they'd hoped for, as they battled the clock and illness during a Thanksgiving weekend unlike any other.

"After we were done with the deal," Hoyer recalled, "I went into his office to find a quiet place to type up the final terms. On Curt's desk was *Negotiating for Dummies*. Theo and I just cracked up."

"I brought it out into the room and shouted, 'So this is your secret?'" Epstein said. "'If you'd told me this is what you were using, we could've gotten this deal done before Thanksgiving!'"

"Curt thought it was pretty funny, though I think he was glad we found it after the fact," Hoyer said.

It took borrowed socks, a *For Dummies* book and a makeshift brownie tray, but Boston's first championship since 1918 was rooted firmly in Thanksgiving dinner at the Schilling house.

WAR COMPARISON

The Red Sox got everything they could have hoped for from Curt Schilling, giving up the WAR equivalent of one season's worth of a bench player to get him. Arizona's stubbornness over Steinbrenner's previous slights caused them to turn down a far better deal for Schilling. The Yankees actually offered more future production than they'd have received from Schilling.

RED SOX RECEIVED	WAR PRE-TRADE	WAR POST-TRADE
Curt Schilling	26.0	17.8
DIAMONDBACKS RECEIVED	WAR PRE-TRADE	WAR POST-TRADE
Casey Fossum	1.3	-1.4
Brandon Lyon	0.4	2.1
Jorge De La Rosa	0.0	0.0
Mike Goss	0.0	0.0
ASKING PRICE FOR YANKEES	WAR PRE-TRADE	WAR POST-TRADE
Nick Johnson	3.2	11.1 over next 5 years
Alfonso Soriano	9.6	16.0 over next 5 years

CHAPTER 3

— AU REVOIR, MONTREAL —

THE STORY BEHIND THE BARTOLO COLÓN TRADE

A city's last stand deserved a better trade.

The Montreal Expos were ready to make a push for the pennant in 2002 and swung a June deal to land stud starting pitcher Bartolo Colón. As is often the case, the Expos had to mortgage some of their future to land the rent-a-star. Among the players the Expos gave up were future Cy Young winner Cliff Lee, outfielder Grady Sizemore and infielder Brandon Phillips. All three players were still going strong by the time the Expos, who missed a playoff berth in 2002 by 12.5 games, had packed up and moved to Washington.

World War II was rough on the Philadelphia Phillies. In 1942, the team finished last for the fifth time in a row and in the bottom two for the tenth year in a row. They lost 100 games for a fifth straight year and, over that span, had finished a total of 263 games out of first place.

The Phillies had a total attendance of 230,183 for the 1942 season. The September 11 game against the Reds attracted a "crowd" of just 393.

The best pitcher on the team was Tommy Hughes, who won 12 out of the team's 42 games and received votes for the NL MVP award. Phillies owner Gerald Nugent hoped to sell him to another team and bring in $100,000 in much needed cash.

Hughes was drafted into the army, however, and wouldn't return to baseball until 1946, wiping out one of Nugent's few potential sources of significant income. Nugent instead traded his second-best pitcher, Rube Melton, to the Dodgers for $30,000 in cash. He also sent first baseman Nick Etten to the Yankees and received $10,000 in return.

That didn't quite get it done, financially. Nugent was two years behind in rent on Shibe Park, where the Phillies played their home games. They also still owed two years on the lease to Baker Bowl, their previous stadium, which they left in 1938.

The Phillies had taken out loans from the National League to stay afloat. All told, Nugent owed about $330,000. Then, after taking Hughes off the table, the war hit the Phillies with another blow.

Prior to spring training in 1943, MLB commissioner Kenesaw Mountain Landis declared that teams had to adhere to the government's wartime travel restrictions. While traveling to Florida for a month would have been expensive for Nugent, likely requiring another loan from the league, it was nowhere near as costly as finding a site in Philadelphia to train.

According to legend, Nugent found a buyer for the Phillies who could get him out of debt. Bill Veeck, the flamboyant marketing genius, wanted to buy the team and stock it with the best players from the Negro Leagues, breaking baseball's long-standing color barrier. Abe Saperstein—who managed the Harlem Globetrotters basketball team and was also involved with several Negro League baseball teams—was going to help Veeck find and sign the top African American players for the Phillies.

Veeck informed Landis of his plan, and the commissioner quickly worked to quash the sale, leaving Nugent without a buyer.

At an owners' meeting on February 9, 1943, the National League took control of the Philadelphia Phillies. They ran the club for nine days, until the team was sold to William Cox, a lumberman who, that November, would become the only owner ever banned from baseball for betting on his own team.

Those nine days were the only time an MLB team was run by the league for the next 57 years, until Jeffrey Loria moved to Florida.

The players' strike of 1994 was rough on the Montreal Expos. By early August that year, they had built a 6-game lead in the National League East and were sitting with the best record in baseball, at 74–40. The Expos' pitching staff—led by future Hall of Famer Pedro Martínez along with Ken Hill and Jeff Fassero—was tops in the league in ERA. The team ranked third in batting average, and the outfield of Moises Alou, Marquis Grissom and Larry Walker was among the best in baseball—both Alou and Grissom made the All-Star team.

More than 1.2 million fans had come to Olympic Stadium to watch the Expos that year, an average of 24,000 per game. It was the best team in franchise history and a favorite to win the World Series that year.

The players' association and the team owners couldn't come to an agreement on a new collective bargaining agreement, however, and on August 12, 1994, the players went on strike, ending the season. For the first time since 1904, there would be no World Series.

Regrouping for the next season, the Expos' ownership was on track to lose $25 million in 1995, so the team traded away its best, and most-expensive, players, including Grissom and Hill, and they let Walker walk away as a free agent. The Expos finished last in the division in 1995, 24 games out.

The combination of anger over the strike and frustration over the dismantling of the team kept fans away from the stadium. Attendance fell by 25 percent per game in 1995. By 1998, attendance had dropped below a million. The following year, it was down to 772,000, and in 2001, it was at 642,743, putting Montreal last in the National League in attendance for the fourth year in a row.

That attendance total would have ranked fourth in the Triple-A International League, behind the Buffalo Bisons (666,202), Louisville Bats (663,961) and Pawtucket Red Sox (647,928). Eleven minor league teams in all had a higher per-game attendance average than the Expos.

A game against the Marlins on September 19, 2001, drew a crowd of 2,887 fans to the 66,000-seat Olympic Stadium. It was the low point in a stretch of four home games that drew a total of 11,854 fans.

Starting in 2000, after a dispute between Jeffrey Loria, then an owner and managing general partner of the Expos, and the Sports Network, the Expos were no longer broadcast on local television. Loria also clashed with the radio outlets, meaning the only way to catch an Expos game outside the stadium was on French-language radio.

Meanwhile, following the 2001 season, baseball's ongoing labor dispute again reared its head. Commissioner Bud Selig and the owners had long claimed that most franchises in MLB were losing money, and several were on the brink of going out of business. Selig would testify before the U.S. Congress in December that 25 of the 30 teams lost money in 2001.

Two days after the 2001 World Series, with the collective bargaining agreement set to expire in a day, the owners voted 28–2 to contract the league and eliminate two teams: the Minnesota Twins and the Montreal Expos.

In addition to the attendance and broadcast woes, the Expos were on the chopping block largely because they weren't located in the United States. Any time baseball went to war over the collective bargaining agreement, the owners were careful not to do anything to jeopardize their antitrust exemption.

Back in 1922, Major League Baseball had won a lawsuit that allowed it to prevent teams from relocating without permission of the other owners. In most industries, this would be considered a violation of antitrust laws, but the Supreme Court ruled that baseball is a game, not interstate commerce, meaning the owners were exempt from antitrust laws. MLB is the only sports league with that exemption.

Contracting a U.S.-based team would anger thousands of voters and make enemies in Congress, which could lead to a movement to reopen an examination of baseball's legal standing regarding commerce laws.

Meanwhile, Carl Pohlad, a longtime friend of Selig's, had owned the Minnesota Twins for seventeen years and was thinking of selling. He would receive nearly a quarter-billion dollars if the Twins were contracted instead.

While it's possible that MLB would have carried out its plan to wipe out the two teams, there is also the possibility that it was all posturing for better position at the negotiating table with the players. Showing that they were prepared to eliminate 50 major league player jobs, as well as countless minor league opportunities, the owners had a significant bargaining chip. The players' association filed a grievance the day after the owners' vote.

The owners' strategy would never be put to the test, however. On November 16, ten days after MLB voted to contract the two teams, a judge in Minnesota issued a ruling in favor of the group that owned the Metrodome, the home stadium for the Twins. On September 26, the Twins had exercised the team's option to play at the Metrodome in 2002.

The stadium lease included language that said, "If the Team ceases to play major league professional baseball games for any reason, the Team shall have breached this Agreement and will be liable for such remedies as may be available to the commission at law or in equity, including, but not limited to, injunctive relief, and orders for specific performance requiring the Team to play its Home Games at the Stadium during the Term hereof."

The judge granted a temporary injunction that required the team to play its entire 2002 home schedule at the Metrodome, in essence making it illegal to contract the Twins. Contracting just one team wasn't an option, because it would leave an odd number of franchises.

The Minnesota Supreme Court refused to hear MLB's appeal of the injunction, and on February 5, Selig announced that contraction had been tabled, at least for a year.

A week later, MLB owners approved a franchise swap that had been originally designed under the assumption that the Expos would be contracted. Marlins owner John Henry sold his team and purchased the Boston Red Sox; Expos owner Jeffrey Loria purchased the Marlins from Henry for $158.5 million.

Unable to eliminate the Expos, MLB instead purchased them from Loria and operated the team for the next two seasons. Not only did the league buy Loria's team from him, for $120 million, but they agreed to loan Loria $38 million to cover the difference in the Marlins' purchase price and the Expos' selling price.

Reportedly, the terms of the loan stipulated that if the Marlins didn't get a new stadium within five years (they didn't), MLB would forgive $15 million of the loan, and the remaining $23 million would be interest-free.

Despite the legal decision on the Metrodome that prevented the elimination of the Twins, the Expos certainly looked as if they'd been contracted. Loria had been planning to take over the Marlins all off-season, as soon as his current team was contracted. He'd already moved out most of the franchise's assets.

The suddenly revived Expos needed a manager, and fortunately, MLB had a former Manager of the Year Award winner working for it. Hall of Fame player Frank Robinson had been MLB's Vice President for On-Field Operations since 1999. He was hired to be Montreal's manager, returning Robinson to the dugout for the first time since 1991.

MLB also hired Mets assistant general manager Omar Minaya to become general manager of the Expos and appointed Tony Tavares as team president.

All three roles were open, because the manager, coaches, GM and most of the front office staff had followed Loria to Florida.

With spring training set to open in three days, Minaya had to fill about 100 front office positions. Those that Loria didn't take with him had found other jobs in baseball, anticipating that the team would be contracted.

"I had seventy-two hours to put the whole staff together," Minaya recalled. "In seventy-two hours, training camp was going to open."

At that point, the Expos had a half dozen employees left in baseball operations—Triple-A manager Tim Leiper, Triple-A pitching coach Randy St. Claire, farm director Adam Wogan, trainer Ron McClain, office assistant Marcia Schnaar and media relations assistant Monique Giroux. Not only that, Loria had moved out most of the equipment that belonged to the Expos—from computers to radar guns. He also took proprietary information like scouting reports. There had long been a life-sized cardboard stand-up of Expos star outfielder Vladimir Guerrero in the business office. Loria took that too.

Despite the skeleton crew and empty offices, the Expos boasted a talented roster in 2002. Right fielder Vlad Guerrero was a legitimate star. He would hit 39 home runs, drive in 111 runs and steal 40 bases that season. Center fielder Brad Wilkerson would belt 20 home runs. Second baseman José Vidro would hit .315 and 19 home runs. Shortstop Orlando Cabrera would steal 25 bases. On the mound, Javier Vazquez would strike out 179 batters. Tomo Ohka would go 13-8 with a 3.18 ERA. Tony Armas would become a third starter to win double-digit games.

The Expos opened their season at home against Loria's Marlins. He didn't bring any of their old office equipment with him. Montreal won on a walk-off single by Cabrera after erasing a two-run Marlins lead in the ninth, and 34,351 Expos fans went home happy. A combined total of 9,322 fans would attend the next two games of the series.

The Expos were in first place for 22 days in April. They won 6 straight and 9 of 11 at the end of the month to move to 7 games over .500. The team came back down to earth in May, but they still finished the month at .500, just 2.5 games out of first.

An 8-game winning streak from June 12 to 21 stamped the Expos as a contender. The team was six games over .500 and jumped from fourth to second place, 4.5 games out.

Prior to the season, commissioner Selig promised that the Expos wouldn't be asked to hold any fire sales. "From this day forward, in terms of decisions they make, they are on their own," he said.

However, the 29 other MLB teams were chipping in to meet Montreal's payroll. While they didn't have any say over the moves Minaya made, they did control the budget. That meant Minaya would have his hands tied in any attempts to add players for the pennant race.

Back across the border, the Cleveland Indians were having a roller coaster year. The defending AL Central Division champs opened the 2002 season with an 11–1 record, including a 10-game winning streak. They immediately followed that up with a 6-game losing streak and dropped 15 of 17 games. On May 3, they were 13–16, in third place. Cleveland hovered around 4.5 games back until June but, by mid-May, the team had lost hope of a repeat division title.

"We began considering our alternatives," GM Mark Shapiro said. "We could either add players or trade players. We felt the picture was too bleak this year to win and it could be worse next year. So we decided we would trade and try to build another championship team."

One of the most valuable trade chips Shapiro had was starting pitcher Bartolo Colón. The right-hander went 18–5 in 1999, finishing fourth in Cy Young voting, and had won at least 14 games each of the previous four seasons. Still only 29 years old, he was well on his way to adding a fifth, holding a 10–4 record by late June.

Shapiro needed to find teams who had prospects that made losing Colón worthwhile.

"About mid-May, we studied all of the organizations and concluded that Montreal had the best young players who could be ready to help us in the next twelve months," said Shapiro. "We talked to all of the contenders and some teams that could be contenders next year, but we felt Montreal had the best fit."

Montreal's Minaya also looked at his situation in May and came to the same conclusion as Shapiro.

"I told myself, 'Just because we're the Expos doesn't mean we can't compete for these players,'" Minaya recalled. "When you have a chance to get a young pitcher like Bartolo Colón, I'm not going to pass this up."

The Expos would be a buyer as the trade deadline approached. And although Minaya couldn't add salary, that limitation was counterbalanced by the fact that he was a short-timer in a lame-duck job. The league was still attempting to wipe out the team he worked for, so he had no reason to worry about keeping minor league prospects for the future.

Minaya's game plan sounded noble, albeit a bit like the plot to a Disney film. "We were trying to save the team by trying to contend," he said. "I didn't know where things were with potential buyers or anything, but we felt if we got into the playoffs, the town would have supported us, and the private sector would offer more support. . . . Our goal was to win. Getting to the playoffs would have created that demand from politicians, entrepreneurs, to say, 'Hey, we gotta step up as a city to save this.'"

Minaya looked to Seattle as a model. The goodwill the Mariners had built up with a playoff run in 1995 helped them get a new stadium.

Shapiro and Minaya talked in early June, while the Indians GM was still gauging interest in Colón and the price he could get for him.

"We had a small conversation," Minaya recalled. "I said, 'Keep me in mind.' We talked about different names. It kept building and building."

By late June, with the Expos still lurking in contention, Minaya was ready to move. "I told Mark, 'If we're going to do this, let's do it this week. The longer this goes on the harder it will be for me to do this.' If we waited for the thirty-first [July 31, the trade deadline], we might not be around the thirty-first. We could be ten, twelve games back and not be a player. If I waited to the thirty-first, there also would be more competition."

Several other teams had checked on Colón, including the A's—who offered first baseman Carlos Peña, who was on his way to 19 home runs in his rookie season, and 24-year-old second baseman Esteban Germán—and the Yankees. But none could match the prospects that the Expos were dangling.

"They needed to get their socks knocked off," Mets GM Steve Phillips said about Shapiro and the Indians. "We didn't think we had the right fit. . . . I couldn't do that deal."

"We played, but we couldn't make the economics work," Reds GM Jim Bowden said.

So, it appeared that Colón would be headed to Montreal. Minaya and Shapiro then set about tackling the tough part of the deal: putting the trade together in a way that didn't increase the Expos' payroll.

"We went through many scenarios," Minaya said. "I finally said, 'We're going to have to think outside the box. I can't add payroll, but let's exchange ideas—because I don't have payroll, but I do have a lot of ideas.'"

Colón had a $4.9 million salary. In order to bring him to the Expos without asking MLB for more money, Minaya included Expos first baseman Lee Stevens and his $4 million salary in the deal. The Indians would make up the $900,000 difference in salary by sending the Expos cash.

After knocking at least 20 home runs in five straight seasons, Stevens was hitting just .190 in 2002, although he had 10 homers in the first half of the season. He'd lost his starting job to 41-year-old Andrés Galarraga, who Minaya had signed for $500,000 in March, gambling—correctly—that the former Expos All-Star still had something left in the tank.

"Atlanta didn't want me, a couple of teams didn't want me, and the Expos gave me the opportunity to play," said Galarraga, who had a battle with cancer two years earlier. "That is something more special, more personal, because the Expos is where I started."

The trade to Cleveland came as no surprise to Stevens. "I knew that, sooner or later, the team would do something," he said after being informed of the deal. "Personally, I was surprised to merit a spot on the team this spring."

The Expos also gave up their top prospect: 21-year-old shortstop Brandon Phillips, who was hitting .327 with 9 homers in 60 games at Double-A Harrisburg. "I didn't want to give him up," Minaya said. "I sat on him for a while. But the more I thought about it, the more I realized it was hard for me to pass up Colón."

Finally, Minaya told Shapiro he was ready to "cross that bridge," if Shapiro was ready to cross his.

The deal included Montreal's top pitching prospect, lefty Cliff Lee. The 23-year-old was 7–2 at Double-A, with 105 strikeouts in 86.1 innings. He was allowing less than one baserunner per inning.

Shapiro also wanted a player from the Expos' major league roster, to help satisfy the fans and Indians players, who would be furious that the popular Colón was gone. His first choice was Brad Wilkerson, the 25-year-old center fielder in the midst of a career year.

"We realized they're trying to win this year and they couldn't do it," Shapiro said of trading Wilkerson. Instead, he took another minor leaguer, outfielder Grady Sizemore, and risked the wrath of the city of Cleveland. Sizemore was a third-round draft pick who was hitting .343 in Class A.

In addition to Colón, the Indians sent the Expos Tim Drew. The former first-rounder had spent the previous three seasons in Triple-A Buffalo, where he won 23 games and earned a few brief trips to the big leagues.

When the deal was announced, on June 27, it sent shockwaves through baseball. The lowly Expos were making a run at the pennant.

"When it came across the wire, people said 'Wait a minute, this don't fit. Montreal is not supposed to be getting these guys, it's supposed to give these guys back,'" Minaya said. "It was fun for me to hear that."

"If anything, it's a morale trade," Minaya continued. "Our players are thrilled and after the way they've played for Frank, it's important that they know we're going to do everything we can to help them try to win. It's important for the fans in Montreal, too. We want them to come aboard and start supporting us."

"I hope it sends a message to our fans and players that we are trying to be competitive and trying to make the playoffs," he added.

Minaya defended himself against criticism that he'd given up too much, prospect-wise. "I would've done this trade even if I had a five-year contract," he said. "Colón is one of the premier pitchers in baseball and when you've got a chance to get someone like him, you've got do it." He pointed out that the 29-year-old Colón still had another year on his contract, too, so it wasn't "any rent-a-player deal."

Minaya then headed to Yankee Stadium to scout another starting pitcher, Orlando Hernández. "Not by a longshot am I done," he said. "I don't know what's gonna happen after this year. We may be relocated, sold or contracted out, but, for now, we're competing and committed. I got no money, but I got ideas."

The "morale trade" had the expected impact in the clubhouse.

"You have to congratulate Omar Minaya on making a great trade," second baseman José Vidro said. "He really showed everybody that he's not thinking about contraction and all that stuff. He's just thinking about making this team better. He promised to everybody that if he had to deal our prospects he would try to make this team better, and he kept his word. We're happy. Everybody's excited."

"Colón gives us a staff," manager Frank Robinson said. "We go into Atlanta now—they go with [Greg] Maddux, [Tom] Glavine, [Kevin] Millwood. Now we can match up with anybody."

"If the way we've competed this year didn't already send a message, then I don't know what would," Robinson continued. "All I know is that this sends a message to the players that we have in this clubhouse that we are serious about putting the best product on the field that we possibly can."

The reaction in Cleveland was as bad as Shapiro had feared.

"It's a big blow to us, a shock," said Indians starter CC Sabathia. "Bartolo was certainly the best pitcher on the staff. He carried the load for this team."

Shortstop Omar Vizquel took it a step further. "Now there are a lot of guys that are very disappointed," he said. "It's hard to see the best pitcher on your team go like that. We felt Bartolo was the next Bob Feller of the Cleveland Indians."

Fans had a virtual riot on sports radio.

"I feel very mixed emotions," Colón said. "It was only this morning, listening to the radio, the fans, the anger, that I realized these are great fans. But I hope to have the same thing in Montreal."

Shapiro didn't earn any points with his statement on the trade: "This very clearly and very definitively demonstrates that we are moving into a formal rebuilding process with players that we all feel are going to be here in the '04 and '05 seasons, which are when we feel we can start to emerge as a contender again. From the start of the offseason, we stated that if the difficult goal of transitioning and contending was not successful, we would have to enter into a more dramatic and profound rebuilding process. That is the juncture where we find ourselves today."

The Expos couldn't have asked for much more from Colón. He matched his first-half performance by going 10–4 for the Expos after the trade. He finished the year a combined 20–8 with a 2.93 ERA.

Minaya also continued to do his part. Two weeks after the Colón trade, he swung an eight-player deal with the Marlins to acquire outfielder Cliff Floyd, who had 31 homers the previous season and was in the midst of a 28-homer year.

"To be able to add Bartolo Colón and Cliff Floyd without taking on money, that's a huge challenge," Minaya said, "but that's why I love this job."

The Expos just couldn't make a run at first place, however. In between the two trades, the team went 6–7. They lost 8 of 9 shortly after Floyd arrived.

Meanwhile, not counting the strike season that still haunted the Expos, the first-place Braves had won the last 10 division titles. They were used to fending off challenges from teams, whether it was the Giants, Mets, Phillies or Marlins. They saw the Expos loading up in their rear-view mirror and hit the gas.

The Braves won 11 of 12, beginning the week before the Colón trade when the Expos were still in negotiations to acquire him. They ran off a streak of 6 wins in 7 games at the start of July and won 6 straight shortly after the All-Star break. The explosion took Atlanta from 12 games over .500 and nursing a 4.5 game lead to 28 over and a 13.5 game margin. The National League East race was essentially over by the end of July. And, just in case the Expos got any ideas, Atlanta sandwiched a 7-game winning streak around the July 31 trade deadline.

Minaya raised the white flag on July 30. The only trade he made at the deadline was to send Cliff Floyd to the Red Sox, 19 days after acquiring him.

"When we acquired Cliff Floyd there were close to seventy games left," Minaya said. "Right now, we have close to fifty games left. We've got five teams in front of us. When we acquired Cliff Floyd, we didn't have five teams in front of us. I think we were second in the wild card. That's one difference."

Another difference was that Floyd hit just .208 in his 15 games with the Expos and struck out 10 times in 57 at bats. He took responsibility for the team falling out of the race.

"I wish we had done better and the situation would have been different but we didn't, and I played a big part of it," he said. "I didn't do as well as I thought I should have in the fifty at bats or so that I got here, but I felt my swing starting to come around so hopefully I can go help their team."

After the season, MLB again failed in an attempt to contract the Expos, and the league's strange custody relationship with the franchise would continue another season. Seemingly punishing the team for its own inability to kill them off, MLB made things even tougher for the Expos in 2003. Selig announced that the team would get a slight increase in their budget for the upcoming season. In order to raise revenue, the team would play half its home games in Puerto Rico, meaning a brutal travel schedule for the Expos players.

Unfortunately for Minaya, Colón was scheduled for a big salary increase. The team had a $6 million option on him for the following year, and the million-dollar raise wouldn't fly. Minaya ended up trading Colón to the White Sox in the offseason, receiving the pitcher he'd scouted the year before—Orlando Hernández—in return, along with pitcher Rocky Biddle (20–30, 5.47 ERA in a five-year MLB career) and Jeff Liefer (a .230 career hitter). Hernández never pitched an inning for the Expos, missing the entire 2003 season to injury and then rejoining the Yankees as a free agent. Biddle and Liefer were both out of the majors by 2005.

Essentially, the Expos traded away Cliff Lee, Grady Sizemore and Brandon Phillips, and all they had to show for it less than a year later was Rocky Biddle and Jeff Liefer.

Against all odds, the Expos competed again in 2003. They spent all but one day in April in first place and were just two games out by the end of May. The team still had a shot at the Wild Card with a September run, but MLB hit them with one last body blow.

Rosters expand to 40 on September 1, allowing teams to add up to 15 minor league players to help provide late-season reinforcements. When Minaya tried to call up prospects from his farm system, the commissioner's office vetoed the promotions, due to "budgetary reasons"—the few thousand dollars it would cost were not in the team's budget.

"That was the lowest point, by far," Minaya said, years later.

"It was a message to the players," Minaya added. "It was a momentum killer. . . . The guys who were there those three years—there was a bond there. We felt basically like David, that's the only way I could describe it. We were David and there were twenty-nine other clubs that were Goliath."

Unfortunately, in baseball, Goliath sometimes wins, and Disney movie endings are few and far between. The Expos played one final year in Montreal, finishing 2004 with a 67–95 record. MLB announced they were moving the team to Washington the following season. Minaya resigned in September.

As expected, by the time the prospects Minaya was willing to deal reached the major leagues, he and the Expos were long gone. After getting traded from Montreal, Cliff Lee went 83–48 for the Indians and won the Cy Young Award in 2008, when he went 22–3 with a 2.54 ERA. He pitched a no-hitter for Cleveland on June 14, 2009, and two weeks later he was traded to the Phillies, whom he would help lead to the World Series. Lee went 4–0 in the 2009 postseason. After a brief stop in Seattle, he joined the Texas Rangers for their run to the 2010 World Series.

Grady Sizemore led the league in doubles and runs scored in 2006. His power, nonexistent when he was in the Montreal farm system, blossomed in the majors; he had four straight 20-home run seasons, including a high of 33 in 2008. He was a two-time Gold Glove Award winner in the outfield.

Brandon Phillips never got a full-season shot in Cleveland, but he developed into a top-level second baseman after he was traded to the Reds prior to the 2006 season. He had a 30/30 (30 homers and 30 stolen bases) season in 2007, drove in 103 runs in 2013 and twice scored 100. He also nabbed four Gold Gloves while with Cincinnati.

All three of the prospects Minaya traded made multiple All-Star teams. All three received MVP votes in at least one post-trade season.

In 2016, a 43-year-old, overweight Bartolo Colón was still succeeding at the major league level. Since leaving the Expos, he played for the White Sox (twice), Angels, Red Sox, Yankees, A's and Mets. He won 21 games for the Angels in 2005 and won the American League Cy Young Award. At age 40 in 2013, he won 18 games for Oakland and led the league with three complete-game shutouts. He posted a fifth straight double-digit win season by going 15–8 for the Mets in 2016 and making the All-Star team.

Colón's flailing style when asked to bat in Mets games was a source of Internet memes, until he hit his first career home run in 2016. Sporting a noticeable gut, he also made a spectacular behind-the-back throw to first base in the field, showing that, despite appearances, he still had plenty left.

According to research by Baseball Essential's Joshua Sadlock, six other former Montreal players tried but failed to catch on with MLB or minor league teams at some point during the 2015 season, making Bartolo Colón the last Expo standing—the final active player who had once worn a Montreal jersey.

At the 2015 All-Star Game, new commissioner Rob Manfred announced that Major League Baseball was considering expansion. One of the cities on the short list was Montreal.

WAR COMPARISON

By WAR alone, the Expos had reasons to regret the Bartolo Colón trade. Cliff Lee, Brandon Phillips and Grady Sizemore all had long careers as starters and All Stars. For giving that up, Montreal received the equivalent of one starter-quality season from Colón, then were fleeced when budget issues forced the Expos to deal him away a year later.

The true loss of the deal can't be measured by WAR, as the city of Montreal lost its team. While it's no guarantee that a playoff run would have prevented that outcome, it would have made it much tougher to leave town.

EXPOS RECEIVED	WAR PRE-TRADE	WAR POST-TRADE
Bartolo Colón	22.6	2.4 with Expos, 9.5 over next five years
Tim Drew	-1.6	-0.5
INDIANS RECEIVED	WAR PRE-TRADE	WAR POST-TRADE
Cliff Lee	0.0	16.2
Brandon Phillips	0.0	-1, 23.7 with Cincinnati after 4 years in Cleveland
Grady Sizemore	0.0	27.5
Lee Stevens	-0.6	0.3
EXPOS RECEIVED FOR COLON, SEVEN MONTHS LATER	WAR PRE-TRADE	WAR POST-TRADE
Orlando Hernández	0.4	0.0
Rocky Biddle	-0.2	-2.8
Jeff Liefer	-0.9	-1.2

CHAPTER 4

— TO HAVE AND HAVE NOT —

THE STORY BEHIND THE QUARTER-BILLION-DOLLAR TRADE

The rare salary dump that produces a good trade.

The most expensive trade of all time took place in late 2012, when two players with $100 million left on their contracts were swapped. Altogether, $260 million worth of salary was swapped in an intricate, complex deal, as the Boston Red Sox accomplished the biggest salary dump in history in a trade with the Los Angeles Dodgers. Unlike most trades involving mega-salaries, however, this one had an impact on the field, not just the balance sheet.

Four years after their most recent World Series title, the Boston Red Sox were bad in 2011. In fact, things were so bleak in Boston that merely bad teams could take solace in the fact that they weren't the Red Sox.

Part of the blame was placed at the foot of the manager, Terry Francona, a pleasant, outgoing former player who had the reputation of being a "player's manager." When the collection of free spirits and goofballs that included Pedro Martínez, Curt Schilling, Manny Ramirez and Kevin Millar won the 2004 World Series, Francona's willingness to give the players room to express themselves and stay loose was considered one of the reasons.

However, when the team went south in the standings, winning just one postseason series in the four years from 2008 to 2011, the blame was placed on Francona's lack of discipline. Suddenly, the inmates were running the asylum. Things imploded down the stretch in 2011. The team won just 6 of their last 24 games as they blew a 9-game lead and missed the postseason. After the season, word leaked out that several pitchers, including Josh Beckett, would frequently go into the clubhouse during games to drink beer, eat fried chicken and play video games, instead of rooting for their teammates from the bench.

It's rare for a starting pitcher to remain in the dugout until the end of the game. Once he's been removed from the mound, he generally goes back to the clubhouse to get treatment on his arm. While icing his moneymaker, it's not unheard of for a pitcher to imbibe in an adult beverage and get a head start on the postgame meal. It's rarer still for a starter not scheduled to pitch that day to remain in the dugout for the full nine innings, without heading back to the clubhouse for some R&R.

The fans of Boston either didn't know this or didn't care. Memories of Schilling's bloody sock—the result of an ankle surgery he had between starts in the 2004 postseason—were still fresh in their minds. Schilling's toughness and leadership contrasted with Beckett's take-it-or-leave-it approach to the sport, while playing under a contract promising him $15.75 million a year for three more seasons. The fact that Beckett pitched twice in the final 7 games of the epic collapse, giving up 6 earned runs and 2 homers in each of them while losing, certainly didn't help.

Francona was fired following the 2011 season, replaced by Bobby Valentine in a textbook managerial move. When a team stops listening to a "player's manager," he's replaced by a drill sergeant. Valentine would take no crap, nor would he back down from an argument. The hope was, he'd whip the lazy Sox into shape and shut down the mid-game locker-room parties.

The move was an unmitigated disaster. Boston players rebelled against the tyrannical Valentine almost immediately, and the team was floundering along at 60–66 in late August, on the way to its first losing season since 1997.

Beckett, whom the team was unable to trade in the offseason, showed his inability to read a room in early 2012. After missing a start in May due to injury, Beckett went out to play golf on an off day, leading fans to once again question his commitment.

Beckett also became lax in his conditioning workouts, despite the pleas of strength coach Dave Page. That led one team insider to grouse to the *Boston Herald*, "It's hard for a guy making $80,000 to tell a $15 million pitcher he needs to get off his butt and do some work."

The Red Sox tried again to deal Beckett prior to the trade deadline, in 2012, to no avail. They offered him to the Dodgers, but Los Angeles was more interested in Jon Lester, another of the chicken-and-beer squad. But since Lester was four years younger and had potential to be the ace of the future, the Red Sox were not looking to trade him.

"If people don't want you, you don't want to be there," Beckett said, just prior to the deadline on Boston sports radio.

One executive approached by Boston about a potential trade explained, "Nobody wants him and he makes a ton of money."

Also making a ton of money was Adrian Gonzalez, one of the best hitters in the game. The first baseman had been acquired by Boston from the San Diego Padres before the 2011 season and signed to a seven-year, $154 million contract before playing a game for the Sox.

Gonzalez seemed worth the money in his first season with the team, when he won a Gold Glove for his defense at first base, a Silver Slugger for his hitting and finished seventh in MVP voting. Still, Gonzalez didn't have the oversized personality, like Pedro and Big Papi (David Ortiz) who won over the fans of Boston. Fans were quick to note his inflated salary—the *Providence Journal* pointed out that he made $134,920.63 per game—and the fact that he hit .183 against the hated Yankees and .131 against Tampa Bay, as the Sox fell behind both division rivals in September.

In the midst of the September collapse, Gonzalez also made the mistake of complaining about Boston's travel schedule. "We play too many night games on getaway days and get into places at four in the morning," he said. "This has been my toughest season physically because of that."

When Gonzalez opened the 2012 season in an uncharacteristic slump, he fell even further out of favor. In early May, he was hitting just .254 with 2 home runs. He also began ducking the media on occasion, after enduring a particularly rough game. Still, silence was probably better than his response on the final day of the 2011 season, when Gonzalez seemingly shrugged off a heartbreaking loss that eliminated the Red Sox with, "It wasn't God's plan for us to be in the playoffs."

Valentine wasn't able to light a fire under Gonzalez. Quite the contrary. Gonzalez led a group of more than a dozen players to meet with ownership in late July, complaining that they didn't want to play for Valentine.

Carl Crawford was another big acquisition prior to the 2011 season. The Sox decided to sign him to a seven-year, $142 million contract. He responded with a season where he hit a career-low .255, 52 points lower than he hit in 2010. His home runs dropped from 19 to 11, RBI from 90 to 56 and stolen bases from 47 to 18. He hit so poorly that the Sox dropped him to seventh in the order, not the spot for a $20 million a year free-agent pickup. In the final game of the 2011 season, with a chance for Boston to salvage a playoff berth, Crawford misplayed a fly ball, allowing the winning run to score.

The 2012 season was even worse. Crawford injured his wrist before the season, and, just when he was ready to return from that rehab, he injured his elbow. Crawford didn't play his first game until July 16, when the season was 90 games old.

Valentine mocked the brittle Crawford and the front office's guideline that he not play in more than four consecutive games in order to avoid injury from overuse. Valentine played Crawford in the first six games he was healthy. Then, after a day off, the manager sent him out for 5 straight games. Following another off day, Valentine had Crawford play the next 20 games in a row. Crawford's elbow gave out, and he had season-ending Tommy John surgery, which would keep him out for nine months.

"I did a manager no-no thing and went against what I was told to do—never to be done again," Valentine said.

But the damage was done. Lazy Beckett, indifferent Gonzalez and injured Crawford: they symbolized all that was wrong with the Red Sox. They were also the team's three highest-paid players. Between them they made more than $59 million in 2012, more than the entire payrolls of the A's and Padres.

It was time for a change.

In Los Angeles, the change had already occurred, and the Dodgers were ready to reap the benefits. Owner Frank McCourt and his wife, team CEO Jamie McCourt, had spent 2009 through 2011 battling in divorce court. The couple spent $20.9 million in payments to divorce lawyers and put the team in bankruptcy.

As one of the most-expensive and nastiest divorces dragged on, details on the McCourts' lifestyle emerged: They'd spent $14 million to tear up tennis courts at their mansion and replace them with an Olympic-sized pool. Jamie's monthly expenses totaled nearly a million dollars, including house calls from hairdressers and makeup artists. Plus, the couple had to decide how to divide up the properties in Massachusetts, Colorado, Wyoming, Mexico and the side-by-side beach houses they'd purchased in Malibu.

Baseball commissioner Bud Selig got involved. He accused McCourt of "looting" the Dodgers' finances for $189 million to help fund his lifestyle and legal battles. Baseball took control of the club while searching for a buyer for one of the sport's showcase franchises.

In the meantime, the crosstown Angels had staked their claim to the title of most-popular team in the Los Angeles area. The Angels were owned by Arte Moreno, who was the first Mexican American to own a major sports franchise, and the Latino population in the area had responded. The Angels outdrew the Dodgers in 2011 for the first time ever, and they followed that up by signing one of the best players in baseball—Albert Pujols—to an enormous ten-year, $254 million contract. The Dodgers needed new ownership and new blood to win back the "City of Angels" from the Angels.

In early 2012, the Dodgers were finally sold. The new ownership group included Magic Johnson, former Braves president Stan Kasten and Mark Walter, the CEO of the Guggenheim Partners investment group. The group purchased the team, Dodger Stadium and the land surrounding it for a record $2.3 billion. The purchase price included a $131 million payment to Jamie McCourt to finally settle the couple's divorce. (A year later, she tried, unsuccessfully, to challenge the settlement in court, in order to receive a bigger share of the sale price.)

The new owners swept in, promising to spend money to build a winner. At the opening press conference, Magic announced that parking prices would be cut from $15 to $10. "We understand that you have to spend money to be good," Johnson said. "We're not going to gouge the fans just because we paid a nice sum for this franchise," he added. "We don't want the fans to think because we wrote a big check, we're going to stop writing checks for talent. We don't want people to think we're short on money now. That's not the case."

In addition to winning over the fans, the ownership group won over the guys in the clubhouse.

"You could feel a difference with the fans instantly," manager Don Mattingly said. "There's been so much negative for the last few years that it just gets kind of old for guys that are playing because people aren't showing up and it doesn't have anything to do with if you win or not. And I think the energy's been great with the new group. Hearing the things these guys are talking about wanting to do, it fits in right with what we want to do. We came to win. These guys come and they work hard, and at the end of the day they want to be fighting for a championship, and it sounds like the group we have coming are all about that."

"It's a cool time," ace pitcher Clayton Kershaw said.

Two days after the new owners took over, the Dodgers signed their first free agent. Bobby Abreu was a former All-Star and Home Run Derby champion who had played with the Angels for the previous three seasons. Past his prime, Abreu didn't do much for the Dodgers on the field, but he gave the new owners a chance to make a statement.

A month later, the new regime made a more significant series of moves. First, the Dodgers signed one of their promising young starts, outfielder Andre Ethier, to a contract extension that would pay him $85 million over five years. Two weeks later, they signed Cuban defector Yasiel Puig to a seven-year, $42 million contract. Other teams were shocked that the Dodgers shelled out so much for a guy who hadn't played competitively in more than a year. One anonymous executive told *Baseball America* the deal was "crazy," while another said, "I don't know what's going on in Dodger Land."

Crazy or not, the new atmosphere revived the franchise. The Dodgers found themselves 12 games over .500 and in first place in mid-August. The front office also had been active at the July 31 trade deadline. Los Angeles picked up infielder Hanley Ramirez from the Marlins, relief pitcher Brandon League from the Mariners and outfielder Shane Victorino from the Phillies. Ramirez was a three-time All-Star due $31 million over the next two seasons.

"If it comes down to a strictly baseball move, we have the right to do whatever we need to," GM Ned Colletti said, "Which is a tremendous position to be in. We're not going to let money stand in the way of a true baseball move."

The Dodgers were still looking to add pitching. They put in a waiver claim on Phillies ace Cliff Lee, who had more than $87 million remaining on his contract, but the two sides couldn't get together on a trade.

Eager to establish themselves as big spenders on the level of the Yankees, Angels and Red Sox, the Dodgers wanted to do whatever it took to win now, and they were in the process of getting a new multi-billion-dollar television deal, which would fill their coffers. So, when one of the other big spenders came along, looking to cut salary, it set the stage for a match-to-powder-keg deal.

The Red Sox and Dodgers pulled off the biggest waiver-period trade in baseball history, and one of the largest, financially, of all time.

A quick primer on August trades in baseball: the July 31 trade deadline usually spurs teams into a maelstrom of activity, but the date is actually mislabeled. On rare occasions, you'll hear it referred to properly, as the *non-waiver* trade deadline. Simply put, up until the deadline, a team can trade whoever it wants, with whatever team it wants. In essence, it's an open market that closes at the end of July.

For the final two months of the season, teams can trade players only after they've passed through waivers. A team needs to inform the rest of the major league teams that it is considering getting rid of a guy, if anybody wants him. That's called putting him on waivers. Other teams can then put in a waiver claim on the player, saying, "Yes, I'm interested." If multiple teams put in a claim, the team with the worst record has priority.

Once a player has been claimed on waivers, the team that waived him has a few options: It can simply give up the player to the team that claimed him; it can pull him back off waivers, saying, "Never mind. We're keeping him;" or the two teams can try to work out a deal.

If a team waives a player and no one claims him, then the team can deal him to whatever team it wants.

Throughout the month of August each season, a game of chess is going on over the waiver wire among team executives. Teams will try to sneak players through waivers so they can be traded. On rare occasions, a team will try to beat the system by putting nearly its entire roster on waivers, hoping to overwhelm the rest of the league and get some players through without a claim, thus allowing the team to trade freely. Teams will sometimes put in claims on a waived player, simply to block a divisional rival from making a deal to improve its roster—but they have to be cautious about claiming too many players, lest they be stuck with someone they don't really want, if the waiving team decides to give him up.

Trades can still get done after the non-waiver deadline, but clearly it's rather complicated. That didn't stop Boston and Los Angeles, however. The two teams managed to put together a nine-player deal that moved $270 million worth of salary, with most of it going west, from Boston to Los Angeles. The teams moved seven players through waivers, convinced Beckett and Crawford to waive their no-trade clauses and cut a quarter of a billion dollars from future Red Sox payrolls.

For the Red Sox, it was addition by subtraction, and it worked out better than even their most optimistic projections. Boston got rid of Crawford, Beckett, Gonzalez and middle infielder Nick Punto.

Punto provided the punchline of Boston's side of the deal. A year later, when Boston writers headed to Los Angeles to do a looking-back story on the trade, the three bitter ex-Sox refused to speak to them, as payback for past criticism.

Punto was the spokesperson for the group. "I have an issue with [Hall of Fame writer and TV commentator] Peter Gammons," he said. "He did a 30-minute segment [on the trade] and didn't mention my name once. Tell him I'm looking for him."

The money involved in the deal underscored the absurdity of baseball's haves and have-nots. Gonzalez was owed $127 million over the next six years. Beckett had two years and $31 million remaining on his contract. Crawford was owed $102.5 million over five years. And Punto? One year, $1.5 million—or a little over 0.5 percent of the salary Boston was dumping.

Remarkably, the Dodgers were absorbing more than 95 percent of the remaining money on the contracts. Normally, when a player with a large salary is traded, the team shedding the contract will need to pony up a portion of the money the player is owed, to make him more palatable to the team trading for him. (See: Alex Rodriguez to the Yankees.) The Red Sox had to pay only $12 million of the $262.5 million remaining on the four players' deals. That money would be spread over the next six years.

The Dodgers didn't care about chicken in the clubhouse or the exorbitant salaries they were adding to the payroll. This was the statement deal that they hoped would clinch them a spot in the playoffs and leave the Angels in their rear-view mirror. Beckett and Crawford were big names and could help the team once they became healthy (Crawford) and motivated (Beckett). The moody first baseman Gonzalez, however, was the key to the deal.

While Gonzalez may not have had the personality Boston fans wanted, he was tailor-made for the laid back LA crowds. Gonzalez was born in San Diego, to David and Alba, both Mexican immigrants. David had played baseball for the Mexican national team. As a young child, Gonzalez and his family moved to Tijuana, where they lived until Adrian was eight years old. At the end of the 2012 season, the new Dodger would be named an "exemplary citizen" by the mayor of Tijuana.

For the first time since Fernando Valenzuela, the pudgy left-hander from Sonora, created Fernando Mania in 1981, the Dodgers had a legitimate star of Mexican heritage. With the greater Los Angeles area home to 4.9 million Latinos, or 9 percent of the nation's total Hispanic population, Gonzalez's nationality presented a powerful marketing opportunity.

In return, the Dodgers sent the Red Sox about $10 million in salary obligations. Most of that came from James Loney, who was making $6.3 million in 2012 and was scheduled to make about $2 million the following year. The other four players heading to Boston were all making the major league minimum (about $480,000) or just over it.

Loney was a 27-year-old first baseman who would have lost his job to Gonzalez had he not been included in the trade. The Red Sox also acquired Allen Webster, a 22-year-old right-handed pitcher in his first full season at Double-A, and 24-year-old infielder Iván DeJesús Jr., the son of the shortstop the Cubs traded for Ryne Sandberg 30 years earlier. DeJesús had played a total of 40 games with the Dodgers over two years. It would take him until late 2015 to play 40 more in the majors.

Three of the four players the Dodgers received—everyone except Beckett—produced more Wins Above Replacement with Los Angeles than they had in Boston. They came at a high cost, however.

The Dodgers paid the newly acquired players $9.3 million per win above replacement (WAR). By comparison, the 2014 Yankees, who had one of the highest payrolls ever for a team that missed the playoffs—$218 million—paid about $6.6 million per win above replacement (WAR) that season.

Rumors of the deal began to pick up steam on Friday, August 24, when Loney was scratched from the Dodgers lineup, Gonzalez and Punto from the Red Sox.

"There's still nothing for me to talk about at this point," Mattingly told the media before and after the Dodgers' home game against the Marlins.

Across the country, as the Red Sox hosted the Royals in a game at Fenway Park, Valentine was also out of the loop.

"I have no thoughts at all," he said. "I saw it scroll on the bottom of my TV. . . . I talked to Ben this afternoon and there was no mention—at all. There wasn't a mention of 'who do you want?' There wasn't any conversation, so I believe it's nothing more than the standard operational of a guy gets claimed, it's a block, it's not a trade and life goes on. . . . I'm sure if there's something that's concrete, it'll be presented to me or I'll get to read it on the scroll."

In addition to the seven major league players that had cleared waivers, two other names were appearing on the scrolls for ESPN and other sports channels. Jerry Sands, an outfielder with 26 home runs at Triple-A Albuquerque, and right-handed reliever Rubby De La Rosa, were rumored to be the eighth and ninth players in the deal, both headed to Boston. ESPN reported the news.

"That's how I found out I'd been traded," Sands said. "I saw my name on the crawl."

De La Rosa had just been called up, two days earlier, to appear in his only MLB game of the season, in which he gave up two runs in two thirds of an inning. He was expected to be optioned to Triple-A on Friday, but the team changed plans at the last minute, sending him to Double-A Chattanooga instead. Meanwhile, in Memphis, where Albuquerque was playing, Sands, along with DeJesús, was pulled from the starting lineup of Friday's game, the first one in two weeks that he sat out. "The manager called me into his office, said, 'It looks like this is happening,'" Sands said.

On Saturday, Magic Johnson's private jet was sent on a cross-country trip, landing in Boston before the trade was finalized. Sands and De La Rosa were still seeing their name on ESPN, although neither had been officially notified they were being traded, by either Boston or Los Angeles.

At 1:45 in the afternoon, in Boston, Punto posted a picture of himself on Twitter, posing with Beckett and Gonzalez, dressed in T-shirts and jeans, with backward caps and gold chains, on Magic's 83-foot, $37 million Gulfstream G III, awaiting takeoff. (Crawford, rehabbing from surgery, wasn't in Boston with the team and traveled separately.) "#dodgers doing it first class!" he tweeted.

It was still radio silence for the last two components in the deal.

"Nobody from the Dodgers got in touch with me," Sands said of the Saturday waiting game. "I went to see the manager (Lorenzo Bundy) and he said he didn't know anything either. He told me, 'I've never seen anything like this.'"

DeJesús wasn't in the clubhouse, and suddenly, Sands' name stopped appearing on the scroll reports of the rumored trade.

When Bundy posted the lineup, an hour and a half after Punto's tweet, Sands' name was listed, batting cleanup and playing first base.

"My wife finally decided to call Iván's wife," Sands said. Sands and DeJesús had played together in Albuquerque for the last two seasons, and the two women had become friends.

The DeJesúses didn't have much time to talk, however. They were busy packing for the move. "They'd gotten a call from the general manager," Sands recalled. "They'd heard from the Red Sox about where he was getting assigned."

Seven players were busy crisscrossing the country to get a new start to their career. Sands and De La Rosa were in limbo. They were the players to be named later.

It was one last numbers game that needed to be played in the complicated trade. In addition to the 25-man active roster that an MLB team can have in uniform for any given game, there's a 40-man roster. The 15 additional names on that list might include players who are on the disabled list in the majors. The rest are the minor league players the team has identified as being most major league ready. A player on the 40-man can be called up at any time, assuming there's a spot on the smaller active roster. More importantly, players on the 40-man are protected in the offseason, while unprotected minor league veterans can be drafted away by other teams promising them a spot in the big leagues.

The whole system prevents an organization from stockpiling players in the minor leagues. But it also requires some creative accounting. The Red Sox were getting more players than they were giving up, and the team didn't have room on its 40-man for everyone.

Sands and De La Rosa were officially pulled from the trade, as announced, and they'd remain in the Dodgers organization. "The Red Sox wanted to wait until the offseason to find room for us on the 40-man," explained Sands.

Although Crawford spent the rest of the season on the disabled list, all three players eventually contributed to the Dodgers, in varying degrees of effectiveness. Beckett battled injuries over the next two and a half years and underwent shoulder surgery in 2013. His most successful season as a Dodger was his last one. He went 6–6 in 20 starts in 2014, split by three stints on the disabled list. His commitment to his craft, so often questioned by fans in Boston, was again criticized early in the season. In a postgame TV interview after he pitched a no-hitter against the Phillies, Beckett said that he was considering retiring after the season.

It turned out he did. Doctors told him that a hip problem would have required surgery. "I just don't see me going through that rehab and coming back to pitch at this point in my life," the 34-year-old said.

Crawford sat out the rest of the season post-trade, but the Dodgers got more from him over the next few years than many observers expected. He played 116 games in 2013 and 105 the following season. While not regaining his All-Star level, Crawford batted .286 and stole 48 bases over the next three years.

Gonzalez was everything the Dodgers had hoped for and more. In his first three years in Los Angeles, he hit 77 home runs and had 306 RBI. He led the league in RBI with 116 in 2014 while winning a Gold Glove and the Silver Slugger Award. He was an All-Star in 2015. Gonzalez quickly supplanted Matt Kemp as the team's best position player, and he led the Dodgers to three straight NL West division titles, matching the team's total for the 17 seasons prior to the trade.

The players headed to Boston didn't have as stable a baseball home waiting for them. Sands, Loney and DeJesús were gone by the end of 2012. De La Rosa and Webster were dealt away in December 2014.

Loney played 30 games for the Red Sox. DeJesús played 8. De La Rosa and Webster played more games for Boston's Triple-A team in Pawtucket than they did for the big-league club. Sands never suited up for a team in the Boston organization. It seemed that the trouble Boston had fitting its new acquisitions onto the roster never cleared up.

Back in 2012, when Sands and De La Rosa had to be left behind in Los Angeles, the Sox hadn't been able to contact them to explain their player-to-be-named situation. Contacting another organization's players is considered tampering. The Dodgers were also keeping mum on the identities of the players to be named. So Sands finished out the season in Albuquerque.

"You just go out and do your job," he said. "You don't know what's going to happen. Things could fall through, so you want to keep doing a good job for your current team, in case you're going to stick around."

The day after the season ended, De La Rosa and Sands became named players. They officially joined the Red Sox organization.

Sands would play for the Pittsburgh, Tampa and Cleveland organizations over the next three years. He saw some time in the majors but spent the bulk of those seasons in the minor leagues, hoping to hold on to a spot on the 40-man roster and get some security, still holding out the dream that one day, he'd be an MLB "have"—one of the players that teams dispatch their private jets to retrieve.

Unlike many teams that trade to dump salary, the Red Sox didn't pocket the savings. Boston typically has one of the highest payrolls in the major leagues, and the mega-trade was more of an effort to press the reset button than to actually cut costs. The Sox got rid of players who had overstayed their welcome, performed addition by subtraction in clubhouse chemistry and freed up money to spend elsewhere.

Boston promptly spent $13 million on free-agent outfielder Shane Victorino, another $13 million on first baseman Mike Napoli and $13.3 million on starting pitcher Ryan Dempster. The Sox also traded for starting pitcher Jake Peavy, adding another $14.5 million. In the blink of an eye, the 2013 payroll was back over $150 million. By the end of the season, it would be at $174 million, higher than the 2012 pretrade payroll.

The new Sox blended well with the veteran stars and developing youth already in Boston. The Red Sox posted a remarkable 28-game improvement in the first full season after the trade, winning the World Series. Napoli and Victorino each homered in the ALCS, and each drove in 4 runs in the World Series, while Peavy started a game in each postseason series.

Off the field, the new blood had a big impact as well. Napoli was one of several Sox players who stopped shaving in spring training. By October, the Sox looked like mountain men and celebrated big plays by tugging on a teammate's facial hair.

"It's funny that we talk about beards," Napoli said, "but the bigger thing is that we're together. . . . We're all having a good time."

And not one of the long scraggly beards was filled with bits of chicken or soaked with beer while teammates were on the field.

WAR COMPARISON

The trade was addition by subtraction for the Red Sox. The players they acquired ended up with net negative production, from a WAR standpoint.

For Los Angeles, Adrian Gonzalez provided the big long-term benefit, although all four players gave a solid production for at least a short time with the Dodgers.

The true benefit for Boston wasn't in the players they obtained, but in the players that the salary reset allowed them to obtain. Boston brought in four high-salary players for 2013 and paid them $8.2 million for each win over replacement they produced. By comparison, the players sent to L.A. cost $9.3 million for every win over replacement they generated.

RED SOX RECEIVED	WAR PRE-TRADE	WAR POST-TRADE
Iván DeJesús	-0.5	-0.3
James Loney	8.7	-0.2
Allen Webster	0.0	-1.4
Jerry Sands	0.1	0.0
Rubby de la Rosa	0.5	0.3
DODGERS RECEIVED	WAR PRE-TRADE	WAR POST-TRADE
Carl Crawford	0.6	3.1
Josh Beckett	22.6	2.0
Adrian Gonzalez	9.9	13.5
Nick Punto	0.4	2.5
HOW BOSTON SPENT ITS SAVINGS	WAR 5 YEARS PRE-BOSTON	WAR WITH BOSTON
Jake Peavy	9.9	0.5
Ryan Dempster	11.1	-0.2
Mike Napoli	14.6	7.9
Shane Victorino	19.1	7.2

CHAPTER 5

A TRADE ABOUT
— NOTHING —

THE STORY BEHIND THE JAY BUHNER TRADE

When comedians use your trade for material, you've made a bad trade.

In 1988, the New York Yankees dealt an outfielder who had not really made an impact on the roster as an everyday player. The Seattle Mariners played him in right field for the next decade, and in the late 1990s, an angry Frank Costanza met George Steinbrenner in a very special episode of Seinfeld. *Frank's first question to the Yankees owner: "What the hell did you trade Jay Buhner for? . . . You don't know what the hell you're doing!"*

Larry David is never all that happy, but 1987 was a particularly bad year. He turned 40 that year and was still looking for his big break.

David thought he'd gotten it two years earlier, when he was hired as a writer for *Saturday Night Live*. His season with the show was a disaster, however. The show tanked in the ratings, and David rarely saw any of his material make it to air. David tried stand-up comedy, but the experience was stressful, combative and, usually, doomed to fail. If only David knew then that he would eventually partner with Jerry Seinfeld to produce one of the most successful comedy TV shows of all time.

But back in the mid-80s, even sports, David's great escape, weren't much solace to his struggling career. His Yankees were in the midst of a down spell. In 1987, they would finish in fourth place, nine games out of first. It had been six years since the franchise's last World Series appearance and nine since its last championship.

A lifelong Yankee fan, David was uncharacteristically optimistic about the future of the team. Kenny Kramer was David's neighbor in the New York apartment building where he lived at the time. Kramer eventually became the inspiration for the wacky neighbor character of the same (last) name on *Seinfeld*.

"All year, he kept talking about this kid in Columbus that he'd seen, Jay Buhner," Kramer recalled. "He's the future of the Yankees."

Buhner certainly provided reason for hope to Yankee fans scouting the minor leagues. The 22-year-old outfielder jumped to Triple-A Columbus in 1987 after playing the previous year in Single A, skipping Double A altogether. He made the International League All-Star Team and led the league with 31 home runs. He also had 85 RBI and an astounding 20 assists in the outfield, most achieved by throwing out runners trying to advance an extra base, unaware of the strength of Buhner's arm.

Then in September, when rosters expanded, the Yankees brought him up. Buhner went 2 for 3 in his second game as a Yankee, after getting an RBI in his debut. It wasn't until his fourth game that he threw someone out on the base paths.

"He's going to save the team!" Kramer remembers David exclaiming.

Given Yankees' owner George Steinbrenner's history with prospects in the 1980s, there was no reason for David to be optimistic. A former assistant football coach, Steinbrenner was a firm believer that fiery speeches and in-your-face management would work as well on the diamond as it seemed to on the gridiron. Steinbrenner also wasn't afraid to spend big on his team. He regularly outbid the rest of the market on top free agents and freely added high-salaried veterans when other cash-strapped teams were looking to get out from under their large contracts.

In the early 1980s, as the seasons since the Yankees' last World Series title in 1978 added up, and the crosstown Mets began building a contender, Steinbrenner looked for a way to keep his team in the Big Apple spotlight. While high-profile Mets stars like Dwight Gooden, Darryl Strawberry, Gary Carter and Keith Hernandez were capturing the city's attention, Steinbrenner sought out big names to add to his roster, and he was willing to part with the jewels of the Yankees' farm system to get them.

The list of prospects the Yankees had and dealt away in the first half of the decade looks like an All-Star Team.

There was Willie McGee. Drafted in the first round by the Yankees, the 21-year-old was taken off the Yankees 40-man roster in 1980, after the team needed the spot for one of Steinbrenner's headline-grabbing acquisitions—future Hall of Famer Dave Winfield.

"When we signed Winfield, somebody had to come off our 40-man roster to make room for him," Yankees' vice president for player personnel Bill Bergesch said. "We decided to outright McGee to our Columbus farm team, which meant he was a 'frozen' player—he couldn't be reacquired by us without going through major-league waivers. McGee couldn't make our Columbus team in spring training (1981), so we sent him to Nashville, where he had a good year."

Indeed, McGee showed plenty of promise in Nashville. He hit .322, the second time in five minor league seasons he'd topped .300. He stole 24 bases, his third year with at least 20, and he showed signs of gap power, setting career highs with 20 doubles and 63 RBI. But the Yankees couldn't call him up.

"We knew that if we tried to get him back through waivers, we'd probably lose him for $20,000," Bergesch said. "So we decided to try to trade him. That way at least we would get a player for him."

McGee was dealt to the Cardinals for journeyman pitcher Bob Sykes. McGee went on to win an NL MVP, two batting titles and make four All-Star teams. Sykes won three minor league games for the Yankees and never made it to the majors in the organization.

The Yankees never bothered to say goodbye to their promising minor leaguer.

"I picked up the paper one day at home, and read about it in transactions," McGee said. "The Yankees never called me. The Cardinals never called me. After two weeks of not hearing from either of them, I finally called the Cardinals."

McGee wasn't surprised by his fate, however.

"In the Yankee organization, we were always told that if you were good enough, you'd make it," McGee said. "But everybody knew that getting traded somewhere else was your best bet because the Yankees sign free agents instead of going with young players."

Just behind McGee in the Yankees system was hard-throwing Dominican righthander José Rijo, who signed with the Yankees as a 16-year-old. Two years later, he won 18 minor league games in 1983, posting a 1.88 ERA.

The Yankees gave him a trial in the big leagues the following year. He struggled to a 2–8 record.

"I was throwing the ball really good until they brought me up," Rijo said. "There was a lot of pressure, but the way they used me was a bigger problem. I got six starts, one here, another two weeks later. And then they started using me in long relief, short relief. That was the big problem."

After the season, the Yankees included Rijo in a package of prospects that brought them Oakland A's outfielder Rickey Henderson. Rijo went on to make an All-Star team, twice finish in the top five in Cy Young Award voting and win the 1990 World Series MVP.

Just behind Rijo in the system was righthander Doug Drabek, who won 13 minor league games at age 23, including nine complete games and two shutouts.

He got called up in 1986, at age 24, and went 7–8 with the Yankees, which meant he was just good enough to be traded. Steinbrenner came close to dealing him for future Hall of Famer Tom Seaver at the trade deadline but was talked out of it by manager Lou Piniella.

As Steinbrenner headed to the winter meetings that offseason, Piniella had one last piece of advice for the owner.

"Whatever you do, don't trade this Drabek kid," Piniella said.

A few days later, Steinbrenner told the manager he had good news. The Yankees had just traded for Rick Rhoden, a veteran pitcher who had 121 career wins in the National League.

"Tell me Drabek wasn't in the deal," Piniella said.

At about the same time, Pirates GM Syd Thrift was announcing the trade, saying, "I wouldn't have traded Rhoden unless I got Drabek. "

"The Drabeks . . . are guys you build your staff around," Thrift said. "They're dominating pitchers."

"If I had a staff of Drabeks," Pirates pitching coach Ray Miller said after a few seasons working with the pitcher, "I wouldn't have much to do. Drabek never blames anybody but himself for anything, and he refuses to be poor at any aspect of the game where he could help himself. He's become a great bunter. He's become a great fielder. He's become a great pitcher."

Drabek went on to win a Cy Young Award and finish in the top five in the voting two other seasons.

There was also Fred McGriff, who hit 493 career home runs, all of them coming after the Yankees traded him for Tom Dodd and Dale Murray. Dodd never suited up for the Yankees; Murray won three games.

There was Bob Tewksbury, traded in mid-July, 1987, for another veteran pitcher, Steve Trout. Tewskbury would go on to finish in the top three in Cy Young voting once and make an All-Star team. Trout had a 6.99 ERA in his one year with the Yankees.

Meanwhile, Buhner found himself on the infamous Columbus shuttle, getting called up for a few games, then sent back down in favor of more playing time for veterans. It was enough to drive a diehard fan of the team like Larry David crazy.

"Steinbrenner! He's ruining my life," he complained to Kramer. "I can't take another season with him. He'll just trade away their best young prospects, just like he did with McGee, Drabek, McGriff."

Buhner spent the first month of the 1988 season in Columbus, then earned a call-up in mid-May. Over the next two months, he'd be promoted to the Yankees three times and sent back down three times.

The constant change affected him. Buhner's average in Columbus dropped by more than 20 points from the previous year. In his longest stint with New York, he endured a prolonged slump, going hitless from June 15 through July 1. During that 0-for-27 stretch, he struck out 14 times.

Buhner also managed only 2 outfield assists. Part of the problem was his position. With his powerful throwing arm, the natural position for him was right field, where the fielder needs to make the longest throws of anyone, from the outfield warning track to third base. However, the Yankees already had a right fielder in Dave Winfield, a future Hall of Famer. He wasn't moving for any rookie, regardless of how many homers the kid might have hit off minor league pitching. So, Buhner was relegated to center field.

While many fans remained confident that Buhner was the Bronx Bombers' savior, his struggle to find a place with the big league club seemed to convince the front office otherwise. Buhner was sent back to Columbus in mid-July. He would never wear Yankee pinstripes again.

As so often happens with players on the fringe of MLB, Buhner's fate was sealed by a seemingly unrelated development. In a game at Texas on July 6, Yankee third baseman Mike Pagliarulo hurt his hamstring. The injury would have seemed to provide Buhner with an opportunity to enter the lineup, but the roster calculus was working against him.

Pagliarulo, who hit 32 homers in 1987, was a left-handed hitter. Yankee Stadium, with its famous short porch in right field, is tailor-made for left-handed power hitters, and the best Yankee teams in history always seemed to have a strong lefty presence in the lineup—from Babe Ruth and Lou Gehrig to Yogi Berra and Roger Maris to Reggie Jackson.

Pagliarulo would play a total of one inning in the next nine games. That left the Yankees with just two left-handed options, first baseman Don Mattingly and outfielder Claudell Washington. Mattingly was a fixture in the lineup; he was in the midst of four straight seasons finishing in the top five in MVP voting. In order to fit Washington into the lineup, however, the Yankees had few options. The team had Winfield in right and another future Hall of Famer, Rickey Henderson, in left. That meant Washington had to play center, leaving the right-handed Buhner, already moved from his natural position on the field, without a home.

It also meant that the Yankees needed to find some lefty power. "We'd like to fine-tune the club," general manager Bob Quinn said. "Our focus on a left-handed hitter has been made more acute because of the unavailability of Pags. That search is now being accelerated."

Across the country, another club was having its own problems.

The Seattle Mariners were having a terrible season. That was nothing new. Since joining the American League as an expansion team in 1977, the Mariners had never finished over .500.

In fact, the 1987 Mariners had been the best team in franchise history, finishing in fourth place, 7 games out of first, 6 games under .500. All three were franchise records.

Hopes were high in 1988, but the season crashed and burned quickly. The Mariners were 10 games out of first by May 8. By June 5, they were 10 games below .500 and fired their manager. On July 4, they were 18 games below .500 and in dead last, more than 20 games out of first place. They'd also played in front of home crowds of 10,000 fans or fewer on 15 occasions.

The Seattle fans weren't the only ones who had seen enough of the team. First baseman Ken Phelps expressed his displeasure with another losing season. "I don't think they want to say they're writing this season off," he said of the front office, "but let's face it, we're not going to make up 20 games. There's just no way it can happen. Obviously, this team has got to start building for the future, because they're not going anywhere this year and everybody knows it."

It wasn't the first time Phelps had criticized the team's decision making, but it would be the last.

The previous October, Phelps made it clear that he wasn't content simply with the Mariners losing less often than usual. He urged owner George Argyros, who was notorious for his low payrolls, to open his wallet and improve the team.

"If George wants to do it right, he's got to go out and spend some money," Phelps told the Spokesman-Review the day after the 1987 season ended. "When there's some good free agents out there, you've got to get a couple of them if you want to win. You see what's going on, and you wonder.

"There are teams out there willing to make the deals, but it's all a matter of spending the money. George doesn't want to spend it. It's obvious."

In the same interview, Phelps ripped the Mariners' stadium and the Seattle fans. "We don't get the fan support here. You play before four to five thousand people—that's a joke. Our fans deserve a better team, and we deserve better support. And we deserve a better facility to play in.

"The Kingdome is not a good place to play in. . . . If I'm the owner of this ballclub, and I've got hundreds of millions of dollars, I build a stadium somewhere else. I put every penny in my pocket into it. If I'm committed to being up here, I will build the stadium."

Perhaps the biggest surprise at the start of the 1988 season was the fact that Phelps was still a Mariner. The team tried to deal him over the winter, and the Yankees, shopping for left-handed power already, came close to acquiring him.

In the early days of advanced baseball statistics, Phelps was a favorite of Bill James, a pioneer in the field. James attacked the baseball establishment for labeling Phelps early in his career. He couldn't field. He couldn't hit left-handed pitching. As a result, he couldn't get a full-time job. James contrasted Phelps' fate with that of Henry Cotto, another Mariners player who got chance after chance, because he "looked like a ballplayer," even though, in James' view, he couldn't play a lick.

The "looks like a ballplayer" line of thinking was one of the flaws that baseball's turn to advanced metrics in the new millennium helped to dispel, two decades too late to help Phelps.

In his 1987 *Baseball Abstract*, James created the "Ken Phelps All-Stars," a team of talented players deprived of an opportunity in MLB because they were labeled early on as having some type of flaw and were never given a chance to prove the label incorrect. In Phelps' case, he was, at best, a platoon player, because he couldn't hit southpaws. Sent to the bench whenever a left-hander came in to pitch, Phelps had no opportunity to demonstrate any improvement in that particular skill.

Ironically, one of the reasons Steinbrenner reportedly wanted to trade for Phelps was because the owner saw Phelps run to first base one time and was impressed. He looked like a gritty player to the Yankees boss.

When he had the chance to play, Phelps produced at a Hall of Fame rate. He set a record for fastest to 100 career home runs, reaching the milestone in 1,330 at bats. That's still the American League record, although Ryan Howard broke the MLB mark two decades later.

In his Mariners career, Phelps hit a home run every 13.65 at bats, a mark that was second in baseball history at the time. Only Babe Ruth, at a homer every 11.76 at bats, went deep more often.

Still, Phelps never played more than 125 games in a season. In 1988 he topped 100 games, the fourth and final time in his 11-year MLB career. The problem, of course, was that Phelps was a platoon player. Only 208 of his 1,854 career at bats came against lefties, as managers refused to give him a chance to confront his limitations. That was despite the fact that Phelps hit 12 points higher and homered at a higher rate against lefties than he did against rights in 1987.

Phelps was the Mariners' franchise leader in career home runs, but it was clearly time for him to move on. Seattle and New York quickly worked out a deal, with the Yankees sending three minor leaguers to the Mariners for Phelps.

Seattle received pitcher Rich Balabon, a right-hander in his fourth year in the Yankees organization and still in Single A. Balabon would never reach the majors. The Yankees also sent a player to be named later, later revealed to be right-handed pitcher Troy Evers, to the Mariners. Evers was also in his fourth year in the Yankees organization and, like Balabon, would never make it to the major leagues.

The third prospect in the deal was Jay Buhner, who, despite the multiple trips to and from the minors, wasn't happy to be leaving the Yankees organization.

"I wasn't really tickled at the time, because let's face it, they (Seattle) weren't going to win," Buhner said, years later.

The Phelps-for-Buhner trade was a setback in the Yankees' rebuilding efforts. For starters, like every other team that had Phelps on the roster, New York had no idea how to use him.

"What we'll try to do is rest Winfield a day a week, Henderson a day a week, and [DH Jack] Clark a day a week," manager Lou Piniella said on the day Phelps was acquired. "Another option is to put Phelps at first and move Mattingly to the outfield."

Still, the Yankees didn't believe they'd spent too much to add Phelps' bat, even if it was as a pinch hitter and spot starter. Although Buhner showed promise, the Yankees were able to hold on to the three most-prized prospects in the system: pitcher Al Leiter, outfielder Roberto Kelly and third baseman Hensley Meulens.

New York never found a spot for Phelps. He started just 28 of the team's final 70 games that season, all at designated hitter. In 1989, he started 46 of the Yankees' first 134 games, all but five at DH. He hit just 17 home runs as a Yankee and only 10 at Yankee Stadium, a park that was supposed to be ideal for his left-handed slugging ability. He averaged a home run every 20.11 at bats with the team, a rate that was a far cry from Ruth and Hall of Famer Ralph Kiner's MLB bests. Instead, he homered about as frequently as Phil Nevin, Don Mincher and dozens of other forgotten sluggers.

The Yankees traded Phelps to the Oakland A's in August 1989, 13 months after giving up Buhner to get him. They received pitcher Scott Holcomb, who never made it to the big leagues.

"I was having a pretty good year in Seattle, and all of a sudden, I was going to the pressure cooker of New York City," Phelps recalled, 27 years after the initial trade. "I didn't know what to expect, and I was pretty stressed."

"When I got traded, at the time, I try to tell people I was a little better than [Buhner]," Phelps said. "I was established at the time. I was rolling. I was hitting about .285 with 14 home runs. I had a head start on him."

Buhner also wasn't entirely comfortable with the trade.

"The Yankees at the time were known for taking all their young talent, pretty much, and using it to make trades and get veteran guys," he said, more than two decades later. "[Seattle] was a great opportunity for me to come over and get a name for myself, get a chance to step into the lineup and play every day. As a young kid, that's all you can ask for. I was a little apprehensive at first. Let's face it, I didn't know much about Washington state. Like everyone, I was thinking Washington, D.C."

Leaving a team with the history of the Yankees for a team that was in its twelfth year of existence was also an adjustment.

"Just the guys that came through that clubhouse in New York," Buhner recalled. "You look around, and you have Whitey Ford and Mickey Mantle walking through the clubhouse. I remember one time we were going through a tough stretch, and I asked Whitey Ford if he ever went through something like that. He said, 'Oh yeah. Of course. There were two years out of the fourteen I was here that we didn't go to the World Series.'"

Buhner was also faced with the task of replacing a proven player, one of the best in the Mariners' bleak history to that point. He showed that he was up to the task. By 1993, he had passed Phelps' Mariner home run total. He topped 40 home runs and 100 RBI in three straight seasons. He was an All-Star, won a Gold Glove and had finished fifth in MVP voting. Buhner also threw out 95 baserunners from right field over his 14-year Mariner career, leading the league in assists twice.

Buhner played 1,440 games for the Mariners. Meulens, Leiter and Kelly, the three higher-rated prospects that the Yankees held on to, combined for 845 games in their Yankee careers. Leiter was eventually traded for another right-handed slugger with a rifle arm—right fielder Jesse Barfield, who was, of course, an experienced veteran whom the Yankees tried unsuccessfully to plug into their lineup.

Eight years after the trade, life was going much better for Larry David. He'd found a steady source of income, partnering with fellow (and more successful) stand-up comic Jerry Seinfeld to develop a "show about nothing" for NBC. *Seinfeld* was wildly popular with critics and viewers.

Seinfeld was as big a baseball fan, albeit of the crosstown Mets, as David. As a result, baseball worked its way into the plot of the show.

From the first episode of the series—which included a storyline that had Jerry trying to avoid finding out who won the Mets game, because he'd recorded it—and throughout its run,

Seinfeld kept returning to the sport for comedy inspiration. Former Mets Keith Hernandez and Roger McDowell were guest stars. Five Yankee players, including Derek Jeter and Paul O'Neill, made guest appearances on the show.

The New York Yankees became an important part of the *Seinfeld* storyline. The character David based on himself, George Costanza, got a job with the team, working for an exaggerated George Steinbrenner character, who never appeared on screen but was voiced by David himself.

In the episode "The Caddy," Costanza goes missing and is feared dead. Steinbrenner contacts his parents to break the news to them.

While George's mother collapses in tears, his father, Frank Costanza, points at Steinbrenner and, in a gravelly voice, shouts, "What the hell did you trade Jay Buhner for? He had thirty home runs, over a hundred RBIs last year! He's got a rocket for an arm!"

"You don't know what the hell you're doing!" he concluded.

The words were very similar to what David himself said back in 1988 upon hearing news of the trade. "Larry went nuts," Kramer recalled, changing his voice to do a rough Larry David impersonation. "How could they trade Jay Buhner? What were they thinking?"

"Those were absolutely Larry's words," Kramer said. "That episode aired in '96. What's that? Eight years later? Larry was still pissed." The George Steinbrenner character on the show gave the excuse that he was just listening to his baseball people, and his baseball people loved Ken Phelps.

When the *Seinfeld* episode aired, Buhner was coming off of a 40-homer, 121-RBI year. Posting their third winning season since the trade, the Mariners finished in first place in 1995 and went to the postseason for the first time in team history; they beat the Yankees in the ALDS. Buhner hit .458 in the five-game series and hit a home run. He also threw out Yankee runners at second and third base, from his spot in right field. He added three more homers during the six-game loss to Cleveland in the ALCS.

Buhner enjoyed the attention at the time, and years after his retirement, he's still thrilled to be the source of Larry David's Yankee angst.

"I still get family members that call me and say the rerun was on last night," he said. "It's a classic—an all-time classic. So to be mentioned on one of the greatest shows ever, it doesn't get any better."

Meanwhile, Phelps had been out of baseball for five years. He played briefly for Oakland and Cleveland before finishing his career with the Giants' Triple-A team in 1991. Phelps hit his last career home run in April 1990, fittingly, in a game that he didn't start. He entered the game with 2 outs in the ninth inning, and his solo homer broke up a perfect game bid by Brian Holman of the Seattle Mariners. Buhner was on the disabled list with a sprained ankle and didn't play in that game. Henry Cotto, the poster-child for "looks like a ballplayer" on the Ken Phelps All-Stars, pinch-hit and scored for the Mariners.

On that January night in 1996, when the *Seinfeld* episode aired, far from New York's budding World Series champions, the former Yankee found himself thrust back into the spotlight.

Phelps had no idea that he was about to become a blip on the pop culture radar. "I had friends back East calling me and saying, 'You've got to watch *Seinfeld* tonight!'" he said. "That's how I learned about the episode for the first time."

The onetime Mariners home run leader appreciates his infamous spot in history. "It's good to be remembered for something—good or bad," he said. "It's good to have guys remember who you are."

And by the time the episode of *Seinfeld* excoriating Steinbrenner's mismanagement of prospects hit the airwaves, the Yankees had a very different look. The team returned to the postseason for the first time in 14 years the previous October and would win the World Series for the first time in 18 seasons before the year was out.

The core of that Yankees team, and the ones that would win three of the next four Fall Classics as well, was made up of home-grown prospects, including Derek Jeter, Bernie Williams, Jorge Posada and Mariano Rivera. The four Yankees stars came up through the farm system and would play their entire careers with the team. Pitcher Andy Pettitte was another key contributor who came up through the farm system.

The primary reason for the Yankees' change in approach was the fact that owner George Steinbrenner was suspended from baseball from 1990 to 1993. Steinbrenner had hired a gangster to dig up dirt on his Hall of Fame right fielder, Dave Winfield—a big-name and high-priced free agent signed prior to the 1981 season. When the commissioner's office found out, they issued an indefinite suspension for the Boss.

While the future of the Yankees was incubating in the minor leagues, Steinbrenner had relinquished day-to-day operations of the Yankees to Gene Michael, who, without pressure from above to win the back pages of the New York tabloids by making big news, was able to hold on to the team's prospects instead of dealing them for veterans with splashy names and high price tags.

"George will admit I have too much patience at times," Michael said at one point after the Yankees' rebuilt. "Maybe it's because I spent seven and a half years in the minors myself."

It took someone who understood life as a young Willie McGee or Jay Buhner to stop the Yankees from trading them all away.

WAR COMPARISON

Advanced metrics were in their infancy in the early 1980s, and WAR was still years from being developed. While the Yankees and their trade partners used more conventional baseball statistics to help make trade decisions, the WAR breakdown quickly shows just how damaging this era of trades was to the Yankees' future.

The four prospects mentioned on *Seinfeld* cost the Yankees a combined WAR of 96.7. Since a war of 8 is considered an MVP-worthy season, that's the equivalent of 12 MVP-caliber seasons. In exchange, the Yankees received six players who gave them a combined WAR of 6.1, the equivalent of about three seasons for a regular starting player.

MAIN PLAYERS TRADED	WAR PRE-TRADE	WAR POST-TRADE
Jay Buhner	-0.2	30.7
Ken Phelps	9.6	1.0
OTHER PROSPECTS THE YANKEES DEALT	WAR PRE-TRADE	WAR POST-TRADE
Willie McGee	0.0	25.5
Doug Drabek	1.6	21.2
Fred McGriff	0.0	19.3
WHAT THE YANKEES RECEIVED IN THOSE TRADES	WAR PRE-TRADE	WAR POST-TRADE
Bob Sykes	-3.7	0.0
Pat Clements	1.8	-0.1
Rick Rhoden	20.5	4.3
Cecilio Guante	4.6	1.6
Dale Murray	2.5	-0.7
PROSPECTS THE YANKEES KEPT INSTEAD OF BUHNER	WAR PRE-TRADE	WAR POST-TRADE
Hensley Meulens	0.0	-1.5
Al Leiter	-0.1	0.8
*Jesse Barfield	29.4	9.9
Roberto Kelly	0.8	12.7

*Veteran the Yankees received for Leiter in a later trade. Leiter went on to post a 42.2 career WAR with three other teams.

CHAPTER 6

THE 180-DEGREE
— RIP-OFF —
THE STORY BEHIND THE JOHN SMOLTZ TRADE

Both teams get exactly what they wanted and then some, the definition of a good deal.

The Detroit Tigers made a trade that clinched them the division in 1987. Doyle Alexander went 9–0 down the stretch, becoming one of the most significant late-season pickups in baseball history. And all Detroit had to give up for Alexander was a prospect by the name of John Smoltz, who went on to a Hall of Fame career with the Atlanta Braves.

Mitch Lukevics is the Tampa Bay Rays' director of minor league operations. The position, referred to in many organizations as "farm director," is perfectly suited for the fatherly Lukevics. The farm director is the man responsible for the development of the roughly 150 minor leaguers in the organization at any given time.

To watch Lukevics work a batting practice for one of the Rays' farm teams is to see a transformation in normally aloof young ballplayers. They approach the 61-year-old Lukevics, who stands to the side, wearing a straw hat covered with Rays logos, with smiles and hugs.

Lukevics is rarely alone when among the minor leaguers, and with good reason—he's scouted many of them in high school and college, drafted and signed the vast majority. They clearly have deep affection and trust for the man, and the feelings are reciprocated.

"The best thing is to tell a guy that he's going to the majors," Lukevics says. "Normally, a manager will get to bring him into his office after the game and give him the good news, but sometimes, if a team is about to leave for another city or something, I get to be the one to make the call." He remembers which players he got to tell, and there's no doubt that the players remember just as clearly that Mitch was the one to tell them.

On the other hand, "Telling someone that you've traded them is hard," Lukevics says, although he admits it's not as tough as breaking the news to someone who's just been released. "You never know how they're going to react. Especially the young ones, who are being traded for the first time. Sometimes they just sit there and don't say a thing. But sometimes. . . ." He doesn't finish the thought, but the pained look on his face makes words unnecessary.

"From the time they were eighteen, nineteen years old, they were Rays. They thought they were going to be Rays forever—that they were going to go to the majors as Rays, retire as Rays, go to the Hall of Fame as Rays. And now. . . ." Again, Lukevics trails off.

"I try to tell them," he continues, "don't think about all of our plans, and our roster numbers and all that. That's business. It had nothing to do with you, or what we thought of you.

Instead of focusing on that, what you need to say to yourself is 'Somebody wants me. Somebody wanted to trade to get me.'"

Lukevics isn't the only farm director to give this advice. Players past and present echo a similar line when they talk about coping with the indignity of being traded for the first time.

"Someone wanted to get me," they'll say, likely thinking fondly of the farm director who told them the same thing, years earlier.

Then again, sometimes a player gets traded because a team wants to get rid of him, and the team acquiring him doesn't fully understand what a pill he is. By all accounts, pitcher Doyle Alexander fell into that category.

Former Orioles general manager Hank Peters, who got his start as one of those affectionate, caring farm directors, once called Alexander, "One of the most disagreeable individuals I've ever known."

The adjectives used to describe him sound like the surly clique of Snow White's friends: prickly, cranky, grouchy, bitter. Detroit writer Mitch Albom compared Alexander's personality to a pit bull's. The *Washington Post*'s Thomas Boswell said, "If you're insulted or defensive, then he's happy."

The former teammates and managers who were willing to talk about Alexander had nothing nice to say about their time with him, using words like "gutless" and "we don't need his crap."

When he played in Toronto (1983–86), Alexander was nicknamed "Dour Doyle," and that was before he presented a handwritten list of "reasons for leaving Toronto" to a local newspaper reporter. The list included criticism of the front office, which "made no changes to improve the team over the winter," an analysis of an increase to the Canadian tax rates, and complaints about the chilly, rainy Toronto weather.

Alexander wouldn't sign autographs. He wouldn't make appearances in the community for the team. When reporters checked to see if he was willing to answer a couple of questions, he would respond noncommittally with, "You can ask."

Throughout his career, Alexander was described as a mercenary and a gunslinger. In the pre–free agency days, he already viewed the sport as a business and set about looking out for number one. Team spirit and camaraderie didn't pay the bills.

"You have to learn to stand up," Alexander said. "You find out once you've been around baseball, you've got to treat negotiations as business. Because they (the owners) always have. It's fun to play baseball in high school. You go into professional baseball, it's a business."

So Alexander always looked to rent, not buy, and didn't get too close to anyone in the clubhouse. "For me, the places we live in summertime, that's a temporary residence," he said.

That attitude, he claimed, had its genesis in the first time he was traded.

Alexander had been drafted by the Dodgers in 1968 and quickly rose through the minor leagues. He played for future Hall of Fame manager Tommy Lasorda at Triple-A Spokane. "You talk about a guy who wanted to *beat* you," Lasorda recalled. "He was tough. He was quiet and introverted but, buddy, when he got out on that mound, he was tough. That's why he's pitched so long."

By mid-1971, Alexander was ready for the big-league club. He finished the season with the Dodgers, then was traded to Baltimore in December, as part of a package for a future Hall of Famer. Alexander either wasn't told the comforting words by a sympathetic farm director, or he didn't listen.

"I found out pretty quick what it was like," Alexander said. "I signed with the Dodgers at seventeen. At twenty, I was in the big leagues pitching for 'em. I guess at that point, I was one of their top young pitchers. That winter, I was in the trade for Frank Robinson."

Alexander spent the rest of his career smarting from the wound of getting traded by the team that drafted him. He would go on to be traded seven times, or once every twenty months, throughout his nineteen-year career.

"Other than the first time I was traded, I've had a hand in every move I've made," he said. "It all goes back to one thing. I wanted to play. If they were not going to play me, or pay me, I'd ask them to trade me."

He fought with the Orioles over salary—he claimed it was a dispute about between $5,000 and $10,000—and the Orioles moved him to middle relief the following year. Alexander was unhappy about his role.

When the team finally had enough and traded him to the Yankees in June 1976, Orioles manager Earl Weaver called him and catcher Elrod Hendricks, also part of the deal, into his office. "I've got good news for you, Doyle, and bad news for you, Ellie," Weaver told them. "The good news is you've been traded to the New York Yankees, Doyle. The bad news, Ellie, is you've also been traded to the New York Yankees."

Four years later—after playing one season for the Yankees, signing with the Rangers as a free agent, and then getting traded to the Braves in December 1979—Alexander held out during contract negotiations in Atlanta, forcing a trade to San Francisco in December 1980. Following the 1981 season, he held out with the Giants, forcing a trade to the Yankees, again, in March 1982. The fact that he'd managed to find a way to get consistent raises, without having to attend Florida workouts all February and March, didn't get him off to a good start with his new teammates.

"We've been in spring training for eight weeks, and he's just coming," griped Yankees outfielder Bobby Murcer. "It's not fair."

A dispute with Yankees owner George Steinbrenner over, of all things, money, led to his release.

In 1982, Alexander was the losing pitcher in Hall of Famer Gaylord Perry's 300th career win. Far from celebrating his opponent's milestone, which at the time had been accomplished by only fourteen other pitchers, and just three since 1924, Alexander broke a finger on his pitching hand after punching the dugout wall in frustration.

He was out for nine weeks and felt so bad about the injury that he offered to give back his salary to the team for the time he was injured.

"I can't help them with my hand in a cast," he said.

After meeting with the players' union the following week, Alexander retracted his offer to surrender a month's pay. Alexander further infuriated the Yankees by refusing to take suggestions from the pitching coach on adjustments to his delivery and approach to hitters.

"Steinbrenner personally had meetings with Alexander to convince him to listen to the coaching staff. Alexander turned him down," a Yankees executive said. "George said he's sorry he signed him. . . . If we could trade him tomorrow, he said he would authorize me to do so."

Toronto was his next destination. Alexander played out the rest of his lucrative contract, which had been signed with Steinbrenner before the trade, wearing a Blue Jays uniform.

He relished beating the Yankees, while they were still paying him, to clinch the 1985 division for the Blue Jays.

When the Yankees' money ran out, so did Alexander's patience. His list of reasons to get out of Toronto—which also included items as minor as postgame traffic and going through customs for every road trip—did the trick. He was dealt back to the Braves.

Despite all the red flags with Alexander, teams never had a problem finding a trading partner. Part of that might have been a "we can fix him" arrogance by the receiving team, but part of it had to do with the other side of being a mercenary gunslinger—Alexander got the job done.

The monetary disputes may have been just another way Alexander kept score in the competitions that drove him. Seemingly the only thing he enjoyed as much as getting paid was winning games.

In his nineteenth and final season, 1989, a line drive broke his jaw. The ball hit him so hard that the fracture showed up on the other side of his face. He didn't miss a start.

"I don't feel I did any more damage to it," Alexander said about his jaw after continuing to pitch. "I felt like the ballclub needed me to pitch more than I needed not to pitch."

Few pitchers were as dominant as Alexander was after landing a new home and new contract. He went 10–5 after being acquired by the Yankees in mid-1976, helping them win their first AL East crown. He won 17 games with the Rangers in his first season with the team. He went 5–2 to start his Giants career and won 7 consecutive games down the stretch in his first half season with the Blue Jays.

Despite starting off the 1987 season 5–10 for a Braves team that would end up losing 92 games, the me-first competitor that was Doyle Alexander would be a strong midseason acquisition for a team looking to make a postseason run.

"What I like best about Alexander," Detroit manager Sparky Anderson said, "is that he is 15–3 in the month of September over the past three years."

That was not a small-sample blip on Alexander's record. For his career, he had 14 more wins in September than any other month of the season and was 52–25 with a 3.34 ERA down the season's stretch run.

Alexander's gunslinger reputation had one blemish, however, and the temperamental pitcher was eager to erase it. As good as he'd always been in September in helping a team wrap up a postseason berth, he was equally bad in October, once the playoffs began.

The Orioles gave Alexander the ball in the final game of the then best-of-five ALCS in 1973. He failed to last four innings and took the loss to the eventual world champion Oakland A's. Three years later, the Yankees called his number for the opening game of the World Series against the Cincinnati Reds. He gave up 5 runs in six innings and took the loss.

He prepared for his next postseason appearance with the Blue Jays in the '85 ALCS. "I think I'm a much better pitcher now than I was then," he said. "I don't think I have anything to prove. I was fairly young then. . . . I think I know my own talent a lot better now. I can rate my stuff better now. I know if I have to change my stuff before I go out to the mound."

The stuff didn't work any better that time around. Alexander gave up 5 runs in 5 innings in the opening game and gave up another 5 in Game Six, taking the loss.

The difference between September Alexander and October Alexander was stark.

In September: 52–25, 3.34 ERA, 1.245 WHIP, .253 opponent average, .366 opponent slugging.

In October: 0–3 in four games, 7.65 ERA, 1.650 WHIP, .350 opponent average, .675 opponent slugging. Even worse, his teams had lost all three postseason series in which he'd pitched.

Toiling for the Atlanta Braves, at the time the worst team in baseball, Alexander seemed far from meaningful in the September and October games. He responded to the frustration the only way he knew how.

"I'm not happy with my situation here, my contract," he told Atlanta papers in mid-June 1987. "I'm not happy with the way things happened here. I'm very disappointed in the way I was treated here. But it's not going to affect how I pitch."

Alexander was about to become a much-desired commodity.

Detroit had won the World Series three years earlier, and most of the team's nucleus from '84 remained. But the Tigers were a rapidly aging team, and time seemed to be running out. Starting pitcher Jack Morris (18–11, 3.38 in '87) and outfielder Kirk Gibson (.277, 24 home runs, 79 RBI) were both scheduled to be free agents following the season. Second baseman Lou Whitaker turned 30 in 1987 and made the final All-Star team of his career. First baseman Darrell Evans was 40. Starters Walt Terrell (17–10) and Frank Tanana (15–10) would never again post as many wins. Reliever Willie Hernandez, who won the Cy Young and MVP awards in the magical 1984 season, had already lost his closer role and had two years left in the major leagues.

As early as May of 1987, it appeared that the window had already closed for Detroit. The Tigers were in sixth place in the seven-team division, 11 games out. They then began to steadily improve, climbing into the race and pulling as close as a half game out of first in late July.

The improvement was remarkable, especially considering Detroit had no reliable starting pitchers after Morris, Terrell and Tanana. Dan Petry, who went 18–8 in 1984, was 6–4 at the end of July 1987 and having a wildly uneven season. He failed to make it out of the fourth inning in 4 of his first 11 starts. Then he ran off 4 wins in a row in June, followed by back-to-back starts where he was knocked out in the second inning. Rookie Jeff Robinson had made his major league debut in April and bounced between the bullpen and the starting rotation until late May. He had an ERA well over 5.00 in July.

Tigers general manager Bill Lajoie had a clear task in front of him—make the playoffs, now or never. And to do that, he needed to add a pitcher.

Unfortunately, the two teams battling Detroit in the American League East were also shopping for pitching. In the first two weeks of August, the Yankees and Blue Jays each spent time in first, second and third place. Despite their rocky history with Alexander, both teams were willing to consider adding the veteran for the playoff push.

The Yankees went with veteran Steve Trout instead, acquiring him from the Cubs in mid-July for three prospects. Trout was a second-generation major leaguer, the son of longtime Tigers pitcher Paul "Dizzy" Trout. His presence in the Yankees locker room probably made for a lighter atmosphere than Alexander's would have, but Steve Trout never won a game for New York. He went 0–4 in nine starts. The Yankees tried him in the bullpen, too, where he fared no better. His low point came on September 13. In his first start in more than two weeks, Trout gave up two singles, two walks and a double while retiring only one batter before being pulled from the game against first-place Toronto. Making matters worse, one of the young pitchers the Yankees gave up, Bob Tewksbury, would go on to win 110 games in 13 big-league seasons.

Toronto also went the safe route instead of trying again with Alexander, and it blew up in their faces as well.

"There were a few pitchers floating around and we probably talked about all of them," Blue Jays general manager Pat Gillick said. "If I had my choice, I probably would've taken Alexander back, but my people here didn't think it would work."

Instead, the Jays traded for Phil Niekro, the 48-year-old future Hall of Famer, on August 9. Niekro lost the first two games he started for the Blue Jays. In his third start, he gave up 4 hits, 2 walks and 5 runs before getting pulled with 2 outs in the first inning. He was released two days later.

With the other two top AL East teams looking elsewhere, Braves general manager Bobby Cox called Lajoie to try to trade pitching for prospects with the Tigers.

"I tried to tell the whole baseball world how good Doyle is, but not many listened," Cox said. Perhaps smarting from the lukewarm response to Alexander, Cox offered the Tigers two other veteran pitchers, Rick Mahler and David Palmer, instead.

"Atlanta was talking to us about other pitchers," Lajoie said, "but they wanted too much for them. Finally, I said 'What about Alexander?' and he got back to me and said OK."

Over his career, the veteran pitcher had won more games against the Tigers (15) than any other opponent. He'd also impressed the Tigers with a dominating seven-inning performance at Tiger Stadium as a Blue Jay the year before.

The Tigers offered the Braves their choice of prospects from a list of four names. Braves scout John Hageman was dispatched to Glens Falls, home of Detroit's Double-A team, to report on the possible trade targets.

Although the four names on the list have never been publicly disclosed, only a handful of Glens Falls players that year went on to have MLB careers of any substance: catcher Chris Hoiles, infielder Doug Strange and pitcher Kevin Ritz. If any of those players were available for Alexander, they didn't impress Hageman during his scouting trip. The report went back to Cox that the Braves should turn down the Tigers' offer.

Hageman did see one player he liked while in Glens Falls, however: a right-hander who threw a bullpen session one day and pitched in a game another.

"I think my words were, 'The best arm I've seen so far,'" Hagemann recalled. "'Top-of-the-rotation guy'. . . . He was raw at the time, but showed me a real live fastball, really good stuff."

Hageman called Cox and suggested that the GM try to get John Smoltz from the Tigers.

"Smoltz?" Cox responded. "Who the hell is he?"

The 22-year-old Lansing, Michigan native had grown up a Tigers fan. His father was an usher at Tiger Stadium and had worked the 1984 World Series. His grandfather had been a longtime and much-beloved member of the grounds crew.

Smoltz had been drafted by Detroit two years earlier, in the 22nd round. He slipped so low in the draft because most teams expected the high schooler to bypass the pros and play baseball and basketball at Michigan State. The Tigers took a chance, and the lure of the hometown team, as well as a promised $100,000 signing bonus, convinced Smoltz to give up his college dreams and sign with Detroit.

Smoltz's contract paid him only $90,000, split over two years, with a vague, unwritten promise to make up the extra $10,000 later. Smoltz's father and grandfather had worked with the team long enough to know some important people, and soon, former Tigers owner John Fetzer found out about the missing $10,000. He made a call to the team president, Jim Campbell, who ordered Lajoie to pay Smoltz his money. Smoltz's 1987 minor league salary was increased by $10,000.

The financial windfall didn't help him on the mound, however. Smoltz was struggling with a 4–10 record and 5.68 ERA at Glens Falls. He'd also walked 81 batters, or more than 5.5 per nine innings.

"We did not have a pitching coach there. I was struggling. Our team was horrible," Smoltz recalled. "I felt like I was just spinning. . . . I just didn't know whether I was coming or going. I didn't know what was going on that year."

Still, Hageman saw talent that could be developed and told Cox to pull the trigger.

The Braves had other scouts checking out other Tigers' prospects, too. Cox also received glowing reports on Steve Searcy, a left-hander at Triple-A Toledo. He had been drafted in the third round, 19 rounds earlier than Smoltz. He was a level higher in the farm system and thus a level closer to the major leagues. The lack of a pitching coach at Glens Falls hadn't fazed him. He'd blown through that level the previous year, going 11–6 with a 3.30 ERA.

The choice should have been a no-brainer: Searcy was a better prospect, closer to the major league level. But he was also out for the rest of the year after getting hit in the kneecap with a line drive. The shot, off the bat of Pawtucket's Dave Sax, bounced from Searcy's knee on the mound all the way to the backstop behind home plate. He had to be taken from the field in an ambulance.

"That was one of the worst I've ever seen," said Searcy's opposing pitcher that day, Pawtucket's Steve Ellsworth.

Cox couldn't decide between a healthy Smoltz and a hobbled Searcy. His advisors with the Braves were split. So he put the onus on the Tigers. He informed the team he'd be happy with either player. Detroit could pick the one they wanted to send him.

Detroit's front office also didn't agree on which pitcher to keep, although, years later, no one was willing to fess up to being a Steve Searcy fan.

"When I asked various people, the consensus was Searcy. The consensus was that he was closer," Lajoie said, discussing who the team wanted to keep. "I didn't feel like I was on real solid ground at the time. I went with the consensus, knowing full well that I should have traded Searcy. With a check and balance system, the president of the club said did this person agree, did this person agree? Yes. Did I agree? No. But with a checks and balances system, that's why it was done."

Ken Madeja, the scout who originally found Smoltz in high school, remembers it differently. He said Lajoie was still upset over getting called out on the missing $10,000 and was willing to get rid of Smoltz.

Joe McDonald, then the Tigers' vice president of development and scouting, said he had a "bad feeling" in his gut over giving up Smoltz.

The front office made its choice—Smoltz was sent to the Braves on August 12. The Tigers were in second place, a game and a half behind the Jays and one ahead of the Yankees.

"Now, here is Alexander with the Tigers. They got him for next to nothing," complained the *Toronto Star*, still bitter over Dour Doyle's time with the Jays and worried about the second-place Tigers.

Detroit, who didn't bother putting a full-time pitching coach at their Double-A affiliate, also couldn't be bothered to employ a gentle farm director to help Smoltz cope with being dealt.

"That was the last thing that I ever expected," Smoltz said on getting traded. "That totally threw me for a loop. It's hard to describe, because of how bad I wanted to play for the Tigers. I didn't know anything about the National League. I was going to the worst team in baseball. I was just crushed." So was his family, who got rid of every Tigers hat, shirt and other piece of Detroit paraphernalia they owned.

As far as veteran-for-prospect trades go, it's hard to find a better prototype. The Tigers couldn't have asked a veteran to do more for them in the short term than Alexander did, and the Braves couldn't have expected any more from a minor leaguer than Smoltz would give them over the long run.

The trade worked out exactly as the Tigers had hoped. Alexander wasn't just good down the stretch, he was perfect. He made 11 starts with Detroit in late August and September. He went 9–0, setting a record for midseason acquisitions that would be matched 21 years later by CC Sabathia. The Tigers also won the two games in which Alexander had a no-decision. He threw 3 complete-game shutouts and had a 28-inning scoreless streak at one point.

His last two starts of the regular season were against the Blue Jays. Alexander pitched into the 11th inning at Toronto on September 27, before the team rallied and won for the bullpen. On October 3, the second-to-last day of the season, Alexander beat the Blue Jays at home to move Detroit into a tie for first. The Tigers won the division the following day.

"The trade itself accomplished what we wanted to do, which was to get into the playoffs," Tigers executive Joe McDonald said. "Alexander got us to the playoffs."

Alexander wasn't able to exorcise his playoff demons. He gave up 6 runs and took the loss in the first game of the ALCS against the Twins. He started again in the final game of the best-of-five series. After a scoreless first inning, the Twins opened the second inning with a single, walk, double, single, groundout, single, hit by pitch and single. Alexander was pulled from the game after giving up 4 runs on 5 hits and retiring just one of the eight batters he faced in the inning. He took the loss, and the Twins went on to win the World Series.

Smoltz reported to the Braves' Triple-A team in Richmond, who had a full-time pitching coach. The team quickly developed Smoltz's raw talent, and he made his MLB debut on July 23, 1988—37 days earlier than the pitcher the Tigers thought was closer to being ready for the big leagues, Steve Searcy.

Searcy went 4–12 in four years with the Tigers before the team let him leave in free agency. Smoltz went on to have a Hall of Fame career with the Braves. By the time the Tigers made the postseason again, in 2006, Smoltz had won 193 major league games, including a Cy Young Award and a World Series ring.

Since Smoltz hadn't been ready to take Alexander's spot in the Braves starting rotation for the remainder of the 1987 season, the team called up a left-hander from Richmond. Future Hall of Famer Tom Glavine made his MLB debut on August 17. He would go on to win 305 games and, with Smoltz, form two-thirds of one of the best starting staffs in baseball history for Atlanta. "It was a two for one," Smoltz said of the trade in his Hall of Fame induction speech.

When Smoltz and Glavine won the 1995 World Series with the Braves, one of the front-office executives who got a ring was Bill Lajoie. The Tigers' GM who dealt Smoltz to the Braves was now a member of Atlanta's brain trust. The flip from the Tigers to Braves was fitting, since the team widely assumed to have "won" the trade did a similar flip. With the benefit of hindsight, the trade went from being a steal for the Tigers to one of the most-lopsided trades in history in the Braves' favor.

In reality, the trade accomplished both teams' goals. "Bill deserves the credit for getting it done, not the discredit," McDonald said of Lajoie. "He made a good trade. It just turned out that he traded away a great pitcher."

WAR COMPARISON

Despite joining Detroit in mid-August, Alexander produced numbers equivalent to an All-Star quality season in two months. The mercenary pitcher took Detroit back to the playoffs and was worth sacrificing a minor leaguer or two to obtain.

Of course, no one suspected that the minor leaguer in question would win 210 games and save 154 over the next 20 years for Atlanta.

TIGERS RECEIVED	WAR PRE-TRADE	WAR POST-TRADE
Doyle Alexander	4.0	6.7, 4.4 in 1987
BRAVES RECEIVED	WAR PRE-TRADE	WAR POST-TRADE
John Smoltz	0.0	67.0, 0.0 in 1987
OTHER BRAVES PITCHERS OFFERED	WAR PRE-TRADE	WAR POST-TRADE
Rick Mahler	14.0	5.4
David Palmer	3.8	0.3
OTHER TIGERS PROSPECTS AVAILABLE	WAR PRE-TRADE	WAR POST-TRADE
Chris Hoiles	0.0	23.4 with Baltimore
Kevin Ritz	0.0	5.2 with Detroit, Colorado
Doug Strange	0.0	0.5 with 6 teams
Steve Searcy	0.0	-2.1 with Detroit, Philadelphia

CHAPTER 7

— THE WHITE FLAG TRADE —

THE STORY BEHIND THE WILSON ÁLVAREZ TRADE

A team pulls the plug too soon with a deplorable deal.

Teams that are out of the running for a division title often try to sell off their tradable assets to stock up on young prospects. The Chicago White Sox tried that in 1997, but they forgot the part about waiting until they were out of contention. At the trade deadline, Chicago was three and a half games out of first. They decided to trade one of their starting pitchers and their closer to the San Francisco Giants, essentially killing their playoff hopes. The White Sox did get plenty out of the prospects they received—they won the AL Central three years later—but it wasn't enough to overcome the bad feelings from the team's unconditional surrender three seasons before.

Hannah Storm set up in the Cleveland Indians dugout for an interview with center fielder Kenny Lofton. It was two hours before Game 3 of the 1995 World Series, and she'd cleared the post-batting practice interview with Lofton.

What she didn't know was that the Indians needed a spark.

Cleveland had lost the first two games of the series to the Atlanta Braves, and their All-Star slugger, Albert Belle, had managed just one single in the two games. Teammates knew that Belle played best when he was angry, and they set about provoking him.

"I've tried to get into his head a little," said Lofton. "I don't think he's as frustrated as I'd like to see him. I want to see Albert breaking a bat or something."

"Every day's a different thing," said shortstop Omar Vizquel. "I've seen him throw water coolers, break telephones, start breaking trophies in the clubhouse. I mean, there are cookies all over the place. He's been real calm here."

When Belle returned to the dugout after batting practice and saw a crowd of reporters blocking the way, the Indians had the spark they needed.

"All you media (bleeps), get the (bleep) out of here now," Belle snarled.

Most of the reporters scattered, but, in one corner, Storm continued to prepare for her interview.

"I'm talking to you, you (bleep)!" Belle screamed. "Get the (bleep) out!"

Storm stood her ground, and Belle responded with an expletive-filled tirade that lasted, according to one observer, for a full four minutes. Storm was shaking in fear by the end of it.

Mission accomplished: Belle drove in a run in the game and homered in the next two games.

He was eventually fined $50,000 for the incident, one of the highest fines in baseball history. Along with the announcement of the fine, the Indians released a statement from Belle: "I very much regret the incident and the ill feelings it has generated. At no time whatsoever was the presence in the dugout of any individual reporter the cause of my actions. I was upset with the sheer number of them in the dugout and not any particular one. But, having said that, many of them were simply doing their job, and it was not for me to decide that they should not be there."

When Belle saw the statement appear in news stories, he went to the Indians and complained. "I told them to take it out," he said. "I apologize for nothing."

Belle had already "apologized sincerely" to Storm privately, if the conversation could be accurately termed an apology.

"You got to stop wearing your hair like that," Belle told Storm. "I thought you were Lesley [Visser, another TV reporter]."

Belle later clarified what he meant. "I didn't even know it was Hannah Storm," he said. "I thought it was Lesley Visser. I wish it was Lesley Visser, because I don't like her anyway."

It was hardly an isolated incident for Belle. He threw a baseball at a *Sports Illustrated* reporter for taking his picture during pregame warmups. When the first toss missed and hit some seats nearby, Belle threw again and hit his target.

"I told you not to take my picture, (bleep)," Belle exclaimed.

In college, Belle went into the stands to try to fight a heckler, earning him a suspension. Earlier in his major league career, he threw a ball at a heckler in the stands, missed his intended target, and hit another fan in the chest. He also once dumped a cup of Gatorade on a cameraman.

Some players get into a zone at game time, and their competitive instincts cause them to lash out at anything that distracts them from their job. Albert Belle was not one of those players. He was just as volatile behind the scenes.

Belle regularly threw full cans of soda at locker room walls after bad at bats, leaving the mess for clubhouse attendants to clean up. The Indians also had to replace two clubhouse thermostats after Belle shattered them with bats, once because another teammate changed the temperature he'd set. Two days after the 1995 World Series ended, Belle chased down Halloween trick-or-treaters who had egged his home, and he hit them—with his car.

When a reporter tried to stand his ground in a confrontation with Belle, teammate Sandy Alomar Jr. took the reporter aside and explained, "You don't understand. He's crazy."

Colleagues described Belle as "Jekyll and Hyde" and a "black eye on baseball."

This was the man that White Sox owner Jerry Reinsdorf decided to make the highest-paid player in baseball, thirteen months after his rampage against Hannah Storm and trick-or-treaters.

Just a few years earlier, Reinsdorf had been one of the owners pushing for a hard line against rising player salaries during the strike that cost baseball the 1994 World Series. Then, when players' union and owners' negotiators worked out a compromise agreement in November 1996, Reinsdorf convinced his fellow owners to vote down the proposed new labor deal, again arguing for "salary restraint."

"It's not in the best interest of fans, players or owners to reach an agreement that doesn't solve our problems," Reinsdorf said. He went on to say that choosing between the current system and the proposed deal was "like choosing which of the Menendez brothers you like best," referring to the brothers who murdered their parents in one of the top news stories of the 1990s.

Seventeen days later, Reinsdorf explained why he led the coup against the owners' own negotiator. "We need some meaningful salary restraint and sharing of revenues, so everyone has a chance to compete," he said. Of course, his words lacked their full impact, since they were uttered after he'd agreed to make Albert Belle baseball's first $10 million a year player.

"Reinsdorf is a split personality, saying one thing and doing another," said Marvin Miller, longtime executive director of the Major League Baseball Players Association. "The most stupid people in the world clearly are the other owners who follow Reinsdorf."

Angry executives from other teams pointed out that, by rejecting the labor deal, which would have placed a "luxury tax" on large payrolls, Reinsdorf saved himself several million dollars by signing Belle when he did.

"I know [signing Belle] isn't going over well outside Chicago, but inside of Chicago is what I'm worried about," Reinsdorf said. "This is the perfect example of labor costs spiraling out of control. Most teams can't do it. The Royals and Brewers couldn't do it. Pittsburgh couldn't do it. But we have to compete within the system as it exists."

The Belle signing was important for Reinsdorf and the White Sox for financial reasons beyond the luxury tax. Attendance at Chicago's new Comiskey Park had fallen by more than 900,000 from the 2.5 million fans the team was averaging before the 1994 strike. Reinsdorf needed a big name to help sell tickets.

With first baseman Frank Thomas, a future Hall of Famer and one of the greatest sluggers in White Sox history, and Belle, one of the most feared hitters in baseball, Chicago appeared to have the lineup in place to make a run at the World Series. And, in the "chicks dig the longball" era of baseball marketing, they promised to have plenty of high-scoring offensive explosions along the way.

Reinsdorf underestimated his fans, however. Many Chicagoans still harbored ill will over the strike, and the White Sox owner seemed willing to risk canceling another World Series simply to avoid paying a luxury tax on contracts. The fact that Thomas and Belle would earn more than the entire payrolls of several teams was also a turn off.

Plus, Belle didn't exactly become warm and cuddly after signing his big contract. He skipped several team autograph sessions early in the season and refused to speak to the media or do anything to help promote ticket sales.

A story in the *St. Paul Pioneer Press* during the 1997 season portrayed the two White Sox sluggers as less interested in winning ballgames than in the lifestyle that their mega-salaries allowed them to pursue. The story opened with Thomas excitedly talking about a CD release party he'd attended, only to be interrupted by a security guard, informing him, "Frank, your suit guy is here."

"There were a lot of unfair expectations coming out of spring," Thomas said in the article. "They were talking about Ruth and Maris, and it was unfair. I think we've handled it pretty well. The first ten days seemed unfair. People were expecting us to hit two or three home runs a game in our first ten games. Baseball is not that easy. There was a comfort level we had to achieve first."

At the same time, the Indians were cruising along, in first place without Belle. "Everything is quiet now that he's gone," said Cleveland's Vizquel. "It's more relaxed in here than fear."

Chicago fans continued to stay away from the ballpark. While attendance went up by about 3,000 fans a game, the White Sox would still finish below two million for the season, a big drop from the prestrike days and good for just eighth best in the American League.

Reinsdorf complained about the relatively low ticket sales all season, and, a few months into the season, general manager Ron Schueler was warning that, due to stagnant attendance numbers, the White Sox would possibly have to let starting pitcher Wilson Álvarez and closer Roberto Hernández leave as free agents following the season.

By midseason, the White Sox were sending signals that they might not be willing to wait. With an increased payroll and nearly flat ticket sales, the team was on pace to lose $15 million in 1997.

As Chicago moved to within two and a half games of Cleveland in the standings, word got out that Álvarez and Hernández might be available at the trade deadline, for the right price. Schueler swore that there was no mandate to trade away high-priced stars but added, "In the right deal, I'll talk about anybody."

Executives in other teams' front offices were left scratching their heads. "We're still wondering why," one unnamed executive said.

Álvarez knew what it meant. "If they trade me or they trade Roberto, they are showing the people that they're giving up," he said.

The White Sox had discussions with the Mets, who were two games out of the National League wild card and desperate for pitching. They also talked with the Mariners, who led the AL West but were seeking a closer.

On July 29, it became clear that the White Sox weren't just talking. They were going to be sellers at the deadline. Chicago traded veteran outfielder Harold Baines to the Orioles for a player to be named later.

Baines was hitting .305 with 12 home runs for the White Sox, but he was also making $1,925,000 that year. The Orioles led the American League East and were looking to hold off the defending world champion Yankees in the stretch run by adding a bat.

"This is not a message that we're giving up," Schueler said. "I want to win. I want to win this year. This gives enough maneuverability."

The following day, trade deadline eve, talks heated up between the White Sox and the San Francisco Giants, who were clinging to a half-game lead in the NL West. The Giants were looking to add pitching. Specifically, they needed bullpen help and a fourth starter. While Shawn Estes, Mark Gardner and Kirk Rueter had combined to win 32 games at that point in the season, the team went 0–8 after the All-Star break in games started by anyone else. However, the only arms that seemed to be available were second or third tier talents. They had pursued, without success, 33-year-old Bobby Witt, who had led the league in walks three times and wild pitches twice, although he'd matured into a 16-game winner the previous season with Texas; Detroit's Willie Blair, a 32-year-old who was pitching as a starter for the first time, after seven seasons in the bullpen; and the Cubs' 34-year-old Terry Mulholland, who was 6–12 on the season. (The Giants did eventually add Mulholland, when the Cubs waived him a week after the trade deadline.)

Then the White Sox made a last, best offer, and, for the second time in eight months, the sport would be stirred into a rage by Reinsdorf.

Giants manager Dusty Baker pulled his pitching coach, Dick Pole, aside while on a flight to Cincinnati and showed him a list of White Sox pitchers:

Wilson Álvarez, a left-handed starter who, at age 27, was already a two-time 15-game winner, had struck out 360 batters over the previous two seasons and was 9–8 with a 3.03 ERA at the time.

Roberto Hernández, a veteran 33-year-old reliever who led the league in appearances the last three years, had saved more than 30 games in three of the previous four seasons, and already had 27 saves and a 5–1 record in 1997.

Danny Darwin, a seemingly ageless 42-year-old right-hander who had been in the majors since 1978, had led the league in ERA back in 1990, and was 4–8 in 17 starts for the White Sox in 1997.

"I thought we'd have to decide on one of them," Pole recalled.

No. The Giants were getting all three. Of the White Sox's 52 wins to that point in the season, the three pitchers on the list had combined for 18 of them, in addition to Hernández's 27 saves.

The Giants had to give up a half-dozen minor leaguers to gain the pitching infusion. They included outfielder Brian Manning, pitcher Lorenzo Barceló, left-handed pitcher Ken Vining and infielder Mike Caruso. All four turned 22 during the year and were in just their second or third (Barceló) year of pro ball. San Francisco also gave up two promising 24-year-old pitchers in Keith Foulke, who had made his MLB debut earlier in the year, and Bobby Howry, who won 10 games as a starter in Double-A the year before, then switched to the bullpen in 1997 and had 22 saves.

The White Sox were just three and a half games out of first place at the time.

"We're extremely excited to get six players of this caliber," Schueler said. "We still believe we can win, but we were burned last year by the Alex Fernandez situation, and we couldn't allow it to happen again." (The previous offseason, the White Sox had watched the 28-year-old ace sign with the Florida Marlins after turning down a five-year, $30 million offer to stay in Chicago.)

The players in the Chicago locker room weren't convinced. A tearful Ozzie Guillén smashed the clubhouse television set when he heard about the deal.

"We have to pick up the pieces and move on," Frank Thomas said. "There's still a lot of talent in this room, and we can still win. But it's going to be different. We definitely lost two all-stars, and Danny Darwin was having a good year, too. . . . We haven't been drawing well. The fans have sent a message they don't like the team."

"I personally don't like it," third baseman Robin Ventura said. "We didn't just lose three pitchers, we lost three quality pitchers. We'll never know if we could have won [the division] because we never got the chance. . . . No-one told me the season ended on August 1."

The trade quickly became known as the "White Flag trade." The Sox were giving up with over two months still to play.

"I don't ever give up," Schueler said. "But what I saw was a club that I felt I had given four months, but we didn't perform as good as I thought they would. We weren't even at the .500 mark and I wasn't at the point where I thought I could go out and add a lot of dollars to make it better."

"Anyone who thinks this White Sox team will catch Cleveland is crazy," was Reinsdorf's explanation.

Jaws dropped open around baseball.

"Signing Albert Belle was one," said one GM. "Doing this is not good for baseball, either."

"It's the Major League Baseball version of 'no mas'," an owner said, referring to boxer Roberto Duran's surrender in a 1980 title fight against Sugar Ray Leonard.

"My God, you give away a good starting pitcher and your top reliever, and you're only three and a half games out of first place—that's just not good for the game," said Hall of Fame manager Whitey Herzog.

"I think it's going to be battered around for weeks, and it should be," said longtime baseball executive Buzzie Bavasi. "Something like this could affect the game. Trading three established players to another club in the middle of a pennant race?"

"I think what Jerry Reinsdorf did was unconscionable to the fans and to baseball in general," Orioles GM Kevin Malone said. "It's disappointing that owners aren't held accountable for the things they do, but that's the nature of the beast. . . . Do you think that's good for baseball when you have a team that's three games out? I just think it's disappointing for baseball if you're going to commit $10 million for one player. It's disappointing because we have to live with the repercussions of the mistakes of others."

"For that particular club to dump salaries when they are right in the hunt, I just don't think that's fair to the fans or to baseball," Malone continued. "Where's the integrity of the game? If we had a strong commissioner like Bowie Kuhn, he might have overruled that deal. When's somebody going to stand up for the game? I think people should be disappointed with what's happening with this game."

The new Giants players wasted no time taking shots at their old team. "I'm happy to be out of there," said Álvarez. "The players, they're great. The fans, they're good—they were good to me all six years I was there. It's the people in the front office. They don't care about the players. All they care about is making money. That's why they're not going to win."

"I've never seen management up and throw in the towel like that when they're so close," Darwin said. "I've never heard an owner come out and say, 'We have no chance of catching the team in front of us.' I've never seen that in twenty-two years of professional baseball."

"They were saying they had tried to talk to our agents [about contract extensions], and they flat-out lied," said Hernández. "I've been honest with them for my whole career. A lot of people thought I was bitter. I'm not bitter. I just don't like being lied to and have the fans being lied to."

"It was a relief to get out of there," he continued. "We tried to get out of there as soon as possible. If there was a jet within fifteen minutes, we were on it."

Incredibly, Reinsdorf attempted to backtrack from his controversial statement. "That's what I said yesterday," he explained. "I don't feel that way today."

When the Giants arrived in Cincinnati for their next game, Baker gathered the team together in the hotel to give them the news.

"He rounded us up in a corner and told us about it," first baseman J. T. Snow said. "I was standing in the back when I heard the news and said, 'Oh, my God.' I think everyone was stunned but very happy. I think management has done the positioning. Now we got to do it from here. It's up to the players."

"Once you sit back and see the quality of the three players, let alone put them in one deal, it is pretty unique," Giants general manager Brian Sabean said.

Sabean wasn't concerned about whether the team could sign the two potential free agents in the offseason. "Our concern is what they can do for us now," he said. "Whatever happens after the season remains to be seen."

The team's ownership group was also thrilled with the deal, in part because of the impact it would have on the bottom line. "They know how important winning is to getting people in the ballpark," said Peter Magowan, the Giants' managing general partner. "We've got a new ballpark coming in the year 2000, and we want to get people invigorated in baseball like they were before the strike."

In Chicago, Schueler continued to work to break up the team. He tried to work out a waiver-wire trade with the Yankees for Ventura, and the two teams even had conversations about Belle, but neither player ended up leaving—at least not that season. Ventura departed for the Mets after he became a free agent in 1998. Belle took advantage of a loophole in his gigantic contract to leave in 1998 as well.

Belle's contract had included a clause guaranteeing that he would be one of the three highest-paid players in baseball. He had three days after the World Series each year to demand that the White Sox increase his salary to keep him in the top three.

By the end of the 1998 season, Pedro Martínez ($12 million a year), Greg Maddux ($11.5 million) and Gary Sheffield ($11.4 million) all made more than Belle's $10 million salary. In fact, Belle was tied for fourth place, with the Cubs' Sammy Sosa.

After the World Series, Belle's agent requested a $1,416,667 raise for his client. Reinsdorf refused, and Belle became a free agent. He signed a five-year deal with the Orioles that would pay him $13 million a year. He lasted two seasons in Baltimore before a degenerative hip forced him to retire.

Álvarez earned the victory for San Francisco as a starter in the first game following the trade, and the Giants went on to win 30 of 53 games to secure the 1997 NL West title. In all, Álvarez won 4 games for San Francisco, while Hernández had 5 wins and 4 saves after the trade.

The postseason run the team had hoped for didn't materialize, however. The Giants were swept in the opening round by wild card Florida. Álvarez started the final game of the series, but took the loss after giving up 4 runs in six innings. Hernández pitched in all 3 playoff games and had a part in all three losses, posting a 20.25 ERA in 1.1 innings.

The Giants weren't able to retain either of the two free agents. Álvarez and Hernández both signed with the expansion Tampa Bay Devil Rays after the season. Álvarez started the first game in Rays history in 1998. Tampa signed him to a five-year, $35 million contract—exactly the same terms that Alex Fernandez got from the Marlins a year earlier. Hernández signed with Tampa for four years and $22.5 million.

Despite the "white flag" message sent by the trade, it wasn't a total mismatch by any means. In fact, based on value produced after the trade, the White Sox won the deal on paper by a wide margin.

The six prospects the Giants gave up were all promising players, and five of them reached the major leagues with the White Sox. Both Foulke and Howry would play a role in the White Sox winning the AL Central in 2000.

"He was untouchable," Giants director of player personnel Dick Tidrow said of Mike Caruso, once the organization's top prospect, "unless we could get an All-Star type of major leaguer back. Otherwise, we wouldn't part with him. He was on a very fast track. We thought he might be up by September of '98."

Chicago had Caruso in the lineup earlier than that. He played 133 games in 1998 and finished third in Rookie of the Year voting after posting a .306 average and 22 stolen bases. The following year, he suffered through a sophomore slump. His average dropped by 56 points, and he was caught stealing more times than he was successful. The White Sox waived him after the 2000 season.

Brian Manning couldn't hit .200 in a brief trial at Double-A and never made it past that level. Barceló pitched in parts of three seasons with the Sox, going 5–3 with a 4.50 ERA, before two arm surgeries cut his career short.

Ken Vining also needed arm surgery, but he managed to get back to prospect status and then had a disastrous stint with the White Sox in his only MLB experience. After retiring three of four batters he faced in his first two outings in May 2001, Vining gave up runs in each of his next six appearances. He ended up giving up 13 earned runs in 6.2 innings for a 17.55 career ERA in the majors. Of the 42 batters Vining faced in his major league career, 23 reached base, and one in every three batters he faced came around to score.

Keith Foulke saved 100 games in six seasons with the White Sox, including 34 as the closer for the 2000 division champs. He would go on to play for Boston, where he finished all 4 games in the Red Sox's historic 2004 World Series victory.

Howry spent five years with the White Sox. He won 13 games and saved 49, including 28 as the team's closer in 1999.

Eight years and three months after the White Flag trade, Astros pinch hitter Orlando Palmeiro hit a weak ground ball to shortstop. Juan Uribe fielded it and threw to first base. Paul Konerko made the catch, Palmeiro was retired and just like that, the Chicago White Sox had won their first World Series in 88 years.

A few days later, after a parade in Chicago, Konerko called the team's owner to the podium. "Mr. Reinsdorf. Jerry, get up here," Konerko said. "Everybody kept asking me over the last couple days what I did with that ball—the last out."

"Well," he said, "it's going to this man right here, because he's earned it." Konerko reached into his pocket and pulled out the ball and handed it to a stunned Reinsdorf.

"I almost lost it when he gave me the ball," Reinsdorf said later. "It was never on my mind. Then, when he called me up and gave me the ball, I really came very, very close to being overly emotional. I was emotional enough as it was. If you take out the birth of children and getting married, certainly, yeah, that was my number one moment with the White Sox. Baseball is the one sport that ties generations together. We were able to give everybody that wonderful feeling. That was the best part of it."

The feeling was enough to make an owner wonder why anyone would ever give up a chance to win.

WAR COMPARISON

The White Sox actually received good value for the veterans they traded away, and the front office deserves credit for choosing prospects who, for the most part, contributed to Chicago at the major league level.

As in real estate, however, timing is everything. The trade drew derision not because the White Sox lost too much value or gained too little. Instead, the problem was that the Sox gave up on the season when they still had a legitimate shot to make the playoffs.

GIANTS RECEIVED	WAR PRE-TRADE	WAR POST-TRADE
Roberto Hernández	10.8	1.1 with SF, 6.3 over next 5 years
Wilson Álvarez	17.4	0.2 with SF, 4.2 over next 5 years
Danny Darwin	1.5	-1.1
WHITE SOX RECEIVED	WAR PRE-TRADE	WAR POST-TRADE
Bob Howry	0.0	5.9
Keith Foulke	-1.3	14.3
Mike Caruso	0.0	1.1
Ken Vining	0.0	-0.6
Lorenzo Barceló	0.0	0.5
Brian Manning	0.0	0.0

CHAPTER 8

— THE THROW-IN —

THE STORY BEHIND THE RYNE SANDBERG TRADE

*A second-thought throw-in turns out to be
a winning lottery ticket in this top-shelf trade.*

*In 1982, the Philadelphia Phillies traded aging shortstop Larry Bowa, who had been one
of the key players on their World Champion team of two years earlier. In exchange, they
received clubhouse peace, as well as the starting shortstop on what would become their 1983
World Series team, Iván DeJesús. The trade would have been a good example of upgrading
a roster, if not for the throw-in—a prospect named Ryne Sandberg, who would become
the face of the Cubs for a generation and change the way people looked at the prototypical
second baseman.*

At age 69, Larry Bowa is still ready for a fight.

Holding a fungo bat, Bowa stops tidying up from batting practice and turns his full
attention to the reporter questioning him.

"They lied to me," he says. The sun glints off his wraparound shades, but his glare is still
apparent from behind the tinted plastic.

Bowa pulls his mouth tight and squares his shoulders, seemingly ready to throw down
with anyone who wants to raise a counterpoint or play devil's advocate.

"They lied to me," he repeats, nodding his head.

After an uncomfortable silence, Bowa, confident that his opinion won't be challenged,
continues reminiscing on the events leading up to his trade.

"I went to . . . who was the general manager at the time? Was it Pope?"

The moment encapsulates Larry Bowa's baseball career. Still angry 33 years after the fact,
Bowa doesn't even remember the GM that so enraged him—just that he hates the man for lying
to him. Anger and a willingness to scrap has fueled Bowa's half century in professional baseball.

While Bowa spent his baseball life wearing his emotions on his sleeve, the manager he was
working for at the time was a polar opposite. Ryne Sandberg, to whom Bowa will always be
linked, was well known as one of baseball's all-time introverts.

Rubén Amaro Jr., a former teammate of Sandberg's, as well as the Phillies GM that hired
him as manager, said, "He's extraordinarily shy about his accomplishments. He gets almost
sheepish about making a good play."

Teammates sarcastically nicknamed Sandberg "Gabby," and Rick Sutcliffe said he rode to
the ballpark with Sandberg for seven years and never heard him speak.

Sutcliffe also recalled the time he had shoulder surgery, and Sandberg visited the recovering pitcher afterward. "I knew he was there to see me, but he couldn't tell me that," Sutcliffe told ESPN. "He had a hard time communicating."

The contrast in personalities between Bowa and Sandberg likely explains why the latter was almost completely overlooked when it came time to trade the former.

While Sandberg was a three-sport star in high school and an All-American quarterback with a scholarship offer from the Pac 10, Bowa was cut from his high school baseball team all four years. To hear him tell the story at banquets, Bowa says he was cut because he was too small. At five foot ten and 155 pounds during his playing days, he was certainly no giant. He was, however, about the same size as his contemporaries at the middle-infield spots. He was the same weight as Dave Concepción and Ozzie Smith, taller than Davey Lopes and Joe Morgan.

In Bowa's mind, however, he was dwarfed by the other players on the field, hopelessly undersized. His genes had stacked the deck against him. A more accurate restatement of history might be that Napoleon had a Larry Bowa complex.

"They thought I was 'too small,'" he said of his high school team. "I don't know anybody that was on it, and none of them made out to be a big-league player. They said I was too small."

"It's a mind-set with me," he told a Philadelphia paper. "When I played, during the winter I'd say: 'I'm going to play 150-plus games every season.' I basically brainwashed myself into thinking that way even though I wasn't very big." The quote was for a story on how Bowa is one of the oldest coaches in MLB to still throw batting practice. He pushes his elderly arm through the daily punishment because, in his mind, he's still too small to belong unless he allows his determination to push him to his physical limits.

More likely, Bowa was cut from his high school team each year because he wasn't that good at baseball, at least in terms of raw talent. "Hitting a ball is hard," he says. "Catching a ball is hard. The easiest thing to do on a field is play hard."

From his high school indignity, Bowa developed a single-minded pursuit of success on the field. Bowa is frequently described as "fiery," but that word doesn't fully capture the sheer force of his drive. A more apt description of Bowa the player is a blowtorch, blasting heat capable of melting metal. Anyone standing in his path has to either step aside or get burned.

Plenty of teammates have gotten scorched over the years. Don Zimmer, a baseball lifer, called Bowa, "The most selfish player I have ever known," and "the most negative man I've ever been around in my life." Zim didn't blurt out the attack while still in the heat of the moment, either. He said it while reading from a prepared statement in the Cubs clubhouse. Zimmer, the team's third-base coach, took the unusual step in defense of manager Jim Frey, who had been ripped by the 39-year-old Bowa for the sin of starting 22-year-old first-overall draft pick Shawon Dunston at short, in place of him.

Confrontation has followed Bowa at every stop of his baseball life. He was discovered by Sacramento City College while playing AAU baseball. When the coach offered him a spot on the junior college's team, Bowa challenged him. "I didn't even make my high school team. Why do you want me?"

Sacramento CC eventually convinced him to come, and he was one of the team's stars. When the Phillies sent a scout to watch him during a doubleheader, Bowa was ejected in the early innings of both games. The scout had to send back a report based on about four innings worth of observation, which may explain its inaccuracy.

Bowa was originally considered a "good field, no hit" shortstop prospect by the Phillies, a good "organizational player" who would put in a few decent years filling out a minor league roster, likely peaking at Double-A.

The report has not been given a pass by Bowa. He points out that his 2,191 major league hits were "pretty good for someone who wasn't supposed to be able to hit." It was good enough to rank him 190th on the all-time hit list (as of 2015). With 400 more hits than elementary-school dropout Shoeless Joe Jackson, Bowa may have the most hits by a player who never played high school ball.

Bowa was investigated by MLB after he allegedly fought a reporter in 1978. He feuded with Phillies manager Dallas Green en route to the 1980 World Series title. Bowa took issue with the equally fiery Green for criticizing him publicly.

He feuded with Cubs teammates Ryne Sandberg and Shawon Dunston, as well as manager Jim Frey.

"Larry Bowa acts like he knows all the answers before I do," a frustrated Frey said during Bowa's final spring training with the team. "There is nothing I could say that would be interpreted the right way."

Once his playing days were over, Bowa became a coach and left a trail of smoldering bridges behind him as he went from team to team. In his one year as a minor league manager, he picked up five fines and two suspensions while leading the Las Vegas Stars to a Pacific Coast League title. He was ejected four times in his first 44 games and had a clubhouse confrontation with one of his best players, outfielder Gary Woods.

Sandberg was more forceful as a manager than as a player, but he was still so unassuming that his players applauded him in the clubhouse the first time he was ejected from a game for arguing with umpires. "We kept wondering if he had it in him," infielder Russ Canzler told ESPN. "Then all of the sudden, he saw something he didn't like and he just ran out there and laid down the law. It was awesome."

Bowa needed no encouragement from his players to get in someone's face. "I expected too much out of Triple-A players," Bowa told the *New York Times*, reflecting on his season. "I expected these guys' work habits to be what mine are."

That attitude didn't change at the major league level. He flamed out as Padres manager, feuding with his players and getting fired 46 games into the 1988 season after leading them to a 97-loss, last-place finish the year before. While pulling pitcher Storm Davis from a game, he had a confrontation on the mound that spilled over into his office postgame. He informed the hurler, "The SD on our cap stands for San Diego, not Storm Davis."

Bowa also benched catcher Benito Santiago, who was on his way to a Rookie of the Year award, for not running out ground balls. He had a clubhouse shouting match with outfielder Stan Jefferson.

During his tenure as manager of the Phillies from 2001 to 2004, he clashed with All-Star third baseman Scott Rolen, All-Star catcher Mike Lieberthal and outfielder Pat Burrell. He was suspended for the second game of the season after arguing with umpires during spring training. After cutting pinch hitter Tyler Houston from the roster, Bowa called him "a loser," adding "fifteen guys [on the team] did back flips after we released him."

Larry Bowa, 155 pounds of fury and sharp edges, is not going to respond well to a lie. And a misunderstanding, like the one that occurred in late 1981, is likely to be interpreted by Bowa as a lie.

At some point following the 1980 championship season, Phillies owner Ruly Carpenter promised Bowa a contract extension that would keep Bowa in town through 1984, when the shortstop would be 39 years old. Carpenter may have been feeling especially affectionate toward one of the leaders of his gritty team following the World Series victory, or since he was already considering selling the team, the owner may have been slightly disingenuous.

"I told Bowa I would give him the extension if I still owned the team," Carpenter told Bill Giles, the leader of the group that bought the team from Carpenter in 1981.

Regardless of the reasons behind Carpenter's declaration, Bowa considered it an ironclad guarantee. The Phillies owed him a new contract, at $400,000 a year.

Bowa didn't have an agent in the early 1970s, when he negotiated his first contract extension with Carpenter. Over the years, when the two had trouble coming to an agreement, Carpenter was known to call Bowa's wife to facilitate the negotiations.

Bowa didn't have the same relationship with Giles, or the team's general manager, Paul Owens, nicknamed "Pope" due to his resemblance to Pope Paul VI. Giles was hesitant to lock up the aging shortstop to a long-term deal, and he let Bowa know that the promised deal was off the table.

Just like that, the new owner found Bowa's blowtorch heat aimed at him. Bowa took his frustration to the Philadelphia media, the same sin he'd gotten angry with manager Dallas Green for committing a year earlier. "I've been here twelve years," he said immediately after the end of the 1981 season, "and now it looks like the whole organization is going to be changed, from top to bottom."

He pointed out that, if he were buying the team, he wouldn't come in and immediately clean house, but he wasn't the new owner. "Obviously," he said, "there's going to be some changes made."

"Bill said he would trade me if I wanted," the 69-year-old Bowa recalled, "and I said, yeah. Get me out of here."

Bowa had been in the majors for more than ten years and with the Phillies for more than five. According to MLB's collective bargaining agreement, as a "ten and five man," Bowa had the right to veto any trade. In essence, Bowa could dictate where the team sent him. And Bowa wasn't going to make it easy on the front office.

Manager Dallas Green left the team following the season, to become general manager of the Cubs. Despite the clashes in 1980, time had helped soften the feelings between the two.

"He doesn't lie to you," Bowa said of Green. "He may not tell you what you want to hear. He tells you what he sees, which, hey, I'll be the first to admit as a player you don't always like it. But you look back on it and say, 'you know what? He was right.'"

It's the same way that current players speak of Bowa, the coach and manager. Former Yankees second baseman Robinson Cano was ridden incessantly by Bowa throughout his early years, when Bowa was a coach with New York in 2006 and 2007. The two didn't speak for a week at one point.

Bowa recalled, "I told him, 'If you want to go and practice once every five days, go do it.

I've got no stake in you. I'm a third base coach. But if you want to be great, you'll do it my way.'" Cano gave Bowa a Rolex watch as a going-away present when Bowa left the organization. Since the two have separated, Cano's work ethic and habits have again been called into question at times.

"He's demanding, but he knows what he's talking about," Troy Glaus said, after then-Angels coach Bowa gave him a crash course in playing third base as a rookie. "He doesn't sugarcoat anything. He's not always going to give you a warm-and-fuzzy answer, but if you're fine with that and understand it, it's all right."

Green was clearly built from the same mold as Bowa. If anyone could wring more from the shortstop than Bowa himself, it was Green.

"Dallas is in Chicago," Bowa recalled telling Giles. "Send me there. I want to play for Dallas."

The worst trades are the ones you're forced to make, but Giles acted thoughtfully and deliberately, considering his options.

The Phillies had two shortstop prospects that Giles and Owens hoped would be ready to take over at shortstop for the big league club by 1983. In five minor league seasons, Julio Franco had never batted below .300. Luis Aguayo spent most of 1980 and 1981 on the Phillies bench but played in 65 games at second and short. Trading Bowa would leave the question of who would man the shortstop position in 1982.

The front office didn't want to saddle either youngster, Franco or Aguayo, with the task of replacing Bowa, a favorite among the notoriously harsh Philadelphia fan base. Bringing the disgruntled Bowa back to play out the final year of his contract would risk blowing up the clubhouse.

Giles had three choices: send Bowa to the Cubs, convince him to accept a trade elsewhere or give in to his contract demands.

"I'm not going to trade him just because he's popping off in the papers," Giles said on January 7, 1982—a Thursday. "I'm going on vacation beginning Saturday. So I'll try to make a deal for him this week, if we can improve ourselves or stay equal."

Owens also had strict requirements on trading Bowa. "I'd like to get a shortstop back," he said, "an experienced shortstop." He mentioned the Cubs' Iván DeJesús and disgruntled Cardinals shortstop Garry Templeton as potential targets. The team also contacted the Padres about a deal for Ozzie Smith. Bowa wouldn't bless a trade to St. Louis or San Diego, however, effectively ending negotiations for Templeton and Smith, a future Hall of Famer, in their infancy.

The Phillies also explored the idea of sending Bowa to the White Sox for Bill Almon. News leaked out, and White Sox GM Roland Hemond backed off the deal publicly. "What they say in Philadelphia, I have no control over. It sounds like somebody is doing our orchestrating for us," he said.

While the Phillies were exploring trade options, Bowa went on Philadelphia talk radio to break a story. According to his agent, he had been traded to the Cubs. The deal included outfielder Dick Davis and Aguayo. The Phillies would receive DeJesús and relief pitcher Bill Caudill.

"Maybe it's more than that," Bowa said on air. "I was waiting for a call this afternoon but I didn't get it. But it looks like it right now. I can't confirm that but I'll go with what he [his agent] said."

The attempt to spur the deal along didn't work. The Phillies denied the deal the next day, as Giles packed to leave for Barbados.

There was plenty of interest in Bowa. The Braves offered pitcher Tommy Boggs, and the Orioles began assembling a package of prospects. As the hours ticked by, however, it appeared that it would be the Cubs or no one, a fact that Cubs GM Dallas Green knew full well.

"Sure, I'd take Larry in a minute," he told the media on Friday. "He's a gamer, a winner. But they want pitching over there, and I'm not sure we can help them with what we have here."

"Dallas is asking for some steep things," Paul Owens griped.

Green knew he had his former team over a barrel. "They had to get rid of him," he said after the fact. "He had that contract problem, and then he went out on a limb and said some testy things. I knew he'd be gone."

The deal appeared to boil down to Bowa for DeJesús. Both teams needed to replace the starting shortstop they were giving up. However, DeJesús was seven years younger than Bowa, meaning the Cubs would be giving up more future production in an even-up swap.

Green began talking up DeJesús in the media, making him sound like a potential gold glover. DeJesús was among the league leaders for putouts, assists and double plays turned at shortstop. But he was hitting just .194, the lowest in the league among regular players. DeJesús was also the anti-Bowa, angering Green by not showing feistiness in the clubhouse or on the field, including an unwillingness to participate in infield chatter during games.

Still, publicly, Green continued to sing the praises of his current shortstop. "I've said all along I'd never trade him one-for-one," he said.

It was time to talk throw-in. The Phillies would need to include a prospect to even out the deal.

Prior to managing the Phillies, Green had been the organization's farm director, so he had a better grasp of the prospects in the system than most opposing GMs. Plus, he'd brought another Phillies executive, Gordon Goldsberry, with him to the Cubs as his right-hand man.

"Gordie and I wanted a young player who could be a building block for the Cubs' future. We agreed that 22-year-old Ryne Sandberg had that potential," Green wrote in his memoir.

Goldsberry had scouted Sandberg as a high school player, and Green was the one who pulled the trigger on him for the Phillies in the 20th round of the 1978 draft. But Sandberg had been stuck behind Bowa and Franco on the organization's shortstop depth chart.

Sandberg was coming off a year in which he hit .293 with 9 home runs and 62 RBI at Triple-A Oklahoma City, numbers that were down from his minor-league career highs set the previous year. He had gotten one hit in six at bats during a brief stint with the big-league club in 1981. His one hit came, appropriately enough, against the Cubs, at Wrigley Field, using a bat he borrowed from Larry Bowa.

Sandberg had played 431 of his 456 minor league games and 5 of his 6 MLB games at shortstop. He had just 18 games of experience at second base, during which he had made 6 errors.

"He was a tremendous all-around athlete, with great speed and hands," Green wrote. "He had mostly played shortstop in the minor leagues, but we felt he could adapt to any infield position."

The Phillies balked at including Sandberg, a testament to Green's knowledge of their system. They tried to sell him on Aguayo. They offered first baseman Len Matuszek, a fifth-round draft pick—15 rounds earlier than Sandberg.

Green and the Cubs stuck to their demands. Hopes for a prevacation agreement waned.

At midday, Friday, Owens left for Houston, for a Saturday luncheon where he was being honored by the American Association of College Baseball Coaches. On Saturday, Giles left the country. Phillies vice president for public relations Larry Shenk was asked if there was phone service in Barbados.

"We'll find out," he said.

Bowa was still a Phillie without a new deal, left to stew for a week.

Tanned, rested and reunited with Owens, Giles took another week after returning from vacation to put together a deal with the Cubs: Bowa for DeJesús, with the Phillies including Sandberg as a sweetener.

On Sunday, January 24, the announcement of the deal came first on talk radio—poetic justice for the Phillies, who leaked the story while Bowa was left in the dark.

"I'm just sitting here waiting," Bowa said when Philadelphia papers contacted him at home in Florida. "I imagine that if something was close, they would have called me."

On Monday afternoon, Giles put a stake in the ground. By end of day Tuesday, he proclaimed, it would be decided once and for all "whether Mr. Bowa will be in a Cubs uniform this year or a Phillies uniform."

Having given in to Green's demand for Sandberg, the Phillies were now asking for more.

"We probably can make a deal if we want to," Giles said on Monday. "But we're trying to expand it if we can."

Philadelphia hoped to obtain Lee Smith, a Cubs reliever with one career save, who would go on to save another 477 over the next 16 years. That effort failed, after the Cubs demanded outfielder George Vukovich, and hopes for a deal again faded.

"We're pretty much where we were a month ago, to be quite honest," Giles said on Monday evening.

Bowa, who earlier in the day had said he was "just sitting back, waiting till they tell me where I'm going," found that the laid-back approach didn't work for him.

When the possibility was raised of staying in Philadelphia and heading to the negotiating table, Bowa said, "I'm sure things could be negotiated, but it's a little late for that, isn't it? They should have been talking from the end of the winter meetings until now. He [Giles] knows he has to talk to me if a trade falls through. Unless, uh, he misunderstood again. He seems to misunderstand a lot."

Tuesday came and went, and more names kept flying. Bob Dernier, Don McCormack, Del Unser and Sparky Lyle were all added to and removed from the deal at various points. Finally, late that night, the deal went back to the three core players.

"We tried to expand it a lot of different ways," Owens said. "We went round and round so many different ways I can't even remember them all."

The Phillies organization took one last potshot at Bowa on his way out of town.

"Iván DeJesús has value," Giles said at the Wednesday press conference announcing the deal. "Julio Franco has value. We found out in trying to trade Larry that his value was minimal."

Bowa would sign a four-year contract extension with the Cubs, paying him $500,000 a year, which more than made up for the barb from Giles, even if Bowa never forgot the comment.

DeJesús, for his part, was hurt by the Cubs' decision to part ways with him.

"I really don't know why they traded me," he said. "I didn't ask to be traded. I suppose the only way they can have a winning team is to make changes. So they changed me . . . but maybe they made a mistake."

DeJesús also wasn't happy that the team's shortstop of the future, Franco, was sitting in Double-A, waiting for him to show signs of aging. "A lot of things can happen to a guy between Double-A and the big leagues," DeJesús' agent, Jim Bronner, reminded everyone on trade day.

Sandberg remembered getting the call while heading home after a game in winter ball. "I'd grown up a Phillie," he said. "They drafted me. I came up all through their system and had just had a taste of the major leagues, and now I wasn't going to be a Phillie after all."

Not only that, but the move didn't really offer him a fresh start with a new organization. "I was a shortstop at the time. I was still blocked, and still blocked by the same guy, since Larry was traded with me."

Sandberg had been working at center field in the winter leagues, but, with Steve Henderson established at that position for the Cubs, that didn't offer him much of a path to being a major league regular either.

As with most post-trade press conferences, the Phillies were bullish on DeJesús' potential, although Owens was careful to downplay his offensive struggles. "I think it was just one of those years," Owens said of the .194 average in 1981.

The team expected him to be better, both in the field and at the plate, thanks to his now playing home games on Philadelphia's artificial turf. The team also had Manny Trillo at second base. He had been DeJesús' double-play partner in Chicago in 1977 and 1978, two of DeJesús' best seasons. He led the league in runs scored in 1977 and in defensive assists among shortstops both years.

The Phillies also thought DeJesús would be able to fill a hole at the top of the order. He'd batted leadoff for the Cubs and would get the chance to win the job for the Phillies. Of course, if his offensive struggles persisted, new Phillies manager Pat Corrales admitted, "We'll have to move him down." But the manager was hopeful for the future.

"We can look back just at the last couple of years," Corrales said. "Pittsburgh won the World Series in 1979 and stayed pat, and it caught up with them. I just don't think Bill Giles and Paul Owens are going to let that happen here in Philadelphia."

"We just think that, not only this year but in the long run, whatever we do at the shortstop position, we'll be better as a ball club," Giles said. "Iván might be here eight years. You never know what's going to happen."

He wasn't there for eight years—three, to be exact. In fact, despite the age difference, Bowa (36) for DeJesús (29) was a virtually even swap. DeJesús played 463 games for Philadelphia and was the starting shortstop for the team's trip to the 1983 World Series. Bowa played 494 games in Chicago over three and a half years and started at short for the team's first trip to the postseason in 39 years.

DeJesús and Trillo only played together for one season before the Phillies dealt the second baseman to Cleveland (with Julio Franco and George Vukovich). DeJesús also didn't work out at the top of the order. He batted leadoff in just 3 games and started 420 games in the eight-hole, batting just in front of the pitcher.

The trade would have been a blip on the radar, hardly worth the effort that the negotiations and spin took over the winter of 1981–82, except for the throw-in. The minor leaguer seeking a position, included just to make the age differential more palatable to the Cubs, ended up being the keystone of the deal—and made for one of the greatest fleecings in trade history.

The pretrade assumption was correct—DeJesús had more left than Bowa. He would produce about double the value Bowa did over the rest of his career. So it made sense that the Phillies would have to include someone else in the deal to even things out. And any of the other six Phillies players—who were either unproven prospects or veterans finishing out their career—would have nearly balanced the scales of the trade.

The Cubs just happened to get the throw-in candidate who was the equivalent of a winning lottery ticket.

"The consensus scouting report on Sandberg from our baseball people was that he couldn't hit well enough to play third and couldn't field well enough to play second," Giles recalled in his memoir.

In other words, Sandberg was a "tweener." He didn't fit at any position, at least according to baseball's traditional view of how a lineup should be fielded. A team's corner infielders—the first and third basemen—are supposed to be power hitters and RBI producers. Sandberg wasn't going to be another Mike Schmidt, who hit 548 home runs as the Phillies third baseman.

Sandberg also wasn't the slick fielder that generally manned the middle infield positions, where hitting prowess wasn't expected or demanded. Of course, Sandberg would eventually revolutionize the position of second base, bringing his ability to produce runs to the spot, once the Cubs were willing to look past the traditional prototype for the position.

One of the reasons that the Cubs were more willing than the Phillies to break the mold and try a nontraditional approach in their infield positions was that they didn't have as much to lose. While the Phillies had won the World Series in 1980 and had five postseason appearances in the previous six seasons, the Cubs were in the middle of one of the longest streaks of futility in the history of the sport.

The team had last appeared in the World Series in 1945—a 36-year drought, at the time the trade was made. Over that span, Chicago had finished in last place eight times, including both 1980 and 1981, and second-to-last 10 times. While finishing in the bottom two places in half of the previous 36 years, the Cubs had finished in second place just three times, most recently in 1972. The Cubs had posted only eight winning seasons since 1945, and it had been a decade since the last one. The team could afford to take a few risks.

The *Chicago Tribune* announced the trade with the headline, "DeJesus Traded for Bowa, Rookie." The story introduced Sandberg as "an untested minor leaguer" and "a 22-year-old middle infielder with good speed but a light bat."

"It would seem doubtful that Sandberg will crack the opening-day lineup," the *Tribune* concluded.

Back in Philly, beat writer Jayson Stark wrote 2,500 words about the deal for the next two editions of the *Philadelphia Inquirer*. Less than a dozen were devoted to the throw-in: "The Phillies also sent along rookie infielder Ryne Sandberg to Chicago," Stark wrote. He devoted 190 words to Julio Franco.

On April 1, 1982, nine weeks after they completed the deal with the Phillies, the Cubs released third baseman Ken Reitz and created a spot for Sandberg in the lineup. Starting 131 games at third base, Sandberg hit .271, with seven home runs, 54 RBI and 32 stolen bases. He finished sixth in Rookie of the Year voting.

That offseason, the team traded for third baseman Ron Cey, chose not to re-sign second baseman Bump Wills and shifted Sandberg to second base. The prospect without a position won the next nine Gold Gloves at second base, added seven Silver Sluggers and nine All-Star starting spots and took the 1984 MVP award.

That same season, the Cubs won the National League East, a division that didn't exist the last time the team had finished in first place. They finished 6.5 games ahead of the Mets (a team that didn't even exist in 1945). The Phillies were in fourth place, 15.5 games out. The Cubs won the first two games of the best-of-five 1984 National League Championship Series, but they went on to drop the next three games, missing out on the World Series yet again.

The Cubs won the division again five years later, and Sandberg finished fourth in MVP voting and led the league in runs scored. Again, the team fell short of reaching the World Series.

Sandberg helped to redefine the role of second basemen, paving the way for future power hitting second basemen like Jeff Kent and Alfonso Soriano. He led the league with 40 homers in 1990 and retired with the most career home runs by a second baseman with 275 (later broken by Kent). Sandberg's number 23 was retired by the Cubs, and he was elected to the Baseball Hall of Fame in 2005.

From the time of the trade until Sandberg's retirement in 1997, the Phillies would start 24 different players at second base. The last of the two dozen players was Mickey Morandini, who was traded to the Cubs in December 1997 to replace the retiring legend.

As for the Phillies shortstops of the future, Julio Franco found that DeJesús' agent was right. Among the things that can happen between Double-A and MLB are trades. Franco was dealt after playing 16 games for the Phillies. He would go on to collect more than 2,500 hits in a 23-year career in the majors—and another 652 while playing in professional leagues in Japan, Korea and Mexico—but he got only 8 hits in a Phillies uniform.

Aguayo stayed with the Phillies as a reserve until 1988. He appeared in 568 games in his ten-year career, never more than 99 in a season.

Larry Bowa has been ready for a fight for more than 50 years in baseball. The one with a general manager he had trouble recalling helped end the Cubs' long postseason drought. It also helped clear up turbulent clubhouse atmosphere in Philadelphia, which played a factor in the Phillies' return to the World Series, without Bowa, in 1983.

That general manager, like most people who came into contact with Bowa, had no trouble remembering him. "Even if you were mad at him," Owens said, "you couldn't help but admire him."

WAR COMPARISON

The Cubs were right. DeJesús for Bowa would have been an unfair deal. While neither shortstop put up huge offensive numbers, the younger DeJesús produced double the wins over replacement as Bowa.

Had the Phillies thrown in Luis Aguayo or Bob Dernier, the trade would have been a relatively even, extremely minor swap. Instead, Philadelphia chose the future Hall of Famer to try to even up the two sides of the trade and created one of the more lopsided deals in baseball history.

CUBS RECEIVED	WAR PRE-TRADE	WAR POST-TRADE
Larry Bowa	21.4	1.5
Ryne Sandberg	-0.1	67.7
PHILLIES RECEIVED	WAR PRE-TRADE	WAR POST-TRADE
Iván DeJesús	8.1	2.9
OTHER CUBS THROW-IN POSSIBILITIES	WAR PRE-TRADE	WAR POST-TRADE
Dick Davis	0.7	-0.5
Luis Aguayo	0.1	3.6
Bob Dernier	0.6	2.5 with Phillies, 3.9 with Cubs after trade 2 years later
Del Unser	1.5	-0.3
Sparky Lyle	0.0	-0.7
Don McCormack	0.1	0.0

CHAPTER 9

NOTHING TO
— CELEBRATE —

THE STORY BEHIND THE MIGUEL CABRERA TRADE

*A once-in-a-generation talent, traded away
for a forgettable package of prospects.*

In 2007, the Florida Marlins were having another fire sale. This time, they dealt Miguel Cabrera and Dontrelle Willis to the Detroit Tigers in exchange for six prospects. Cabrera went on to win a Triple Crown and be one of the best hitters in the game for seven seasons. On paper, the trade looks bad enough, but the Marlins were supposedly also considering dealing Cabrera to the Dodgers for Clayton Kershaw and Matt Kemp, to the Red Sox for Jacoby Ellsbury, and to the Angels for Howie Kendrick. They decided that Cameron Maybin and Andrew Miller were their best bet.

As is often the case with bad trades, the Marlins weren't thinking about on-field performance when they traded Miguel Cabrera.

The 24-year-old, described as a "hitting savant," was one of the best young sluggers in baseball. Cabrera had received MVP votes all five years of his career and made the All-Star team four years in a row.

Looking at advanced stats, as all baseball front offices were doing in 2007, Cabrera was even more valuable. In an off year—for him—in 2007, Cabrera was still fifth in the National League in runs created. The year before, he was third in the NL in offensive WAR, and in 2005, he was fifth in the league.

The Marlins had just finished their second fire sale in a decade and were looking to build around young talent. No young player was as talented as Cabrera.

The team's front office decided that off-field issues, most resulting from Cabrera's attitude, made him a poor choice to build around.

There was also a heavy financial component to the decision to put Cabrera on the block. Even though he was young, Cabrera started early in MLB and had five years in at the end of the 2007 season.

Five years is a significant milestone in baseball. It means arbitration and the prospect of free agency. In other words, it means teams will have to start paying more to keep their players.

Cabrera, in the Marlins' view, was a poor choice to invest in as the centerpiece of the team.

There was a risk in cutting ties with the savant. The team knew his best years were still ahead of him. They just didn't know how good those best years would be.

When the Marlins signed a sixteen-year-old Cabrera out of Venezuela in 1999, their general manager was Dave Dombrowski. At the time, Cabrera's deal was one of the biggest international contracts in history, although the $1.8 million the Marlins spent would be dwarfed by contracts to come over the next decade. Florida's manager was Jim Leyland, who, four years later, had the twenty-year-old rookie Cabrera on his roster when the club won the 2003 World Series.

"I knew there were some issues," Leyland said, years later.

"You hear things," Dombrowski said, looking back with the benefit of hindsight. "And for me, with [Cabrera] that goes back for years. But a lot of guys go out at night and have something to drink. If you thought it was something of major, major consequence and you had proof of it, you would approach those things at the time. That never happened."

Cabrera essentially grew up in professional baseball. He signed a contract as soon as he turned sixteen and was playing Rookie League and Class A ball as a seventeen-year-old. He hit .365 with 10 home runs in his first two months at Double-A, earning a promotion to the Marlins just 63 days after his 20th birthday. He hit an 11th-inning walk-off home run in his MLB debut. He hasn't slowed down since.

On the field, Cabrera has been one of the top baseball talents in recent history. He's received MVP votes every year of his career and has made 10 All-Star teams in his first 13 seasons. He hit 25 or more homers 11 straight years, and 30 or more in nine of them. He also had a string of 12 straight 100-RBI seasons and hasn't hit below .292 since his rookie year.

"I think he's one of those players who comes along only every twenty years," said former Marlins teammate Alfredo Amézaga. "He's different from the rest of us. He does things so easily. He adjusts to pitchers so quickly. To me, that's incredible, because the hardest thing to do in sports is hit. It appears that for him, it isn't."

As a rookie, Cabrera hit .333 with 3 home runs and 6 RBI in the Marlins' NLCS win over the Chicago Cubs. He gave the Marlins an early lead in Game Seven with a 3-run blast off of Kerry Wood in the first inning. After Chicago had taken the lead, Cabrera drove in another run to tie the game in the fifth. In Game Four of the World Series, Cabrera homered off of Yankees ace Roger Clemens—after getting knocked on his rear by a brushback pitch—to give Florida an early lead.

Cabrera was versatile in the field. He spent time playing left field, right field and third base in his first two years with the Marlins.

Despite the on-field accomplishments, Cabrera's behavior off the field was occasionally cause for concern. Early in 2005, the *Fort Lauderdale Sun-Sentinel* interviewed his father, who warned, "He has a responsibility to get home early. He can't be out there partying."

One day, later that season, Cabrera stopped shagging fly balls during batting practice, earning a scolding from Marlins coach and Hall of Famer Tony Pérez. He often played with a soccer ball on the field instead of stretching. At a game in Houston, he made light of his own tardiness by showing up shortly before stretching and announcing, "Don't worry, guys. I'm here. Don't worry."

In late September, Cabrera's behavior became even more erratic. After leaving a game early after fouling a ball off his knee, he arrived late for treatment the next day. Manager Jack McKeon pulled him from the lineup as punishment. Three days later, Cabrera showed up for a game in Atlanta 45 minutes before first pitch and missed batting practice. He claimed he overslept. He was given a one-game benching.

On September 27, upon his return to the lineup, reporters asked him if he needed guidance from older players to improve his work ethic. Cabrera responded with "[Bleep] the veterans," using a Spanish expletive. "They haven't told me anything and they better not come tell me anything, either. I don't want to hear anything else. I want to play baseball, give what I have to give on the field of play, and win. That's all I want. . . . I'm not going to go crazy worrying about these things."

The veterans responded by having a closed-door meeting to read Cabrera the riot act.

"All of a sudden they said, 'Get everybody in here. We're going to have a meeting,'" Lenny Harris recalled, "and I saw Miguel with his head down. I asked Luis [Castillo] what's going on and he said, 'Oh, man, they just got all over Cabrera.'"

"Guys got things off their chest," center fielder Juan Pierre said.

"People are pissed," pitcher Josh Beckett said. "He's a grown-up man."

It became clear that something had to be done with Cabrera. The team needed to either bring him in line with some tough love or send him out of town. As it turned out, the Marlins' business interests quickly determined which way the team would go.

Cabrera came up on a World Series champion, Florida's second in six years, but two years later, the Marlins set about tearing apart a championship team for the second time in recent history. Catcher Iván Rodríguez and pitcher Ugueth Urbina were allowed to leave as free agents at the end of 2003. First baseman Derrek Lee and outfielder Juan Encarnación were traded before the 2004 season. Brad Penny was shipped off at the 2004 trade deadline. Carl Pavano left as a free agent following an All-Star performance in 2004.

After the 2005 season, the Marlins' fire sale shifted into high gear. Beckett and third baseman Mike Lowell were traded to Boston. Gold Glove second baseman Castillo was sent to Minnesota. Juan Pierre went to the Cubs. Alex Gonzalez and Jeff Conine left as free agents.

By the time the 2006 season started, the only two players that remained from the Marlins 2003 championship team were Cabrera and pitcher Dontrelle Willis, who was a year older than Cabrera.

Cabrera was in position to be the leader of a team in the middle of a youth movement.

"Miguel is the type of player who has to carry himself first," Harris said. "Everybody knows what an impact player he is on the field, but it takes a different kind of guy to lead in the locker room. He could be a leader. It all depends if he accepts that role or not."

Cabrera didn't show any desire to do so.

"I'm ready to play," he said. "I don't worry about these guys. They have to play hard. If we play together, we'll have a chance to win."

In January 2006, police were called after Cabrera was involved in a scuffle outside a nightclub in his hometown of Maracay, Venezuela. He claimed the problem was caused by an autograph seeker, and he never threw a punch.

The following month, Cabrera skipped a $200-a-plate dinner where he was supposed to receive the team's MVP award. He also skipped a FanFest event at Dolphins Stadium.

Cabrera put on weight—he reported for spring training in 2007 at 260 pounds, 80 pounds more than he weighed when he signed with the Marlins—which limited his defensive ability. He led the league with 23 errors that season. In July, he had a dugout altercation with pitcher Scott Olsen, who was upset about Cabrera's lackadaisical effort in the field.

While the off-field issues and questionable attitude frustrated the Marlins, Cabrera committed an even greater infraction, in the eyes of the team brass, prior to the 2007 season: He got a big raise by winning in arbitration. After making $472,000 in 2006, one of the biggest bargains in baseball history, Cabrera won the third-highest arbitration award in history. He would earn $7.4 million in 2007.

The reaction of the Marlins front office signaled trouble on the horizon.

"It was a lot of money either way for a great player," said GM Larry Beinfest, who had offered Cabrera $6.7 million. Beinfest and team president David Samson also ripped Cabrera for skipping FanFest and other promotional events again, earlier in the month.

"It's very disappointing," Samson said. "[Owner Jeffrey Loria] and the rest of us are very disappointed that he's not here with every one of his teammates. All the players are here except Miguel. We have tried to contact him and we were told he couldn't be here for personal reasons or whatever the case was. Hopefully, when we see him, he will explain to us and the fans why he wasn't."

When asked if the pending arbitration hearing was a motivation for Cabrera's absence, Samson replied, "Miguel's an adult. He knows it's a business."

"He was disappointed they brought it up," Cabrera's agent, Fernando Cuza, said of the FanFest absence. "He didn't attend prior years, and they never brought it up publicly before."

After another outstanding season—34 homers, 119 RBI and .320 average—the hitting savant would likely merit a $10 million contract. The Marlins didn't want another arbitration battle. At the general managers' meetings in Orlando that November, they made it clear Cabrera was on the block, and they wanted him moved by December.

The *Palm Beach Post* reported that the Marlins were concerned about his weight and "frustrated with his overall attitude and approach."

In a controversial column, five years afterward, the *Palm Beach Post*'s Greg Stoda crystalized the reasons for the Marlins' decision:

Miguel Cabrera was 24 years old when the Marlins gave up on him.
They had their reasons, and you can arrange the forthcoming sequence in whichever reason you choose:
A) money
B) off-field concerns (see: drinking)
The Marlins didn't want to pay Cabrera the big bucks necessary to keep him in the long term—he'd already won an arbitration case against them—and wondered if he'd someday ruin his own career through self-destructive behavior.
They weren't willing, in other words, to take the financial and social risks involving Cabrera, and went looking for somebody who was.

The Yankees checked in almost immediately. They were facing the prospect of losing Alex Rodriguez, who had filed for free agency, and were shopping for a power-hitting third baseman. They were willing to part with outfield prospect Melky Cabrera (no relation), but Yankee general manager Brian Cashman was hesitant to give up any of the team's top pitching prospects in Joba Chamberlain, Phil Hughes and Ian Kennedy.

Cashman didn't rule out including one of the stud pitchers, but he made it clear it wasn't likely. "I'm sure I'll be challenged like I have been in the past on those guys," Cashman said.

"No one is untouchable, but some guys are less touchable than others, and those guys fall into that category. I will be tested a lot and this organization will be tested a lot on that."

The Yankees had just completed their first season under manager Joe Girardi, who had managed the Marlins in 2006. "I didn't have any problems with him," Girardi said of managing Cabrera. "I had him and I know what he did for me. He's a great player and a smart player. He really understands the game of baseball. I loved having him."

New York was willing to part with some of their next-best minor league prospects: Alan Horne, Humberto Sánchez, Ross Ohlendorf and José Tábata.

"The Marlins have evidently let it be known that he's available, so we're looking into it," Hank Steinbrenner, the Yankees owner and co-chairman, said. "But everything is really very preliminary."

Later, Steinbrenner said, "My sense is that it might be too much but we'll see. It's early."

The Yankees could afford to be picky, because re-signing A-Rod was an option. Although eight years older, Rodriguez was still one of the best players in the game. A-Rod had topped Cabrera in WAR in four of the five years Cabrera had been in the major leagues. Getting a younger, cheaper replacement for Rodriguez was desirable, but a luxury. The Yankees eventually decided to bring Rodriguez back instead of dealing away their prized pitchers. Paying him $10–20 million more than Cabrera over the next several years, the Yankees saw Rodriguez outperform Cabrera in WAR just once—in the 2008 season.

One National League executive told the *New York Daily News* that the Marlins would be selective in their negotiations. "They know what they want and they don't make many mistakes in evaluation," he said. "I suspect, like with Beckett, they will target a few teams they know have what they want. They are not going to open this up to 29 teams. This will not be an auction. They will ask a big price, and if anyone says yes, they will do it."

It turned out the unnamed executive grossly underestimated the avalanche of interest in Cabrera. As the December winter meetings drew closer, talks shifted into overdrive. Virtually every team expected to contend in 2008 was checking in on Cabrera's price.

Other teams were intrigued by the possibility of landing Dontrelle Willis, the other remaining holdover from the 2003 champs. He was earning $7 million in 2007, making him a prime target for the Marlins to deal.

The Cardinals balked when the Marlins asked for Colby Rasmus in exchange for Cabrera. The 21-year-old outfielder was one of the top players in the St. Louis system. He was a first-round draft pick in 2005 and hit 29 homers for Double-A Springfield in 2007. St. Louis instead traded for Toronto third baseman Troy Glaus to replace veteran Scott Rolen at the hot corner. Glaus made slightly more than Cabrera would get in 2008 and produced better WAR numbers, but only for a year.

The White Sox also tried hard to acquire Cabrera. Chicago's manager was Ozzie Guillén, who had been a Marlins coach in 2003. Like Cabrera, he is from Venezuela, and the two are close friends. When Cabrera had his weight issues the previous season, the outspoken Guillén called Cabrera a "fat boy from Venezuela."

The message from Chicago hit home. Cabrera said, "If he says I have to lose weight, then maybe I do."

The Sox weren't sure where they'd put Cabrera, but Guillén said, "We'd find a place for him."

The real problem facing the White Sox wasn't lack of a position, however, but lack of suitable prospects to exchange for Cabrera. Chicago was dangling pitcher Gio González and infielder Josh Fields. González was a 22-year-old left-hander who had been drafted in the first round in 2004. He won 13 minor league games as a 19-year-old and struck out 185 batters in 150 innings at Double-A Birmingham in 2007. Fields was 25 and also had been a first-rounder in 2004. He was promoted to the White Sox in 2006 and homered in his first MLB at bat. In 2007, he was rated the second-best prospect in the Chicago organization and again earned a promotion to the bigs, where he hit 23 home runs for the White Sox.

The two youngsters weren't enough. The Sox would likely have to trade established starter Jon Garland to somewhere else to obtain another prospect, whom they would in turn send to Florida for Cabrera. The talks came to an end. The White Sox gambled that incumbent third baseman Joe Crede, who missed most of 2007 after having back surgery, would recover. He made the All-Star team in 2008, but was out of MLB two years later.

The Red Sox backed off after the Marlins requested both outfielder Jacoby Ellsbury and pitcher Clay Buchholz, although they were willing to part with Ellsbury. Boston stuck with third baseman Mike Lowell, whom they'd acquired from the Marlins two years earlier, when the fire sale in Miami was in high gear.

The Indians did the same after shortstop Asdrúbal Cabrera (again, no relation) and pitcher Adam Miller weren't going to be enough for Florida. The 22-year-old Cabrera was an Eastern League All-Star in Double-A and was promoted to the Indians in late 2007 after hitting .310 with 25 steals in the minors. Miller, a 23-year-old right-hander, won 15 games in 2006, split between Double-A and Triple-A, but he'd battled elbow problems.

Every one of those teams was wrong to cling to their prospects. Cabrera would be better than any package of prospects that the Marlins demanded from St. Louis, Cleveland, Boston, New York or Chicago, as well as the third basemen that the teams went with instead of Cabrera.

Cabrera would take hitting savant to another level over the next eight years. He led the league in home runs with 37 in 2008 and 44 in 2012 while hitting a total of 270 homers over his first eight seasons in Detroit. He strung together seven straight 100-RBI years, leading the league twice, and led the league in batting four times in five seasons. In 2012, Cabrera became the first player to win the Triple Crown in 45 years. He was named the American League MVP in back-to-back years in 2012 and 2013.

That's not to say that every team that discussed trades with the Marlins should have parted with the prospects that came up in discussions. Some were right to back away from the deals.

The San Francisco Giants had been in the running for a while. The Giants were looking to replace 40-year-old Pedro Feliz, who was a free agent.

Sources said that the Giants offered Tim Lincecum, although GM Brian Sabean denied this when asked by members of the media following up on the rumors. Lincecum had been chosen sixth overall in the 2006 draft. He made it to the majors almost immediately and won seven games for San Francisco in 2007.

The Marlins weren't happy with Lincecum alone. They also wanted 22-year-old pitcher Matt Cain, who was a first rounder in 2002 and had spent two years in the Giants' starting rotation, and two other players from San Francisco's major league roster, outfielders Rajai Davis and Fred Lewis.

Lincecum and Cain were the two prizes in the potential packages the Giants offered. Lincecum would lead the league in strikeouts for the next three seasons and won back-to-back Cy Young Awards in 2008 and 2009. He'd win at least 10 games a year for the next seven years.

As Lincecum's star faded, due to arm trouble, Cain's was on the rise. He peaked with a 16–5 season in 2012. The two pitchers would form the backbone of the Giants' rotation for the team's run to three World Series titles.

The Giants tried to move the Marlins off of Cain and onto Noah Lowry, a 27-year-old lefty who had been in the rotation for three years, winning 13 and 14 games in two of those seasons. The Marlins wouldn't bite. The Giants ended up getting another Marlin to play third base for them in 2008. José Castillo, a 27-year-old utility infielder who had signed with Florida in the offseason after being released by Pittsburgh, was waived by the Marlins near the end of spring training. The Giants, desperate for a third baseman, signed him and started him. He ended up having a negative WAR, meaning that he was less valuable to the team at his position than an average minor league call-up.

In an incredible rumor, reported by Fox Sports' Ken Rosenthal, the Los Angeles Dodgers had been the leaders in the Cabrera hunt and nearly acquired him before Thanksgiving.

LA was looking to replace Nomar Garciaparra, a former shortstop shifted to third as he aged. Garciaparra would be 34 in 2008, and his production had been in decline.

The package included outfield Matt Kemp, first baseman Andy LaRoche and pitcher Clayton Kershaw. Kemp was an outfield prospect with developing power. He hit 27 home runs at Class A Vero Beach in 2005. He also stole more than 20 bases in 2005 and 2006. He hit .342 with 10 home runs in 98 games after being called up to Los Angeles during the 2007 season. LaRoche showed power in the minors and retained it as he rose through the system. He hit 23, 30, 19 and 18 homers in his four seasons in the Dodgers' system.

Then there was Kershaw. He would turn twenty years old during spring training before the 2008 season. The hard-throwing left-hander was drafted in the first round, number seven overall, in 2006, straight out of high school. He went 2–0 with a save in rookie ball in 2006, striking out 54 batters in 37 innings. In 2007, he won 8 games and struck out 163 in 122 innings.

The Marlins wanted a fourth player—either pitcher Chad Billingsley or outfielder James Loney. Loney had been a first-round draft pick who hit 15 homers in 96 big league games in 2007. Billingsley was yet another former first-rounder. He went 12–5 in a season split between the starting rotation and the bullpen.

Assuming the details of the Dodgers deal are accurate, the Marlins should have jumped at the chance to make Los Angeles the winner of the Cabrera sweepstakes. Florida didn't need to have a fourth player added; they would've fleeced the Dodgers even without Loney or Billingsley.

Kemp would finish runner-up for National League MVP in 2011 after leading the league in runs, with 115; homers, with 39; and RBI, with 126. Kershaw, however, was the top prospect in any deal offered to the Marlins. He'd twice win 21 games, leading the league both times, and he'd lead the league in ERA every year from 2011 to 2014, including microscopic ERAs of 1.83 and 1.77. He also led the league twice in strikeouts and won three Cy Young awards in four years.

The Dodgers went with rookie Blake DeWitt at third base in 2008. After mustering just a 1.6 WAR in his first year in the bigs, DeWitt was traded by the Dodgers for Indians journeyman Casey Blake at midseason, who took over the spot.

In the end, the Marlins narrowed down the list of suitors to two teams: the Tigers and the Angels.

The Angels' package included a combination of prospects. Second baseman Howie Kendrick, whom the Angels had held on to over the last two off seasons despite multiple trade offers, was on the table. So were minor league prospects Brandon Wood and Nick Adenhart. The fourth player the Marlins sought was a catcher, either prospect Jeff Mathis or starter Mike Napoli. When the Angels tried to pull back Wood, the Marlins asked for pitcher Ervin Santana.

On November 19, the Angels swung a deal involving a Cabrera, but not the one making headlines. The team dealt Gold Glove shortstop Orlando Cabrera to the White Sox for pitcher Jon Garland, the pitcher Chicago was hoping to flip for a prospect to seal the deal with the Marlins.

Instead, the Angels added Garland to a deep pitching staff. Garland won 10 or more games for six years, including back-to-back 18-win seasons in 2005 and 2006. Adding the veteran made the young pitchers Adenhart and Santana expendable in a Miguel Cabrera deal.

"Tony is not done," manager Mike Scioscia said, referring to GM Tony Reagins. "He's going to keep moving forward. Every club he's talked to wants pitching. . . . Obviously, there's a lot of focus on the offense, and now he has the tools to do the things we need to do."

"This gives us opportunities to strengthen our club in other areas," said Reagins. "It's a positive step forward. It gives us flexibility to do some other things. . . . We're looking at every opportunity available to make the club better."

The Marlins also considered throwing in second baseman Dan Uggla to help seal the deal with the Angels.

The Angels decided to stick with emerging talent Chone Figgins at third base. The 30-year-old had finally found a spot at the hot corner after playing utility infield for several years. He would produce a two-year total WAR of 10.0 in 2008 and 2009, which topped Cabrera's production over that span.

While the Marlins and Angels moved players in and out of the deal, the Dodgers offered reliever Jonathan Broxton as the fourth player in their package, but the Marlins weren't interested. Florida insisted on getting a fourth player off of Los Angeles' major league roster. Broxton eventually became a two-time All-Star and saved 118 games.

As it turned out, the Tigers pulled off a stunner of a deal. They landed not just Cabrera but also Dontrelle Willis, adding two All-Stars and the final two pieces from the Marlins' 2003 World Series team. Detroit gave up six prospects for the pair.

Why was Detroit willing to give up a half-dozen minor leaguers? It could have something to do with the man calling the shots in Detroit.

Signing Cabrera and helping to assemble the talent that would eventually win the 2003 World Series for the Marlins, was General Manager Dave Dombrowski. The Tigers hired him as president and CEO prior to the 2002 season.

Dombrowski was the one who was willing to pay more for Cabrera than anyone had spent in the past. He was the one willing to ignore the warning signs and bring Cabrera to the big leagues so early.

In 2007, Dombrowski was again willing to ignore the off-field issues and just let Cabrera do his thing. Baseball history is filled with head cases who partied hard and gave management headaches with off-field antics, from Babe Ruth to Manny Ramirez. Teams were able to win with those types of players because their rare ability to hit a baseball like no one else playing at the time trumped everything else. After five years in MLB, Cabrera had done nothing to dissuade Dombrowski from his belief that the mercurial third baseman could be one of those hitters.

Dombrowski made the decision despite the fact that the team didn't need Cabrera. The Tigers had Brandon Inge, who had posted a 4.9 WAR in 2006. Inge contributed on both offense and defense, unlike Cabrera, who was a liability with the glove. The Tigers also had shortstop Carlos Guillén, whom they would move to third base in 2008, allowing Inge to play a variety of positions as a super-utility man. Both Inge and Guillén would make AL All-Star teams in the next two seasons.

It didn't matter. When it came to someone like Cabrera, Dombrowski was willing to make room. Detroit's first baseman in 2007 was Sean Casey, who was the anti-Cabrera. A friendly, outgoing guy, Casey was nicknamed "the mayor" for his popularity both in his clubhouse and with opposing players. He had finished third in the AL in fielding percentage in 2007, but was just a fraction above replacement level at the plate.

The Tigers moved Cabrera to first base, at least until he was ready to become a full-time designated hitter.

The Marlins received pitcher Andrew Miller, the number six overall selection in the 2006 draft. He made the Tigers by the end of that season and won 5 games in 2007. The Tigers also sent Florida their first-round pick from the previous year's draft, outfielder Cameron Maybin. He had shown power and speed while hitting over .300 both years in the minors. Maybin joined the big league club by the end of the 2007 season. Miller and Maybin were the two top prospects in the Tigers' system. The Marlins also picked up the catching prospect they were seeking in Mike Rabelo.

Florida received three more propping arms in the deal. Right-hander Burke Badenhop had won 14 and 12 games as a starter in his previous two minor league seasons. He spent time in the Arizona Fall League working out of the bullpen. Right-hander Frankie De La Cruz was a 23-year-old minor leaguer who also had experience in the rotation and bullpen. Dallas Trahern, another righty, went 13–6 at Double-A and Triple-A in 2007.

On paper, the deal looked like a win-win. The Marlins picked up the top pitching and position players in the Detroit system and also added a catcher and three other arms.

Still, Cabrera's move to Detroit sent shockwaves through the American League.

"There's a lot of American League pitchers that just got real nervous. We're one of them," said Red Sox manager Terry Francona of the Tigers, who now included seven All-Stars. "That's quite a lineup."

"Wow. That's unbelievable," Detroit closer Todd Jones said. "I'm just blown away. I thought it was a big typo when I first saw it. It's a great day in Detroit. I'm going to go get my season tickets right now."

"We feel we made offers that were competitive offers," Reagins said, after finding out the Angels finished runners up. "It takes two teams to get something done."

When Guillén found out that Cabrera wouldn't be joining him in Chicago, but would instead be joining a divisional rival, he called his wife, Ibis, to give her the news.

"That's funny," she said. "He's sitting in the car right next to me." She was driving their friend to the airport in Miami so he could visit home in Venezuela.

While Florida was used to seeing its best players sent away, the news still hit the players on the roster hard.

"It was kind of like, wow, when I heard. I halfway expected one of them to get traded, but not both in the same deal. So it's a little bit of a shock," outfielder Josh Willingham said. "It's deflating because they're great teammates and good friends. It's going to be hard not seeing them around. I know we got some good players in the deal, but Miguel and Dontrelle are proven big league players, and it's going to be tough to fill those roles. . . . It will be tough to replace those guys."

While Cabrera alone made the trade worthwhile, Willis struggled to live up to his promise. Told about the deal while on vacation in Mexico, Willis said, "I'm excited. They're good. I just don't want to go in there and mess anything up."

What got messed up was his control. Willis lost command of the strike zone and then struggled with anxiety disorder. He would win a total of two games for the Tigers and just four games over the rest of his career.

The Marlins, meanwhile, didn't get the return they'd hoped for from their half-dozen prospects.

"I think my first year or two in Florida, I mean, you just couldn't get away from [the trade]," Miller said. "I tried to do everything I could to say it was irrelevant and act as though it was irrelevant, but I think I tried to do too much for a while to maybe—not to live up to him, just to prove that I was worth being a part of the blockbuster trade. . . . Going to a new place is never easy, and I feel like I was given a great opportunity in Florida, but, you know, I certainly didn't take as full advantage as I would've liked to."

Miller went 10–20 with a 5.89 ERA in three years with the Marlins. Badenhop was a middle reliever for four seasons in Florida.

"That's the thing I'm linked to the most," Badenhop said of the trade. "When you've been traded for arguably the best player in the last decade, it's tough not to give it a little bit more attention."

He joked, "I was traded straight up for Dontrelle, it was the other five guys who were traded for Miguel."

Rabelo, De La Cruz and Trahern combined to play 40 games with the Marlins. Maybin appeared in 144 games in three seasons in Florida, never getting a shot at a full-time role.

Dodgers GM Ned Colletti offered a snarky reaction when informed of the deal. "That's a lot of players," he said. "They got what they wanted. Apparently, Detroit did too."

Colletti said that that Marlins called him one last time before agreeing to the Tigers' deal. Apparently, had the Marlins simply backed off on the fourth player, they would have gotten Kershaw and Kemp, and still had Willis to deal at the 2008 trade deadline. But, with a promise of a half dozen prospects from Detroit, they held tight.

"Everything was the same," Colletti said. "The same names going out, the same name coming back and the same answer from me."

Cabrera continued to struggle with off-field issues, seeking treatment for alcohol at one point, but Dombrowski and the Tigers stuck with him. Dombrowski even drove him home from jail after one incident in 2009.

On September 16, 2011, Cabrera had caught the final out of Detroit's 3–1 victory at the Oakland A's to clinch the American League Central Division title. The players jumped, hugged, and dog-piled on the field, as teams do after wrapping up titles. Then, they moved the party into the clubhouse, out of view of the fans—as teams do.

Miguel Cabrera sat on an exercise bike, sipping from a bottle of water, his feet resting on a couch. In front of him, gleeful debauchery was taking place in the Detroit Tigers clubhouse.

The Tigers were provided with dozens of cases of champagne and beer for the celebration. They poured it into one another's open mouths and over one another's heads. Eventually, puddles formed on the plastic sheeting that had been put up to protect the clubhouse, and players took turns playing slip-n-slide across the clubhouse floor.

The Tigers made sure that nonalcoholic champagne was available, should Cabrera want to take part in the festivities, but he chose to stay at a distance, watching with a smile on his face as his teammates celebrated.

WAR COMPARISON

Other than the Tigers, every team involved in the Miguel Cabrera negotiations made the worst possible decision.

The Marlins lost Cabrera, who produced the equivalent of six MVP seasons with the Tigers. In exchange, they received a half dozen players who gave them the equivalent of one Triple-A call-up's production.

If they had taken the players offered by any other team that they contacted, the Marlins would have made out better than they did with the Tigers' prospects.

Similarly, the other teams involved in the negotiations balked at further sweetening the deal by adding more players to the pot. The numbers show that, other than the Dodgers, any of the other teams could have significantly upgraded their offers and still come out ahead.

TO TIGERS	WAR PRE-TRADE	WAR POST-TRADE
Miguel Cabrera	18.2	46.5
Dontrelle Willis	17.1	-1.1
TO MARLINS	WAR PRE-TRADE	WAR POST-TRADE
Burke Badenhop	0.0	1.9
Cameron Maybin	-0.4	1.9
Andrew Miller	-0.3	-2.4
Mike Rabelo	-0.2	-0.2
Frankie de la Cruz	-0.2	-0.9
Dallas Trahern	0.0	0.0
WHITE SOX PACKAGE	WAR PRE-TRADE	WAR POST-TRADE
Gio Gonzalez	0.0	6.8 with Oakland, 12.9 with Washington
RED SOX PACKAGE	WAR PRE-TRADE	WAR POST-TRADE
Jacoby Ellsbury	0.6	20.5
INDIANS PACKAGE	WAR PRE-TRADE	WAR POST-TRADE
Asdrúbal Cabrera	1.6	19
GIANTS PACKAGE	WAR PRE-TRADE	WAR POST-TRADE
Either Tim Lincecum	1.1	8.8
Or Matt Cain	8.9	22.8
DODGERS PACKAGE	WAR PRE-TRADE	WAR POST-TRADE
Matt Kemp	1.4	19.8
And Clayton Kershaw	1.4	45.8

CHAPTER 10

— FOR SALE TO THE —
SECOND-HIGHEST BIDDER

THE STORY BEHIND THE ALEX RODRIGUEZ TRADE

*A bad free-agent contract leads to months of offseason melodrama
that frustrated everyone except producers of sports chat shows.*

Alex Rodriguez was the best player in baseball and deserving of the highest contract in baseball. However, he signed a contract so large that it kept his team owner from being able to afford to surround him with players capable of lifting the team out of last place. In 2003, after three years, the owner was ready to find someone with a bigger wallet to take A-Rod off his hands. That led to a series of negotiations with baseball's superpowers that involved five All-Stars, filled the entire offseason with checkbook drama and shifted the balance of power in the American League.

Alex Rodriguez came to the plate to start the eighth inning at Toronto's Skydome to face former Rangers pitcher Esteban Loaiza. He drove a 1–2 pitch over the wall in left center for his second home run of the game. It was August 17. There was still a month and a half to go in the 2001 season, and Rodriguez's monster game brought him to 37 home runs and 104 RBI on the season.

Rodriguez also doubled in the game, his 28th of the year. The 3-for-4 day brought his batting average to .321 and his OPS to 1.005. The performance was exactly what Rangers owner Tom Hicks hoped to get when he signed Rodriguez to a 10-year, $252 million contract prior to the season.

It was $2 million more than Hicks paid for the Rangers franchise in 1998. That transaction included the team's home ballpark and 270 acres of Arlington land surrounding the stadium.

"I like to win," Hicks said at the press conference announcing the Rodriguez signing. "I like to win any competition. What we've had a chance to do here is leapfrog into an arena where we've never been."

Critics attacked the exorbitant deal for being so far above market value that it would inflate salaries of lesser players for years to come. They also questioned Hicks' ability to afford A-Rod and still manage to surround him with enough quality players to build a contender.

In the first season of the deal, the critics appeared to be right. A-Rod's big game against the Blue Jays helped to underscore that fact. Both of his home runs were solo shots, and his second one cut Toronto's lead over the Rangers to 11–3.

An inning later, the Blue Jays wrapped up the win by the same score, dropping Texas to a 52–70 record, good for last place in the AL West, 35 games out of first.

Texas wasn't able to afford pitching. The staff's 5.71 ERA, 1,670 hits allowed and 596 walks surrendered were all worst in the league by large margins. In A-Rod's two-homer game, Rangers pitchers allowed utility infielder Jeff Frye, who entered the game hitting just .219 on the season, to hit for the cycle. They also surrendered four homers in the sixth inning, allowing the Blue Jays to set a team record.

"It was embarrassing for me. It was embarrassing for the team," said Rangers reliever Pat Mahomes, who became the tenth pitcher in AL history to give up four homers in an inning. "Tonight they kicked my butt, I'll be the first to say it. When I stink, I stink."

Out of the 156 home runs Rodriguez hit as a Ranger, 61 of them came when the team was losing the game, including 19 when the team was behind by 4 or more runs. By comparison, Rodriguez hit 189 homers as a Seattle Mariner before signing the huge deal with Texas. Only 60 came while the team was losing, and 17 came with the team down by 4 or more.

Including the loss to the Blue Jays, Texas had a 10–8 record when A-Rod hit two or more homers in a game. While he was with the Mariners, the team was 12–3 when Rodriguez went deep more than once.

Two years, and two more last-place finishes, later, Hicks was facing the reality that his critics were right on the money.

It's hard to imagine A-Rod doing any more on the field to live up to his salary. In three years, he'd won three home run titles, two RBI titles, led the league in runs scored twice, total bases twice and slugging percentage once. He'd finished sixth and second in MVP voting and was the favorite to win the 2003 award, despite playing for a last-place team. Rodriguez had also been durable, missing only one game in his three seasons with the Rangers.

But Hicks' team had gotten worse: 16, 18 and 20 games below .500 in the three seasons, respectively. Texas had gone through three managers and two general managers during A-Rod's tenure with the team. Texas' team ERA was worst in the AL in two of the three seasons and was never below 5.15.

Hicks realized his team was no closer to leapfrogging into the arena he'd envisioned.

He was ready to make a change.

Following the 2003 season, general manager John Hart spoke to Rodriguez about his situation. "Things have changed," Hart told Rodriguez.

After taking time to digest the message that things on the cash-strapped team weren't going to improve, Rodriguez told Hart to try to trade him. He had a no-trade clause in his contract, but A-Rod gave the Rangers "flexibility," offering a short list of teams he'd waive his clause to join.

There weren't many teams that could afford to take on the financial commitment that a trade for A-Rod would entail. He was still owed $179 million for the remainder of his contract. One of the first calls the Rangers made was to the aptly named Cashman, general manager of the team that year after year had the highest payroll in baseball.

With postseason hero Aaron Boone and Yankee captain Derek Jeter manning the left side of the infield, Cashman told Hart he had no room for Rodriguez.

Hart threatened to shop Rodriguez to the Red Sox, the team that had been nipping at the Yankees' heels for years, trying to dethrone New York as the team to beat in the American

League East. Their long-standing rivalry had included off-field sniping, on-field brawls, and bad blood all around.

The threat didn't sway Cashman. "He said, 'I understand. I don't think that's going to work for us,'" Hart recalled.

Hart lived up to his word and called his counterpart in Boston, GM Theo Epstein. With a nine-figure contract on the table, however, the discussion was above Hart and Epstein's pay grade.

On October 20, three days after Boone had ended Boston's season, Rangers owner Tom Hicks called Red Sox CEO Larry Lucchino to clear the way for the two general managers to begin negotiations. Hart's next call was to A-Rod.

"We got back to him and said New York wouldn't play, but Boston looked like they might," Hart said.

He told Rodriguez, "We're going to pursue this. Just making sure you're on board."

Rodriguez said he was, and the Red Sox and Rangers began to work out a mega deal. The problem was, contrary to popular demand, Theo Epstein had to stay within his budget.

"There's a tendency to look back on it now and say, 'Oh yeah, the Red Sox and Yankees were the two big superpowers of the era. Financially, they could do whatever they wanted.' But there was a huge difference between where the Yankees were and where the Red Sox were," Epstein said, years later. "We had great resources—make no mistake—but the Yankees were in another stratosphere."

The Sox brought a third team into the mix—the Angels—and tried to structure a deal that would send each team's shortstop to new homes. Boston would get A-Rod and send their own elite shortstop, Nomar Garciaparra, to the Angels, who would give Texas their starting shortstop, David Eckstein. That deal, discussed at the general managers meetings in early November, fell apart and eventually was leaked to the press.

The Rangers tried, unsuccessfully, to deny the negotiations. On the third day of the meetings, Hart told the media, "I think we've got the best player in the game. We love him. We have no interest in dealing Alex Rodriguez. We're not having any conversations with any team about Alex Rodriguez. If anybody were to call, of course we'd listen, but we're not interested in any way, shape or form in trading Alex Rodriguez."

At the same time, Texas manager Buck Showalter, whose relationship with A-Rod had been rocky at best, said, "It would be less than honest for me to say we're not listening. If people call you about a player, even if it's a player you love the way we love Alex, you have to at least listen."

The following week, Rodriguez was named the American League MVP. While on vacation in Mexico, he spoke to reporters on a conference call. He confirmed that the team was shopping him to "three or four teams."

"I did not approach management; management approached me," he said. "I'm just going to leave the door open, give Tom Hicks some choices. That means I could be back with the Rangers. I'm leaving that door open too."

The Red Sox and Rangers continued to work on a deal, and Epstein continued to find creative solutions to stay under budget. There was no way to add Rodriguez to the roster and continue to pay outfielder Manny Ramirez, a flaky but prolific slugger who was halfway through an eight-year, $160 million contract. The Rangers agreed to take Ramirez, whose contract, while exorbitant, was still nearly $100 million less than A-Rod's. They also demanded Boston's top pitching prospect, Jon Lester.

Epstein then set about trying to find somebody who might be able to replace Ramirez in the lineup. He worked out a deal with the Chicago White Sox that would send Nomar Garciaparra, left without a position if Boston finalized the A-Rod deal, for outfielder Magglio Ordóñez. The Chicago slugger just missed extending his streak of 30-homer and 100-RBI seasons to five in 2003, when he hit just 29 homers and drove in just 99 runs. Chicago was also willing to replace the pitching prospect Boston was giving up to Texas by throwing Brandon McCarthy into the deal.

All told, the Red Sox were cutting loose Ramirez, Garciaparra and Lester, while adding A-Rod, Ordóñez and McCarthy. The two deals were finalized at December's winter meetings.

"It was three in the morning, maybe later," recalled Jed Hoyer, then Boston's assistant to the general manager. "We knocked on Tito's [manager Terry Francona] door, who had just been hired a week before, and we wrote out the lineup for him. He literally started dancing in his hotel room in his underwear."

One hurdle remained. Despite ridding themselves of the hefty contracts of Ramirez and Garciaparra, and with the Rangers agreeing to pay part of the remaining money owed Rodriguez, Epstein still couldn't add A-Rod without going over budget. They would need him to restructure his contract and agree to take about $28 million dollars that would be owed him in upcoming seasons and defer it until far into the future.

Deferred salary is a fairly common tactic that teams use to help solve short-term budgetary problems. Ramirez will receive deferred money from that $160 million contract until he's 54 years old, and the Mets will be paying off deferred money on a contract Bobby Bonilla signed in 2000 until the year 2035.

The Red Sox sent a contingent to meet with Rodriguez in person. Epstein and Hoyer left the winter meetings in New Orleans and snuck away to New York City, trying to avoid attracting any more media attention.

The executives arrived at the Four Seasons hotel, where Rodriguez had a suite, between two and three in the morning.

"We were disgusting," Epstein said. "We were tired and needed a shower." Instead, they went straight to Rodriguez's room. He answered the door in a suit and tie, and the Red Sox executives and A-Rod held a pair of negotiating sessions before sunrise.

"After the second negotiating session that night, we had a deal," Hoyer recalled. "Somewhere in my files is a signed Red Sox contract from A-Rod."

In exchange for deferring $28 million in salary, Rodriguez got the rights to market his own image and renegotiated the opt-out in his deal, to give him more flexibility. Instead of Rodriguez being able to break the contract and become a free agent after seven years, the Red Sox were willing to give him that option after six.

Rodriguez had the opt-out put in his contract in the first place because he wanted the chance to leave Texas for the Mets, so he could play in New York.

With the renegotiated deal signed by Rodriguez, it appeared that the Red Sox had landed the best player in baseball and managed to stay under budget.

"Our entire focus was how do we make those massive pieces fit, and for a brief moment we had all those pieces fitting," Hoyer recalled.

The deal was derailed by the Major League Baseball Players Association, which had to approve any contract restructuring that involved deferred money. Union head Gene Orza refused to allow the $28 million deferment, saying it reduced the value of A-Rod's contract, then the highest in professional sports history. He allowed a maximum of $12 million to be deferred, and everyone was sent back to the negotiating table.

Years later, Orza explained his decision. "Theo came over to try to convince the PA [players' association] that giving A-Rod an opt-out after six years rather than seven was worth $30 million," he said. "It was a valiant effort on Theo's part, but preposterous."

"It's unfortunate that the players' association felt it necessary to take a legal position which prevented the player and at least two teams from effectuating an agreement that they felt was beneficial," complained Bob DuPuy, MLB's chief operating officer.

Rodriguez quickly got back in lock-step with the players' union, releasing a statement that read, "In the spirit of co-operation, I advised the Red Sox I am willing to restructure my contract, but only within the guidelines prescribed by union officials. I recognize the principle involved, and fully support the need to protect the interests of my fellow players. If my transfer to the Red Sox is to occur, it must be done with consideration of the interests of all major league players, not just one."

At that point, baseball commissioner Bud Selig gave the teams a 72-hour negotiating window to complete the deal.

Symbolizing the growing gulf between A-Rod and the Red Sox, after the initial deal had been done in person, the follow-up negotiations were all conducted by telephone. Texas offered to back off on their requirement that Boston pay $5 million of Ramirez's salary each year, to help the Red Sox get under budget, but it wasn't enough. The negotiating window expired.

"The proposed trade between the Boston Red Sox and the Texas Rangers is dead," said Boston's Larry Lucchino. "The players' association's intransigence and the arbitrary nature of its action are responsible for the deal's demise today."

Years later, Lucchino said, "Too much was at stake for Alex to change his contract. He was the poster child for the union, with a $252 million deal."

Not everyone was as pessimistic as Lucchino. "There is a likelihood the deal is dead," Texas GM John Hart told the Associated Press. "But at the same time, we haven't issued a statement that it's completely dead."

A-Rod's agent, Scott Boras, also held out hope. "Is it going to happen?" he said. "I can't say. Normally when you give two sides a $12 million [deferred] benefit, that's something that usually brings them to the table."

The Red Sox and Rangers did continue to negotiate for nearly a week, trying the deal in several other iterations. Finally, Texas owner Tom Hicks gave a deadline of 5:00 p.m. on December 23 to finalize a trade. That deadline came and went without a deal.

"It is time for the Texas Rangers to look forward to the 2004 season with Alex Rodriguez as our shortstop and leader," Hicks said.

"He has indicated he would not accept a trade for A-Rod in the immediate future," Boras said of the Rangers' owner.

The Red Sox released a statement declaring, "No further discussions regarding this transaction are planned."

The Alex Rodriguez trade was dead.

More than a month later, on January 25, Rodriguez and Hicks were in New York City for the annual baseball writers dinner. At the event, Hicks said, "There is no possibility he will be traded. It looked like a possibility at one time. It didn't work out. We're going to put it behind us." Rodriguez was named captain of the Rangers at the dinner, and he was officially presented with his American League MVP trophy. Then he returned to his seat on the dais—next to Yankees GM Brian Cashman.

Ten different players received first-place votes in the 2003 American League MVP voting, the second most in history. Rodriguez received just six first-place votes, the fewest by an MVP winner since 1951. He beat runner-up Carlos Delgado by a mere 29 points, and only 112 points separated the top five finishers. By comparison, the National League MVP was claimed by Barry Bonds, with a 123-point edge over second place. The previous year, the MVP winner's margin was 102 points in the American League, 172 in the National. If just a few voters had changed the order of names on their ballots in 2003, someone else from the crowded pack of American Leaguers might have edged out A-Rod. Cashman would have found himself sitting next to Delgado or his own Yankee catcher, Jorge Posada, at the banquet.

As it happened, Cashman was shopping for infield help, thanks to a basketball injury.

When Aaron Boone first walked into a locker room after being traded to New York, he said, "It's nice to walk into this room and know it's about winning games. That's how I like to play." That explains why he went for the loose ball.

"I figured I'd run up and down the court a little," he recalled. Instead, three minutes into the five-on-five full-court pickup game, his competitive instincts took over, and he forgot he was just playing to get in a little offseason cardio work.

"I was just hanging on the outside," he said. "One time, there was a loose ball, and I went to tip it and take it the other way, and this guy cut me down."

Boone, hero of the 2003 ALCS win over the hated Red Sox, dropped to the floor, clutching his left knee.

Baseball contracts are an interesting read. They promise players millions of dollars for playing a game—Boone's contract, signed in December 2003 with the drama of his series-clinching walk-off home run still fresh in everyone's mind, would pay him $5.75 million for the 2004 season.

After investing that much money in a player, a team is going to make sure that its asset is protected. That means putting in clauses preventing players from doing anything that might risk injury. After all, they're getting paid all that money to play one specific game.

According to research by USA Today, the New York Yankees, who spent the most on players by a large margin, also had the strictest limitations on outside and offseason activities. The list filled an entire page and banned piloting any type of aircraft (the activity that ended the life of Yankees catcher and team captain Thurman Munson in 1979), sky diving, rodeo sports, hang gliding, pole vaulting, windsurfing, boxing, wood chopping, log rolling and tree climbing.

Those restrictions seem perfectly logical. The inherent danger is part of the appeal of each of them. However, the standard Yankee contract also prohibited cosmetic surgery, cave exploration, golf, darts, swimming, bowling, shuffleboard and Ping-Pong.

The standard Yankee contract, like the one signed by Aaron Boone on December 1, 2003, also prohibited playing pickup basketball.

It was a clause the Yankees were willing to negotiate with some players. Pitcher Mike Mussina, a teammate of Boone's, received permission to play pickup games during a three-week offseason window, prior to January 1, and only on his own personal court at his house. Now, clearly, Mussina didn't have a custom court installed in his home, only to have it sit idle for 49 weeks out of the year. And it's likely that more than a few Yankees have taken a dip in the pool or played a round of golf or two.

In a practical sense, the Yankee contract doesn't prohibit players from participating in those activities—it prohibits them from getting hurt while participating in them.

Boone said it was the only time that offseason that he played basketball, and there's no reason to suspect him of lying. After all, he admitted that he injured his knee on the basketball court, and that bit of truth cost him $5.75 million. It would have been easy enough for Boone to swear the other nine players on the court that day to secrecy, perhaps with a few thousand dollars each for their troubles, and then tell the Yankees that he slipped on the stairs. That fib would have kept his 2004 salary guaranteed.

"I've got a lot of respect over how he went about it. He didn't try to cover it up," his brother Bret, then a second baseman for the Mariners, said. "That's the thing about him. He has character and is honest. You have to respect someone who is honest from the get-go. As a professional athlete, it's tough to do that."

As a result of his honesty, the Yankees voided Boone's contract and released him, about six weeks after he tore his ACL going for a loose ball. Instead of paying him his full salary, the Yankees only had to pay 30 days of termination pay, or $917,553.

"We're exercising our rights in the contract," Yankees general manager Brian Cashman said. "Would we want to pay him the full salary despite the injury? That wouldn't make any sense whatsoever from a business perspective."

Soon, though, the Yankees would find a suitable replacement to play third base.

Boone's injury occurred on January 16, 2004, more than a month after baseball's winter meetings, meaning most teams that had players available for trade had already consummated their deals. It was just over a month before pitchers and catchers reported for spring training; most big-name free agents had already found homes.

Simply put, it wasn't the best time for a team to lose its starting third baseman. "We're going to come up with a game plan," Cashman said. "But obviously it's the back end of the market."

On the Yankees' own roster, the best options for third base were Enrique Wilson and Miguel Cairo, two backups who combined for a .240 average with 8 homers and 47 RBI the previous year. Neither was a full-time third baseman. In Triple-A, they had Drew Henson, who hit .234 with 14 homers and 78 RBI. He was also less than two months from signing a contract to play quarterback for the Dallas Cowboys, also a prohibited activity that would cause him to lose about $12 million in signing bonus money from the Yankees.

The trade market was equally bleak. The Yankees were looking at options like the Dodgers' Adrián Beltré, who hit just .240 the year before; Tampa's Geoff Blum (.262, 10 home runs); and Padres utility infielder Jeff Cirillo (.205, 2 homers).

For nine days, Cashman and the Yankees considered their options, none of them good. Then the general manager went to the awards dinner, and a solution fell into his lap.

It was another in a long list of what-ifs. If Boone hadn't gone for the loose ball in that pickup game, or if Boone's brother-in-law hadn't been visiting and told him about the pickup game in Costa Mesa, the Yankees wouldn't have needed a third baseman. If Boone had decided to lie and protect his salary, Cashman might have been looking for a short-term fix at the position, expecting Boone to return late in the season and finish his contract, instead of a replacement for the soon-to-be-released contract violator.

If the epic Boston-Texas negotiations had taken slightly different turns at any number of points, Cashman might have found himself seated next to his arch-rival's newest acquisition.

Rodriguez had met with Hicks, Hart and Showalter for five hours while the group was in New York for the writers dinner. They worked out their differences and were ready to move on.

Then it was dinner time.

"I spent the entire night sitting there, having dinner with Alex on the dais, talking about what happened and why Boston didn't happen," Cashman recalled. "The Rangers, the Red Sox, the union involvement—it turned into a little bit of a roadmap. I started to get the idea that we might have something we could do."

Cashman called Hart to ask about the Rangers' reserve third baseman, Mike Lamb, who had appeared in 28 games and hit .132 in 2003. As they talked about the Yankees' dire third-base situation, Cashman brought up A-Rod's name.

"His initial reaction was, 'Oh, you're not going to do this to me,'" Cashman said of Hart.

After the public nature of the failed Red Sox negotiations, they didn't want the press to find out about the further discussions. They also didn't involve their owners at the start.

"I didn't tell anyone about it," Cashman told Ian O'Connor in a biography of Derek Jeter. "I didn't even tell my owner I was working on that deal." Team president Randy Levine found out through a friend in Miami he shared with A-Rod.

Hart also didn't bring Hicks into the discussions, at first. He and Rodriguez were acting as if all wounds had been healed. A-Rod appeared at the team's preseason banquet with fans. The following day, he went to a birthday party for Hicks. The day after that, February 8, he visited Hicks at home.

Meanwhile, Cashman and Hart were working on the deal. The negotiations had a far different feel than the Red Sox talks. The Yankees had no interest in meeting with Rodriguez or his agent, Boras, to work things out. They had the Rangers convey their requirements to the player.

"I'm not talking to Boras," Cashman remembered saying. "He'll try to extract something from us. You guys have to tell Alex he's got to waive his no-trade clause, and that he's got to play third base.

"That was the biggest hurdle," Cashman said. "It was one of surprise because you just don't know. When John Hart called back and said, 'This is one area we can proceed on,' that was a surprise, but certainly a welcome one."

Hicks was brought into the negotiations after Rodriguez left his house on February 8. Eventually, the Rangers' owner agreed to pay $67 million of the remaining $179 million on A-Rod's contract. To add enough value to the contract to satisfy the players' union, the Yankees agreed to give Rodriguez a suite on road trips and to help promote his personal web page on the team's site.

In exchange for Rodriguez, the Yankees offered All-Star second baseman Alfonso Soriano, who had hit 77 home runs and stolen 76 bases over the previous two years. They also agreed to send a player to be named later, which would be selected from a list of five prospects in the Yankee organization. The list included:

- 19-year-old shortstop Joaquín Árias, who stole 12 bases and hit .266 at Class A Battle Creek, a year after hitting .300 in rookie ball;
- 21-year-old second baseman Robinson Cano, who hit .277 with 6 home runs in a 2003 season split between Class A and Double-A;
- 20-year-old outfielder Rudy Guillen, who had 13 home runs and 13 stolen bases at Battle Creek;
- 22-year-old Ramon Ramirez, a Dominican right-hander who had reached Triple-A Columbus in his first year in pro baseball; and
- 20-year-old outfielder Bronson Sardinha, the Yankees' first-round pick in the 2001 draft.

In late April, the Rangers selected Árias. It wasn't a bad choice—the infielder eventually became a semi-regular at the major league level, playing in 112 games and batting 319 times in 2012 as a member of the San Francisco Giants. It was the second-best career of any of the five prospects on the list.

Unfortunately, it was second-best by a wide margin. Cano would finish runner up for the 2005 Rookie of the Year, as a member of the Yankees. He would go on to become a six-time All-Star and a top-five finisher in MVP voting four times. He'd win two Gold Gloves and five Silver Sluggers, and had nearly 250 home runs and 1,000 RBI through his first 11 seasons in the majors, still going strong in his early 30s.

"I look back on it, but I don't second-guess it," Hart said of the Árias pick. "The reports I had on Cano were that he was talented but moody, and we were not sure what he was going to be. The young shortstop had reports off the chart. He was gifted, could run, had a cannon arm, could hit. Cash didn't blink putting Cano in and told me we picked the right guy with Árias."

The news hit Boston like Boone's home run had in October.

Ever since word of the Boone injury broke, the Red Sox were dreading the possibility. "We looked at each other in the office and said, 'If A-Rod's willing to play third, he's a Yankee,'" Epstein said. "Then it started to leak out—he's going to play third. It was just a matter of time. We were just waiting for the ax to fall."

Epstein compared it to Lucy pulling the football away from Charlie Brown. "Everything works out for the big, bad Yankees, and we were doomed."

Hoyer said he was "devastated." "I wanted to puke, I was sick to my stomach," he said.

Lucchino said, "We had fallen back into the abyss. We had tried, and the Yankees had succeeded."

The Yankees celebrated yet another triumph over the rival Red Sox, and the media piled on. Tony Kornheiser of ESPN and the *Washington Post* began a column by saying, "Nice try, Red Sox. Nice try, Larry Lucchino. Nice try, Theo Epstein. Better luck next year. Or the year after that. Or by 2018, 100 years after the last World Series you won. The Curse of the

Bambino Lives. The Evil Empire triumphs again. The Yankees just got Alex Rodriguez, right from under your noses. So enjoy that Patriots Super Bowl victory, Beantown. Because that's the only victory coming to Boston anytime soon."

As it turned out, Kornheiser was wrong. Boston would win two World Series before Rodriguez and the Yankees returned to the Fall Classic. When the Red Sox broke their 86-year championship drought that October, Manny Ramirez, the man who had been headed to Texas in the aborted A-Rod deal, was named the World Series MVP.

When Boston added a second title in 2007 and a third in 2013, Jon Lester, the throw-in prospect in the failed Rangers trade, went 3–0 in World Series games. He allowed a total of 1 run in 21 innings pitched.

Rodriguez would spend a productive but controversial tenure with the Yankees. He won two MVP awards and was a key contributor to the 2009 World Series championship team.

A-Rod struggled to fit in with the tightly knit Yankees team, however. Scandal seemed to follow him, from embarrassing personal details on the back pages of tabloids to his admission that he'd used performance-enhancing drugs, ironically, in an attempt to live up to his gigantic contract.

"When I arrived in Texas in 2001, I felt an enormous amount of pressure. I felt like I had all the weight of the world on top of me and I needed to perform, and perform at a high level every day," he told ESPN.

Near the end of his career, the Yankees were looking for ways to disassociate themselves from A-Rod, even as he was hitting career milestones like 700 home runs.

Meanwhile, out from under the massive contract, the Rangers were able to invest in their entire roster. The Rangers improved to fifth in the league in pitching in 2004, winning 89 games.

That October following the Rodriguez trade, in another dramatic ALCS between Boston and New York, the Red Sox became the first team in history to come back from a three-games-to-none deficit in a seven-game series, winning the final four games against the Yankees. Rodriguez went 2 for 17 in the four losses.

In the eighth inning of Game Six, the Yankees were trailing 4–1 but appeared on the verge of one of those rallies that seemed to break the Red Sox's hearts each year. Miguel Cairo, the infielder who wasn't good enough to replace Boone at third, doubled, and Jeter singled him home. That brought Rodriguez to the plate. He hit a slow roller up the first-base line. Boston pitcher Bronson Arroyo fielded it and laid the tag on Rodriguez, but the ball came loose. Jeter ran all the way around to score from first base, pumping his fist as he crossed the plate, and cut the Boston lead to one. Rodriguez, the potential tying run, stood at second base. The Yankee Stadium crowd was in a frenzy.

The umpires conferred, however, and, when they broke their huddle, they declared A-Rod out for interference. Replays showed the call was the correct one: Rodriguez had slapped the ball out of Arroyo's glove.

Fans rained debris down onto the field, and players headed to the dugout for safety. When play resumed, Jeter returned to first base, where he remained until the end of the inning. The Yankees didn't manage another hit that game, and the Red Sox completed the comeback the following day with a resounding 10–3 win.

"I don't know what I was trying to do," Rodriguez said after the game. "It was a big momentum changer."

In the end, Alex Rodriguez was a key factor in the Red Sox winning their first World Series in nearly a century. Just as everyone had expected, eleven months earlier.

WAR COMPARISON

Had the Red Sox been able to complete the trade, they would have received nearly as much value from A-Rod and Ordóñez over the next five years as the Yankees got from a dozen years of Rodriguez alone.

The most striking aspect of the trade is how much worse off the Rangers were, from a player value standpoint, because the players' association vetoed the trade. Instead of getting Manny Ramirez at near All-Star level for several seasons, Texas got one good year from Alfonso Soriano.

RED SOX WOULD HAVE RECEIVED	WAR PRE-TRADE	WAR POST-TRADE
Alex Rodriguez	25.5	37.7 over next 5 years
Magglio Ordóñez	24.3	13.7 over next 5 years
RANGERS WOULD HAVE RECEIVED	WAR PRE-TRADE	WAR POST-TRADE
Manny Ramirez	16.6	16.6 over next 5 years
Jon Lester	0.0	30.7 with Boston, 8.6 over next 5 years
WHITE SOX WOULD HAVE RECEIVED	WAR PRE-TRADE	WAR POST-TRADE
Nomar Garciaparra	41.1	3.3 over next 5 years
TO YANKEES	WAR PRE-TRADE	WAR POST-TRADE
Alex Rodriguez	25.5	55.5
TO RANGERS	WAR PRE-TRADE	WAR POST-TRADE
Alfonso Soriano	9.6	3.6
Joaquín Árias	0.0	-0.1

CHAPTER 11

WHO IS
— RICK SUTCLIFFE? —

THE STORY BEHIND THE RICK SUTCLIFFE TRADE

Perhaps the best midseason pickup in history leads the Cubs to the postseason.

In 1984, the Chicago Cubs were ravaged by back trouble, arm trouble and hepatitis. Plus, they hadn't made the postseason in 38 years. One trade solved all their problems, as Rick Sutcliffe became the most significant midseason pickup in history.

Rick Sutcliffe needed another World Series ring, because he refused to wear his first one.

Unfortunately for him, the two teams that employed him in 1984—the Indians and the Cubs, had gone a combined 112 years without winning a title and a combined 75 without making the World Series.

In fact, of the 24 teams in existence when MLB added an extra round to the postseason in 1969, only four teams hadn't made the postseason over the first 15 years of League Championship Series play—the Washington Senators/Texas Rangers, the San Diego Padres, the Indians and the Cubs.

In his first 98 games in the major leagues, Sutcliffe had been a small part of two World Series teams and one champion. Incomprehensibly to Cubs and Indians fans, winning didn't make him happy.

Sutcliffe was a member of the 1981 Dodgers, who beat the Yankees in six games in the World Series.

"In 1981, I got a World Series ring; I got the check; I got the trophy. But my pride won't let me wear that ring." he said. "Now I want one I can wear."

Sutcliffe doesn't feel like part of the '81 Dodgers, because the team left him off the postseason roster. In the team's defense, Sutcliffe was the one who vowed, "I'll never (bleeping) play for you again," after leaving the manager's office in shambles and the manager a little shaky as well.

The Dodgers took Sutcliffe in the first round of the 1974 draft, choosing the powerful starting pitcher out of high school. He made his major league debut two seasons later with a late-September start. After another brief cup of coffee with the Dodgers at the end of the 1978 season, he won the National League Rookie of the Year award in 1979, going 17–10 with a 3.46 ERA.

Inexplicably, the team tried to make a reliever out of him the next year. His ERA ballooned to 5.56 and he went 3–9.

He hoped to return to the starting rotation in 1981, but a portly left-hander from Mexico, Fernando Valenzuela, arrived on the scene. Valenzuela won his first eight decisions with the Dodgers, and Fernando Mania spread across Los Angeles.

The Dodgers also had veterans Jerry Reuss, Burt Hooten and Bob Welch in the rotation, leaving no room for Sutcliffe. He made four starts in April, going 2–1 with an impressive 2.30 ERA.

In back-to-back starts in early May, he was pulled from the mound after two innings. He gave up four runs in each. He didn't pitch for 15 days, and he was banished to the bullpen for the rest of the season. He appeared in just 8 more games, and only twice when the Dodgers had a lead.

In September, Sutcliffe met with manager Tommy Lasorda and pitching coach Ron Perranoski. He asked to be given the chance to start a game.

"I'd like to have five innings in one game, to see if I can pitch or not," Sutcliffe told Lasorda.

"You've got it," the manager replied.

Instead, he sat and waited. He pitched the final inning of a game the Dodgers lost 8–2 on September 15. It was his first work in over a month and just his second appearance since the All-Star Break. Four days later, he pitched the final two innings of a 7-3 Dodgers loss. He allowed one baserunner in his three innings of work.

Meanwhile, reliever Bobby Castillo got a start on September 3 and pitched five innings. Ted Power, called up from Triple-A Albuquerque with the September roster expansion, got two starts near the end of the month and went five innings each time.

"There were three of us there, and he gave me his word," Sutcliffe said of the first meeting with Lasorda.

On the second-to-last day of the regular season, Sutcliffe went into Lasorda's office for a second meeting and closed the door.

"I asked why he had started Power and Castillo, and he said he wanted to give the younger pitchers a chance," Sutcliffe said, "but Power and Castillo were both older than I was!" Indeed, both pitchers are more than a year older than Sutcliffe.

"I said, 'Why? Why did you lie to me?' And he said, 'The opportunity didn't present itself.' Well, that was the biggest lie I'd ever heard," Sutcliffe recalled. "We were already in the playoffs from our first-half finish, and the Dodgers had brought in a reliever before the seventh inning in 20 of 31 games."

The 6-foot-7 Sutcliffe jumped up and knocked everything off Lasorda's desk.

"I'll never (bleeping) play for you again!" he shouted. "You lied to me, and you had no reason. I've done everything you've ever asked."

Sutcliffe flipped the desk over.

"I grabbed a chair and I was about to smash the wall with it," Sutcliffe recalled.

Lasorda's office was famous for his celebrity wall. Hollywood stars frequently took in Dodger games, and Lasorda made sure to host them in his office whenever possible. He had framed photos of him posing with each of his guests covering his office wall.

"I saw the picture of Frank Sinatra, and I felt I'd seen enough of him," Sutcliffe said. "But before I could throw the chair at the wall I decided that having the Dodgers mad at me was bad enough. Having Frank Sinatra mad at me also might have been a little dangerous."

Lasorda shouted at the pitcher, "You've got no right being upset at me. The way you've pitched, you don't even belong in the big leagues!"

"That's when I picked him up by his uniform collar," Sutcliffe said. "I wasn't exactly choking him, but I guess my hands were sort of around his neck—and I held him in the air and said 'If you weren't fifty years old, I'd kick your (bleep).'"

Two months after winning the World Series, Lasorda pushed to have him traded to Cleveland, the MLB equivalent of Siberia.

Sutcliffe didn't mind the change, however, since it came with a chance to pitch regularly. He won 14 games in 1982 and led the league in ERA. In 1983, he won 17 games. But the way his 1981 season ended still haunted him.

"I keep saying I've forgotten about it," Sutcliffe said after a win in May 1983, "but here, I've shut out the Royals. I beat my hometown team. I struck out George Brett, and instead of getting excited, all I can think about is the guy who said I don't belong in the big leagues."

"When your manager tells you you don't belong in the majors," he continued. "I just take it one start at a time now."

Sutcliffe also set another goal for himself, in addition to getting another ring.

"Probably, if I have any goal in my career, that would be it. I want to prove I belong in the major leagues," he said. "I'd like to be in the National League, just to face that ballclub."

It was clear by the end of the 1983 season that playing in Cleveland wouldn't get him very close to either goal. The Indians finished sixth in the seven-team American League East in 1982, and seventh in 1983. They were a combined 29 games below .500 and 45 games out of first in the two seasons.

As a five-year veteran, Sutcliffe had an option to demand a trade after the season. "I have to let the Indians know by October 1," he explained. "If I do, they have to trade me by March 15 or I am a free agent."

"I'm not worried about a long-term contract," he said. "One year is fine with me, and I'm not after a lot of cash. But I do want to play for a winner, and I have some doubts about where the Indians are going."

Sutcliffe informed the team he'd like to be traded. As part of his option, he could give the Indians a list of six teams that were off-limits. On his list were the Chicago Cubs.

Sutcliffe eventually changed his mind and withdrew his trade after the Indians tore up his contract and gave him a new deal for $850,000, nearly triple what he made in 1983. He started the 1984 season with the Indians. By early June, they were in last place again, already 13 games below .500, already more than 20 games out of first place.

The record wasn't the only reason Sutcliffe was miserable. In spring training, 1983, he had oral surgery and suffered complications from the procedure. Throughout most of that season, he suffered headaches, equilibrium problems and even temporary loss of hearing in one ear.

Prior to the 1984 season, when the problem hadn't gotten any better, it was time to do something. "I decided to seek help," he said.

He got a second opinion, and the new dentist told him infection had set in. The dentist began to drill.

"It was like an explosion," Sutcliffe said of the pain. "I was there for four days, and two days later, I was pitching in Yankee Stadium."

The dental problems set him back. "I wasn't throwing all that hard, and I was working to gain my strength back," Sutcliffe said. "I wasn't feeling well . . . I had lost weight."

Sutcliffe struggled to a 4–5 record and 5.15 ERA by June 11.

While Sutcliffe was struggling in Cleveland, the Chicago Cubs had a disgruntled player on their hands.

In spring training, the Cubs lost 11 straight games. "I didn't have a leadoff man, and we didn't have an outfielder who could catch the ball. I started to wonder what I had gotten into," manager Jim Frey said.

At the end of spring training, general manager Dallas Green decided his locker room didn't have the fire he wanted to see.

"We needed a screamer, a holler guy, a leader," Green said.

He needed someone like Gary Matthews. A rookie of the year in 1973 and an All-Star in 1979, Matthews' true value came behind the scenes. He was nicknamed "Sarge" for the tough leadership he provided.

"I mean, when I realized we could get him from the Phillies, I couldn't say yes fast enough," Green said. "This guy talked when it was time to talk and produced when it was time to produce."

Green acquired Sarge and speedy center fielder Bob Dernier from the Phillies for a package that included reliever Bill Campbell. The trade solved one problem, but it created another.

Mel Hall was a promising outfielder for the Cubs. He sped through the team's minor leagues, hitting .319 with 24 homers and 95 RBI in Double-A and .329-32-125 in Triple-A. Hall had a combination of power and speed, showing a prowess for stealing bases in the minors.

He joined the Cubs as a regular in 1983 and finished third in the Rookie of the Year voting. He split that season between left field and center.

The trade with the Phillies took away both of those spots, however. Matthews took over left field, and Dernier went to center. Hall was put into a platoon with Keith Moreland in right field, with the left-handed Hall playing against right-handed pitchers and the righty Moreland starting against southpaws.

Moreland was coming off a year in which he hit .302 with 16 home runs while starting 150 games in right field. Needless to say, he was not happy with the new arrangement. He started 4 of the Cubs' first 10 games in 1984 and 6 of the next 10. He was hitting just .224 at the end of April.

Then his time seriously began to dwindle. He started in just two of the next 10 games. He was hitting .238 and hadn't homered since opening day.

He demanded that Green trade him somewhere that he could play every day. He complained to the media about his playing time and would sing, "Please release me, let me go," in front of reporters in the clubhouse.

"I have nothing against the new players on the team," Moreland said. "Matthews and Dernier are good players. I just want to play, too. If that means going to another ball club, well, that's how badly I want to play."

The Cubs' front office discussed the Moreland problem and came up with a solution.

"We knew we had to trade Hall," Jim Frey said, years later.

The decision wasn't made out of loyalty to Moreland. The Cubs simply thought that Hall would bring them more of a return on the trade market. "We thought we could get a pretty good pitcher," Frey said.

The Cubs suddenly found themselves in need of a pitcher. Veteran starter Dick Ruthven, a two-time All-Star who won 12 games for the Cubs in 1983, started feeling tingling and weakness in his pitching arm. He lasted just 23 innings in a five-start stretch and gave up 21 earned runs in those games.

On May 18, Ruthven was x-rayed, and doctors found that an artery was being compressed when he threw. He had surgery five days later. The team said it wasn't career-threatening, but it would require a long recuperation.

Around the same time another pitcher went down. Scott Sanderson suffered back spasms and missed consecutive starts in May. He was then out the entire month of June.

On May 15, the Cubs lost their backup catcher, Steve Lake, when he was diagnosed with hepatitis. Doctors were shocked that he had the strength to walk, let alone hit a homer one week earlier.

"I was lying there in that dark hospital room in Chicago last summer, having problems breathing because my liver was enlarged," Lake recalled.

Dallas Green was able to solve all the team's problems with one trade. On June 13, the Cubs got Sutcliffe from the Indians, along with reliever George Frazier and catcher Ron Hassey.

In exchange, the Cubs gave up four promising young players: Mel Hall, Triple-A outfielder Joe Carter, Triple-A pitchers Don Schulze and Darryl Banks.

It was a steep price to pay. Carter, Schulze and Banks had all been first-round draft picks. Carter was chosen second overall in 1981. Hall, who already had a season of MLB experience under his belt, was "only" a second-rounder.

Schulze was 21 years old, Hall 23, Carter and Banks 24. Plus, Sutcliffe was scheduled to be a free agent after the season, meaning the Cubs might have been mortgaging their future for half a season from him.

"It wasn't just another deal," Frey said. "It was a big deal; it took a lot of nerve."

"We hate to give away good players," Green said, putting his arm around Hall. "This guy has done a heck of a job for us, but we ran into a situation we could do very little about. We got two pitchers who are necessary additions to our staff, and the making of the trade rested on Hall being part of it."

"Sutcliffe has had success," Green continued. "He's a 200-plus inning pitcher, and he can anchor our staff. Frazier will help with middle relief, and, with the Lake problem, we were going to kill (starting catcher Jody Davis) if we're not careful and didn't get him some help."

Indians president Gabe Paul was just as happy on his side. "It shores up our front line. It shores up our bench," he said. "We've got a good bench now for the first time. It weakens our pitching. We've got to get more pitching strength, but we're doing one thing at a time. I think that this is a greatly improved ball club today over yesterday. (Manager) Pat Corrales was ecstatic when we talked about it."

"Money had nothing to do with this," said Indians GM Phil Seghi. "The trade follows the pattern we began in the winter. We want to get the best young players we can and see what they can do. Hall and Carter are outfielders with some pop. Carter is a good prospect and Hall hit 17 homers for the Cubs. He (Carter) hits for power and average. Carter and Hall can also run."

Carter was more than a good prospect. He was in the process of tearing up the American Association at Triple-A Iowa. At the time of the trade, Carter was hitting .310 with 14 homers,

67 RBI and 11 steals after just 61 games.

The previous year, he'd hit .307-22-83 with 40 stolen bases and was named American Association Rookie of the Year. It was a letdown to return to Triple-A in 1984, but, as Keith Moreland could attest, the Cubs outfield was crowded.

"My full season in Triple-A, I played almost every game," Carter said at the start of the 1984 season. "You go out there and hope to play 162 more, plus the playoffs. You try to become a little bit better. You can set your goals a little bit higher; try to do what I did this year and a little bit more. It's gonna be tough, but I'm not saying it can't be done."

Needless to say, news of the trade, which reached Carter between games of a doubleheader, was welcome.

"I was happy," he said. "Chicago was in first place, but I was in Triple-A. I didn't want to be in Triple-A the rest of the year. I wanted to make something happen, so they'd either bring me up or trade me away. I was just happy to get my chance to play in the big leagues. I didn't care where it was, as long as I was given a chance to play—something I'd dreamed of playing for a long time."

Sutcliffe was also thrilled with the change of venue. "I picked up 25 games in one night," he said. "That's a Houdini type of move!"

Sutcliffe wasn't worried about his impending free agency. "I don't know anything about that yet. I just want to do the best job I can and help this club win the pennant," he said. "I talked to Dallas Green about a week before the deal and we discussed some things then. But we'll talk later."

The other former Indians were just as happy to be joining a first-place club.

"I just want to have a chance to pitch. I'll do whatever they say," Frazier said. "No one ever thinks about getting traded but now that I'm here, I want to do the best I can."

Like Sutcliffe, Frazier had a postseason score to settle. As a Yankee in 1981, he lost 3 games in the World Series, posting a 17.18 ERA.

Hassey was happy to take on the backup role. "I'm available. I'll do what I'm asked to do. I think it will be exciting to play on a contender," he said.

There was one last hurdle to the trade, however.

Somehow, Dallas Green forgot to put Hall and Carter through National League waivers before trading them. They had to be put through the process—giving any team the opportunity to claim them and knock them out of the trade.

MLB's trade rules were even more complicated in 1984 than they are now. Currently, there is a July 31 deadline for teams to trade players without having to put them through waivers first, then, a month later, there's then another deadline for trading players that have cleared waivers. In 1984, the trade deadline depended on which teams were involved in the deal. There was a June 15 nonwaiver trade deadline, but that was only for trades between teams in the same league. The nonwaiver deadline for interleague trading had passed on April 1, meaning that the players swapping between the NL Cubs and AL Indians had to clear waivers.

That put the two new Indians outfielders in limbo for five days. Hall remained in Montreal, where he'd played his last game as a Cub before being traded. He wasn't even allowed to join the Indians. Carter, because he was a minor leaguer, was able to travel with the Indians while waiting to clear.

If anyone claimed Carter or Hall, they would return to the Cubs and couldn't be traded until the end of the season. The Indians and Cubs would have to negotiate some other compensation.

Hall ripped the Cubs for trading him and then botching the deal in the process. "Who is Rick Sutcliffe?" he said. "I hope I face him sometime."

On June 19, Hall and Carter completed their waiver period. Carter batted sixth in the lineup and singled in his first at bat for Cleveland. Hall arrived from Montreal the next day and pinch hit in the game. He also singled in his first Indians at bat.

The same night that Carter played for Cleveland, Sutcliffe made his Cubs debut. He pitched eight innings, struck out nine, allowed five hits and beat Pittsburgh, 4–3.

Five days later, in his Wrigley debut, he shut out the Cardinals, striking out a then-career-high 14 and walking just one in a complete game victory. It was the most strikeouts by a Cubs pitcher in 13 years. He would top it in September with 15 strikeouts against the Phillies.

"It was thrilling, especially pitching before a sellout crowd. We didn't have too big a crowd when I pitched in Cleveland," Sutcliffe said after the St. Louis win.

The day before he pitched at Wrigley, his wife attended her first game there. "I'll never forget, after the game, when I walked out, my wife was just crying with excitement," he recalled.

"Are all the games like that here?" she asked.

"There were more people in the park that day than we would normally see in a month (in Cleveland)," Sutcliffe said.

In his next start, June 29, Sutcliffe returned to Los Angeles. He finally got the chance to achieve his goal of facing Lasorda's Dodgers.

Steve Sax led off the game with a triple against Sutcliffe. After Sutcliffe walked the next batter, Sax stole home. Sax also tripled against Sutcliffe in the fourth inning, driving in a run.

Lasorda was in Sutcliffe's head, and the pitcher struggled, allowing 7 runs in four innings. Sutcliffe and the Cubs lost 7–1.

He wouldn't lose again that season. Sutcliffe went on to win his final 14 decisions of the year, leading the Cubs to first place for the first time since 1945.

Sutcliffe shattered the team record for consecutive wins. He was an astounding 16–1 as a Cub and reached 20 wins, combined for the two teams, on the season. His ERA, over 5.00 for Cleveland, was 2.69 for Chicago. He had 7 complete games for the Cubs and struck out 155 batters in 150.1 innings.

Sutcliffe won the National League Cy Young Award, despite starting the season in the American League.

"That year for Sutcliffe was enchanted," said pitcher Steve Stone.

Fittingly, Sutcliffe was on the mound on September 24, when the Cubs won 4–1 at Pittsburgh to clinch the NL East division. He threw a complete game two-hitter, allowing one run and no walks and striking out nine.

"This ballclub has suffered for 39 years, and that's long enough," Frey said. "Everybody said this club had a monkey on its back. Now the monkey's off."

Matthews, the clubhouse leader, drove in the eventual game-winning run. He then instituted a "no high-five rule" in the dugout until after the seventh inning. "We don't want to show anybody up," he said. Once again, his teammates listened to the Sarge.

Longtime Cubs broadcaster Jack Brickhouse sounded a cautionary note during the postgame celebration. "There's this nagging thing in the back of my head that tells me it's okay to celebrate, but let's stop short of hysteria," he said. "Until we beat San Diego [in the NLCS], until we've won the league championship, we haven't won anything. Look at the White Sox last year. They had that big celebration in Daley Plaza, and then Baltimore beats them, and you never saw such a pall over a city. I don't want anyone tearing Wrigley Field down brick by brick because of a division title. If they don't win the World Series, that's not that important to me. But the important thing is to get into the World Series."

Keith Moreland wandered back onto the field at Pittsburgh's Three Rivers Stadium to watch video of the celebration on the streets of Chicago, being shown on the stadium scoreboard. "I'm going to savor the hell out of this moment," he said.

Since the trade that gave him a full-time job again, Moreland had lifted his average 40 points, to .279. He matched the previous season's 16 homers and had 80 RBI, then a career high. He was named National League player of the month for August.

Rick Sutcliffe won again in the first game of the best-of-five NLCS. He pitched seven shutout innings and hit a home run as the Cubs rolled 13–0 at Wrigley.

Chicago won the second game at Wrigley as well, but the Padres rallied in San Diego to even the series. Sutcliffe started the deciding fifth game.

The Cubs scored two runs in the first inning and another in the second to give Sutcliffe a 3–0 lead. Sutcliffe continued to help his own cause at the plate, singling in his first at bat.

Through five innings, Sutcliffe had allowed three baserunners. None had gotten to second base on him. That's when his magic ran out.

The Padres started the sixth with two singles and a walk, then scored 2 runs on back-to-back sacrifice flies.

In the bottom of the seventh, Sutcliffe was back on the mound, protecting a one-run lead. Following a walk and a bunt that advanced the runner to second base, first baseman Leon Durham made an error on a ground ball, allowing the tying run to score. Sutcliffe then gave up 3 straight hits. By the time the dust cleared, the Padres were up 6–3. The Cubs wouldn't score again.

Just like that, Chicago was eliminated from the postseason.

Sutcliffe filed for free agency in the offseason but chose to re-sign with the Cubs. He remained with the team for seven more seasons and posted an 82–65 record, including a league-high 18 wins in 1987, when he finished second in Cy Young voting. He concluded his 18-year career with two seasons in Baltimore and one with the Cardinals.

Sutcliffe would return to the NLCS with the Cubs in 1989, this time facing the Giants. He doubled in his second time at bat, extending his NLCS hitting streak to 3 games, but he left his Game Three start with the score tied. The Cubs went on to lose the game and the series. It was Sutcliffe's final postseason appearance. He never made it to the World Series.

Sutcliffe would go 8–4 against the Dodgers in his career, with a 3.22 ERA.

Although the Indians did receive some coveted talent in the trade with the Cubs, the team was unable to rise out of the bottom of the standings. Through the rest of the decade, Cleveland finished as high as fifth place only once—in 1986, their lone winning season during that time—and finished dead-last twice, in two 100-loss seasons.

Joe Carter would spend six years with the Indians, and he earned MVP votes in three of those seasons. He hit 151 homers for Cleveland, with a career-best 35 in 1989, and led the league in RBI with 121 in 1986. He went on to play in Toronto, where he hit a World Series winning home run in 1993.

Hall didn't reach the same level of stardom as Carter, although he did have a 13-year major league career. He spent five years with the Indians and then four with the Yankees before playing three seasons in the Japanese professional leagues.

Hall achieved the goal that he stated while waiting to clear waivers. He got to face Rick Sutcliffe 10 times in his career. He went 6 for 9 against him with a double, homer, sacrifice fly and 4 RBI. No one with at least 10 plate appearances against Sutcliffe had a higher average than Hall's .667

But it was Sutcliffe's amazing run during the 1984 season that remains the most significant outcome of the trade.

As the Cubs players destroyed the clubhouse that September night in Pittsburgh, spraying champagne and beer, Sutcliffe thought back to his bitter experience the last time one of his teams made the postseason.

"I've seen a lot of wine in dressing rooms, but I was never a part of it," he said. "I was usually just heading for the showers when the party started. I was never a part of it."

WAR COMPARISON

Rick Sutcliffe posted a 3.9 WAR in the second half of 1984, leading the Cubs to the postseason. Up until that point, he'd only had one full season with a WAR as high. He'd go on to post a 6.1 WAR season in 1987, when he finished runner up for Cy Young.

While the Indians clearly came out on the short end of the trade, Cleveland couldn't be too unhappy with its acquisitions, led by Joe Carter, who had several years of All-Star–quality production.

CUBS RECEIVED	WAR PRE-TRADE	WAR POST-TRADE
Rick Sutcliffe	8.6	21.8
George Frazier	0.7	-2.0
Ron Hassey	8.0	0.4
INDIANS RECEIVED	WAR PRE-TRADE	WAR POST-TRADE
Joe Carter	-0.6	14.3
Mel Hall	3.1	2.9
Don Schulze	-0.5	-0.6
Darryl Banks	0.0	0.0

CHAPTER 12

— 541 —

THE STORY BEHIND THE VON HAYES TRADE

Paying a big price for a poor fit leads to a much-mocked trade.

After the 1982 season, the Phillies wanted Cleveland Indians outfielder Von Hayes, and they were willing to put up a king's ransom to land him. The Philadelphia Phillies sent their starting middle infielders, a reserve outfielder and two prospects to Cleveland, raising expectations among notoriously hostile Phillies fans. For the rest of his career, Hayes would be saddled with the nickname "Five for One."

It was bad enough when Von Hayes wasn't hitting, but then, suddenly, he wasn't playing either.

In his third year with the Phillies, Hayes, in a 1-for-22 slump, which included 16 straight hitless at bats, found himself on the bench for a June game. Manager John Felske inserted him as a defensive replacement in the ninth inning.

"I was scuffling," Hayes recalled. "I think I was about 0-for-19 [*sic*] at the time. I walked into the clubhouse, and I wasn't in the lineup."

On June 10, Hayes was out of the lineup again. He entered the game in the seventh inning as part of a double switch. When the lineup was posted on June 11 and he wasn't in it, it was time for Hayes to take a stand.

"To be an everyday player, especially as a left-handed batter, where they're looking for situations to sit you down, you have to fight for your playing time," he said.

Hayes went into Felske's office and told the manager, "Listen, I'm not going to break out of this if you keep sitting me down."

Felske agreed—perhaps he was waiting for his temperamental left fielder to stand up for himself.

"Well, yeah, okay," Felske said. "What we'll do is: we'll lead you off today. That way you'll get an extra at bat, and maybe you'll break out of it."

Hayes had batted leadoff just four times in his career prior to that, but the change seemed to work. Instead of watching two teammates bat ahead of him, giving him time to think and rethink his approach, the first pitch that Hayes saw from New York Mets starter Tom Gorman came when he was standing in the batter's box.

"The first time up, I didn't even use my own bat," Hayes said. "I grabbed Jeff Stone's bat because it felt a little lighter to me. And I hit a home run. I hit it pretty good, but it barely got out of the ball park. It was what we call a 'paint-scraper.'"

It would be Hayes' only home run to lead off a game in his career.

The Phillies went on to send eight more batters to the plate that inning, bringing Hayes back up to bat in the first. Philadelphia led 4–0, and the bases were loaded.

"I hit another one," Hayes said. "And this was another one that I thought I had hit really good and it barely got over."

It was his first grand slam, and one of just two he'd hit in his career. Hayes also became the first major league player to hit 2 home runs in the first inning. Years later, he'd name his boat in honor of the accomplishment: *Two in the First.*

It was his greatest day as a Phillie, and he accomplished the feat in front of the home fans at Veterans Stadium. But Hayes was still worried.

"After hitting those two home runs, I was afraid it would put me in another slump," he told reporters after the game. "I'm not really a home run hitter and I have to keep myself from swinging for the fences."

Worried, Hayes had to look closer at what was going on. "The third time I came up [in the game] I grabbed Jeff Stone's bat again, but this time I grabbed it with my bare hands," Hayes said. "I didn't have my batting gloves on. And [the bat] had a hairline crack in it. So that explained why I thought I'd hit both of those balls really good and they barely got out. So I put that bat down and didn't use it again."

When the Hall of Fame called, asking for memorabilia from his accomplishment, Hayes overthought that too.

"You're going to send a bat to the Hall of Fame, you want your name on it, right?" he said later. So he sent them a Von Hayes model bat and kept the cracked Stone one. "It was there for quite a few years," he said. "Then, about three or four years ago, I went to the Hall of Fame. . . . They took me through with a group of people so I could look at my accomplishments. . . . And at that time, I fessed up. I said, 'I've got to admit to something. That's not the bat I hit them with.'"

The Phillies scored nine runs in the first inning of the game on June 11, 1985, and added seven more in the second. Hayes singled in the middle of that second-inning rally, to give him three hits, nine total bases and five RBI in three plate appearances. He came up again in the fourth inning, with the Phillies riding a 16–5 lead, and struck out. A murmur went through the crowd.

"I go out to left field and the fans are going crazy and having a great time," he recalled. "I get a ball that was hit off the end of the bat in front of me, I run in to get it and make a shoestring catch. I ran right into the lights and the ball hit me in the heel of the glove and I dropped it."

And the boos rang down from the stands at Veterans Stadium.

"It was pretty short-lived," Hayes said of his love affair with the Phillies faithful.

Anyone familiar with the legend surrounding Philadelphia sports fans wouldn't be surprised by the fast turnaround. One thing that Philly fans love almost as much as putting up 26 runs against the hated Mets is booing one of their own when he falls short.

Frank Olivo understood Philadelphia fans. He was one of them. In 1968, the Eagles of the NFL were dreadful, losing their first 11 games of the season, but not dreadful enough. A 2-game winning streak cost them a shot at the top pick in the upcoming NFL Draft. So, after the Bills selected O. J. Simpson, Philadelphia chose the next best running back, someone named Leroy Keyes.

As he did every year, Olivo went to the last game of the 1968 season dressed up in his Santa Claus suit. The weather was frigid and heavy snow kept the halftime act from making it to the stadium in time. Eagles officials decided to improvise. They pulled Olivo out of the stands, gave him an equipment bag to carry, and sent him onto the field to wave to fans.

As "Here Comes Santa Claus" played over the sound system, fans booed. They booed the terrible season. They booed missing on a shot at O. J. They booed the halftime act that didn't show. And they booed the last-minute substitution.

Future Pennsylvania governor Ed Rendell was in the stands as a spectator. "The fans were in such a bad mood. None of us wanted to see Santa Claus to begin with," he said.

Olivo got it. "They're not booing me," he recalled thinking. "They're booing everything."

Then the first snowballs started landing. By the time he traveled from one end of the field to the other, Olivo was receiving a steady stream of flying snowballs. "If it doesn't snow, they probably throw beer bottles," he said.

Olivo estimated he was hit by at least 100 snowballs. One knocked off his white Santa eyebrows, which he never recovered.

Olivo, a true Philly fan, gave it as good as he got it. "You're not getting nothing for Christmas," he shouted to a fan whose snowball missed from point-blank range.

Philadelphia sports fans are commonly referred to as working-class or blue-collar. They respect their own. From Rocky Balboa to Pete Rose to Allen Iverson, they get behind the undersized guy with the nasty streak who did more than anyone expected. It was the players for whom things came easily that the fans lost patience with. Mike Schmidt got booed. Donovan McNabb and Flyers legend Eric Lindros were both booed.

And Von Hayes was booed mercilessly.

Hayes came to Philadelphia as a golden boy. He was tall, six foot five, and athletic, with long arms. Scouts called him a five-tool player, good in everything a ballplayer is expected to do. He was drafted by the Indians, and it took him just two seasons to rocket through the farm system, from Class A to Triple-A to the majors.

In his autobiography, Phillies president Bill Giles called Hayes "a young, sweet-swinging outfielder/first baseman, who was only 24 and was being heralded as the next Ted Williams."

That alone would have given Phillies fans reason to distrust him. Dripping with potential is potential for disaster in the eyes of that fan base. No matter what he might accomplish, there was always room for more. That should have been a concern for Phillies management. They knew what their fan base was like and what it could do to a young player unaccustomed to the constant pressure. Would Hayes be able to handle the spotlight, and the booing that was sure to result at some point in his Phillies career? If the Phillies ever considered Hayes' mental makeup while pursuing him on the trade market, they miscalculated by a large margin.

Even the best Phillies players often complained about the harsh home fans. "I'll tell you something about my playing in Philadelphia," Schmidt said near the end of his Hall of Fame career. "Whatever I've got in my career now, I would have had a great more if I'd played my whole career in Los Angeles or Chicago, you name a town, somewhere where they were just grateful to have me around."

Philadelphia doesn't have a monopoly on tough fans and a harsh spotlight. Pitcher Ed Whitson struggled after signing a free-agent contract with the Yankees. Fans responded by leaving nails in his driveway and harassing his family in the stands. "When he got out on the mound it was like being in Vietnam," his agent said.

Decades later, future Hall of Famer Randy Johnson joined the Yankees and immediately showed he wasn't ready for the big stage, getting into a confrontation with a cameraman while on his way to a physical that finalized the trade.

After the 1982 season, Von Hayes was still in the Indians organization, but he was on the radar of Giles and the Phillies. Cleveland needed help up the middle in their infield. The previous season, two light-hitting youngsters had manned second base and short for the Indians. The double-play combination of Jack Perconte and Mike Fischlin had combined for no home runs, 36 RBI, a .255 average and 20 errors. (As an interesting side note, Fischlin and pitcher Bill Caudill would become the first two players represented by super-agent Scott Boras, who had been a high school teammate of Fischlin's.)

The Indians wanted an upgrade at both positions, and the Phillies were loaded with young middle infielders. Julio Franco was probably the best shortstop prospect in the Phillies organization. The team had once considered him untouchable and still sounded that way publicly. They'd turned down a trade with the Toronto Blue Jays the year before that would have netted them ace pitcher Dave Stieb in exchange for Franco.

However, as Giles wrote years later, the team had concerns about Franco. According to Giles, Franco was "a 24-year-old shortstop we suspected was older than that and who had an awkward batting stance that we didn't think would allow him to hit major league pitching." There were also concerns about Franco's defense.

The two teams began negotiating in early November 1982. Giles and GM Paul Owens had lunch with Indians president Gabe Paul and GM Phil Seghi at the general managers meetings on November 11.

"They're asking for too much, but we think we can really help them, and we're keeping communications open," Giles said afterward.

A week later, Giles made it clear that Franco was on the table. "If we could get a good young player like a Von Hayes in return," he said, "we would consider giving up Franco. But we will not give up Franco for an older player."

By the start of December, the possibility of a five-for-one trade was raised for the first time. Giles told the media he'd offered a quintet of prospects for Hayes, but the Indians said it was "not enough."

At the same time, Owens began talking about all the different ways the Phillies could use Franco the next season. "I'm not going to trade him unless it's for a star player," Owens said. "He could play quite a bit at second and third, fill in some at short, and we could even try him in center field."

Philadelphia's All-Star second baseman Manny Trillo was also taking up some of Giles' and Owens' attention. He wanted a contract extension. The team had prospect Juan Samuel waiting in the wings, however, and didn't want to commit to Trillo for longer than two or three seasons.

The Phillies were also working on a variety of trade possibilities with the Giants. Philadelphia wanted to add relief help, and San Francisco had three relievers—Greg Minton, Al Holland and Gary Lavelle—who would fit the Phillies' needs well. The Giants were also trying to sign their own veteran second baseman, future Hall of Famer Joe Morgan, to a new contract.

The December winter meetings were in Hawaii. As front office personnel from the Phillies and Indians prepared for their flights to the islands, there was a bit of public posturing.

"Von Hayes is our number one goal right now," Owens said. "At this point, they're asking for more than we want to give up. They're talking about three or four pretty good ballplayers."

"Of course, Paul Owens and Bill Giles want Von Hayes," Seghi said. "Everyone wants Von Hayes. We'll listen to them like we'll listen to everyone."

Prior to leaving for Hawaii, the Phillies announced one deal—they signed shortstop Iván DeJesús, acquired the previous year, to a new five-year contract. The commitment to DeJesús sent out clear messages about the eventual fates of Trillo, who didn't get a new deal, and Franco, who was now blocked by DeJesús.

"If there has been a change in our thinking toward Franco, it is partly due to our satisfaction with Iván as our shortstop," Giles said. "But we are not going to trade Julio unless it is for what we're looking for—namely, a quality young player."

At that point, the deal on the table was Hayes for four players: Trillo, Franco, pitcher Dick Ruthven and Philadelphia's top minor league outfielder, Alejandro Sanchez. That was too expensive for the Phillies.

Giles didn't want to spend the entire winter meetings trying to land Hayes, so he gave a three-day window. "I told Gabe that we would like to know by Sunday if we have a chance," he said. "Up to this point, we have basically been concentrating entirely on that one deal. That deal would determine so many other things we might want to do. But if it does not look like we're going to do it, then we want to know early in the week so we can try and go a different way."

The deal hit a snag due to Trillo's contract status. He made it clear he wasn't thrilled about negotiating a long-term extension with the Indians, and Cleveland didn't want to make the deal if they only had him for the one remaining year on his contract. The Phillies couldn't sign and trade him, thanks to a new rule that resulted from the 1981 players' strike.

"Manny's a six-year player," Owens explained. "Under the terms of that side letter, if we sign him to a new contract, he's only obligated to play the 1983 season for the Indians. He's entitled to ask the Indians to trade him by March 15 of '84. It's something that has a lot of general managers in a bind. . . . Before this damn side letter went into effect, I might have been able to make this deal in an hour. The problem is not the quality of the players offered, but the contract status of one of the players."

Sunday came and went. Owens said, "We will make every effort to get it settled one way or another in a day or two. We're going to retrench a little and meet again sometime Monday."

The next move was to cut Trillo out of the deal. The Phillies contacted the Seattle Mariners, who were shopping second baseman Julio Cruz. A three-way trade that would send Cruz to Cleveland, in exchange for utility men Luis Aguayo and Len Matuszek from Philadelphia, was discussed. Phillies outfielder George Vukovich was identified as another potential piece for the Indians.

The inclusion of the Mariners complicated things significantly, however. Cleveland began negotiating a separate deal with Seattle, offering first baseman Mike Hargrove straight up for Cruz. Philadelphia countered by shopping Franco to the White Sox, who were offering pitching.

By Tuesday, it was looking like the Phillies would take the long flight home from Hawaii without landing Hayes.

"If we make the deal, it will be Julio Franco, a second baseman and two more players for Von Hayes," Giles said. "The problem is, everybody we approach about a second baseman wants either Franco, Juan Samuel, or Bob Dernier. It's the opinion of my people that we can only afford to trade one of those three." Giles declared that there were two chances of swinging the deal: "slim and none."

"They want 5-for-1 or 7-for-2," Owens said. "It's just too heavy, particularly when they're asking you to give up some of your good kids. We feel we can go pretty deep in numbers for the right player, but not that deep."

"Our trade discussions? Right now, that's a subject too painful to talk about," Owens concluded.

Midweek, the Phillies brain-trust retreated into their hotel suite and imposed a news blackout, only dropping hints that something big was afoot.

"I hit my low ebb just before noon Wednesday," Owens said. "It seemed like we were dead in the water because of the Indians' unwillingness to risk not being able to sign Trillo. Then, just before noon, Gabe told me that they were willing to gamble."

By Thursday night, the deal was sealed. Von Hayes was headed to Philadelphia, in exchange for Franco, and, as Giles described in his autobiography, "a solid but past-his-prime second baseman (Trillo), a reserve outfielder (Vukovich), a minor league pitcher we weren't real high on (Jay Baller), a minor league catcher we weren't real high on (Jerry Willard)."

Five for one.

Teams almost never give up five players to get one. It simply doesn't happen. The Mariners traded five prospects, including future star outfielder Adam Jones, to the Orioles for left-handed pitcher Erik Bedard in February 2008. Two months earlier, Baltimore had swung another five-for-one, getting a handful of prospects from the Houston Astros for Miguel Tejada. Seven and a half years later, baseball is still waiting for its next five-for-one.

The rare five-for-one deal for Hayes earned praise from Hall of Fame baseball writer Peter Gammons. "He's an outstanding young talent," Gammons said of Hayes. "He has great natural ability and is nowhere near his full potential."

"The fans in Philly will love him," Gammons concluded.

In retrospect, the fans might have loved him, if only he'd arrived with some company. If the Phillies had asked the Indians to throw in anyone else—a minor league stiff, an unheralded Single A player with no future or a veteran close to retirement—it would have cleared the way for Hayes. "Six for two" doesn't set the bar anywhere near as high as "five for one."

First impressions are everything, and Hayes seemed to go out of his way to make a bad one with Philadelphia fans. On the night the trade was announced, he was contacted at home in Stockton, California, and complained that the Phillies played on artificial turf.

"It's not my favorite surface," he said. "I like to play an aggressive right field. I dive for a lot of balls and come in hard on balls hit in front on me. You can't do that on turf or the ball's by you or bouncing over your head."

Hayes also sounded somewhat aloof in his reaction to joining the Phillies. "It might take a few days for it all to set in," he said. "I don't think it has really hit me yet, but I was excited by all the attention I've got, by the fact that the Phillies thought enough of me to give up five good players. And playing for the Phillies is going to be a real experience. I think it will give me a real incentive. I had been really tired after playing winter ball for two years, but this is going to make baseball very exciting for me. And being with Philly is going to make it a big challenge for me."

Still, the Phillies were building up expectations for Hayes. "He has superstar potential," manager Pat Corrales said. "He's an outstanding young player who can only get better. I don't know where he'll bat in the order, but it'll be somewhere near Mike Schmidt."

"I'm never afraid to trade four for one or five for one, if that one is the one we want," Owens said. "And Von Hayes is the one we wanted."

It's important to note that Von Hayes did everything the Phillies expected of him. Immediately after the trade, Corrales said, "He's got the potential to hit 15–25 homers, drive in 90–100 runs, and steal 30–40 bases."

In eight years with Philadelphia, Hayes had seasons where he hit 16, 19, 21, 26 and 17 home runs. He drove in 98 runs in 1986. He stole 48 bases in 1984.

From a WAR standpoint, the Phillies won the trade by a comfortable margin. Hayes more than doubled the value produced by Franco and outproduced all five players he was dealt for, combined. Furthermore, the Phillies got nearly Franco's production from the two prospects they were able to keep—Samuel and Dernier.

Hayes gave the Phillies nine years of production that ranged from solid starter to borderline All Star. What Hayes didn't do was match five players' worth of production in the eyes of the fans. Of the players traded for Hayes, Vukovich would have the shortest career, playing just three more seasons in Cleveland. Manny Trillo had seven years left in him, including an All-Star season in 1983. The other three players all played in the major leagues longer than Hayes. Jay Baller's last appearance was in 1992, 12 days after Hayes' last game. Jerry Willard lasted until 1994, and the ageless Julio Franco played 22 more seasons after leaving Philadelphia. He was selected to three All-Star teams and won five Silver Slugger awards for being the best hitter at his position.

From the outset, Hayes was saddled with the label "Five for One." Pete Rose, a gritty player who had as little patience for golden boys as the people of Philadelphia did, gave Hayes the nickname soon after they became teammates.

"For me, looking back on that first year, whenever you're traded to a new team, you want to fit in," Hayes recalled. "You want to be comfortable, and, in order to do that, you have to play. That year, right out of the gate, I got hurt in spring training. I started the season out on the disabled list. I'd never really been hurt previously in my career. It just seemed like I got off on the wrong foot. It took me awhile to get going again."

He hurt a shoulder in spring training. Then he hurt his thigh. Then he re-aggravated the shoulder problem. Hayes wasn't ready for Opening Day, and he went 0 for 4 in his Phillies debut a week later. On May 20, he was hitting .111.

"When you're already in the major leagues and all of a sudden, boom, something like that happens—you go from just one of the players to all of a sudden now you're a number-one-pick type—then it becomes kind of tough to deal with," Hayes said, adding that Phillies fans expected "a perennial most-valuable-player-type" performance from him.

There was a disconnect between what the fans expected and what Hayes delivered. "Disconnect as far as being booed out of the stadium and not being happy about it? Yeah, there was definitely a disconnect there."

Hayes simply wasn't a good fit for the situation. He was an intense player who put a lot of pressure on himself in normal situations. The added pressure of being known as "Five for One" ("541" for short) and being booed whenever he fell short was just too much to handle.

Hayes also tended to overthink things and analyze small, seemingly inconsequential details—many coaches commented on how he would think himself out of hot streaks and into slumps. As a result, his approach to the game, dating back to his comments about playing on turf, tended to sound like whining to fans already predisposed to be suspicious of him.

Later in his Phillies career, he explained away an 0-for-25 slump with, "I know how this started. The new contract required me to take a physical exam. We flew back from Pittsburgh at 4:30 [a.m.] and I had to be in the doctor's office at 8. That night we played the Mets and the game went until 2. I could hardly stand up when it was over. I was still exhausted the next day. I took back-to-back oh-fers and it got worse from there. You get in a hole like that and it's tough to get out."

Fans didn't want to hear about how an early doctor's appointment, scheduled so he could sign a rich new contract, caused an inconvenience for him.

Hayes was also a rich, attractive young bachelor, and his social life often made the papers. He dated a former Miss America for a while. He also had a relationship with a soap opera actress. All of which served to further distance him from the fans.

Hayes struggled to fit in on the veteran team as well. As the Phillies went on their World Series run in 1983, led by the aging Rose, Morgan (added in a trade to replace Trillo) and Schmidt, the media crowned them the "Wheeze Kids" (a tongue-in-cheek nod to the 1950 Phillies team known as the "Whiz Kids"). The all-time greats had little patience for a five-tool player who didn't have time to listen to advice.

"I was pretty hardheaded, and felt like, it was almost like it was touching your manhood. I have to be able to deal with this. I've got to figure out a way to deal with this on my own," Hayes said. "My whole career was like, if I could figure this out, it'll make me better in the long run. Hitting, anything. So I was very stubborn about getting advice, or getting help from the outside. It's probably one of my worst traits."

"He'll hit," Phillies hitting instructor Dennis Menke said near the end of Hayes' tenure with the club. "His only problem is that he wants everything to be perfect."

Despite Hayes' early struggles, the Phillies made the postseason in his first year with the club. Anticipating the added pressure of October, manager Pat Corrales decided to pull Hayes from the starting lineup, as they had done at times throughout the season. Unlike during the regular season, however, when he came off the bench to play in nearly 40 games, Hayes saw his playing time dwindle to nearly nothing in October. He batted just twice in the NLCS and three times in the World Series. Hayes went hitless in his five postseason at bats.

The following spring, the Phillies brought in the greatest hitter of all time, Ted Williams, to tutor Hayes during spring training. The scene was captured by legendary baseball writer Roger Angell, who was able to depict the curse of Hayes' intensity and anxiety.

Hayes "looked pale with concentration" as Williams told him he needed a smaller bat and spun stories about Stan Musial, Rogers Hornsby and Harry Heilmann.

Williams told Hayes he was "swinging down on the ball."

"Hayes looked startled," Angell wrote. "'I thought it was straight up,' he said. He swung again and then again.

"'Well, it's still down,' Ted said quietly.

"Hayes, who has a long face, looked sepulchral now, and no wonder, for no major leaguer wants to retinker his swing—not in the springtime, not ever."

The pressure of meeting the Hall of Famer and trying to absorb the advice was evident to all observers, and Williams, who made an art of gruffness and grouchiness, even changed his tone to one of gentle encouragement by the end of the session.

Hayes also tended to let his frustration show, often taking it out on water coolers or batting helmets. He once got into a shoving match with then-manager Lee Elia after he made an out in the ninth inning, threw his helmet and hit the manager with it.

"I'm not going to lie to you," Hayes said. "There was a tremendous amount of pressure involved."

As a result, Hayes saw his Phillies career alternate between hot streaks and prolonged slumps.

"There have been times when he was the hottest hitter in the league over a period of months," Elia said. "I guess he's the kind of guy that you keep looking at every year and see how close he's come for periods of time. In a six-month championship season, for two of those months, he is a premier ballplayer. I guess everybody waits."

As his career went on, Hayes began missing time due to injuries. He had elbow surgery during the 1988 season and appeared in only 104 games. In 1990, he fouled pitches off his shin and foot on back-to-back nights. When he came back, he favored the injured leg and aggravated a tendon in his arch.

Hayes also cut his finger while moving an exercise machine in his home, requiring twelve stitches. As if cutting his pinky on his home gym weren't enough to get the fans started, Hayes' explanation trolled them further. "When we leave the ballfield, we don't lock ourselves in a room until the next game. We're as susceptible to freak accidents as anybody else. I had planned to go out that day. I wish I had. It would've kept me out of trouble. But when you get bored around the house, you start looking for something to do. . . . In a way, maybe this was a blessing. When I come back, I'll be 100 percent."

Once the finger healed, Hayes was sent to Class A Clearwater on a minor league rehab assignment, but even that was high-pressure for Hayes.

"People don't understand that's a tough situation," he said years later. "I remember coming down to the minor leagues on rehab assignments after playing in the big leagues for ten years. You go down there to A ball and everybody gets a hit on the team except for you. It's the worst feeling in the world. You're put in the situation—it's actually a different kind of pressure. Everybody expects something of you. It's harder to produce in those situations sometimes."

Eventually, the pressure from the fans, and himself, was too much for Hayes to take. "At some point, you feel you deserve some respect," he told reporters in his final season with the team. "What was happening had begun to destroy my enthusiasm for the game."

GM Lee Thomas traded Hayes to the Angels on December 8, 1991. Nearly nine years to the day after he was obtained in a five-for-one deal, Hayes left town in a two-for-one, with the Phillies picking up pitcher Kyle Abbot and outfielder (and future general manager) Rubén Amaro Jr.

At the Phillies Winter Caravan—a series of autograph signings and town meetings with fans around the Philadelphia area, meant to sell season tickets—fans cheered Thomas for finally trading Hayes away. It got to the point that when PA announcer Dan Baker, who emceed the events, sensed that he was losing the crowd, he'd mention the trade again to get a positive reaction.

"That was the darndest thing, wasn't it?" Thomas said. "I was totally taken aback by that reaction. I'd like to think that there were a few people in the room who started it spontaneously and it just grew from there.

"When I first came to Philadelphia [in 1988], he was the one guy I said I wouldn't trade," Thomas recalled. "We were going to build around him. But it just didn't work out. I almost feel like it got to the point where no matter what Von did—if he went 10 for 10 and then he made an out the 11th time—he was going to let the fans get to him."

WAR COMPARISON

On paper, the Phillies won the Von Hayes trade, getting more value from him than the Indians received from their five prospects. As is always the case when discussing Von Hayes' career, the key word is *potential*.

Philadelphia expected a Hall of Fame career from their five-for-one star. Instead, it got nearly a decade of production just good enough to keep Hayes in the starting lineup. The fact that the players the Phillies gave up to acquire Hayes didn't do great things in Cleveland doesn't change the disappointment over what they received from Hayes.

PHILLIES RECEIVED	WAR PRE-TRADE	WAR POST-TRADE
Von Hayes	3.5	27
INDIANS RECEIVED	WAR PRE-TRADE	WAR POST-TRADE
Julio Franco	-0.1	13.6
Manny Trillo	6.7	0.5
Jay Baller	0.0	0.0
George Vukovich	0.3	1.8
Jerry Willard	0.0	2.3
PHILLIES KEPT (INSTEAD OF FRANCO)	WAR PRE-TRADE	WAR POST-TRADE
Juan Samuel	0.0	11.8 (with Phillies)
Bob Dernier	2.3	0.8 (with Phillies) 4.3 (overall)

CHAPTER 13

— A GIFT FROM GOD —

THE STORY BEHIND THE DAVID WELLS TRADE

Choosing the wrong package of prospects leads to years of regret.

In 1995, the Detroit Tigers unloaded David Wells, trading him to the Cincinnati Reds. They almost sent him to the New York Yankees, and thus missed out on the opportunity to add one of the game's best closers. The Reds then passed on a chance to trade Wells to New York for two future greats a few months later.

José Rijo's elbow hurt. That was nothing new. It started hurting when he was seventeen years old. Now 30, the hard-throwing right-hander had been in the major leagues for a dozen years. Elbow pain was as much a part of the job as throwing strikes.

Besides, there was nothing that could be done about it. When the pain started, in his second year of rookie ball, the teenage Rijo waited until after the season to have his family doctor in the Dominican Republic take a look. The doctor ordered an x-ray and informed him he had a bone abnormality in his elbow that was causing the discomfort.

Rijo didn't know it, but between that x-ray in 1982 and the 1995 season, the bone spur had grown to two and a half times its original size. When the Cincinnati Reds finally found out about his pain, the team sent him to see Dr. James Andrews, the orthopedic surgeon who pioneered the elbow-reconstruction procedure known as Tommy John surgery.

"I'm so old, I played with the guy who had the first Tommy John surgery," Rijo said. He and Tommy John had been teammates on the Oakland A's in 1985.

Rijo had previously had elbow trouble, diagnosed as tendinitis, in 1988 and again in 1992. In between, he had a string of major injuries on an annual basis. There was a stress fracture in his back in 1989, a shoulder strain in 1990 and a broken ankle in 1991.

Dr. Andrews gave Rijo an MRI on June 2 and diagnosed him with a recurrence of the tendinitis. The Reds placed him on the disabled list and began to worry about their starting pitching.

The only reason the Reds sent Rijo to the doctor in the first place was that they noticed he refused to throw his slider in his start on June 1. "That's why basically he threw all fastballs," Reds general manager Jim Bowden said. "That's why he didn't throw the slider when the slider was called, and the ones [he did throw] didn't work. It's because his elbow has been hurting him."

When the Reds won the 1990 title, Rijo had posted a 14–8 record during the season and went on to be named MVP of the World Series, after winning two games and allowing just one run in 15.1 innings. He won 15 games in each of the next two seasons and led the league in winning percentage (.714) in 1991. He led the league in strikeouts in 1993 and started more games than any other National League pitcher in both '93 and '94.

Rijo was the leader of the Reds' staff in '95, and, with the team tied with the Chicago Cubs for first place in the NL Central, hopes of making the postseason seemed to rest on a quick and complete recovery for his elbow.

"He said you could have him miss one start and bring him back, but he said probably if you want him healthy and you want to win a pennant, you ought to have him miss two starts and not have him throw for seven days," Bowden said.

Rijo returned from the disabled list in mid-June and was the starting pitcher for the game on June 17. He pitched one inning before a long rain delay forced him to leave the game after just 11 pitches. That was probably for the best, because the elbow became inflamed again the next day. The team doctor gave him a cortisone shot to relieve the swelling and pain. The Reds scratched him from his next start and waited to see how his arm reacted.

"This is sort of a last-resort type of measure," Bowden said. "If he has to have his elbow operated on, he's done for the year. . . . All along we've tried to at least nurse him through the year."

Rijo would make 5 more starts that year, battling pain each time. On July 18, he left a game against the Padres in the third inning and was shut down—prohibited from throwing.

The next time José Rijo would pitch in a major league game was August 17, 2001, six years and 30 days later. He would be the first player ever to pitch in a game after receiving a Hall of Fame vote.

He underwent his first Tommy John surgery on August 21, 1995.

By early July, the Reds had known they were facing the prospect of not having Rijo for the stretch run. They were in first place by 5 games at the All-Star break. The top of the rotation featured John Smiley, who was 9–1 at the time, and Pete Schourek, who was 8–4. The Reds would need at least one more reliable starter, maybe two.

Bowden began making phone calls and assembling a list of possible pitchers the team could add. He presented the list to notoriously cheap owner Marge Schott.

"We gave Marge our options, in order," said Bowden. "My recommendation, for financial reasons, was to get none of them and try to hang on with two solid starters. Marge listened, looked up with a stern eye, and said, 'Go get [David] Wells,' who will make $2 million this year and $3 million in '96."

Wells was a workhorse of a left-handed pitcher, but teams paid for his on-field performance with a seemingly never-ending string of off-field headaches. He was inconsistent on the mound, looking unbeatable in some starts and unfathomably bad in others. The uneven performance was blamed on his conditioning and bad habits. Coaches tried unsuccessfully to keep him from eating himself out of shape and to curtail his drinking and nightlife.

There were also clashes with management. During one start in 1992, when manager Cito Gaston came to the mound to remove him from the game, instead of handing the ball to his skipper, Wells fired it into the crowd and stormed off the field.

One season after he won 15 games for the Toronto Blue Jays, he was released by the team. He was immediately snatched up by the Detroit Tigers. Manager Sparky Anderson, manager of three world champions, called him, "The best left-handed starter I've ever had."

Wells battled with his weight throughout his career and at times was sidelined by diabetes and gout. He also had a notorious love for the nightlife. In Toronto, early in his career, he convinced the team that his various nighttime injuries—including a lacerated thumb from breaking a window and bruises from a fall—were due to an undiagnosed sleepwalking condition.

Despite his rocky relationship with team management at several stops on his career, Wells was popular with two of the hardest-to-please owners in Major League Baseball. In addition to getting Schott to open her purse to pay his salary, Wells also eventually developed a strong relationship with Yankees owner George Steinbrenner.

Schott and Steinbrenner were, by almost all accounts, architects of brutal work environments, with their overbearing personalities casting shadows throughout their respective organizations.

Schott and Steinbrenner both had something else in common: Each had been suspended by Major League Baseball and were in their second seasons back in control of their respective teams. Steinbrenner was suspended from 1990 to 1993 for hiring gangsters to "dig up dirt" on Dave Winfield, who was one of his players at the time. Schott was suspended for the 1993 season for racist statements, including referring to her African American players as "million-dollar (n-word)s."

Without Schott, the Reds fell to fifth place in their division, a losing season that was sandwiched in between second- and first-place finishes with Schott at the helm.

Without Steinbrenner involving himself in trade talks that would cost the organization some of its top prospects, the Yankees began to develop their farm system in the years the Boss was away from the team. Many of those developing players were on the verge of contributing at the big league level, provided Steinbrenner didn't revert to his old management style and throw them into deals.

In mid-1995, both Schott and Steinbrenner were interested in adding David Wells to their pitching rotations.

Wells had won nine straight starts and was 10–4 for a terrible Tigers team in 1995 as the Reds began their search for a replacement for Rijo. They weren't the only team with pitching injuries, however.

In his first two years with the New York Yankees, Jimmy Key was one of the best pitchers in baseball. He won 18 games in 1993 and a league-high 17 in 1994, when he finished runner-up for the American League Cy Young award. Any chance that the Yankees had at ending their playoff drought, which had reached 13 years with the cancellation of the 1994 postseason due to the players' strike, seemed to rest on Key's left arm. The team had been protective of Key during his two seasons in New York, putting him on a limit of 110 pitches or seven innings in each start.

Despite the precautions, Key needed arthroscopic surgery on his shoulder following the 1994 season. The shoulder gave him trouble again early in 1995. Key made his fifth and final start of the year on May 16. A cortisone shot on June 5 didn't help, and, like Rijo, he found himself in the office of Dr. James Andrews. He had surgery to repair a tear in his rotator cuff. The Yankees' ace was done for the year.

Yankees starter Scott Kamieniecki also faced an uncertain future. "The last game of spring training in 1995, I felt something I never felt before, and I knew something was wrong," the 30-year-old righty said.

Thus began a two-year stretch of elbow problems for Kamieniecki. He missed more than two months early in the 1995 season and returned in mid-July. His likelihood of making it to the end of the season seemed shaky at best.

The Yankees had the best record in the American League in 1994, but as late as June 20, 1995, they were in last place in the American League East. The front office made it clear that the team would need to show it could contend before the purse strings would be loosened to bring in reinforcements.

Owner George Steinbrenner visited the team on a road trip in early July and dismissed questions about the Yankees trading for a pitcher, saying his payroll was already high enough.

Manager Buck Showalter agreed with the decision. "We talked more about the people we have here," Showalter said, "and what we could do to improve them. I'm certainly not going to ask someone who has spent $50 million on our club already to spend more money."

As a result, the first place that the Yankees looked for pitching wasn't the trade market, but their Triple-A affiliate in Columbus, Ohio. The Yankees promoted several promising young pitchers and gave them shots at filling in for the injured starters. Left-hander Andy Pettitte made his MLB debut as a reliever in late April and his first start on May 27. He would win 12 games that season. Fellow left-hander Sterling Hitchcock was another success story. After pitching out of the bullpen in 1994, he was moved into the starting rotation and won 11 games for the Yankees.

The young right-handers were more of a mixed bag. Brian Boehringer also made his MLB debut in late April 1995. After four relief appearances and three starts, he had a blown save, a 0–3 record, and a 13.75 ERA. He was returned to Columbus.

A 25-year-old Panamanian named Mariano Rivera made his MLB debut in 1995, too. He was shelled in his first start, allowing five runs in 3.1 innings on May 23. After a second start, and his first career major league win, Rivera was sent back to Columbus. He returned in June and gave up 7 runs in 4 innings, then 5 runs in 2.1 innings. He went down to Triple-A again.

In a game on June 30, veteran starting pitcher Mélido Pérez had to leave his start after 2.2 innings due to soreness and tightness in his shoulder—the same shoulder that had been surgically repaired the previous year.

After talking to GM Gene Michael about Pérez's health status, Showalter noted that Michael understood that the team was going to need another pitcher by July 4, Pérez's next scheduled start. For the first time, the Yankees manager mentioned the possibility of the Yankees trading for a starter.

"There are some quality pitchers available," Showalter said. "But only if we're willing to give up guys we think have bright futures. And I don't think we're willing to do that. . . . I trust Gene to do what he thinks is in the best interests of our organization."

"We're not going to mortgage our system with some of the quality people we have," he added. "At the same time, we're going to try and compete here. It's a fine line. Gene has walked it very well. I'm sure he'll be able to continue to do that."

Rivera got the call and responded with what would be the best start of his career. He pitched eight shutout innings against the White Sox, striking out 11 and allowing just 2 hits. That helped change the nature of a deal that, despite the Yankees' denials, was already in the works.

New York had reached out to some of the teams with veteran pitchers available on the trade market. That included Toronto's David Cone and Detroit's Wells.

Gene Michael contacted the Blue Jays and Tigers and asked for a list of Yankee prospects that each team would be interested in obtaining in exchange for their stud pitchers. However, he first gave the teams a list of his own—the untouchables. There were four prospects that the Yankees wouldn't consider trading under any circumstances: Andy Pettitte, Sterling Hitchcock,

Triple-A shortstop Derek Jeter, who had made a brief appearance with the Yankees early in the year, and Double-A outfielder Rubén Rivera.

Mariano Rivera was not on that list. He was promising, but with a fastball that was limited to 88–91 mph following 1992 arm surgery, he didn't have dominating stuff. The Yankees would consider trading him.

The Blue Jays wanted some of the Yankees' best pitching talent for Cone. The demands from Toronto GM Gord Ash included some combination of reliever Bob Wickman, Mariano Rivera and the top pitching prospect in the organization at the time, Matt Drews. Drews had been the Yankees' first-round draft pick in 1993 and was in the midst of a 15-win, 140-strikeout season at Class A.

Michael chose to wait out the Blue Jays and hope the price would come down. There was plenty of pitching talent available on the trade market, including Ken Hill, Jim Abbott, Bret Saberhagen, Mike Morgan and Kevin Tapani. Michael had plenty of options, and he was confident there wouldn't be a bidding war, considering the glut on the market.

He turned his attention to the Tigers. The list they submitted of players they were interested in for Wells included Mariano Rivera. Michael began negotiating a deal with Detroit.

"I never said yes," Michael said years later. "And right about that time, Mariano's velocity in the minors jumped to 95–96. I didn't believe it when I saw our report, but I checked it out with scouts from other teams who were there, and it was true. At that point there was no way I was trading him."

Rivera took two weeks off to rest a sore shoulder, and he claimed that resulted in the jump in velocity.

Brian Cashman, a Yankees front-office employee who would eventually become general manager, said the sudden increase in Rivera's velocity was "one of the amazing mysteries of the game."

In his first game back, Rivera threw a rain-shortened 5.2 inning no-hitter against the Rochester Red Wings. "It's the first time I've pitched in 15 days," he said after the game. "I was feeling great. I went out to do my job. I threw the way I know I can throw. . . . I know I'll be back with the Yankees. I never lost my confidence. Even if I had struggled, I know I can pitch."

"He throws a high fastball and he threw it right by us," said Rochester manager Marv Foley.

His catcher that day was another future Yankee: Jorge Posada. "They had guys who were in the big leagues and guys that were future prospects," Posada later said of Rochester. "He was ridiculous, going through them like nothing. I knew Mariano from 1991, but not until 1995 did everything click."

Rivera was officially off the market—an honorary untouchable. Michael called him back up to the bigs, and on July 4, everyone saw what the new Rivera could do.

"The scouting report we had said that he throws about 85 or 86," White Sox outfielder Dave Martinez said after that game. "He was throwing a lot harder than that."

"Mariano had as good a fastball as I've seen him have," Showalter said later in the month.

So good, in fact, that Rivera would end up losing his spot in the starting rotation. The team decided to convert him to the bullpen, where he could retire batters with his newfound speed.

"It was a gamble," Michael said. "You never know for sure, but we guessed right. . . . He was sneaky fast and he had such great control. We thought he might fit as a late-inning guy."

As Michael had expected, other teams took advantage of the wide array of available pitchers. Four days before the July 31 trade deadline, the AL Central leading Indians acquired Ken Hill from the Cardinals, and the AL West leading Angels got Jim Abbott from the White Sox. That knocked out two of the teams that had been bidding for the Blue Jays' Cone. Sure enough, Toronto's price began to fall.

One day later, on July 28, David Cone was a Yankee. The Blue Jays didn't get any of the prospects they'd originally requested. Instead the trade netted them Double-A pitcher Marty Janzen and two lesser pitching prospects, Jason Jarvis and Mike Gordon.

Over in the National League, Cincinnati was still in first place in the Central Division, although the lead had been trimmed to three and a half games. Part of the reason the Reds were able to remain in front is that, like the Yankees, they were able to find a capable injury replacement from within their own system. C. J. Nitkowski, the Reds' top draft pick in 1994, made his major league debut on June 3, one year after being drafted.

"In fact, I made my first start exactly a year to the day after I signed," he recalled.

"He's a young guy who can throw three pitches over the plate at any time in the count," pitching coach Don Gullett said. He went on to say that, even if Rijo was able to return to the team, they'd find a spot for the promising rookie.

"He's temporary, but he's thrown seven shutout innings so far and he's looked very good out on the mound," Gullett said of Nitkowski. "It's great experience for him and it gives us a chance to evaluate where he is. If he keeps pitching that well, we're not going to run him out of the big leagues, I don't think. We'll have to find a place for him, because he was drafted number one for a reason."

Nitkowski struggled as the year wore on, however. In three July starts, he gave up 15 earned runs in 9.1 innings and was sent back to Triple-A to recover.

Another starting pitcher, Tim Pugh, pulled up lame with a bad back, sending the Reds scrambling again to find quality starters. On July 22, they resorted to giving a start to Rick Reed, a replacement player the team had tried out when the major leaguers were out on strike in spring training.

That same day, the Reds made a trade to bring in reinforcements. They dealt center fielder and two-sport star Deion Sanders to San Francisco to get starter Mark Portugal and reliever Dave Burba.

"It would be very difficult to hold off Houston without another starter," Jim Bowden said. "We need pitching. We've had too many injuries, and our young guys have not stepped forward. We can't go with two solid starters and three maybes."

The Reds reached out to the Tigers to see if they could make a deal for Wells. They didn't know it at the time, but another suitor was pursuing the big left-hander, Cincinnati's cross-state rival. The Cleveland Indians, prior to obtaining Hill, were also in negotiations for Wells.

Cleveland offered right-hander Albie Lopez, a 24-year-old reliever and spot starter who couldn't get a regular spot on the first-place Indians' staff. He had dominated in the minor leagues while waiting for a shot with the Indians. He went 12–4 in 1992, 10–4 in 1993, and 13–3 in 1994 in the minors.

Cleveland started Lopez in the first game of a July 14 doubleheader in 1995, likely showcasing him for Tigers scouts. It was his first MLB appearance in twenty days and his only start until September 3. He struck out 5 and allowed just 2 hits in 5.2 innings.

Detroit didn't take the bait, however, and closed on a deal with the Reds.

David Wells did his part to keep his value high. He simply would not lose. After dropping to 1–3 on the year with a loss on May 18, he didn't lose another game as a Tiger. Amidst the trade rumors swirling in early July, Wells was named to his first All-Star team. His winning streak reached 10 games, continuing on into his stint with his new team. In the months of June and July, Wells gave up 4 runs in a start only one time, 3 or fewer ten times.

As the deadline approached on July 31, the Reds and Tigers came to an agreement. Wells would go to Cincinnati. In exchange, Detroit would get C.J. Nitkowski, pitcher Dave Tuttle and a player to be named later.

Nitkowski said later that he was in "denial" leading up to the deadline. "The Reds drafted me ninth overall in 1994," he said. "At the deadline in 1995, there were rumors I would be on the move. I thought that was impossible. My team just drafted me thirteen months ago; how could it possibly trade me already? I ignored the rumors. This predated cell phones. I walked into my apartment in Triple-A Indianapolis in the early evening to my landline phone ringing. 'Hey, C. J., we just traded you to Detroit for David Wells.' I was in disbelief."

Wells had a good idea he would be traded, but he was still surprised. "At 32 years old, with a contract rising above the two million mark, there was no way I was going to fit into Detroit's dirt-cheap, baby-faced future," he wrote in his autobiography. "When the Cincinnati Reds came calling, offering two very young pitching prospects for one David Wells, the Tigers bit hard. I never even saw it coming."

The Reds didn't play on July 31. Wells claims he learned about the trade from ESPN's *Baseball Tonight*.

"All of a sudden, I see my name and picture on ESPN in a video-doctored Cincinnati Reds hat. Peter Gammons is telling America that I'd just been traded. I actually remember punching Gammons' face on the screen, just for being the messenger. 'What the (bleep) is going on here?' I shout at him. . . . I literally sat there in my house crying. 'You've got to be kidding me.'"

Wells said good-bye to his Detroit teammates, many of whom asked him to take them along.

"The flag's up," said Detroit DH Cecil Fielder. "They must have thrown in the towel. We don't have a run going, so they gave away our best pitcher. They quit. They quit on August 1, but we've got to play until October 2."

The Tigers were 7 games under .500 at the time, 8.5 games out of first place. They were only 4 games out in the Wild Card, but there were seven teams in front of them in that race.

"David Wells is having an outstanding season," Detroit GM Joe Klein said, "but we feel with the amount of good young arms we are developing in our system, with the addition of two more, we are putting together what could turn out to be an outstanding young pitching staff within the foreseeable future."

The mood was much lighter in Cincinnati.

"When you get to this point in July and you have a chance to improve your team you have to go out and do it, even if it means giving up a top prospect," Bowden said.

"We're still envious of the Braves' starting pitching," said Reds manager Davey Johnson, "but not as envious as we were a week ago."

Four of the six division leaders added starting pitchers at the 1995 trade deadline. Only the Braves and Red Sox stood pat with their rotations.

David Cone won his first four starts with the Yankees and went 9–2 for them overall, as New York clinched the first-ever American League Wild Card. The Yankees won the first 2 games of the best-of-five division series against Seattle, but lost the next 3. The two wins were provided by Cone and Mariano Rivera. Now a reliever, Rivera pitched in 3 games in the series and didn't allow a run.

Wells won four of his first five decisions as a Red. He faded down the stretch, however, finishing just 6–5 with them. Still, the Reds wrapped up the Central Division title and were headed to the postseason. They swept the division series against the Dodgers, then lost in four straight to the Braves in the NLCS. Wells earned the series-clinching win against the Dodgers. In Game Three of the NLCS, he pitched five scoreless innings before giving up a 3-run homer in the sixth to lose.

On November 16, the Reds sent infielder Mark Lewis to Detroit as the player to be named later. Lewis had been the second overall pick by Cleveland in the 1988 draft, but he struggled with a .258 average in four seasons with the Indians. In his first year in Cincinnati, in 1995, he hit .339 in a part-time role. Lewis went 2 for 6 in the postseason and hit a grand slam to break open the final game of the divisional series sweep of Los Angeles.

In Detroit, Lewis was given the unenviable task of replacing Tigers legend Lou Whitaker at second base. Whitaker retired in the offseason, as Detroit went to a full-blown youth movement. Lewis lasted one year in Detroit and changed teams seven times in the final seven years of his career.

Like Lewis, C. J. Nitkowksi struggled to live up to his draft status. He went a combined 3–7 with Detroit over the next two seasons, posting ERAs of 7.09 and 8.08. He would go on to be traded three more times and released eight times in a ten-year MLB career.

After getting traded to Detroit, Dave Tuttle posted a 21–33 overall record in five minor league seasons. He didn't make it past Class A in two years in the Detroit organization and topped out at Triple-A with the Diamondbacks.

By the time Cincinnati finished paying the price to Detroit to acquire Wells, he had already pitched his last game for the Reds. Cincinnati was forced to deal Wells in the offseason, after owner Marge Schott tightened the purse strings again. Bowden had to cut $10 million from the $38 million payroll.

Wells still has hard feelings about playing for Schott.

"The woman was psycho," he said, years later. "She's nuts—cheap as can be. You had to go in, if you wanted a pair of socks or sleeves or stirrups, whatever it was, you had to go up in her office, and it was like a cave in there . . . you had to buy them from her. She taxed our meal money. We would fly on a plane with everybody else, it was commercial. But we would be in the front section, or the back section, wherever they did that. And then we'd get our meal money, and we'd have pennies and nickels and dimes in it. I hated her! She was terrible. She was a bad person."

In December, the Tigers traded Wells to the Baltimore Orioles. "The trade was made for financial reasons," Bowden said.

"We've definitely accomplished a lot in the last month," Bowden added. "It's fun building a team. It's not as much fun taking it down."

Wells would eventually join the Yankees and win a World Series with them in 1998. Wells won one game in that World Series, and it was saved by Mariano Rivera.

In early 1997, while warming up in the bullpen, Rivera had another miraculous step forward in his development as a pitcher. No less remarkable than the sudden, inexplicable increase in velocity, Rivera's cut fastball, or cutter, suddenly took on remarkable movement that made it uncatchable by the bullpen catcher, let alone hittable by opposing batters. Rivera considered both developments to be gifts from God. He went on to save an MLB record 652 games and is a sure bet for the Hall of Fame.

It almost never happened. The Yankees made another run at Wells in December 1995 before losing out to the division-rival Orioles.

"The asking price was too high," Gene Michael said. "They wanted two of our top minor leaguers. That's why we backed off. We couldn't do that."

That December, Hall of Fame *New York Times* baseball writer Murray Chass cited an unnamed source involved in the trade talks. The source told Chass that, late in the negotiations, George Steinbrenner called Reds GM Jim Bowden and offered him catcher Jorge Posada and pitcher Mariano Rivera for David Wells.

WAR COMPARISON

David Wells had a strong career after his trade to Cincinnati. Unfortunately for Marge Schott and company, most of it was with teams other than the Reds. According to WAR, the players the Tigers received for Wells actually made the team slightly worse.

None of that, however, is what makes the trade a disaster for Detroit. Instead, the real tragedy for the Tigers is what they could have received for Wells from a desperate George Steinbrenner. Acquiring Jorge Posada and Mariano Rivera would have changed the face of the American League for fifteen years.

As if making the offer wasn't bad enough for the Yankees, the fact that Posada and Rivera both produced more than three of New York's four "untouchables" makes the near-miss even more harrowing.

REDS RECEIVED	WAR PRE-TRADE	WAR POST-TRADE
David Wells	10.1 with Tigers	0.8 with Reds, 20.6 over next five years
TIGERS RECEIVED	WAR PRE-TRADE	WAR POST-TRADE
CJ Nitkowski	-0.6	-0.9
David Tuttle	0.0	0.0
Mark Lewis	0.7	-0.4
YANKEES FINAL OFFER	WAR PRE-TRADE	WAR POST-TRADE
Jorge Posada	0.0	42.7
Mariano Rivera	0.1	56.5
YANKEES UNTOUCHABLES	WAR PRE-TRADE	WAR POST-TRADE
Derek Jeter	-0.2	72
Rubén Rivera	0.0	0.9 with Yankees, 4.1 over next five years
Andy Pettitte	2	32.2
Sterling Hitchcock	2.1	0.7 with Yankees, 6.5 over next five years

CHAPTER 14

"I'M THE DECIDER, AND
— I DECIDE WHAT'S BEST" —

THE STORY BEHIND THE SAMMY SOSA TRADE

The trade bad enough to help win an election.

It's rare that a trade is bad enough to get a president elected, but that's the deal the Rangers pulled off in 1989. Texas traded Wilson Álvarez, who would go on to win 67 games with the Chicago White Sox over the next few years. The Rangers also gave up a rookie outfielder who struck out too much: Sammy Sosa. While on the campaign trail in 2000, former Rangers owner George W. Bush was asked about his biggest regret. "Trading Sammy Sosa," he answered.

Barney Bush lived in the White House for both of George W. Bush's presidential terms and had a series of videos on the White House website, but the true title of "First Dog" belonged to Spot Fetcher.

Spot was the only one of the Bush family dogs—they had three at various times during his two terms in office—that George W. allowed into the Oval Office. "She understands the decorum of the Oval," he said, "so she gets to go in."

Spot was born in the White House in March 1989, to then First Dog Millie Bush, when George W.'s father George H.W. Bush was president. A month and a half later, First Lady Barbara Bush brought the puppy to Texas, as a gift to her grandchildren.

Mrs. Bush was in town to throw out the first pitch at a Texas Rangers game against the Yankees on May 4. Her oldest son, George W., had just led a group to purchase the team during the offseason. Despite only putting up a small sum of his own money, W. was the managing partner and face of the franchise.

W. gave out books to children in attendance, to help support the First Lady's literacy program. Barbara took the mound in high heels, wearing a blue Rangers warm-up jacket over her red flowered dress. When she saw the catcher set up at home plate, 60 feet, 6 inches away, she waved for him to come closer. When he was about 15 feet away, Mrs. Bush tossed a strike and became the first First Lady in history to throw out a first pitch.

Spot didn't have a name at the time. The Bush family voted on what to name the new pet. George W. wanted to call the dog Rangerette, but he was outvoted by wife Laura and the couple's seven-year-old twin daughters, Jenna and Barbara. The dog would be named Spot—

full name Spot Fetcher—in honor of young Barbara's favorite player, Rangers shortstop Scott Fletcher.

Fletcher was the first athlete in the Dallas–Fort Worth Metroplex—also home of the NFL's Dallas Cowboys and the NBA's Dallas Mavericks—to earn a million-dollar salary. He signed a three-year, $3.9 million contract prior to the 1989 season, despite the fact that general manager Tom Grieve said Fletcher had "a below-average arm, below average power and average speed."

Fletcher wouldn't get to collect a million dollars from the Rangers in 1989, however. Less than three months after George W. Bush's daughters voted to name the family pet after him, he was traded away. The Rangers traded Fletcher, along with two prospects, to the White Sox for DH Harold Baines.

More than a decade later, while running for president, George W. Bush would make the trade a campaign issue, but not because he allowed the team to trade away his daughter's favorite Ranger. Instead, Bush focused on one of the prospects the team threw into the deal.

On January 7, 2000, the candidates for the Republican presidential nomination met in Columbia, South Carolina, for a debate. Bush, the reigning governor of Texas, had a comfortable lead in the polls, with more than half of Republican voters saying they'd choose him for the nominee. Senator John McCain was in second place with 18 percent support in the polls. Senator Orrin Hatch, businessman Steve Forbes, former ambassador Alan Keyes and the Family Research Council's Gary Bauer were all polling in single digits.

Midway through the debate, Stephanie Trotter, a reporter for NBC's Greenville, South Carolina, outlet, WYFF addressed the candidates. "Gentlemen, I'm curious," Trotter asked. "As an adult, what is the biggest mistake that you've made, and what lesson did you learn from it?"

Hatch asked Trotter to repeat the question, which she did. Governor Bush then volunteered to answer first, an offer that moderator Brian Williams of NBC declined.

Hatch asked Trotter to repeat the question once more, then made a joke about having made so many mistakes, it was hard to choose just one. He then said that his biggest mistake was joining the 2000 presidential race so late. "But don't worry," he added. "Don't count me out."

Keyes went next and took offense at the question. "I think about the biggest mistake I might make as an adult would be to treat that as if it's a question that is appropriate to be asked," he said, drawing applause from the crowd. "I think that we have to understand that there ought to be in our public life a certain decorum, a certain dignity. There are things that I'll tell my priest in the confessional that I will not tell you or any other American."

Keyes finally said that his biggest regret "was not to have spoken out on the issue of the life of the unborn before I did."

McCain made a joke about his experience as a prisoner of war, saying his biggest mistake was volunteering for the mission where he was captured. He then said that his biggest mistake was his involvement in the Keating Five Savings & Loan scandal in the late 1980s.

Bauer took a shot at Bill Clinton, saying that the current president could write an essay on the mistakes he'd made. He then mentioned a time that he met with President Ronald Reagan and talked about poll results. "His face turned blood-red and he pointed his finger at me and he said, 'Gary, don't cite polls. Tell me the best thing to do for America,'" Bauer recalled.

Williams next presented the question to Bush. "Well, as you know, I've had a perfect background," the candidate said, drawing applause.

"Haven't we all, sir?" Williams fired back.

"After all, I was raised by Barbara Bush," Bush said, drawing laughter and applause for a second time.

"As you may remember, I was in the business world at one time," Bush continued. "I was the managing partner, managing general partner of the mighty Texas Rangers. I signed off on that wonderful transaction—Sammy Sosa for Harold Baines."

Bush brought up the trade again on March 6, when he was a guest on the *Tonight Show* with Jay Leno.

Leno asked Bush about mistakes in his past, and Bush cut him off, saying, "Because you want me to admit how terrible the Sammy Sosa trade was. That's why you brought this up—I know these gotcha [questions]. . . . It is because I want to carry Chicago in the general election, right?"

It made sense that Bush would lean on his baseball experience while running for president. Bush's tenure as managing partner of the Rangers helped jump-start his political career.

Bush would sit field-side at home games, wearing custom-made cowboy boots embossed with the team logo, and interact with fans. "The Rangers helped George be seen as someone other than an Ivy League guy who was son of the president," team president Tom Schieffer told ESPN during the 2000 campaign. "What baseball allowed George to do is show his true personality, that he's very egalitarian and democratic. . . . People would say, 'George, he's OK. He's like you and me.'"

As managing partner, Bush also pushed for a new ballpark for the team. Within five years, the team moved into the $191 million ballpark in Arlington.

The unveiling of the Ballpark coincided with Bush's run for the governor of Texas, and he had a very tangible reminder for voters of what he was capable of accomplishing. "When all those people in Austin say, 'He ain't never done anything,'" Bush said at the time, "well, this is it."

With legendary Texan and Rangers pitcher Nolan Ryan campaigning on his behalf, Bush defeated incumbent Ann Richards in an upset in 1994 and was reelected in a landslide four years later.

Bush's office in the state capitol reflected his love of the sport. One observer cracked that he had "more autographed baseballs than books" in the office.

A year before his run for governor, Bush was approached by a search committee about his interest in serving as commissioner of baseball, replacing family friend Fay Vincent, who had been ousted in a vote of owners, over Bush's protests. Bush and his future Secretary of State, Colin Powell, were the only two potential candidates to turn down the offer. Bush had a loftier goal in mind.

While campaigning for president in 2000, Bush played the John Fogerty baseball anthem "Centerfield" at political events, used a Texas Rangers garment bag to carry his suits and toted his workout clothes in a Rangers duffel.

As Bush rocketed into national prominence, going from businessman and baseball team owner to the highest office in the land, one player had a similar upward trajectory.

"People forget," Tom Grieve said, "at the time we traded him, Sammy Sosa was six feet tall, one hundred seventy pounds. Anyone that says they knew what he would become must have had a crystal ball."

"He wasn't a power hitter," Grieve continued. "Speed was his thing at the time. We projected him as being a right fielder with his strong arm, but the power wasn't there. We thought it would develop, but we had him projected as a 20–25 homer hitter, not 60."

A seventeen-year-old, 165-pound Sosa hit just four home runs in 229 at bats during his first season as a pro in 1986. The following year, at Class A Gastonia, he hit 11 in 519 at bats. He had 9 in 1988. In three full seasons in the minors, he had 24 home runs, or 4 fewer than he would hit in one month, in June 1998.

Sosa had 42 stolen bases in 1988 and topped 20 steals in three straight minor-league seasons. (He was also caught stealing 46 times over those three seasons.)

Sosa would pack on 60 pounds of muscle over the next few years, becoming one of the faces of baseball's steroid era. His 1998 home-run duel with Mark McGwire resulted in both players topping Roger Maris' single-season record, which had stood for 37 years. Sosa had 66 home runs that year, finishing second to McGwire's 70 and becoming one of the most popular players in the sport.

Sosa's ascension to superstardom made the 1989 trade appear to be a lopsided disaster, worthy of mockery in a political campaign. In addition to Bush's own lines poking fun at the deal, the opposition took aim at the candidate for the eleven-year-old trade.

"Does America want a president who would trade Sammy Sosa?" Clinton advisor Paul Begala asked *Texas Monthly* magazine during the 2000 campaign.

While preparing for the presidential debate, Al Gore was prepared to defend any attacks on his judgment (which never came) with the line, "At least I never traded Sammy Sosa."

Fifteen years after the election of 2000, postdebate fact-checks are part of most news networks' political coverage. Like many politicians' claims, Bush's "blame" for the Sosa trade has a grain of truth, but exaggeration and spin have obscured the full story.

"It's a good line," Grieve said, "but it's not accurate. President Bush was the managing partner, and any time we made a trade, the managing partners had to sign off on the trade. But that was mostly to make sure they were okay with the finances of the deal. I don't recall them ever refusing to sign off on anything, and for them to turn down a trade because of baseball reasons? That couldn't have happened. It just wouldn't have made sense."

"We had reports from our farm director on the prospects we included and our major and minor league scouts on the players we were getting. We'd sat down as an organization to assess our strengths and weaknesses and set our priorities before entering into a trade negotiation. The managing partners didn't have access to any of that information."

In other words, with Baines' and Fletcher's salaries matching up almost exactly—a survey by *USA Today* found that Baines made $4,281 more for the year—Bush's role in the trade was merely as a rubber stamp. Any blame should be heaped on the shoulders of team president Schieffer and general manager Grieve.

"The mistake in that trade wasn't including Sammy Sosa," Grieve said. "We made two mistakes with that trade, but Sammy wasn't one of them."

In 1981, Al Oliver hit .309 for the Rangers and was the starting DH in 101 of the team's 105 games in that strike-shortened season. Despite an additional 57 games played in each of the next seven seasons, only one Rangers DH matched Oliver's 101 starts at the position— Larry Parrish, the man Oliver was traded for in the 1981 offseason.

Parrish started 118 games at DH in 1987, while six other Rangers split the other 44 games. Parrish hit a career-high 32 home runs that season and drove in 100 runs, making the All-Star team for just the second time in his 15-year career.

Parrish turned 34 after the 1987 season and got old in a hurry. His average dropped 51 points, to .217 in 1988. He hit fewer than half as many homers (14) and drove in just 52 runs. Parrish still led the Rangers in starts at DH in 1988, with 67, but a total of 13 players were listed in the lineup at the spot. The Rangers released Parrish in July, and he was out of baseball by the start of 1989.

In the first four months of the 1989 season, the Rangers tried fifteen different starters at DH, with no player starting more than 32 games in the season's first 101 contests. It was clear that they needed a dependable bat for the DH spot, if they were going to contend in the American League West. Even with a hole in the order at that position, Texas was doing better than expected. The team was in first place for much of April and, as late as June 28, was just 2 games out of first place.

The first-place Oakland A's would be hard to catch, however. Led by sluggers Mark McGwire and Jose Canseco, a starting rotation that featured four 17-game winners, including ace Dave Stewart, and the game's best closer in Dennis Eckersley, the A's made it to the World Series in 1988 before losing to the Dodgers in an upset.

Adding to their embarrassment of riches, Oakland acquired MLB's best leadoff hitter midway through the 1989 season, stealing Rickey Henderson from the Yankees for prospects Greg Cadaret, Eric Plunk and Luis Polonia.

"We weren't going to catch Oakland," Grieve said, decades later. "That was our first mistake. When we took over, we had a plan to rely on young players, take our time and build things the right way. We let the pressure of contending earlier than we expected get to us. It wasn't the time to trade prospects for veterans. It was a year or two early. We tried to move up the schedule."

The Rangers had the prospects to acquire a big-hitting designated hitter; it was just a question of which one they were willing to give up. "We knew Sosa was a good prospect," Grieve said. "But we had Juan González."

González was eleven months younger than Sosa and signed with the franchise a year later. While Sosa was projected to be a speedy singles hitter, González's power had developed in the minor leagues. He was in the middle of a 30 double, 21 homer, 85 RBI season at Double-A Tulsa.

Still, it would be tough enough for the Rangers to find room for one of the two prospects in their outfield, let alone both. In left field, they had 25-year-old Pete Incaviglia. The eighth-overall pick in the 1985 draft, Incaviglia made his MLB debut without ever playing in the minors and hit 30 home runs as a rookie.

Covering center field was 26-year-old Cecil Espy. He'd finished eighth in Rookie of the Year voting the previous year and would steal 45 bases in 1989.

In right, Texas had 23-year-old Rubén Sierra, who would lead the American League in triples, RBI and slugging percentage in 1989 and finish runner-up in the MVP race. His arm was even better than Sosa's. He led outfielders in assists in 1987 and would finish second and third each of the next two years.

Both González and Incaviglia were projected to be the Rangers' DH of the future, but the team needed someone to tide them over at that spot. Incaviglia had suffered a neck strain in mid-June and went to the disabled list. The Rangers decided to give Sosa a trial run as his replacement, while also showcasing him for potential trade partners.

Sosa made his MLB debut on June 16, batting leadoff and playing center. He singled on the second pitch he saw and was promptly caught stealing. He doubled and scored later in the game but also made an error in the field.

Sosa hit his first career home run five games later, off of Roger Clemens. At age twenty, Sosa became the youngest Rangers player ever to homer.

He cooled off quickly, however, going hitless for 21 straight at bats at one point. He was sent to Triple-A in mid-July, when Incaviglia returned. At the time, Sosa was hitting .238 with no walks and 2 errors. He'd been thrown out both times he attempted to steal.

In late June, catcher Geno Petralli, who had caught the first pitch from the managing partner's mom earlier in the season, suffered a knee injury. That left the Rangers in search of a left-handed hitter, as well as catching depth.

Grieve began shopping Sosa to teams that could meet one or both of his needs. He spoke to the Blue Jays about trading Sosa for backup catcher Greg Myers, and in late July, Toronto GM Pat Gillick flew to Oklahoma City on a scouting mission.

But by then, Grieve was working on a better deal involving Sosa. "Larry Himes was the general manager of the White Sox," Grieve recalled, "and his projections for Sosa were a little higher than ours. He really loved him as a prospect."

The Sox were in last place at the time and would finish 30 games below .500 that season. Himes was looking to add prospects by cutting loose some of his veteran talent. He offered Harold Baines, a 30-year-old DH who batted left-handed.

Baines was remarkably consistent. He'd hit 20 or more homers six times and had at least 80 RBI for the last seven seasons. He would hit .309 in 1989, the fifth time in six years he'd hit at least .290, and he made his fourth All-Star team in five years.

The Rangers offered Scott Fletcher, the million-dollar shortstop. Chicago already had an established shortstop in Ozzie Guillén, but the team hoped to convince Fletcher to move to second base, giving them a solid double-play combination. The White Sox had been using reserve infielder Fred Manrique at second base, and Himes was willing to send him to Texas as well.

That left the issue of Texas prospects to even up the deal. The two sides agreed on Sosa. "They wanted Juan [González] but would take Sammy," Grieve recalled. "We wouldn't have traded Juan under any circumstance."

Then Grieve made his second mistake.

"We never should have included Wilson Álvarez," he said.

A nineteen-year-old left-handed pitcher, Álvarez became the youngest player in the majors that year. Rangers pitcher Charlie Hough—22 years Álvarez's senior—was forced to miss a July 24 start due to injury, and Álvarez was called up from Double-A to fill in. He faced just five batters, giving up a single, back-to-back homers, and 2 walks while taking a loss.

Álvarez was more effective in the minor leagues. He won 7 games at Class A, posting a 2.11 ERA. Promoted to Double-A Tulsa, he went 2–2 with a 2.06 ERA.

Going against the long-range plan and giving up a lot of talented prospects, Grieve finalized the deal and presented it to ownership for final approval: Fletcher, Álvarez and Sosa for Baines and Manrique.

When the deal was first announced, it appeared that the Rangers got the better end.

"For the past several years we've been trying to acquire a designated-hitter specialist," Grieve said at the time. "We feel we now have the best designated hitter in baseball."

"We're not thrilled about dealing two of our best prospects," he added. "But to get a player of Harold Baines' caliber, you have to trade quality."

Himes was left trying to explain to White Sox fans why he traded Baines, one of the team's more popular players and a bright spot during a disappointing season. Baines had played all ten years of his career in Chicago. He was the franchise's career leader in home runs and in the top five on the White Sox career lists for games, runs, RBI and hits.

"Baines came as close as anyone to being Mr. White Sox," Himes said. "It's unfortunate that we had to deal him, but I feel strongly about this trade improving our club."

Baines' former teammates didn't feel the same way.

"I don't have much good to say about that," White Sox catcher Carlton Fisk, a future Hall of Famer, said. "Harold and Freddy for one major-league player. The No. 3 man right out of our lineup. Take the No. 3 hitter out of any lineup throughout the major leagues and see what happens."

"Two major leaguers for one," Fisk continued. "And not just a major leaguer. Harold Baines. Harold Baines. You know what I mean? Harold Baines."

Despite his history with the team, Baines was ready for a new start. The White Sox were on a West Coast road trip when he heard the news. Within an hour of being told he was traded, Baines was packed and checked out of his Anaheim hotel room. He was in the Rangers' clubhouse 90 minutes before game time that same night.

"I love to play baseball," he said. "I didn't want to waste any time. . . . After being in one place for ten years you get settled in. But I was tired of losing. I'm happy to be going to a new team with a new direction."

The Rangers were just as excited to get Baines in the lineup. First baseman Rafael Palmeiro, who would go on to have 3,020 hits and 569 homers in the major leagues, was moved to second in the lineup, with Baines taking the three hole. Batting behind him would be Julio Franco and Rubén Sierra, who were among the league leaders in RBI.

"Those are four guys who've hit third in the major leagues," Texas manager Bobby Valentine said. "That's a pretty good lineup. Those four are as good as anybody in the major leagues."

"This is a hitting team with a chance to win it," Baines said. "This is a good hitter's ballpark. I'm going to get a chance to see better pitches."

Fletcher wasn't thrilled with the move, after having chosen the Rangers as a free agent in the offseason, but he understood the business. Just eight years since his major league debut, this was his third time being traded. The White Sox had traded him to Texas less than four years earlier.

"I was at home when Tom Grieve called me and said I was traded to the White Sox. That was some wake-up call," Fletcher recalled years later. "Jeff Torborg called me and said he wanted me in the lineup that night in Anaheim. I had to pack like two months' worth of clothes in a few minutes. The trade was a surprise, but at least I knew a number of people in the organization; I knew the city and I was comfortable being with the White Sox."

At the time, however, Fletcher sounded lukewarm. "If you've been around baseball long enough, nothing is really a total surprise," he told the press.

Fletcher was no more effusive about the position change. "It doesn't really matter," Fletcher said of moving to second base. "I enjoy playing both. Ozzie has been a very good shortstop for them."

White Sox manager Jeff Torborg was more optimistic after his conversation with Fletcher. "I talked to Scott already, and he looks forward to being back with us," Torborg said. "I asked him whether it'll be a tough adjustment going over to second. He said some of the angles are different but that it should be no big problem."

"Manrique did a super job," Torborg said of the other player the White Sox gave up. "We're giving up two players who can really help them, but we wanted to bring in young players with speed and defense. We tried to solidify our defense and improve our team speed."

The Rangers would replace Fletcher with utility player Jeff Kunkel. "Kunkel has more range and a better arm [than Fletcher]," Valentine said. "We made this trade because this makes us a much better team."

Grieve defended his decision to deal two of the organization's top prospects. "We have six or seven outfielders who compare favorably with Sammy Sosa," Grieve said at the time. "And we have the same kind of pitching depth."

"They envision Sammy Sosa as their center fielder of the future and Wilson Álvarez as a cornerstone of their staff," Grieve added. "For us, this isn't a trade for the last two months of the season. It's not a stopgap. I see no reason why Harold Baines can't be a productive player for us for the next four, five, six years."

It didn't quite work out that way. At the time of the trade, Baines was hitting .321, with 13 home runs and 56 RBI. His average fell to .285 in Texas. He hit only 3 homers and had 16 RBI after the trade.

Baines started the 1990 season very similar to 1989. He was hitting .290 with 13 homers and 44 RBI at midseason. Then the Rangers decided to cut bait and traded him to Oakland for two players to be named later, who would turn out to be Joe Bitker and Scott Chiamparino. Bitker would appear in 14 games for the Rangers, going 1–0 with a 5.32 ERA. Chiamparino made 15 starts over three years, going 2–6 for Texas.

The lineup didn't gel. After hitting over .270 for the first three months of the 1989 season, Texas hit just .253 in August. Palmeiro slumped, hitting .234 in August. He also managed just 1 home run and 10 RBI from the two-spot in the lineup.

The Rangers lost 7 of their first 10 games after the trade and went 28–33 the rest of the way, which was just one game better than the White Sox. As expected, the A's ran away with the division and went on to win the World Series. The Rangers finished a distant 16 games back.

The Rangers' promising young outfield didn't turn out to be as impenetrable as it appeared in mid-1989. Incaviglia hit a career low .236 in 1990, and, after he hit just .231 with 1 home run and 1 RBI in spring training 1991, the Rangers released him before the season to save money. Espy played in just 52 games in 1990 and was allowed to leave as a free agent after the season.

Juan González got called up near the end of the 1989 season and broke Sosa's record as the youngest Ranger to hit a home run. González did his part to make Grieve look like he had made the right call. He led the American League in home runs in 1992 and 1993 and added an RBI crown in 1998. He was named AL MVP in 1996 and 1998. In the latter season, Sosa won the National League MVP.

Álvarez made Grieve regret the trade when he returned to the majors with the White Sox in 1991. He promptly threw a no-hitter. Álvarez would win 15 games twice, finish runner up in ERA in 1993 (2.95), and make the 1994 All-Star team. He would finish a 14-year career with a 102–92 record and a 3.96 ERA.

But it was Sosa who made the trade a lighthearted campaign issue in 2000. In June of that year, as he prepared to accept the presidential nomination at the Republican National Convention the following month, Bush spoke regretfully about the deal.

"He'd just come up and gotten a quick look," Bush said of Sosa. "We were coming down the stretch, chasing Oakland. We were either going to kick in and stay or fade. It just didn't work out. Harold, he just didn't kick in."

In March 2001, two months after his first inauguration, Bush hosted a special event at the White House. The president invited all 62 living Hall of Famers for a luncheon and celebration of the sport, to kick off the baseball season. Forty-seven of them accepted.

"One of the great things about living here is that you don't have to sign up for a baseball fantasy camp to meet your heroes," Bush said. "It turns out they come here."

While such legends as Hank Aaron, Yogi Berra, Sandy Koufax, Stan Musial and Ernie Banks were in attendance, Bush saved one Hall of Famer for a special introduction. "Big Texas is here," Bush said of former Rangers pitcher Nolan Ryan. "The reason I like to keep Nolan around is he is a reminder that when we got done with the Sammy Sosa trade, there was still some talent left on the Rangers."

Sosa became a superstar, not on the White Sox, but across town, with the Cubs. He played three years for the White Sox and was just showing signs of developing power. He hit 15 home runs in his second season and 10 (in 38 fewer games) the following year.

After being fired by the White Sox following the 1990 season, Himes took a job as Cubs general manager a year later. "One of his first moves was to trade for Sosa again," Grieve recalled. "He loved him as a prospect with the White Sox in 1989, and he loved him just as much with the Cubs in 1992."

With the Cubs, Sosa exploded. He hit 33 home runs in his second year with the team, a number that increased to 40 in 1996. Two years later, he hit 66, five more than any player had hit in history up until that point, although it was good for second place to Mark McGwire's 70.

The home-run derby that McGwire and Sosa staged during the 1998 season captured the nation's attention, with Sosa's infectious smile and media-friendly quips making him the favorite over the at-times surly McGwire.

Sosa would top the 60 homer mark twice more and finish his career with 609 home runs, becoming just the fourth member of the 600 home run club. With the steroid cloud hanging overhead, however, his accomplishments would eventually be marked with an asterisk in the minds of baseball fans, if not in the record books.

On January 20, 2004, President George W. Bush, who would win reelection later in the year, entered the Capitol Building to give the State of the Union Address. In the crowd, at the president's invitation, was New England Patriots quarterback Tom Brady. The Super Bowl–winning quarterback was active in community service, but there was another reason to have him seated in the gallery, near the first lady.

"To help children make right choices, they need good examples. Athletics play such an important role in our society," Bush said as the cameras showed the fair-haired Brady.

"Unfortunately, some in professional sports are not setting much of an example," Bush continued. "The use of performance-enhancing drugs like steroids in baseball, football and other sports is dangerous and it sends the wrong message: that there are shortcuts to accomplishment and that performance is more important than character. So tonight I call on team owners, union representatives, coaches and players to take the lead, to send the right signal, to get tough and to get rid of steroids now."

Congress scheduled hearings about performance-enhancing drugs in 2005. Many of the sluggers from the late 1990s were called upon to testify, and they didn't commit themselves well. McGwire ducked questions by saying, "I'm not here to talk about the past."

Sosa, the more quotable player in the 1998 derby, seemed to struggle with the English language, making it difficult for Congress to question him and get straightforward answers. Rafael Palmeiro, part of the Rangers lineup that Baines joined following the trade, waved his finger at Congress and declared, "I have never used steroids, period. I do not know how to say it any more clearly than that." He tested positive five months later.

Eventually, many of the players from the home run era that McGwire and Sosa reigned over were tainted by the steroid scandal. Some tested positive. Others, like McGwire, admitted their use. Many, including Sosa, were just assumed guilty, due to the mountain of circumstantial evidence—sudden changes in body type and production numbers and an inexplicable crash in production once testing for performance enhancers began. Juan González, the other prized Rangers prospect, and Wilson Álvarez, one of the pitchers involved in the deal, were both implicated in the avalanche of finger-pointing stories that followed.

In a 2002 interview with the Dallas–Fort Worth media, Sosa looked back on his time with the Rangers and being traded by Bush.

"If he would have known I would hit sixty home runs three times, he would've said, 'No, no, no. Don't do it!' At the time, I was younger. They had to get rid of someone, and I was the one."

"The President of the United States traded me," Sosa marveled. "That still surprises me . . . but I voted for him."

It's not known whom Sosa voted for in November 2004.

WAR COMPARISON

President Bush has a point: the Rangers certainly didn't receive very much value for Sammy Sosa. After a long, productive career, Harold Baines had very little left when he came to Texas.

Even ignoring Sosa's inclusion in the deal, the Rangers got fleeced by Chicago, as Wilson Álvarez was a very productive pitcher for the White Sox. It probably did Rangers fans', and Bush's, heart good to see that the White Sox made an even worse trade involving Sosa than theirs.

WHITE SOX RECEIVED	WAR PRE-TRADE	WAR POST-TRADE
Sammy Sosa	-0.3	1.1 with White Sox, 33.9 over next 10 years
Wilson Álvarez	0.0	17.4
Scott Fletcher	12.3	2.6
RANGERS RECEIVED	WAR PRE-TRADE	WAR POST-TRADE
Harold Baines	24.5	0.9
Fred Manrique	1.7	1.2
WHITE SOX LATER RECEIVED	WAR PRE-TRADE	WAR POST-TRADE
George Bell	1.4	-2.7
CUBS RECEIVED	WAR PRE-TRADE	WAR POST-TRADE
Sammy Sosa	1.1	58.5
Ken Patterson	1.5	-0.6

CHAPTER 15

THE RENT IS
— TOO DARN HIGH —

THE STORY BEHIND THE MARK TEIXEIRA TRADE

The Braves get held up in a failed attempt to prolong their dynasty.

The trade that should have ended the midseason rent-a-player deals took place in 2007. With a year and a half left on his contract, Mark Teixeira was sent by the Texas Rangers to the Atlanta Braves at the trade deadline. In exchange, the Rangers got a package of prospects including Elvis Andrus, Neftali Feliz and Matt Harrison, who would help form the nucleus of their World Series teams. The Braves dealt Teixeira 363 days later, at the following year's deadline, when it was clear they weren't going to be able to keep him.

The pair sit on an old beige couch, similar to ones found in college-guy apartments all across the country. Dressed in ripped jeans, a blue golf shirt and a throwback Atlanta Braves hat is Tyler Crawford, a twenty-year-old Auburn undergrad and future partner in an accounting firm. Next to him, dressed in a T-shirt, shorts and baseball cap, is Andrew Hall, a future certified project manager. Both are dyed-in-the-wool Braves fans.

Crawford hunches over a guitar and begins to play a catchy tune.

Hall is getting married in less than a month, to Crawford's sister, but a different love motivates him on August 10, 2007. When Crawford finishes his opening lick and slaps the guitar to keep the beat, Hall begins to sing.

> Four and a half games back and I don't care-a
> You know why? We got Mark Teixeira
> Got a new Braves jersey that I'm gonna wear-a
> And written on the back is Mark Teixeira

Mugging for the camera and, at times, fighting off the laughter that ruined their first three takes, Hall and Crawford come up with a remarkable number of phrases that rhyme with Teixeira: The first-place Mets will see their lead "narr-a." It "just ain't fair-a" to add a player of his caliber to a roster that already included Chipper and Andruw Jones ("a mighty nice pair-a").

"A side effect is mild hysteria," Hall sings to end the second verse. "The medical reason is Mark Teixeira."

Hall and Crawford save their best lyric work for the final verse, however, ending the song with a rapid-fire flourish.

Pitchers beware cause he's gonna scare ya
Throw him a strike now if you dare-a
He could probably steal on Yogi Berra
Biggest thing in Georgia since Scarlett O'Hara
If I were a woman I'd probably marry ya.
And that's not gay, 'cause it's Mark Teixeira

"From the moment we heard about the trade, and [Teixeira] flew to Atlanta and came out in that Braves uniform. It was just so exciting. We just had to do something," Crawford recalled. "He went to Georgia Tech and now he was coming back to Atlanta. At the time, we thought he was going to win two or three championships and be a Brave forever."

He wasn't. Teixeira spent less than a year in a Braves uniform, before the team shipped him off for prospects. The 363-day Teixeira era gave Hall, Crawford and the rest of the Atlanta fanbase the chance to feel both sides of the rent-a-player experience, thanks to a short-sighted attempt by Braves management to keep an aging dynasty alive for one more year. As a result, Atlanta dealt away the core of what could have been the next generation of Braves' playoff teams.

It's easy to understand why Teixeira inspired Braves fans into song in his first week with the team in August 2007. By most accounts, he's a real-life action hero or pro wrestling good guy. Sportswriters in the 1930s and '40s ignored players' drinking and nighttime carousing to make them sound like Mark Teixeira actually is.

A *Sports Illustrated* profile opened with teammates talking about how Teixeira stands at attention during the national anthem 190 times a year—no gum chewing, no looking around aimlessly, no snickering at particularly bad renditions of the song.

"He stands perfectly straight, head down, shirt tucked in every single time," said Torii Hunter, a teammate of Teixeira's in Anaheim in 2008. "He doesn't say a word. He doesn't even have a hair out of place."

Teixeira was an honor student at private school and then went on to Georgia Tech for college. He eats a peanut butter and jelly sandwich before each game and says he has a "plan for every day." He funds scholarships. He decided not to sign with his first choice of an agent after the representative was late for a meeting with him, because that's not the way Teixeira does things.

Teixeira was a casting agent's ideal for a baseball star, as well. He hit 26 home runs as a rookie in 2003 and was on his way to a fourth straight 30-homer season in 2007, with a streak of 100 RBI years to match it. Teixeira also had a streak of 507 consecutive games played snapped in June when he went on the disabled list for just the second time in his career. In his first four seasons he had accumulated two Gold Gloves, two Silver Sluggers and an All-Star selection.

But Teixeira, or "Tex," couldn't carry the Texas Rangers to a playoff berth. The team was on its way to a fourth losing season in his five-year career, and its second time finishing in last place; the other three years they finished next to last in the American League West.

The only blemish on Teixeira's reputation in his young career was a confrontation with manager Ron Washington early in the 2007 season. Some reports said that Washington, in his first year as a major league manager, was upset that Teixeira didn't work the count more. It's an odd charge, since Teixeira walked 89 times the year before and was on his way in 2007 to posting the highest on-base percentage in his career to that point.

On Teixeira's side, the relationship with Washington was strained because the manager cursed too much and smoked cigarettes in the dugout during games. The two men didn't see eye to eye, and it resulted in some type of dust up.

"It was a one-night thing where something happened in a ballgame and I called him on it," Washington said. "From that point on, I guess he disliked me. Other than that I always felt I gave him the respect that he deserved. . . . If he'd have stayed around long enough, he'd have understood better what I meant by questioning him on some things. But the next thing you know, it was out of hand. I never had animosity toward him, but when I had something to say to him I said it.

"One time I had something to say and he was the guy I said it to," Washington added. "He said something back. And I went right back at him. It was just about the game of baseball, his ideas versus my ideas. But I am the manager."

Whether it was the message, the way it was delivered or the man who delivered it, Teixeira didn't take it well.

"We were losing our ass at the time. I was trying to change things. That creates friction," Washington said. "But if he'd been here longer he'd have seen where I was trying to take things. What I wanted to do was the right thing for the organization. Tex made it clear he didn't want to be around here. If that's because of me, I am sorry for that. . . . Obviously he'd gotten a bad taste of me and there wasn't enough time for that to change."

With the Rangers spiraling through another lost season, and their star player looking to leave town, general manager Jon Daniels had the unenviable task of trying to get suitable value for Mark Teixeira.

Daniels felt even more pressure than the average general manager in his position would, because of his rocky early history on the job. Daniels became the youngest GM in major league history when the Rangers hired him following the 2005 season, a month after he turned 28. Daniels broke into baseball as an intern just four years earlier, and many were skeptical of his rapid ascent at such a tender age.

For his first trade on the job, Daniels got rid of Alfonso Soriano, the All-Star the Yankees had sent to Texas in the Alex Rodriguez deal in 2004. The prospect included in the earlier trade (Joaquín Árias) failed to pan out, so Soriano was all the Rangers had to show from that A-Rod trade.

Daniels sent Soriano to the Washington Nationals for aging outfielder Brad Wilkerson, who would be out of baseball within three years; Armando Galarraga, who would pitch 542 innings in the majors but just 8 and ⅔ of them with the Rangers, since Daniels dealt him away for a prospect that didn't ever reach the big leagues; and outfielder Terrmel Sledge, who wasn't long for the team. Soriano made three more All-Star teams and finished in the top 20 in MVP voting three more times.

Daniels' second trade didn't make fans forget the first misstep. He traded away Adrian Gonzalez, a future star who was stuck in the minors because he played the same position—first base—as Teixeira. Daniels also included Sledge and pitcher Chris Young in the deal, sending them to the Padres for three players who didn't have a lasting impact on the club.

Daniels also made mistakes in free agency. He signed 31-year-old pitcher Kevin Millwood to a five-year, $60 million deal in 2006. Millwood had led the league with a 2.86 ERA the year before Daniels signed him. He promptly turned in ERAs of 4.52, 5.16 and 5.07 in his first three years as a Ranger. In the final year of his contract, Millwood led the league in losses, going 4–16 for the Orioles after Texas dumped him.

Prior to the 2007 season, Daniels again opened his checkbook. He signed infielder Michael Young to a five-year, $80 million contract extension that seemed far above his market value.

Daniels needed a win, and, with an elite player like Teixeira asking to be dealt, the trade would determine his future as a front office man.

One unnamed American League executive summed up the situation well. "This is going to be his signature trade of his tenure, so it has to work and, therefore, I think his asking price will be too high for anyone to accept."

Rent-a-player trades take place every summer as the trade deadline approaches. Teams out of contention for a playoff spot realize that the value will never be higher for their best veteran players. Teams still competing to make the postseason will be looking for one extra piece to put them over the top, while also keeping a potential contributor out of the hands of their competitors.

A skillful general manager can take advantage of the situation to create a bidding war for their rent-a-veterans, getting valuable prospects from contenders. As one of Daniels' predecessors as Rangers GM, Tom Grieve, explained, the different goals of the "sellers" and "buyers" at the trade deadline allow both teams to get exactly what they want, the hallmark of a good trade.

Thanks to his job status, however, Daniels gave no impression that he was at all concerned with whether his trading partners were happy with their side of the Teixeira trade. His approach to trade negotiations took away any subtlety of the annual prospects-for-vets swap. He set out to rip somebody off.

The only problem with that plan was Teixeira's contract status. He would become a free agent after the 2008 season, meaning that any team that traded for him would just be "renting" him for a season and change. And the agent that Tex chose after punishing his first choice for tardiness was Scott Boras, one of the game's toughest negotiators. There was little question that Teixeira and Boras would want to test the free-agent market.

In June 2007, Texas offered Teixeira an eight-year, $140 million contract extension. He and Boras promptly turned it down, which helped give an idea of just how much the pair would be expecting on the open market.

A team like the Yankees or the Red Sox would be able to sign Teixeira after 2008, and all it would cost them was cash. There was no sense for New York and Boston to ship off their top prospects just to get Teixeira's services a little earlier.

Scaring away teams without the big budgets of the Yankees and Sox was the fact that Teixeira would be eligible for arbitration following the 2007 season. Arbitration is a difficult, antagonistic process that teams and players generally try to avoid at all costs. Before a player is eligible for free agency, he can fight for a salary increase with his current team, in front of a third-party arbitrator.

The player picks a salary that he thinks captures his true worth and states his case to the arbitrator. The team names a lower figure and argues, in front of the player, that he's not all that good, listing all the reasons he's not worth what he's asking. The arbitrator then picks one of the two figures. He can't suggest a compromise in the middle. Hurt feelings often result, and usually, teams and players will come to an agreement somewhere in the middle before going to arbitration. However, with Boras in his corner, there was a good chance that Teixeira would be willing to go through the process.

Daniels began floating trial balloons two months before the trade deadline. On May 26, he addressed the possibility of trading Teixeira in an interview with the *Philadelphia Daily News*, saying, "We're not in a position where we can't at least listen to what's out there."

Most of the teams with the prospects and finances to make acquiring Teixeira feasible checked in with Daniels. Among teams showing interest were the Dodgers, Orioles, Angels, Braves, Red Sox, Giants and Tigers.

"It was actually a lot of fun," Daniels said, after all the negotiations were completed. "We were looking at the best young players in other organizations, trying to find the best combination. The whole organization was involved. Our international scouts and pro scouts were all out there somewhere, and our amateur scouts had dealt with a lot of these players in preparing for the draft.

"Typically, teams look for three things in these deals," Daniels said. "Quality, as far as impact at the big leagues; quantity in getting multiple players and a chance of hitting on one or two; and proximity to the big leagues. We felt we wouldn't get all three, so we made a choice. We had ownership's blessing to look long-term rather than immediate gratification. We went for quality and quantity and did not focus on established big league players."

That direction seemed to give Daniels a green light to ask for the moon when teams called to discuss a trade. He set about trying to hold someone up for his best player, and, while he may have enjoyed the process, he made sure it wasn't much fun for the other teams in the negotiations.

As expected, New York dropped out quickly. GM Brian Cashman informed Daniels that the Yankees' top three pitching prospects—Joba Chamberlain, Ian Kennedy and Phil Hughes— were all off the table when it came to negotiating a trade for Tex. Despite the Yankees' reputation as big spenders who are free with their prospects when it comes to a trade, Cashman is deft at waiting out trade partners and getting them to settle for less than they initially asked for.

It wouldn't work with Daniels. "The Yanks have zero shot at Teixeira," the *New York Daily News* quoted a source familiar with the negotiations in June. "No chance they [the Rangers] settle for a lesser deal."

The Dodgers were the next to fall by the wayside. Los Angeles offered first baseman James Loney and outfielder Andre Ethier, both of whom are still starting in the majors nearly a decade later. Daniels essentially answered with, "And what else?" When Daniels tried to get the Dodgers to add pitcher Chad Billingsley or future three-time Cy Young winner Clayton Kershaw to the package, Los Angeles backed out.

The Tigers wouldn't part with pitcher Andrew Miller, a first-round draft pick (sixth overall) just one year earlier, or outfielder Cameron Maybin, a first rounder (tenth overall) the year before that. (The two prospects were later included in the deal to Miguel Cabrera from Florida.)

Teixeira is originally from Severna Park, Maryland, and the Orioles desperately wanted to bring the hometown boy back. Daniels, however, refused to even listen to an offer from

Baltimore unless it included left-hander Erik Bedard. The 28-year-old Bedard was the ace of the Orioles rotation. He won 15 games in 2006 and was on his way to finishing in the top five in Cy Young voting in 2007. He seemed to be the exception to Daniels' "no established big league players" rule, but the Orioles didn't have much else in their system that interested Daniels.

The Giants dropped out after Texas, according to rumors, asked for pitcher Jonathan Sanchez and future 16-game winner and three-time All-Star Matt Cain.

For the most part, the Red Sox stayed out of the trade discussions, coming in late with what was described as a "significant offer." The two sides eventually worked out a trade for another Rangers veteran—closer Eric Gagne—but Teixeira was a no-go, because Texas wanted either Boston's top pitching prospect, future 17-game winner Clay Buchholz, or its top position player prospect, outfielder Jacoby Ellsbury, a future MVP runner up.

When the dust cleared, two teams—the Angels and the Braves—were left standing, willing to at least consider Daniels' exorbitant demands.

In exchange for Teixeira, the Rangers wanted a package of three players from the Angels. The teams came to agreement on two of them. First baseman Casey Kotchman, a former first-round draft pick who, at age 24, was in his first full season as an MLB regular, would go to Texas to fill the void the trade would leave at first base. ESPN had reported earlier in the process that the Angels offered Kotchman and Reggie Willits, a 26-year-old speedster outfielder, for Teixeira. The Rangers turned down that two-for-one.

Joe Saunders, a 26-year-old left-handed starting pitcher, was the second player who would be headed to Texas with Kotchman. In 2006, Saunders went 7–3 in his first season in the Angels rotation, and he was 4–0 as the trade deadline approached in July 2007.

Texas took some time to scout Angels' minor leaguers before coming back with their request for a third player. The Angels were expecting a throw-in, perhaps, according to some reports, 25-year-old outfielder Terry Evans or 27-year-old outfielder Nathan Haynes. Evans had made his MLB debut in June after hitting 34 home runs the previous year in the low minors. Haynes was a former first-rounder, although it was back in 1997. He made his MLB debut in May after starting the season hitting .386 in Triple-A. Although they weren't Grade-A prospects, the outfielders were better than the average throw-in player, and both had earned promotions to the major leagues.

Daniels wasn't interested in a throw-in, however. After collecting input from the scouting staff, he sent Angels GM Bill Stoneman a list of four players to choose from:

- 20-year-old right-hander Nick Adenhart, considered the top pitching prospect in the organization after going 15–4 in the minors in 2006;
- 22-year-old infielder Brandon Wood, the Angels' top position player prospect, who hit 43 home runs with 115 RBI at Class A in 2005, then added 14 more homers in 29 Arizona Fall League games;
- 24-year-old infielder Howie Kendrick, who was in his second year with the Angels and the team's starting second baseman; and
- 24-year-old right-hander Ervin Santana, who won 16 games for the Angels in 2006 and was in his third year in the Angels' starting rotation.

Stoneman had seen enough. "What we were being asked for was going to hurt us more than the deal would help," he told the media on July 30, the day before the trade deadline. "We are looking at this season and setting ourselves up in the best position for getting in the postseason. We're not going to destroy our ability to compete for next year or future years just for a shot at now."

At this point in the season, the Angels had held or shared first place every day since April 25 and would go on to win the division by six games with 94 wins.

Manager Mike Scioscia agreed with his GM. "Considering the names that were bantered around on our side, I wouldn't call it disappointing because I think it would have been creating a huge hole in what we need to do," he said.

Arte Moreno, who had made several high-profile, and expensive, acquisitions in his short time as Angels' owner, supported the decision to walk away from the deal. "I could have told Bill, 'I want this thing done and send them three players,'" he said. "But, if all the advice I'm getting from the people I pay is not to make the deal and I'm not listening to them, why are they there?"

"We get him [Teixeira] for two months this year, and next year, and then you have to negotiate with Scott Boras," Moreno continued. "If you could guarantee me a World Series, we're going to empty out everything. Does he get us to the World Series if we don't have the pitching?"

Daniels now could afford to be greedy with the Angels, because the Braves, despite essentially bidding against themselves, appeared to be close to giving him everything he wanted. He'd initially inquired about two players: shortstop Yunel Escobar, a 24-year-old who would finish sixth in Rookie of the Year voting that year despite not making his MLB debut until June, and Jarrod Saltalamacchia, a switch-hitting catcher. Saltalamacchia made his MLB debut in May after hitting .309 at Double-A Mississippi to start the year. He was the crown jewel of Atlanta's minor league system.

The Braves balked at including Escobar and tried to keep Saltalamacchia out of the deal for a while as well. By late July, however, it was clear that "Salty" was the centerpiece of the package the team was negotiating for Teixeira. The Braves already had Brian McCann, who made his second straight All-Star team at catcher earlier in the month. He hit 24 home runs and had 93 RBI in 2006.

On Friday, July 27, 2007, four days before the deadline, the Braves players were mingling in the visitors' clubhouse, a few hours before a game against the Arizona Diamondbacks. ESPN's SportsCenter ran on the television at one end of the room, and the anchors engaged in a discussion of the trade.

Veteran pitcher Tim Hudson broke the tension, calling across the room, "See ya', Salty. Adios, buddy."

At that point, the Braves were discussing a three-player package for Teixeira. In addition to Saltalamacchia, the Rangers would get left-handed pitcher Matt Harrison. He was a 21-year-old starter who had 6 complete games over the previous three seasons, a rarity for a minor league pitcher.

The third player would be one of two infielders. Elvis Andrus was an 18-year-old shortstop known for his defense. He also had 25 stolen bases already at Class A Myrtle Beach. At 23, shortstop Brent Lillibridge was the old man of the group. He had 10 home runs, 28 stolen bases and a .287 average in half a season at Triple-A Richmond.

Then Braves GM John Schuerholz did something that most of the other teams' executives, startled by the Rangers' high asking price, didn't try. He opened up the deal and asked Daniels for more.

The Braves needed relief help. In Atlanta's incredible fourteen-year streak of winning the NL East division and making the playoffs, shaky relief had been the team's downfall in far too many Octobers. Now, facing the possibility of returning to the playoffs after a one-year absence, Schuerholz wanted to add another bullpen arm to prepare for the high-pressure late-inning situations that had usually ended in heartbreak in years prior. He asked the Rangers to add one of three pitchers to the deal: closer Eric Gagne, left-hander C. J. Wilson or left-hander Ron Mahay.

Despite Hudson's attempts to poke fun at the elephant in the room, the ongoing negotiations made for a tense, awkward situation in the Braves clubhouse.

"John [Schuerholz] will tell you, a lot of times these rumors of trades don't come to fruition," third baseman Chipper Jones said. "So until it happens, not too many guys are getting too excited. . . . You don't want to act too elated, because somebody's usually going the other way in a trade. Salty's rumored to be going. Salty could be a cornerstone to a lot of organizations, including this one. We're all getting used to seeing him. It'd be sad to see him go."

Still, Jones couldn't help but let his mind wander to the possibility of adding Teixeira.

"He's a pretty versatile hitter," he said, presumably with Saltalamacchia out of earshot. "It'd be nice to have a couple guys in the middle of the lineup who hit for average and power. . . . It's nice to know our front office is giving us a shot of new blood and cares about us continuing on in the playoff chase. Hopefully we can make a move to get us over the hump."

By the end of the weekend, the deal was taking shape. The Braves would get Tex and Mahay. In return, the Rangers would get Saltalamacchia, Andrus and two pitching prospects: Harrison and Neftali Feliz, a nineteen-year-old right-hander who had struck out 70 batters in just 55.1 innings.

Things hit a snag, however, when Texas found out that Harrison had been pitching with a sore shoulder. One option was to make Harrison a player to be named later. The Rangers' scouts could then continue to monitor him for a few more starts while their medical staff pored over his charts. If Texas wasn't happy with the condition of his shoulder, they would substitute another pitching prospect as the player to be named.

That required another negotiation to determine a list of players Texas could choose from, in the event they rejected Harrison. The Braves fought successfully to keep Jo-Jo Reyes, a 22-year-old rookie who went 12–5 in 2006 and 12–1 in 2007 in Atlanta's minor league system, off the list.

By the time the dust had cleared, Daniels estimates that he spoke to Schuerholz between twelve and twenty times, just counting the serious conversations.

In the end, there was no need to keep Harrison's name out of the deal. Texas took him, and, in exchange, the Braves also sent another pitcher, twenty-year-old Beau Jones, a southpaw who was Atlanta's first-round pick in the 2005 draft, to help quell Daniels' concerns about Harrison's shoulder.

It was a huge price to pay for Teixeira. Saltalamacchia, Andrus and Harrison were rated the number one, two and three prospects in the Braves' system, respectively. And the Braves also included two other young pitchers.

The first thing Schuerholz did after the trade was finalized was call the team's scouting director, Roy Clark. After the GM traded away the prize gems from Clark's minor league system, leaving the cupboard bare, one might assume that there would be some testiness between the two men.

However, the mood was festive. Clark understood that his job was to develop players for the organization to use. Some of them would be used in the Braves lineup and pitching staff. Others would be used as trade chips.

Schuerholz said he called "to congratulate him once again" on a job well done.

"Boss, we had a great day," Clark responded, "and now we have to go build it back up again."

"Roy really understands," Schuerholz told the media the day after the trade.

What neither Clark nor Schuerholz understood, or at least weren't willing to admit at the time, is that it wasn't the way the Braves had done things in the past.

On their way to 10 straight divisional titles, the Braves relied on home-grown talent. Future Hall of Famers Chipper Jones and Tom Glavine were both drafted by the Braves. John Smoltz was acquired as a minor leaguer. Other key contributors, including Andruw Jones, Javy López, Kevin Millwood, Ryan Klesko, Mark Wohlers and John Rocker, all began their careers with the Braves. So did Rafael Furcal, Ron Gant, David Justice, Steve Avery and Jeff Blauser.

Most of the veterans the Braves acquired, including Hall of Famer Greg Maddux and National League MVP Terry Pendleton, were signed as free agents. While they were winning NL East titles, the Braves rarely dealt away their prospects for short-term veteran help.

The change in personality for the organization was an attempt to keep the dynasty alive for one more year. Schuerholz and Clark weren't the only ones blind to that fact in the joy that followed the Teixeira trade.

Teixeira made an immediate impact, both on the field and with the fan base. He traveled to Atlanta the night of the trade deadline. A few hours after the trade was announced, he showed up in the Braves dugout, in uniform. Watching on TV, two fans began writing lyrics of praise.

On Wednesday, Teixeira took the field, and the excitement really began. His first time up, he drove in a run and later came around to score. Later in that game, he capped a Braves win with a three-run homer. The next night, he hit a two-run home run to tie the game in the fourth inning. The following night, he homered again.

The combination of Teixeira's Paul Bunyanesque debut with the team and the commitment the team showed to returning to the World Series by making the deal caused an explosion of interest in Braves baseball. In the first six home games of August, attendance went up by 4,000 over the team's season average. Games on regional cable saw a 72 percent increase in ratings, while Braves games on national superstation TBS were up 35 percent.

"This is the most buzz around the team . . . in the last four years," Derek Schiller, the team's executive VP of sales and marketing, said.

Crawford and Hall's song added to the excitement. The fiancée of outfielder Jeff Francoeur discovered the video online.

"That's how it went through the clubhouse," Crawford said. The players loved the video, and Francoeur offered the two YouTube stars free tickets to a game. The team had other plans, though.

"We didn't realize how big it had become," Crawford said. "Fox SportSouth found it, and they were playing it all the time. It was a huge hit in Atlanta. We were in Alabama, and we had no idea that was going on over there."

The team flew the pair in to perform the song at Turner Field at a game in late August. To make the duo feel more at home, the team also shipped in their comfy couch, itself a star of the video.

Unfortunately, there would be no Hollywood ending for the 2007 Braves. The YouTube song mentioned that the Braves were four and a half games back. From August 18 until September 24, the team would never be that close again. They fell as far as nine and a half games back. The team was in third place when Teixeira joined, and, after moving into second for a few days, Atlanta remained in third from August 26 until season's end.

The playoff fever was completely cured by the 2008 season. After playing at or near .500 for the first two months of the season, a 6-game losing streak at the start of June and a 5-game skid near the end of the month sealed the Braves' fate. Atlanta lost another five in a row leading up to the trade deadline, and, almost exactly a year after sending five minor leaguers to Texas for him, the Braves traded Mark Teixeira on July 29, 2008.

"Teixeira did exactly what we thought he would do when he got here," Schuerholz said. "None of us planned on our pitching staff being decimated by injuries after we got him. We had some trouble winning one-run games, too, but that was a function of being able to keep healthy pitchers out there. I'd be dishonest if I didn't tell you that there was a lot of conversation and contemplation about, 'Should we do this? Is this the right guy? We know he's going to be a free agent, and we know that his market price is going to be so steep that we might not be able to match it. But if we can get back in the playoffs and we can re-energize our community, our team and our fans, then it's worth it.'"

The Texas Rangers reached the World Series for the first time in franchise history in 2010, then returned in 2011, losing to the Giants and Cardinals, respectively. Elvis Andrus started every World Series game at shortstop, getting 11 hits and scoring 7 runs. Two of the 12 World Series games were started by Matt Harrison, who picked up losses in both. Of the 4 World Series wins posted by the Rangers in franchise history, Neftali Feliz has saved 3 of them.

After the 2011 season, four years after the trade, Jon Daniels was still the youngest GM in baseball. "It had a symbolic impact on our organization," Daniels said of the trade. "It was a clear point in time when we changed our approach on how we would build our team."

"We didn't know at the time that we had traded nearly half of the Rangers' lineup to them," Crawford remembers of the glory days of his YouTube singing career.

The Braves sent Tex to the Angels, who gave up Kotchman and minor league pitcher Stephen Marek, a 40th-round draft pick out of a junior college in Texas.

The rent wasn't as high as it had been a year earlier, but the lease didn't last as long, either. The Angels had Teixeira for the last two months of the 2008 season. He helped them make the playoffs, where they lost to Boston in the first round. Teixeira hit .467 in his first postseason experience. Then, in the offseason, he signed with the Yankees as a free agent, for an 8-year contract worth $180 million.

Orioles fans, angry that he spurned his hometown team to sign with a division rival, wrote a song titled "Boo Teixeira," which became a short-lived YouTube hit.

Teixeira, the baseball action hero, won a World Series in his first season with the Yankees. It continued his history of making a good first impression on his new team. When he was traded to the Angels in 2008, he had 2 hits in his second game with the team and hit a grand slam in his fifth.

In fact, he made such a good impression in Anaheim that Tyler Crawford and Andrew Hall got a phone call. "Fox Sports Los Angeles wanted to know if we'd come out and do an Angels version of our song," Crawford said. "I mean, we thought for a second about it. It was a free trip to Los Angeles. But who did they think we were, that we'd do something like that?"

"We're Braves fans," Crawford concluded.

And unlike the players they root for, fans cannot be rented.

WAR COMPARISON

Things turned out well for the Rangers, but Jon Daniels' approach to the trade negotiations eliminated most of the potential partners, who were turned off by his aggressive demands. Despite demanding the best prospects in other teams' farm systems, most of the prospects targeted by Daniels didn't pan out. Despite his promise to focus on acquiring up-and-coming players, most of the WAR generated by the players Daniels requested were from guys who were established MLB veterans at the time.

Atlanta's John Schuerholz was essentially bidding against himself and offered far more than other teams were willing to surrender. He ended up getting one solid year from Teixeira, then got fleeced again when he dealt him to the Angels less than a year later.

TO BRAVES	WAR PRE-TRADE	WAR POST-TRADE
Mark Teixeira	21.5	6
Ron Mahay	4.3	0.8
TO RANGERS	WAR PRE-TRADE	WAR POST-TRADE
Elvis Andrus	0.0	20.4
Neftali Feliz	0.0	8.4
Matt Harrison	0.0	9.2
Jarrod Saltalamacchia	0.4	0.5
Beau Jones	0.0	0.0
Braves traded Teixeira a year later, getting Casey Kotchman, who gave the team 0.7 WAR		
Teixeira went on to post WAR of 27.2 over the next eight seasons		

DANIELS' DEMANDS OF DODGERS	WAR PRE-TRADE	WAR POST-TRADE
James Loney	2.5	5.4
Andre Ethier	3.3	18.7
Chad Billingsley	4.9	11.7
Or Clayton Kershaw	0.0	47.2
DANIELS' DEMANDS OF ORIOLES	WAR PRE-TRADE	WAR POST-TRADE
Erik Bedard	12.7	4.6
DANIELS' DEMANDS OF GIANTS	WAR PRE-TRADE	WAR POST-TRADE
Jonathan Sanchez	-0.5	2.9
Matt Cain	8.7	23.0
DANIELS' DEMANDS OF RED SOX	WAR PRE-TRADE	WAR POST-TRADE
Eric Gagne	-0.2	-0.5
Clay Buchholz	0.8	14.8
Or Jacoby Ellsbury	0.4	26.0
DANIELS' DEMANDS OF ANGELS	WAR PRE-TRADE	WAR POST-TRADE
Casey Kotchman	3.0	4.4
Either Reggie Willits	1.7	-1.0
Or Joe Saunders	1.7	7.1
One of:		
Nick Adenhart	0.0	0.0
Brandon Wood	-0.3	-3.4
Howie Kendrick	3.8	24.8
Ervin Santana	-1.2	1.3

CHAPTER 16

— WHITE RAT RUN AMOK —

THE STORY BEHIND THE 1980 WINTER MEETINGS

It's the Whitey Herzog show as a series of shrewd deals helps build dynasties.

In a four-day span in December 1980, St. Louis Cardinals manager/GM Whitey Herzog changed the face of baseball for the next half decade. The Cardinals, Padres and Brewers embarked on a series of trades that sent fifteen players between the three cities, including a future MVP, two future Cy Young winners, and all three teams' starting catchers. The 1982 World Series would match up many of the players who had been packing bags during that fateful week.

Whitey Herzog decided his team needed a come-to-Jesus meeting. The Cardinals were struggling, so Herzog stood up in front of his players for one of those motivational talks that are far more common in sports movies than in actual locker rooms.

"A lot of you thought we had a chance to be pretty good this season," Herzog said. "And so did I."

Herzog paused and looked at the players in front of him for a long moment.

"It's time to (bleep) or get off the pot," he said.

End of motivational speech.

Herzog took his seat. The date was April 12, 1985. St. Louis had opened the season with a 2–4 road trip—and he was speaking in front of hundreds of Cardinals fans at the annual Welcome Home Banquet.

Former Cardinals pitcher Lary Sorensen was long since traded, but the speech wouldn't have surprised him. "Whitey would give it to you straight," Sorensen said. "He would tell us, 'My door is open. You can come in and ask me anything. But you'd better be prepared to hear my answer.'"

Dorrel Norman Elvert Herzog grew up in New Athens, Illinois, less than an hour from St. Louis. It was a small, blue-collar town made up primarily of German immigrants and their descendants. Herzog's mother worked in a shoe factory, his father in a brewery. The town was the real-life embodiment of a black-and-white sitcom or a Republican family values speech. Kids learned the value of a hard day's work—and a beer or two after the work was done.

When he was just seventeen years old, in 1948, Herzog signed with the New York Yankees as an outfielder for a $1,500 bonus and $150 a month salary in the minor leagues. He's proud to point out that his deal was better than the one offered to another outfield prospect by the name of Mickey Mantle. Born nine days before Herzog, Mantle signed for $1,150 and $140 a month.

Despite investing more in Herzog, it quickly became clear that the Yankees' future lay with Mantle. While the Oklahoma Kid established himself as a star, Herzog spent much of spring training on the bench, talking to the team's Hall of Fame manager, before getting sent down to the minors to start the season.

"Casey Stengel saw something in me," Herzog said. "I'm not sure what. He would tell me that I would become a leader and took me under his wing."

"He never said this, but he used to play with Buck Herzog, and I'm pretty sure he thought I was his grandson. I never told him anything different. He'd say, 'How's granddad?' and I'd answer, 'Oh, he's fine.'"

Stengel gave him advice on managing games, the clubhouse and the media, and Herzog took it all in.

On April Fool's Day 1956, after five years in the Yankees farm system and two years in Korea with the Army, Herzog got the news from Stengel: he'd been traded to Washington, as the "player to be named later" in an earlier deal. With Washington, he'd have a chance to make the major leagues—just not with the Yankees.

"The Yankees were always my team, and then I signed with the Yankees," Herzog said. "The saddest day of my life was when I was traded by the Yankees."

Stengel told him not to worry. If Herzog had a good season, Stengel would make another trade to get him back.

Herzog didn't, and neither did Stengel. Herzog bounced around baseball for the next seven years. "I was the kind of player everybody wanted, then when they got me they didn't know what the hell to do with me," he said.

Finally, Herzog was released by the Tigers in 1963. "We can't all be Mickey Mantle, can we?" he concluded, and began his post-baseball life, still only 31 years old.

It didn't last long. He quit his job as a construction foreman instead of laying off two dozen people, and he accepted a job with the Kansas City Athletics, first as a scout, then a coach. After a stint managing in the minor leagues for the Baltimore Orioles organization, he took on a variety of roles with the New York Mets.

He started as a third-base coach—"maybe the best I ever saw," broadcaster Ralph Kiner said. Herzog showed an ability to anticipate and a willingness to roll the dice when deciding whether to send a runner home.

"When a base runner has a chance to score, you've got to remember that the percentage is with him. It's like being a gambler—you'll force the other side to make either a perfect play or a damaging mistake," he said at the time, estimating (or perhaps overestimating) that a good third base coach can win 16 to 17 games a season for his team."

"I'll bet Casey Stengel walked me down the third-base line 75 times a day teaching me that good base running boils down to anticipation and knowledge of the defense," he added. "You can steal a lot of runs."

The Mets determined that Herzog's knowledge could be worth more to the team in a front-office role. He was put in charge of the team's fledgling player development department. "There were five minor league teams," he recalled. "And we had five managers, five trainers, a roving pitching coach and me."

Herzog set about finding the players that would go on to form the nucleus of the 1969 Miracle Mets world champions, as well as the 1973 pennant winners.

"He had a crystal ball," first baseman Ed Kranepool said. "He could look at players to see how good they'd be later on, especially with seventeen- or eighteen-year-old kids."

Under Herzog's watch, Hall of Famer Tom Seaver and All-Star Jerry Koosman made their MLB debut. Herzog also helped develop another promising arm in the farm system.

"I knew him from the time he was eighteen," Herzog said of Hall of Famer Nolan Ryan. "I was on his ass a little bit in the Instructional League, and made him work a little bit harder. A couple times, when he'd doze off, I'd say 'Nolan! Wake up!' or something like that."

In Herzog's first year as farm director, the Mets acquired outfielder Amos Otis and drafted outfielder Ken Singleton and pitchers Jon Matlack and Gary Gentry. In his second year, the Mets traded for Tommy Agee and drafted Tim Foli and John Milner. The team also selected future major leaguers Mickey Rivers and Burt Hooten in the draft but couldn't sign them. Ron Hodges, Bob Apodaca and Wayne Garrett were brought into the organization under Herzog's watch.

In the party following the 1969 World Series win, Herzog attempted to congratulate manager Gil Hodges, only to be beaten to the punch by the skipper.

"He jumped out of his chair and gave me a big ol' handshake," Herzog recalled. Hodges told the shocked Herzog, "For three years now, every time I called you about what I need, you sent me the right player."

The honeymoon ended in 1972, when Herzog was passed over for the Mets managing job following Hodges' death. He said the team wouldn't even let him leave the instructional league to attend Hodges' funeral.

"I've never forgiven them for that," he said.

It was the second unforgivable act by the franchise in a year. Following the 1971 season, the Mets cut bait on Nolan Ryan and traded him to the Angels without telling Herzog.

In December, Herzog was told to break the news to outfielder Leroy Stanton that he'd been traded for Jim Fregosi.

"I said, 'For Fregosi? I wouldn't trade Leroy Stanton for Fregosi,'" Herzog recalled. "'Leroy's got a chance to be a pretty good outfielder. I just saw Fregosi play in Kansas City and he can't play anymore.' [GM Bob Scheffing] didn't even tell me about Ryan being in the trade. I picked up the paper the next day and I saw that Ryan was in the deal. I couldn't believe my eyes."

Two years earlier, the team had ignored his arguments to hold on to Amos Otis, whom he called "the best piece of property we've got." Instead, the team dealt Otis to the Royals for someone named Joe Foy.

Clearly, Herzog was on the outside of the Mets power structure. So, for the second time in three baseball jobs, Herzog resigned. He'd also quit his Athletics coaching job when owner Charlie O. Finley wouldn't give him a raise. "Get your donkey to coach third base," he said, taking a shot at the team's mule mascot.

In 1973, Herzog took a job managing the Rangers, thanks, in part, to the recommendation of Hall of Famer Ted Williams. True to form, Herzog was blunt and honest upon arriving in Texas. "This is the worst excuse for a big league club I ever saw," he said at his introductory press conference.

Herzog was as good a judge of talent—or lack thereof—as ever. The team was terrible. Prior to the season, he ripped catcher Rich Billings, saying, "If he's our starting catcher again, we're in deep trouble."

Billings responded with, "He's obviously seen me play."

The Rangers went 47–91 under Herzog, but he was building a team. "I had some good young players—Jeff Burroughs, Toby Harrah, Davey Nelson, Joe Lovitto," he said. "I didn't have any pitching. By June, I had cleaned out all five starting pitchers. But then we got [Jim] Bibby and signed David Clyde."

Plus, he had plans to make trades during the offseason. "I'd have had a pretty good team the next year," he said.

Instead, owner Bob Short offered to make him general manager. "He told me on Saturday that I was the best manager he'd ever had," said Herzog. "Of course, that wasn't saying much because the only manager he'd ever had was Ted Williams." (Williams, a Hall of Fame player and one of the greatest hitters of all time, had a subpar career record of 273–364 as a manager and lost more than 90 games in three of his four seasons as skipper.)

Herzog turned down the offer to move into the Texas front office.

The next day, news broke that the Tigers had fired Billy Martin—another former Yankee and protégé of Casey Stengel. In the dugout before the Rangers game, Herzog overheard Short telling someone, "I'd fire my grandmother to hire Billy Martin."

By Tuesday, Herzog was the grandmother.

"It was probably the best thing that ever happened to me. It made me realize I wasn't so damn smart," he said.

After a brief stay on the coaching staff of the Angels (he also served as interim manager for four games when Bobby Winkles was fired), Herzog landed back in Kansas City, this time with the Royals. He took over as manager about two-thirds of the way through the 1975 season. He admits he fell into a great position there. Kansas City was a team on the verge of greatness, with third baseman George Brett, his former Mets prospect Otis in center field and a group of solid pitchers.

Herzog made a few changes to the lineup to emphasize the team's speed and tailor the Royals' game to the artificial turf at Royals Stadium. He gave second baseman Frank White and outfielder Al Cowens full-time jobs and got out of the way—at least for a while.

White recalled that Herzog told them, "As long you make good decisions, you'll never hear from me. For the first six innings, just play the game aggressively."

"He let us put our own hit-and-runs on and he let us play the defense the way we wanted to play defense," White continued. "But he said, 'If we haven't caught up by the seventh, then it's my game.'"

Pitcher Paul Splittorff remembers a pregame speech at the start of an important series against a divisional rival. "We'll beat these guys," Herzog said. "Actually, you guys play them even. I know I'm five games better than their manager."

"He's the best I ever saw at game management," catcher John Wathan said. "He'd be two or three innings ahead of everybody. Whitey would have been a pretty good chess player."

Herzog led the Royals to three consecutive American League West titles, but they lost to the Yankees in the ALCS all three years. Herzog blamed the fact that he didn't have a reliable closer, while the Yankees had two—Sparky Lyle and Rich "Goose" Gossage. Even in the mid-70s, the difference between large and small-market teams was hard to overcome.

"They go out and sign Reggie Jackson, Sparky Lyle and Gossage," Herzog said outside the clubhouse in 1978, following the third consecutive ALCS loss. "And who do we sign? [Reserve infielder] Jerry Terrell. . . . All we needed was Gossage and if we'd paid him $600,000, we could have had him but they wouldn't do it."

The team struggled in 1979.

"In July of '79, we lost 14 out of 15," Herzog recalled. "Our pitching fell apart." Herzog also feuded with management over money, and the Royals decided to part ways with him following the season. Herzog shook off the firing. "You get fired the first time, it hurts, because you've never been fired before," he said. "But you get fired the second time, hell, it ain't nothin'."

In 1980, the Cardinals fired manager Ken Boyer between games of a doubleheader on June 8, with the team in sixth place and holding an 18–33 record. Owner August Busch announced the hiring of Herzog, calling him the team's first choice. "We think his aggressive style of play is exactly what is needed to help turn the Cardinals into a winning ball team."

Herzog went 38–35 with the same team, earning him a promotion.

On August 18, general manager John Claiborne was fired. Herzog replaced him a little over a week later, moving upstairs and allowing Red Schoendienst to finish the season as manager. Including Jack Krol, who finished the doubleheader on the day Boyer was fired, Herzog was the only one of the team's four managers that season to post a winning record.

At the end of the season, Herzog approached Busch and offered him a deal.

"I told Gussie what I wanted to do: I want to be general manager and manager and try to put this thing together," he said. "I would take both jobs for the price of one."

There would be no more trades without his knowledge, no more frustration over not getting the players he needed. Herzog would be his own boss.

The team made the announcement in late October. "We realize that this is unique in baseball," Busch said, "but we strongly believe that Whitey is capable of handling both jobs."

Herzog explained that sitting in the press box and watching games, like any other GM, "wasn't my cup of tea."

"I had a spittoon in my office, but I never had one in the press box," Herzog said.

Herzog had the power and a plan. What he didn't have was much time to implement it. The winter meetings would begin in six weeks, and he had a team to rebuild.

"One man in charge, no committees, no crap," Herzog wrote in his autobiography. "It was the first time in my career as a manager I'd had good, solid access to the owner of the club, the man who would give me the authority to make the decisions I needed to make. . . . Gussie had decided I was the guy he wanted to put on the team."

Herzog could build on much of the experience he gained in Kansas City. Like the Royals, the Cardinals played their home games on artificial turf in a cavernous stadium. Herzog knew the stadium wouldn't be kind to sluggers—like catcher Ted Simmons, right fielder George Hendrick and rookie Leon Durham. Instead, Herzog wanted to pack the batting order with speedsters and line-drive hitters, who could run all day while the ball rolled around in the gaps at Busch Stadium.

The 1980 Cardinals had a strong offense. The team led the NL in batting and runs scored but was about at the league average in home runs and near the bottom in stolen bases. Herzog knew that if he could tailor the offense to the stadium, it would free up some assets to help with the pitching the Cardinals so desperately needed.

The Cardinals were last in the league in pitching. While the stadium's sheer size would neutralize the power edge he planned to yield to the opposition, he needed guys that would keep opposing batters off the bases. He also learned from the Royals' postseason failures that he needed a lights-out closer. The 1980 Cardinals led the league in complete games and finished last in saves—in other words, the pitching staff was the anti-Herzog. He made a list of the players he wanted, then he gave himself "cauliflower ear" spending so much time on the phone, setting the stage to acquire them.

From his October press conference, Herzog made it clear that everyone on the roster—except for shortstop Garry Templeton—was available, for the right price. And that price? "What we all know we need here: three kinds of pitching—right-handed, left-handed and relief."

"He'd give me budget," Herzog said later of his relationship with August Busch, "and I'd have to stay within $500,000 of it. When I was wearing both hats, all I had to do was let him know if I traded somebody before it made the papers."

That sounds easy enough, but, at the 1980 winter meetings in Dallas, it required quite a few long-distance phone calls to Busch.

The winter meetings are the oldest annual event in baseball history. As long as owners have been paying players, they've been meeting after the season to trade them. The first meetings were held in 1876, following the inaugural season of the National League. Owners elected a league president and threw two teams out of the league for skipping their final road trip of the season. The winter meetings have been held annually since 1901.

In December 1941, the owners had just arrived in Chicago when news of the bombing of Pearl Harbor broke; the winter meetings went on as scheduled. Two weeks after Kennedy was assassinated, in 1963, the winter meetings went on as planned in San Diego—future Hall of Famers Nellie Fox and Jim Bunning were both traded. When the 1994 labor dispute wiped out the end of the regular season and the World Series, the meetings were still held.

The winter meetings are part business meeting, part convention, part Comic Con. Every MLB manager and general manager attends, along with any agents with MLB clients. Every affiliated minor league team is invited to send representatives as well.

The Rule V Draft, where teams can select unprotected minor leaguers from other organizations, is traditionally held near the end of the winter meetings. But the highlight of the week is the seemingly endless stream of player transactions.

In the pre–cell phone days, most of the Winter Meeting business was done in the hotel lobby. White Sox owner Bill Veeck put up a sign reading "Open for business" at his table in the hotel lobby one year.

General managers would divide up their staff, with each person assigned specific teams to approach in the lobby, to check on potential trades. Former Orioles GM Roland Hemond used walkie-talkies to try to organize the reports from his staff one year.

Some of the biggest deals in baseball history—both trades and free-agent signings—have taken place at the winter meetings. But Whitey Herzog put them all to shame in 1980.

A then-record 59 players were traded in five days at the Dallas Anatole Hotel during the 1980 winter meetings. Herzog was responsible for nearly 40 percent of them. He swung trades involving a total of 23 players, sending away a dozen Cardinals—nearly half his roster.

The players he moved, in one direction or the other, had combined for 24 All-Star appearances and one Cy Young Award at the time. They would go on to make another 12 All-Star teams, win three more Cy Youngs and a pair of MVPs. Herzog made three trades involving future Hall of Famers, including two trades with reliever Rollie Fingers in the course of four days. In the process, he changed the landscape of his team, as well as several others, and helped determine the World Series participants for the first half of the decade.

Some of Herzog's moves seemed random, almost nonsensical. "There were something like six .300 hitters on that 1980 team," Herzog recalled, years later. "I traded so many good players, they wanted to lynch me in St. Louis. . . . Nobody else would have had the guts."

By the end of 120 hours in Dallas, order emerged from the chaos, as it usually did with Herzog.

"Whitey Herzog has a plan for everything he does," remarked pitcher Lary Sorensen, who was traded by Herzog in back-to-back winter meetings. "From his first cup of coffee in the morning to everything that comes afterward. And he's usually thinking three or four moves past everyone else." Herzog made his first move the day before the 1980 winter meetings started, and it was a head-scratcher. The Cardinals signed free-agent catcher Darrell Porter to a five-year, $3.5 million contract. Porter had hit .249 in 1980 with just seven home runs and 51 RBI for Kansas City. He'd also missed the start of the season, because he was in rehab for drug and alcohol addiction.

The move would have been puzzling at any position, but catcher was the one spot on the field where the Cardinals seemed to be set. Ted Simmons—whom Hall of Fame pitcher Tom Seaver called the "toughest out" in the National League—hit .303 in 1980, which was ninth best in the league that year. Simmons hit 21 home runs, the fourth season in a row that he went deep more than 20 times, and more than Porter's career best in any season. Simmons also drove in 98 RBI, good for sixth best in the league.

Behind Simmons was Terry Kennedy, who as a backup nearly matched Porter's production in 1980, and was the likely successor to Simmons. The Cards also had third-stringer Steve Swisher and promising minor leaguer Glenn Brummer. The last thing the team needed was a weak-hitting catcher who had battled personal demons the previous year.

Porter had played for Herzog in Kansas City, and the signing was criticized as cronyism.

"Where will the Cardinals finish? Somewhere between the Mets and the infernal regions. Why? Because of the impulsive negligence of that quail-shooting, beer-guzzling know-it-all Herzog," ranted one angry letter to the editor.

Herzog, however, knew that power-hitting catchers were a valuable commodity, prized slightly more than up-and-coming young catchers. He now had three of them that he could offer. Although he never went to college, Herzog learned at the feet of the Old Professor—Stengel—and he knew that you should always add before you subtract.

In fact, he was already in talks with teams to deal Simmons and Kennedy. He was including Kennedy in negotiations with the Cubs to land closer Bruce Sutter and talking to the Pirates about swapping Simmons for closer Kent Tekulve. He'd also reached out to the Blue Jays, who were desperate for a catcher, about a trade for starters Dave Stieb and Jim Clancy. All this before the winter meetings had even begun.

And if all the deals fell through, leaving Herzog with a logjam behind the plate? He had prepared for that possibility as well. He planned to move Simmons to first base and shift Keith

Hernandez, cowinner of the 1979 MVP Award, to left field, a spot where the Cardinals were trying to upgrade.

Kennedy had also started getting some work in left field, the first time in his career he'd played the position, in 1980. His first game in left had been on June 16, less than a week after Herzog took over as manager. Months before he was even named GM, Herzog was already working on a safety net, should his plan to deal catchers in Dallas fall through.

Of course, Simmons had a no-trade clause in his contract, and he didn't want to play first base. That didn't stop Herzog, who negotiated not one, but two deals sending him out of town, then let the catcher decide which team he wanted to waive his no-trade clause for. One of the trades was with the Yankees, for a package that included left-handed pitcher Ron Guidry. New York planned to use Simmons extensively at designated hitter, a spot even less palatable to him than first base. That leverage helped Herzog send Simmons toward the deal the GM/manager really wanted to consummate.

First things first, however. Herzog had another catcher to deal. On December 8, he kicked off the official start to the meetings with an 11-player trade. He shipped Kennedy to the Padres, along with Swisher, pitchers John Littlefield and John Urrea, infielder Mike Phillips, and minor leaguers Al Olmsted and Kim Seaman. In exchange, Herzog received future Hall of Famer Rollie Fingers, one of the best relievers in baseball. The Padres also sent starting pitcher Bob Shirley and a pair of backup catchers, Gene Tenace and Bob Geren.

"We need pitching," Herzog told the media, and fellow teams, when announcing the trade. "We still need pitching and we'll make another deal. One won't do it."

The next morning, Herzog strolled through the crowded lobby, relishing the attention. "My manager's doing such a good job here," he said, "that I'm thinking of giving him a raise."

"I don't think there's any more pressure on me in both jobs," he added. "Many general managers are brilliant men. But they know the players mainly from their statistics, and there's more to a baseball player than his stats: his mind, his heart, his character, the way he travels. Only the field manager knows him that well."

"My bridge game may lose a little because of these two jobs," he said, still playing the crowd. "But when I leave here, I'll have a ball club. If it doesn't work out, I'll know who to fire: the manager."

Herzog then stirred the pot by planting a rumor about Ted Simmons, intended to get other trade partners, and Simmons, worried. "I've got a date at 4 with [Orioles manager] Earl Weaver," he said. "You know, if they got Ted Simmons, he could be the best switch-hitting designated hitter in history."

Herzog finished his monologue with more bluster. "I'm the only guy here who does something every day," he crowed. "The next announcement will be at two o'clock."

His lobby audience laughed, until two o'clock came, and everyone realized that Herzog was serious. That's when the press conference began, announcing that the Cardinals had made a trade with the Cubs. Herzog gave up Leon Durham, a young power hitter who didn't have a position; third baseman Ken Reitz, who had been convinced to waive his no-trade clause; and outfielder Ty Waller. In return, the Cardinals received Bruce Sutter. Like Fingers, he was a future Hall of Famer, and, like Fingers, he was one of the best relievers in the game.

After entering the winter meetings with shelves stocked with catchers, Herzog had now built up an inventory of another valuable commodity: elite relief pitchers. He was ready to enter another round of trade talks with extra parts to deal.

The Milwaukee Brewers believed that they could compete with the Yankees in the AL East, if only they had a reliever to match New York's Goose Gossage, the same pitcher that Herzog had begged Kansas City's front office to get him, years earlier.

"We wanted Rollie Fingers or Bruce Sutter," Brewers general manager Harry Dalton said. "And we thought we had the inside track on getting Fingers from the San Diego Padres, but the next thing we knew, the Cardinals got Fingers, so we started thinking about concentrating on getting Sutter from the Chicago Cubs but then the Cardinals got Sutter, too."

In fact, Dalton had negotiated a deal for Sutter on the first day of the meetings, a one-for-one trade that would have sent future Hall of Famer Paul Molitor to the Cubs. His advisors were deadlocked, 4–4, on whether or not he should make the deal, so he decided to sleep on it, and in the meantime, he lost Sutter to the Cardinals.

Now the Brewers had to deal with Herzog, if they wanted a reliever. Herzog was also dangling Simmons, since Milwaukee was looking to upgrade with a solid hitter and leader behind the plate.

In addition to working out trade details with Herzog, the Brewers also needed to come to an agreement with Simmons. It was no coincidence that Herzog's other negotiations involving Simmons were with the Brewers' AL East rivals, the Orioles and Yankees. It was also no coincidence that both of the other potential landing spots wanted Simmons as a DH, a position the catcher was reluctant to play, which made the potential of a Brewers trade more palatable to him. While Simmons and the Brewers negotiated a waiver of his no-trade, Herzog was the one holding a gun to their heads. Finally, after twelve hours of negotiations, the Brewers agreed to pay Simmons an extra $750,000 if he'd come to Milwaukee.

"We didn't want the deal to blow up," Dalton said. "We'd heard that the Yankees also were highly interested in [Cardinals pitcher Pete] Vuckovich and Simmons, so we decided to wrap it up and we did."

The trade was finalized on December 12, the final day of the winter meetings. Simmons, Fingers and Vuckovich went to the Brewers in exchange for pitchers Dave LaPoint and Lary Sorensen and outfielders Sixto Lezcano and David Green.

A year later, Fingers won the AL Cy Young and MVP, and the Brewers made the playoffs. The Cardinals had the best record in the NL East, but the split season resulting from the strike kept them home for the postseason.

A year after that, Milwaukee and St. Louis met in the World Series. Vuckovich went 18–6 and was the AL Cy Young winner that year. LaPoint went 9–3 for St. Louis. Green hit .283 as a reserve outfielder. Sutter won 9 games and saved a league-best 36, playing a role in nearly half of the Cardinals' 92 wins.

As one of the pitchers he acquired in 1980 soon learned, Herzog was always thinking far down the line, both in the dugout and in the GM's office. Lary Sorensen recalled his first start of the 1981 season, four months to the day after being acquired by Herzog at the winter meetings. Herzog allowed him to bat for himself with a runner on second base in the bottom of the sixth inning and Sorensen holding a 5–3 lead over the visiting Phillies. Then, after Sorensen faced one batter in the seventh, Herzog came to the mound and replaced him with closer Bruce Sutter, who got the final 9 outs of the game.

Remembering that Herzog said players could "ask me anything," Sorensen stepped into the manager's office a few days later to ask about the decision to pull him from the game when he did. Sorensen couldn't understand why Herzog had such a quick hook for him in the seventh inning. It was still early in the year, and he could have gone longer. Plus, there was no sense burning out your closer so early in the season with unnecessary innings. Furthermore, if he was going to pull him anyway, why did he let the pitcher bat for himself, instead of trying to add another run by sending up a pinch hitter?

"Well, he mentioned about eight things that I'd never thought of," Sorensen said, "about match-ups and the bullpen. Then he said, 'Plus, we're going to Philadelphia in six weeks, and I wanted them wondering about how I use my pinch hitters and closer.'

"I thought I was thinking ahead, because I wanted to save the closer for tomorrow's game," Sorensen said. A few months later, Sorensen was gone, dealt in the 1981 winter meetings as part of Herzog's ever-evolving plan.

"When I found out I was traded to the Cardinals, I was in a hot tub with [Brewers pitcher] Mike Caldwell. They told me I had a phone call," Sorensen recalled. "The next year, I was fishing with Bruce Sutter. When we came back from the lake, they told me to call Whitey right away. I said, this can't be good."

Shooting straight, like always, Herzog told the pitcher, "You know I need a left fielder."

"That's when I knew for sure," Sorensen said. "I asked him, 'Where am I going.'"

Herzog told him he'd swung a deal for Lonnie Smith, a slap-hitting speedster for the Phillies who would steal 68 bases for the Cardinals the following year.

"I thought, well, okay, Philadelphia's a nice town. That's when Whitey said, 'But I'm sending you to Cleveland,'" Sorensen said.

Herzog had orchestrated a three-team, five-player trade with the Indians and Phillies.

At the same winter meetings, in 1981, Herzog also dealt, to San Diego, the one player he'd declared untouchable the year before, swapping Garry Templeton for another shortstop—future Hall of Famer Ozzie Smith.

When the smoke cleared, the core of the St. Louis team that would win the 1982 World Series and National League titles in 1985 and 1987 was formed. So were some of the key players on the 1984 NL champion San Diego Padres (who beat the Cubs and first baseman Leon Durham in the NLCS that year) and the 1982 AL champion Brewers.

All told, in five of the next six seasons, the World Series would feature teams either managed by Herzog or with players dealt to them by Herzog in prominent roles. The '82 Cardinals finished first in stolen bases, first in triples and last in home runs, with 67. For much of the season, Herzog joked they weren't sure if they'd be able to beat Roger Maris (who set the single-season home record by hitting 61, twenty-one years earlier). At a time when the man who would later bring on-base percentage to the forefront of player analysis, Billy "Moneyball" Beane, was hitting .211 at Double-A Jackson, Herzog's Cardinals led the league in on-base percentage.

Every player on the St. Louis roster was offered up in trade talks at some point over the winter meetings of 1980 and 1981. Everyone was expendable, if the deal fit the needs of the one man the Cardinals most needed at the time.

"Whitey Herzog is the one St. Louis could least afford to lose," Giants manager Roger Craig said. "You can't give him enough credit."

WAR COMPARISON

WAR understates the impact of the Cardinal acquisitions, because many of them spent so little time in St. Louis, thanks to Herzog's itching trade trigger. Still, at the 1980 winter meetings, Herzog orchestrated deals that moved players who had combined 134.9 wins above replacement and would go on to produce another 66.9.

CARDINALS RECEIVED	WAR PRE-TRADE	WAR POST-TRADE
Rollie Fingers	5.1	0.0 (traded again before ever playing for St. Louis)
Bob Shirley	4.9	-0.6
Gene Tenace	19.7	3.6
Bruce Sutter	18.5	6.4
David Green	0.0	2.2
Lary Sorensen	12.3	1.0
Dave LaPoint	-0.6	3.2
Sixto Lezcano	18.9	0.5
Bob Geren	0.0	0.0

CARDINALS TRADED AWAY	WAR PRE-TRADE	WAR POST-TRADE
Terry Kennedy	-0.3	16.9
John Littlefield	0.0	0.1
Al Olmsted	0.7	0.0
Mike Phillips	0.3	0.0
Kim Seaman	0.3	0.0
Steve Swisher	-0.2	-0.6
John Urrea	-0.7	1.1
Leon Durham	1.4	15.0
Ken Reitz	0.8	-0.8
Ty Waller	-0.1	0.0
Rollie Fingers	0.0*	7.9
Ted Simmons	44.8	5.9
Pete Vuckovich	9.1	5.1

CHAPTER 17

— THE BLEEPING TRADE —

THE STORY BEHIND THE BUCKY DENT TRADE

A prospect-for-veteran trade works to perfection.

Another deal that looked lopsided one way at first, then the other: the Chicago White Sox sent shortstop Bucky Dent to the New York Yankees in April 1977. In a year and a half, he would improbably break Boston Red Sox hearts and lead the Yankees to a World Series title. Among the players the Yankees gave up in that deal was future 1983 Cy Young winner, LaMarr Hoyt.

Bucky Dent was an athletic player with matinee idol looks. He would dabble in acting and film a talk-show pilot. The man he would replace as Yankees shortstop was a gawky, awkward man nicknamed "Chicken."

"I actually met Mr. Steinbrenner in 1973 or '74," Dent recalled. "It was at a Bulls [basketball] game. He was sitting in front of me, and the gentleman who was with me said, 'Do you know who that is?' . . . I tapped him on the shoulder and introduced myself. He says, 'Boy, I've been trying to get you.' I said, 'I'd love to play for the Yankees someday.' Three years later or so, here we go."

All it took was a trip to the doghouse for the Chicken and a change in the entire financial structure of baseball. From his nickname, it was clear that Fred "Chicken" Stanley wasn't in the majors for his power-hitting ability. In 1976, he learned that there's nothing wrong with being a good-field, no-hit shortstop, until you make an error.

Stanley had nine seasons with five extra base hits or fewer, more than any other major leaguer in the last 55 years. He finished his 14-year career with just 10 homers, 120 RBI and a .216 lifetime batting average.

Stanley joined the Yankees in 1973, George Steinbrenner's first year owning the club. Through the 1976 season, the team had had more managers (3) than Stanley had home runs (2). He was a solid fielder who could play both second base and shortstop, two spots where a team could hide a weak hitter, as long as he wasn't a liability in the field.

In 1976, Stanley had completed his second straight season as, more-or-less, the Yankees' starting shortstop. He had career highs in at bats, hits, RBI and walks. His .238 average was his highest since his rookie year.

The Yankees won the American League East that year, making the postseason for the first time in twelve years, as well as the first time with Steinbrenner at the helm.

That's when Stanley's glove got him noticed by the Boss.

In Game Two of the ALCS, Stanley made one of the Yankees' five errors, as the Royals won to even the series at one game apiece. The Yankees went on to win the series on a walk-off home run by Chris Chambliss in Game Five. Stanley had just the one error in the five games.

After dropping Game One of the World Series at Cincinnati, the Yankees were tied with the Reds 3–3 going into the ninth inning of Game Two. New York starting pitcher Jim Hunter retired the first two batters in the bottom of the ninth, and, when Ken Griffey hit a slow grounder to shortstop, the game appeared headed to extra innings.

Stanley charged the ball and threw off-balanced to first base. It wasn't even close to on-target. First baseman Chris Chambliss had no shot to get a glove on the ball, and it flew into the Reds dugout, allowing Griffey to move to second base.

After an intentional walk, Tony Pérez singled Griffey home for the game-winning run—an unearned run, courtesy of Stanley. The Reds went on to sweep the Yankees in 4 games, embarrassing and infuriating Steinbrenner.

When the team's front-office brain trust met to discuss a game plan for the offseason, the first thing Steinbrenner said was, "We are not going to win a championship with Fred Stanley at shortstop."

In addition to the normal hot-stove trade market, the Yankees had a new tool available to them to upgrade the roster: 1976 was the first year of widespread free agency in Major League Baseball. After two players were named free agents in 1975, nearly two dozen players qualified in the winter following 1976. Compared to modern-day free agency, the market in 1976 was anything but free.

MLB teams conducted a dispersal draft on November 4, in which teams selected free agents to negotiate with. A team could draft as many players as it wanted, but each player could only be selected by, and negotiate with, twelve teams.

Teams could only sign two free agents, or the number of free agents that they lost, whichever number was higher.

The Yankees selected nine players to enter negotiations. The group included only one true shortstop—34-year-old Bert Campaneris. They also drafted Bobby Grich and Dave Cash, who were primarily second basemen, and Billy Smith, a seldom-used middle infielder with the Angels, with the hopes of turning one of them into a shortstop.

When the Yankees set their priorities before the draft, they decided that Campaneris probably wasn't the solution at short, since he was too old. Instead, they would focus on landing Grich, who had played shortstop in the minor leagues.

On November 18, the Yankees outbid everyone for pitcher Don Gullett, using one of their two free-agent spots.

Grich wanted to sign with the Angels. He'd come up through the Orioles organization with Angels DH Don Baylor and considered him a close friend. Angels GM Harry Dalton told Grich's agent that the team didn't have any money left to make an offer, however.

Grich said he would take a lower offer from the Angels, as long as it was fair. Dalton got permission from owner Gene Autry to exceed the team's budget.

Before Grich heard the Angels' offer, Steinbrenner made his sales pitch, promising Grich that he was the missing piece in a World Series championship for the Yankees. He also offered more money than anyone else. Baltimore offered Grich $1.2 million to re-sign. The Angels finally offered $1.5 million. The Yankees' offer was for $2.2 million, "but my dream was to play for the Angels, and in front of my parents," the Los Angeles native said.

To Steinbrenner, Grich said he'd have to think things over.

Steinbrenner wasn't used to not getting his way, and he resorted to bullying the second baseman.

"I later found out that Steinbrenner did everything he could to sign Grich," Reggie Jackson said in his memoir. "He even told Bobby the Angels had manipulated the market, and that he was going to file a protest with the league commissioner, maybe go to court. He told Grich he'd win the protest, and then Bobby would be left out in the cold."

Grich wasn't intimidated. After the meeting, he called Dalton to see if the Yankees could actually win the protest. Assured that they couldn't, Grich signed with the Angels for $700,000 less than the Yankees offered.

"The Boss bluffed a lot, but he wasn't very good at it," Jackson concluded.

Five days after Grich spurned them to sign with the Angels, the Yankees signed their second free agent. Reggie Jackson agreed to a five-year contract worth $3 million.

That left two problems for the Yankees' front office: they still faced the prospect of heading into the season with Fred Stanley as their shortstop, and they now had two right fielders.

In addition to Jackson, the Yankees had Oscar Gamble, a free-spirited outfielder who had just completed his first year with the team. Prior to coming to the Yankees, Gamble had been an up-and-coming outfielder with the Indians. He allowed his hair to grow out into an oversized Afro. "I think it was fourteen or fifteen inches at the time," he said. "I would go like a size and a half too big on my hats and pull it down as far as I could, but it would still fall off as I ran."

In 1975, the Indians held a contest, soliciting ideas from fans on how Gamble could wear a hat over his enormous hair.

"We're open to all suggestions, except a haircut," Gamble said.

Gamble also owned a disco and dressed in wild 1970s outfits, including a pair of red, white and blue plaid slacks and elevator shoes.

The hair and clothes were all in fun but caused many in the conservative baseball establishment to view Gamble as a troublemaker.

"Yeah, people always ask me about my hair. I liked it, but I guess it did cause me to get a bad reputation," Gamble said later. "People took one look at that hair and thought I was a bad guy. There were some sportswriters who wouldn't even talk to me. They thought I was some kind of militant with my beard and my hair."

The Indians traded Gamble to the Yankees for pitcher Pat Dobson in November 1975. The acquisition of Gamble produced a potential collision of ideals, and fashion sense, in New York. When Steinbrenner bought the Yankees, he instituted a grooming policy. Players aren't allowed to have beards or sideburns—only mustaches—and long hair is prohibited.

It's a policy that has lasted for more than 40 years, even after the Boss' death. Famous long-hairs Jason Giambi and Johnny Damon would get trims before donning the pinstripes, and Gamble was no different.

The confrontation took place in spring training, 1976, and there was no question who was going to win.

"(GM) Gabe Paul saw Gamble in the parking lot," former Yankees PR director Marty Appel recalled. "He called me and said, 'His hair is still long. You have to get it cut.'"

Appel asked, "Why me?"

Paul responded, "You're the PR guy. If that hair isn't cut, we're not going to let him play, and that's a PR problem."

So Appel enlisted the help of former Yankees catcher Elston Howard. He was a coach with the team and, more importantly, an African American. He offered to go with Gamble to the barber and offer moral support. Gamble had to pay for the cut himself, however. "It cost about $75–80, even back then," he said.

"I sort of knew it was going to happen," Gamble recalled. "I went in and talked to Billy (Martin), because, when I showed up in the locker room, there was no uniform in my locker."

Gamble told the manager, "Everyone else is getting dressed. Where's my uniform?"

"George says you have to get a haircut first," Martin replied.

The policy cost Gamble an endorsement deal. Afro Sheen had offered the new Yankee money to do a commercial.

Steinbrenner wasn't moved, although he later reimbursed Gamble for the money he would have earned from Afro Sheen.

Gamble found other ways to express himself while on the Yankees. During one game, he came up in the late innings with a runner on base. He got the sign to bunt and refused it. Third base coach Dick Howser called him over and said, "Billy wants you to get the guy in scoring position."

Gamble responded, "Tell Billy I'm already in scoring position when I'm at the plate."

If there was one player who was always in scoring position, however, it was Reggie Jackson. Gamble had 17 home runs, 57 RBI and a .232 average for the Yankees in 1976. Reggie was coming off a year in which he had 27 homers, 91 RBI and a .277 average as a member of the Orioles, and he was just two years removed from leading the league with 36 homers. He also stole 28 bases in '76. When Grich shunned New York and the Yankees took right-fielder Jackson, Gamble became expendable.

As for the Fred Stanley problem, Gabe Paul and the Yankees were busy looking to trade for a shortstop. With the Rangers signing Bert Campaneris, the Yankees checked to see whether Texas' incumbent shortstop Toby Harrah might be available.

The two teams had some talks. Harrah wasn't an elite defensive shortstop—he'd set a record earlier in the season by going an entire doubleheader without handling the ball—but he was the rare middle infielder with 20-home-run power. He was essentially the anti-Stanley. The Rangers intended to hold on to Harrah, however, and move him to third base.

The Yankees also spoke to the White Sox about shortstop Bucky Dent. Chicago was having trouble negotiating a contract with Dent. White Sox president Bill Veeck had offered Dent $500,000 for three years. Despite the fact that that would triple Dent's salary, the shortstop turned it down.

He was unsigned at the time—a situation that could lead to him joining the new free agency circus the following offseason. Veeck, the Chicago president, was a longtime owner, innovator and showman who would be inducted into the Hall of Fame in 1991. He's the one that planted the ivy on the outfield walls at Wrigley Field and convinced announcer Harry Caray to sing "Take Me Out to the Ballgame" during the seventh-inning stretch.

Veeck was the first to put names on jerseys and have obnoxious sound effects and scoreboard pyrotechnics. He also introduced the idea of revenue sharing in the 1940s, 60 years and several work stoppages before the rest of baseball got around to considering it. He signed Larry Doby, the first black player in the American League.

There were also the crazier ideas. Veeck once signed a three-foot-seven little person and sent him to the plate as a pinch hitter, wearing the uniform number ⅛. He also held "disco demolition night," where fans could burn disco records in an on-field bonfire. The ensuing riot left the field unplayable, forcing the team to forfeit a game.

Veeck was always thinking of a new way to buck the system and stay a few steps ahead of everyone else in baseball. As he once said, "I don't break the rules. I just test them for elasticity."

While the Angels came up with one scheme for beating the new free agency system, Veeck took another angle. Whereas the Angels looked to add bit players who were about to become free agents, giving the team extra opportunities to sign new players, Veeck looked for players on the brink of free agency who could contribute to his team in the short term.

His thought process was that the players would be motivated in their last season before free agency. They'd want to put up big numbers to impress future bidders for their services. Veeck decided to give his "rent-a-player" scheme a test run in the 1977 season.

First, he had to find a home for his disgruntled shortstop. The Yankees and White Sox worked on a deal for Dent for four months, to no avail. Veeck wanted the Yankees to include a skinny 25-year-old left-handed pitcher named Ron Guidry.

Guidry was a reliever who had pitched out of the Yankees' bullpen briefly each of the previous two seasons. He hadn't done much to impress. In 1976, his ERA was 5.62. Steinbrenner initially agreed to include him in the trade.

Other members of the Yankees' front office had a fit. Guidry was dominating at Triple-A Syracuse in 1976. He went 5–1 with a 0.68 ERA. He allowed just 16 hits in 40 innings and struck out 50. GM Gabe Paul threatened to quit if Guidry was included in the trade. Steinbrenner relented.

Veeck tried to get reliever Sparky Lyle instead. Lyle had led the league in saves in 1976, but he was supposedly expendable, because the untouchable prospect Guidry was going to replace him as closer. Except that Guidry hadn't proven he could pitch at the major league level yet.

The talks dragged on into spring training, and it appeared that there would be no deal. On March 14, the Yankees dealt reserve outfielder Terry Whitfield, who was playing without a contract, to the Giants for middle infielder Marty Perez, also playing without a contract.

Perez hit .257 the previous year, split between the Braves and Giants. He wasn't Grich, Harrah or Dent, but he was an alternative, at least until Steinbrenner saw him in a few spring training games and decided he couldn't hit.

Perez would play a grand total of one regular-season game with the Yankees—he went two-for-four in that game.

Four days after the Yankees acquired Perez, a Florida paper did a story on Stanley, calling him the "scapegoat" for the Yankees. In it, Stanley commented that he finally felt "needed" by the Yankees, and he defended his abilities.

"Okay, I'll give you Campaneris and Grich," Stanley said, "but name me another shortstop in the league who is better than me."

The comments were like waving a red cape in front of a bull. Steinbrenner went back to trade talks with a vengeance, determined to find a shortstop better than Stanley.

Finally, the day before the regular season, Steinbrenner and Veeck were able to complete the trade.

Gamble went to the White Sox and was bitterly disappointed. After going to the World Series in his first year with the Yankees, he was hoping to return, and win, in 1977. Instead, he'd been caught off guard by a last-minute trade to a team that had lost 97 games in 1976.

Before reporting to the White Sox, he demanded a $25,000 raise, to $100,000, or he might retire. Cooler heads soon prevailed, and Gamble joined a crew of other newly acquired White Sox who were playing for new or better contracts.

Gamble would hit a career high 31 home runs in 1977 and drive in 83 runs. Another offseason acquisition, Richie Zisk, would hit 30 homers and drive in 101.

The White Sox would hit a club record 192 home runs in 1977, bettering the old mark by 54. The Sox also shattered the team record for slugging percentage. They became known as the South Side Hitmen.

The Sox won 6 of 7 games in May to move within a half game of first. On June 19, they'd move into first place. Chicago swept four games from Minnesota to highlight a 6–1 homestead and then won 22 games in the month of July.

The Sox faded, though. They opened August with a 4–12 stretch, and their 5.5 game lead became a 5.5 game deficit by Labor Day.

Next came the downside of Veeck's plan. After their career years earned them a higher asking price on the free-agent market, Zisk left for Texas and Gamble for San Diego. The team went from 90 wins in 1977 to 90 losses the following season.

The Yankees got Dent. They signed him to a three-year, $600,000 contract, which was $100,000 more than Veeck's best offer.

The Yankees also sent the White Sox minor league left-hander Bob Polinsky. The 25-year-old had been converted from starter to bullpen at Triple-A in 1976. He hadn't posted a winning record in the last three seasons, however, and would never pitch in the major leagues.

That was the deal originally agreed upon. In addition, the Yankees would send the White Sox $705,000.

Commissioner Bowie Kuhn stepped in and put a stop to the deal, however. He imposed a $400,000 cap on all cash transfers in trades. The Yankees agreed to give up a relief pitcher and send a lower cash amount—$200,000.

It took some convincing, but Gabe Paul finally made Bill Veeck believe that LaMarr Hoyt would be able to contribute as a member of the bullpen.

Hoyt came from a checkered background. His parents went through a bitter divorce, and, in his first year of life, each parent kidnapped him and tried to disappear. Hoyt was finally stashed with his father's sister, who ended up raising him.

"I raised him and tried to give him love and a home and a security that his parents didn't," his aunt, Margaret Hiller, said. "I didn't do it for roses, I did it because I loved him."

Hoyt was drafted by the Yankees in 1973. He showed up at rookie ball in Johnson City, Tennessee, a day early. There was no one there to meet him, and, after a few hours in a hotel room alone, he headed back home to Columbia, South Carolina.

His aunt talked him into returning, and he quickly rose through the Yankees system. He won six games in Johnson City, went 13–4 at Class A Fort Lauderdale the next year, and, in 1976, he dominated Double-A. Playing for West Haven, he won 15 games and posted a 2.50 ERA. He had 14 complete games and 4 shutouts.

At the time Gabe Paul was convincing Bill Veeck that Hoyt was the answer to his bullpen needs, Hoyt had pitched 90 minor league games for the Yankees organization and started 82 of them. He wasn't a strikeout pitcher, the type usually selected to be a team's closer.

When the Yankees informed Hoyt that he was traded, they softened the blow by telling him he had a good chance of making Chicago's major league roster. Instead, the White Sox had him report to Triple-A Iowa.

While Hoyt was fighting the disappointment of missing the big leagues, he made an equally sour impression on his new team.

Iowa manager Joe Sparks greeted his new player and asked him to pitch, saying, "Let's see what you've got."

Hoyt had pitched seven innings in a spring training game the day before. He replied, "You guys scouted me. You ought to know how I throw."

He finally agreed to throw a few tired-arm pitches, to which Sparks said, "Son, I don't know how you've gotten guys out before, but you won't get guys out here with that (bleep)."

Hoyt made 6 starts in Iowa and was demoted further, to Double-A, after posting a 7.20 ERA.

The young pitcher was convinced that Sparks hated him. The manager said, "I didn't have any trouble getting along with LaMarr, but every time out, I'd look up in the second inning, and we'd be down 4–0 or 5–0. It happened time and again. He'd get hurt with a slow curve. But I liked him. I thought he was a super person."

Hoyt went 4–13 at Double-A Knoxville and appeared to be regressing. He demanded $500 for moving expenses after being demoted, and when the White Sox didn't pay, he threatened to quit.

Hoyt boycotted one game at Double-A and only returned when the team came through with some of the money—$176.

"I think they thought I was a jerk," Hoyt recalled. "There was a lack of communication."

A minor league pitching coordinator met with Hoyt after the season and asked him what they could do to help him become a better pitcher.

"If you put me in the big leagues and leave me alone, I think I'll be okay," he answered.

Instead, they put him on the list of minor leaguers they planned on releasing. The list went to Veeck for approval.

An angry Veeck got a hold of farm director Charlie Evranian and gave him the facts: he'd already spent the $200,000 they got from the Yankees. Gamble was going to leave as a free agent. He wasn't going to cut one of the two minor league pitchers he had left to show from trading Bucky Dent.

"When LaMarr Hoyt goes out the door, you can go with him," Veeck told Evranian.

Instead, the Sox sent him to Class A. He went 18–4 with 13 complete games and four shutouts, overmatching 19- and 20-year-old batters.

He was sent to winter ball, where he met manager Tony La Russa.

"Tony rescued me," Hoyt later said. La Russa taught him to mix pitches and speeds and work the edges of the plate.

Hoyt followed La Russa up through the White Sox system, arriving in the majors for two games in 1979 and to stay the following season.

Hoyt put up 9–3 records in 1980 and 1981, adding 10 saves in '81. La Russa gave up the bullpen experiment after that and returned Hoyt to the rotation.

Hoyt led the league with 19 wins in 1982. In 1983, he won the Cy Young Award with a 24–10 record, as the White Sox won the American League West.

Always heavy, Hoyt's weight began to get out of control. He weighed 250 in his Cy Young season, then showed up the next year 15 pounds heavier.

"Don't be fooled, LaMarr's well conditioned to do the things he has to do," said pitching coach Dave Duncan. "He's mentally and physically tough. For a big man, he's in great shape. He runs on the sidelines, he does all the light weight work that he must. I've never been concerned with the weight of a pitcher, unless it takes away from his stamina and productivity. LaMarr's weight has never been a problem for him."

Hoyt continued to put on weight during the season, and his 13–18 record in 1984 was blamed on his excess weight. He agreed to shed some pounds in the offseason.

However, when he showed up for a team event, he was even heavier than before. "That worried us," GM Roland Hemond said. "We didn't know what weight he could possibly be up to between December and the start of the season."

The White Sox traded Hoyt to San Diego at the Winter Meetings, creating a stir among Chicago fans.

"People were shocked that we would trade a big winner like Hoyt," Hemond said. "I like it when trades like this are not applauded. We also were unpopular for trading Dent to New York for Hoyt. We try to perpetuate things like that. Some day, we may trade one of these guys from San Diego and people won't like it."

Hemond's prediction that one of the "guys from San Diego" would become a fan favorite was correct. Among the prospects the Sox received was shortstop Ozzie Guillén, who would become one of the most popular players the franchise had. After his playing days, Guillén returned to manage the team to its first World Series title in 88 years.

Meanwhile, Hoyt had one more All-Star season in him, when he went 16–8 for San Diego in 1985. Then a shoulder injury and drug problem forced him out of baseball after the 1986 season. He was arrested four times and served two prison sentences by the end of 1988.

Like Hoyt, Bucky Dent was raised by his aunt. His given first name, Russell, was abandoned after a grandmother called him "Cooterbuck" as an infant. "It's a Southern expression," Dent said. "I don't know what it means. After a while, I got embarrassed by it and it just became Bucky."

He also doesn't go by his given last name—O'Dea. His aunt and uncle brought him home from the hospital and raised him as their own, using their last name—Dent.

Dent didn't meet his birth father until he was 25 years old, when he was the shortstop for the World Champions, following the 1977 season.

Also like Hoyt, he didn't make a great first impression on his new team.

"It was the last day of spring training," he recalled. "The phone rang—I was putting a box in the car—and I ran back in to answer the phone. I heard this crowd in the background."

"Bucky Dent?" said the gruff voice on the other end. "This is George Steinbrenner."

"Get out of here," Dent said.

Steinbrenner attempted unsuccessfully to convince Dent that it was really him.

"I thought it was a prank, because all spring I was supposed to be traded and it never happened," Dent explained later. "I told my good friends to stop calling me about it. I don't want to worry about it anymore."

Dent finally excused himself, hung up and called his agent to confirm the news.

Dent quickly assumed the shortstop position for New York. His presence made Perez, the infielder the Yankees obtained in spring training, superfluous. They dealt Perez on April 27, six weeks after trading for him. The deal also sent pitcher Dock Ellis to the A's, upsetting manager Billy Martin, who was an Ellis fan.

The Yankees received pitcher Mike Torrez in the trade. Torrez won 14 games for the Yankees in 1977, plus 2 games in the team's World Series victory over the Dodgers.

He left the Yankees after the season and signed with the Red Sox as a free agent. Torrez was on the mound for Boston when the Yankees and Red Sox had a one-game playoff to break a tie for the 1978 AL East title.

Torrez had a 2–0 lead with two outs in the seventh inning. The Yankees had two runners on, when Bucky Dent came to the plate. Dent had 4 home runs on the season and would hit 40 in his entire career, but he drove a Torrez pitch over the Green Monster to give the Yankees an improbable lead and break Red Sox fans' hearts once again.

The homer earned the shortstop the nickname "Bucky [Bleeping] Dent" in Boston for eternity.

The Yankees won the ALCS and advanced to their second straight World Series. Dent hit in all six games of the World Series as the Yankees beat the Dodgers. He finished the Series with 10 hits in 24 at bats, for a .417 average. He scored 3 times and had 7 RBI, including driving in the run that put New York ahead to stay in the deciding game of the Series. Dent was named World Series MVP.

He would go on to start at short for New York for five and a half years. One of the more popular Yankees of the late 1970s and early 1980s, Dent was elected to the All-Star starting lineup in the fan vote twice.

It was the home run against the hated Red Sox, however, that will cause Dent's name to live on in fans' memories.

It was a storybook moment in a Yankee career that began with trade rumors, an embarrassing call from the owner and Dent's eventual arrival in the clubhouse of his new team.

"The first thing they told me, once I got traded to New York," Dent recalled, "I walked in the door and Billy Martin says, 'Get a haircut.'"

WAR COMPARISON

Veeck and Steinbrenner got together for a surprisingly even trade that helped both teams reach the postseason.

In addition to the dramatic home run against the Red Sox, Dent gave the Yankees several years of starter-quality play at shortstop. Hoyt's Cy Young season was one of two strong years he gave the White Sox out of his three in the starting rotation.

YANKEES RECEIVED	WAR PRE-TRADE	WAR POST-TRADE
Bucky Dent	4.3	12.5
WHITE SOX RECEIVED	WAR PRE-TRADE	WAR POST-TRADE
Oscar Gamble	2.8	3.6
LaMarr Hoyt	0.0	11.2
Robert Polinsky	0.0	0.0

CHAPTER 18

— JUST SEVENTEEN —

THE STORY BEHIND THE BIGGEST TRADE IN HISTORY

The more the merrier as the Yankees and Orioles put together a gem.

The New York Yankees and Baltimore Orioles made the biggest trade in baseball history in 1953, swapping seventeen players and a player to be named later (who never was). The trade was so big that one sportswriter, when informed of the deal, asked the general manager if he was drunk. Included in the swap were Bob Turley and Don Larsen, who helped build the Yankees World Series pitching staffs for the rest of the decade.

In 1954, veteran AP baseball writer Joe Reichler was the one to break news of the biggest trade in baseball history. He received a call at home from White Sox general manager Frank Lane. Although the Sox weren't involved in the deal, the trade sent shockwaves through front offices across baseball, and executives wanted to talk about what had just happened.

Reichler was grateful for the tip, but skeptical. "When he told me the deal involved seventeen players, I said, 'C'mon, Frank, are you drunk?'" Reichler recalled. "Frank said, 'I've never had a drink in my life; I'm telling you, it's a seventeen-player deal.' I sat down and wrote the story and phoned my office, where Orlo Robertson was on the desk. As soon as I told him about the seventeen players, Orlo said, 'C'mon, Joe, are you drunk?' I told him, no, I wasn't drunk, this was really a seventeen-player deal. The story went out on the wire."

The teams involved in the trade were the New York Yankees and the Baltimore Orioles. One was a team that had come to treat the World Series as a birthright. The other was a team just trying to find a footing in a new city.

The trade was so large that there's been confusion over how many players were actually involved. Sources have anywhere from sixteen to eighteen players changing teams. Part of the problem results from the inclusion of a player to be named later who appears to have never been named.

In 1954, the Yankees and Orioles both had unusual seasons. Despite winning 103 games, the Yankees didn't finish first, and despite losing 100, the Orioles didn't finish last.

The Yankees had just completed a record run of 5 straight World Series titles, but, despite winning the most games in Hall of Fame manager Casey Stengel's career in 1954, they finished 8 games back of the Cleveland Indians, who set a then-AL record with 111 wins in '54.

Despite their own gaudy win total, the Yankees were looking to revamp their roster. The pitchers who had helped carry the team to World Series success were all aging. Allie Reynolds, Eddie Lopat, Johnny Sain and Jim Konstanty were all 35 or older, while Tommy Byrne would turn 35 the following year.

Hall of Famer Phil Rizzuto was also feeling the effects of age. At 36, he was four years and a far cry removed from his MVP season of 1950. He hit just .195, and his days as a starting shortstop were coming to an end. Yankees scouts spent the last few months of the 1954 season scanning the majors in search of at least two pitchers to supplement the aging staff, along with a new shortstop.

Yankees GM, George Weiss, thought he had a chance to meet both goals with one trade. He tried to get the White Sox's Lane to send him starting shortstop Chico Carrasquel and pitchers Billy Pierce, Bob Keegan and Sandy Consuegra. Carrasquel was eight years younger than Rizzuto and, in 1954, made his third All-Star team in his five-year career. Pierce was 27, and the other two pitchers were both 33. All three had been All-Stars in at least one of the previous two seasons.

Despite being nicknamed "Trader," Lane turned down the Yankees' overtures. Weiss went looking for another partner who had what he needed.

The Orioles, meanwhile, completed their first season in Baltimore after moving from St. Louis, where they were known as the Browns. A new city didn't change the results on the field. The franchise suffered through its ninth straight losing season and ninth straight year finishing in sixth place or worse. Baltimore lost 100 games, finishing an astonishing 57 games out of first. (The Philadelphia Athletics were three games worse.) They had plenty of young pitchers, but the Orioles needed position players. Even more, the Orioles needed a star—someone for hometown fans seeing their first Major League Baseball to connect with.

The Browns had been infamous for their frugality, and that attitude followed the team to Baltimore. "We had operated very conservatively that season," Orioles accountant Joe Hamper said. "The mind-set was clubs like the Yankees and Red Sox had the big bucks, and we were not in that category."

The team decided to change its outlook in year two in the new city and spend whatever it took to become competitive. The team fired manager Jimmy Dykes and GM Arthur Ehlers and replaced them both with one man: Paul Richards.

Richards had managed the White Sox and had an army of private scouts who followed him from job to job. He was ready to "open the keys to the cash box," as Hamper said.

"Overnight, we went from a conservative organization to a very aggressive and, in some respects, reckless organization," Hamper said.

Richards doubled the signing bonuses the team paid out to get amateur prospects under contract. He also ran through players, using 54 different Orioles in the 1955 season. In 1956, he would try to exchange the team's entire 25-man roster with the 25-man roster of the Kansas City A's. In 1964, while with the Astros, he tried an even bigger deal, offering the team's entire 40-man roster, plus $5 million, to the Braves for their entire 40-man.

So, when Weiss called Richards, looking to see what it would take to get the team's best pitcher, it was like striking a match to a powder keg. Weiss inquired about "Bullet" Bob Turley, the 24-year-old ace of the Orioles' staff who won 14 games in '54 and led the majors in strikeouts, with 185. He also led the majors in walks, with 181, the fourth-highest total in a season since 1900.

Turley had won the first game in Baltimore's Memorial Stadium, pitching one of his 14 complete games and striking out 9 batters in a 3–1 win. A local paper called it "the most thrilling day in Baltimore history since the bombardment of Fort McHenry in the War of 1812."

"I pitched the whole game," Turley said. "Had to. Back then, if you didn't go nine, they sent you back to the minors."

A bright spot in a dismal season, Turley quickly became one of the most popular Orioles. "The fans were friendly in every sense of the word," he said. "When my first son was born that season, people gave us a crib and free diapers. They treated us royally."

Fans also voted him team MVP and most-popular player. He received a Cadillac, $1,000 and other gifts.

Richards was willing to give up Turley, but he needed to stock his lineup. He requested Gene Woodling and Gus Triandos from New York. Woodling was a 32-year-old left fielder who had been with the Yankees for all five World Series from 1949 to 1953. He played in just 97 games in 1954, due to a broken arm. Triandos was a 22-year-old catcher who had hit 19 and 18 homers in his last two minor league seasons.

The Yankees didn't have a regular role for either player. Woodling platooned with Hank Bauer, and Triandos was blocked by future Hall of Famer Yogi Berra. Weiss was willing to give up both players to land Turley, but he needed a backup catcher to fill the role he had envisioned Triandos eventually playing. Weiss asked for Darrell Johnson, who had played just 90 games at Triple-A the previous season.

Back and forth they went, adding players to the transaction. On November 18, Reichler announced the deal. The Yankees acquired three players and sent six to Baltimore. The trade included an astounding nine players to be named later.

In phase one of the trade, the Yankees landed Turley, as he found out when the show he was watching was interrupted with breaking news. "I was at home feeding the baby his bottle and watching *The Tonight Show*," Turley recalled, "when, boom, my picture flashed overtop that of Steve Allen."

Underneath his picture, the headline blared, "BOB TURLEY, MULTIPLE PLAYERS TRADED TO NEW YORK."

Turley stood there with his infant, stunned.

"Nobody from the Orioles ever told me I was traded," he said. "To this day, I'm still waiting for that call."

Turley had decided, for the first time, to spend his offseason in the city where he played. "I started working in the off-season at Hecht's [department store], in sporting goods, signing autographs and greeting people for $200 a week," he said.

"Richards talked to me and said I was going to be one of the players they'd build the club around," Turley said. "But then within 30 days, they traded me."

Orioles fans also weren't happy. "The next morning, when I went out to the car, someone had written 'Damn Yankee' on it in the dust," Turley said.

Fans flooded the team, as well as Baltimore newspapers and stations, with complaints. One poll found fans 10 to 1 against the trade. "It's like trading skilled mechanics for laborers," one fan complained.

Other than the shock and frustration over finding out about being traded from a television update, Turley was happy to be headed to New York.

"It really gives you a shock to hear you've been traded, and I certainly didn't know anything about it," he told the AP when reached for comment. "I hate to get traded from

Baltimore, where I've been treated so wonderfully, but that's something you just can't turn down—going to a first-division club. That's a ballplayer's dream, to play with a first-division club. I had hoped it would be with Baltimore."

Years later, he was a little less tactful. "I'd have crawled to New York," he said. "What did I learn from that '54 season? That I never wanted to be on a loser for the rest of my life."

Hank Greenberg, the GM of the defending American League champion Indians, responded to questions about the trade by complaining, "Why did you have to bring Turley into the conversation? Are you trying to ruin my day? I'd feel a lot better about our chances of winning the 1955 pennant if the Yankees hadn't pried a pitcher of Turley's class from the Orioles."

The Yankees also landed Billy Hunter, the Orioles' starting shortstop. He was ten years younger than Rizzuto and had been an All-Star in 1953.

The third named player headed to the Yankees was Don Larsen. The 25-year-old right-hander led the league in losses in 1954, going 3–21 with the Orioles. Teammate Joe Durham described Larsen as "a real loosey-goosey type person," but the stress of the terrible record wore on Larsen.

Marty Marion, manager of the Browns in 1952 and 1953, considered moving Larsen to the outfield, but he was fired after the move to Baltimore, leaving Larsen on the mound to endure a rare 20-plus loss year.

"I managed to keep my sanity until the last game of the season, when Jimmy Dykes decided to start me," Larsen wrote in his autobiography. "At a time when I wanted to crawl into the woodwork, I was stuck going to the mound. . . . My heart simply wasn't up to the task. It's the only time in my career that I can remember not wanting to play."

"When a ballplayer's in a slump or on a losing streak, he tries everything he can think of to snap out of it. . . . I tried too hard. I'd overthrow and things just got worse," he wrote. "About the time I felt like I was back on track with good pitches, the other team would hit them. So then I'd make bad pitches and walk batters. It was like a continual upset stomach. The more I tried, the worse the results."

Two of his three wins in '54, however, were against the Yankees, impressing the team enough to take a flyer on him. "I think that's why the Yankees wanted to trade for me after the season," he said. "They had seen what I had done against them. I don't know why I pitched well against them, but I did."

The problem was never Larsen's arm. It was his head. The young pitcher enjoyed a good time, whether it was playing pinball, reading comic books or enjoying a few drinks.

One of his longtime friends found himself in Baltimore in 1954 and decided to surprise Larsen. He contacted the team to find out where Larsen lived.

"I explained who I was . . . that Don had been best man at my wedding and so forth," the friend recalled. "Finally, the lady says, 'I'll give you the name and address of three bars where you can look for him. And, by the way, if you do find out where he lives, please let us know, because we don't know.'"

"He's been a fella' who should be able to pitch good, but he don't always pay attention to business," Yankees manager Casey Stengel said.

Dykes said of Larsen, "The only thing he fears is sleep."

Moving from Baltimore to the Big Apple didn't promise to help Larsen curtail his nightlife. Neither did joining a team that included known carousers Mickey Mantle and Billy Martin.

The first phase of the deal accomplished what Weiss needed—two pitchers and a shortstop. To acquire them, the Yankees sent Baltimore Woodling and Triandos, as well as four other players. One of them was another catcher, Hal Smith. Also blocked by Berra, Smith led the Triple-A American Association in batting by hitting .350 at Columbus in 1954. The Orioles would replace Hunter at short with Willy Miranda, who had flopped in his attempt to replace Rizzuto as the Yankees' shortstop, hitting just .250 and committing 12 errors in 88 games at the position in 1954. The Yankees also gave up two pitchers—spot starter Jim McDonald and Harry Byrd. Byrd went from 1952 Rookie of the Year to 20-game loser with Philadelphia in 1953 before going 9–7 for New York in 1954.

Despite the outcry from Oriole fans, Richards defended his deal. "Yes, Woodling had a mediocre year in 1954, largely due to injuries, but he's a great clutch player, and I'm planning to use him as my clean-up hitter."

That didn't work out. Woodling hit just three home runs in 47 games with the Orioles before being traded to Cleveland in June. He had a 19-homer season as an Indian in 1957 and then returned to Baltimore, where he made the All-Star team in '59.

Richards was also bold in his assessment of the swap of pitchers. "I'll venture to say right now that Byrd and McDonald will bring in more victories than the 17 which were contributed by Turley and Larsen in 1954."

They didn't. McDonald and Byrd combined for 6 wins with the Orioles in 1955 and had just 11 wins, combined, over the rest of their MLB careers.

"Fans also overlook the youngsters we picked up," Richards continued. "They don't know that the Yankees turned down a $200,000 bid by the Cardinals for Hal Smith. I expect Smith to take his place among the game's great catchers."

Smith was the Orioles' starting catcher in 1955. He played 135 games, had 115 hits and drove in 52 runs. All were career highs. Baltimore traded him to Kansas City in 1956, after he lost the catching job to another player in the trade, whom Richards had slated for first base.

Gus Triandos played one year at first for the Orioles, then moved to catcher, where he became a three-time All-Star, hit 30 home runs in a season—which tied Yogi Berra for the American League record for catchers—and made Orioles fans forget how much they once loved Turley. Fans nicknamed him Gus Tremendous and created a fan club in his honor. When Triandos moved to a new home in 1962, the housing development responded by renaming his road Triandos Drive.

While the Orioles would have bigger stars in the years to come, Triandos was the first. He gave Baltimore fans a reason to follow the O's and became the face of the new franchise.

Miranda, not even mentioned in Richards' defense of the deal, played for the Orioles for the next five seasons, recording at least 100 games in four of them.

The other players in the trade were agreed upon at the time but not announced until two weeks later. On December 1, the Yankees received their backup catcher, Johnson, as well as pitcher Mike Blyzka, outfielder Jim Fridley and first baseman Dick Kryhoski. The four acquisitions combined for 26 games as Yankees, all by Johnson.

New York reportedly was also supposed to receive pitcher Lou Kretlow, but the Orioles changed their mind and kept him, leading to the confusion about the number of players involved. Kretlow didn't do anything to make the Yankees regret the change in terms. He went 0–4 in 1955, then moved to Kansas City, where he went 4–9 in his final year in MLB.

The four new Orioles named on December 1 were outfielder Ted Del Guercio, an outfielder who never reached the majors and once punched his minor league manager, second baseman Don Leppert, lefty Bill Miller and infielder Kal Segrist. The quartet played 52 games as members of the Orioles.

Segrist was called up in September 1955 after hitting 25 home runs in the minors. He was hampered by a leg injury, however, and didn't make an impression on the big league team. Another young infielder, signed for $4,000 as part of Richards' spending spree, took his place as the team's third baseman of the future—Brooks Robinson.

While the new Orioles players didn't vault the team into the first division, Triandos and, to a lesser extent, Miranda, gave the team two lineup regulars for years to come and helped change the team's identity from its days in St. Louis.

As Richards explained, everyday players were more valuable to a team looking to connect with a fan base. "Frankly, you can't win a pennant, or get into the first division, with one player, even a Turley," Richards said. "At best, he can work every fourth day. I've got to have ballplayers of ability who can produce for me every day."

At the 1954 winter meetings, Casey Stengel agreed with Richards' assessment. "Richards made a wonderful deal," he said. "I think the Baltimore fans are fortunate. They can see these good players every day instead of coming out to watch Turley or Larsen pitch once every fourth day. I know what talent I gave away, but I don't know for sure what I got in return."

Triandos worked well with the young pitchers the Orioles turned to in succeeding years, including knuckleballer Hoyt Wilhelm, who left the catcher with dozens of passed balls and body bruises. He also took the team's young position players under his wing, including Robinson, the slick-fielding third baseman and future Hall of Famer.

"He was so good-natured and such a wonderful teammate. I learned a lot from Gus," Robinson recalled. "The Orioles were lucky to have him for a stretch when they were struggling, because he was so terrific."

Triandos would frequently see Robinson and another young Oriole, Ron Hansen, eating together in restaurants on the road.

"The waitress would come over and say, 'Your check has been paid by that gentleman over there,'" Robinson said. "It was Gus. He had a big heart. He'd tell us, 'When you guys become veterans, you'll take care of the rookies, too.'"

Things worked out much better for the Yankees' three key acquisitions in the deal. Turley won 17 games and struck out 210 batters in 1955, as the Yankees returned to the World Series. Three years later, he had a career year, going 21–7 and leading the league with 19 complete games while winning the Cy Young Award and World Series MVP. Turley won two games and saved another against the Milwaukee Braves in the 1958 World Series, but he became just the second pitcher acquired by the Yankees in that trade to win World Series MVP.

The team's first World Series win following the trade was in 1956, and Don Larsen provided one of the most memorable moments in World Series history en route to that championship.

Larsen had been criticized as inconsistent and uneven, but in his first four seasons with the Yankees, he posted records of 9–2, 11–5, 10–4 and 9–6, and ERAs that ranged from 3.06 to 3.74.

Larsen fit right in with Mantle, Martin and Whitey Ford, staying out late and closing bars. Prior to the 1956 season, he crashed his car into a telephone pole at 5:30 a.m. during spring training. Displaying the long leash he gave his hard-drinking regulars, Stengel told reporters that he suspected Larsen wasn't out late but up early, mailing a letter.

In the 1956 World Series, Larsen started Game Two, and the Yankees staked him to a 6–0 lead over the Dodgers in the second inning. He didn't last through the bottom of the inning, however, walking 4 batters and giving up four runs while getting just five outs. By the end of the inning, the score was tied, and the Yankees went on to lose the game. It was the second time in two years that Larson had looked bad in losing a World Series game to the Dodgers. It wasn't clear whether Larsen would get another shot at a Series start.

The Yankees evened the Series at two games each with a Game Four win on Sunday afternoon. Legends about the rest of the day and early hours of the next morning vary wildly, leaving a hazy picture of what exactly transpired.

Outfielder Bob Cerv claims he and Larsen were out drinking until 4 a.m. Turley claimed that Larsen got a half hour of sleep before heading to the ballpark. Larsen swore he was safely tucked in at his hotel by midnight. Legendary bar owner Toots Shor said that Larsen was at his place that night, drinking with, of all people, Supreme Court Chief Justice Earl Warren.

Regardless, when Larsen arrived at the stadium at 10:30 Monday morning, he found a ball in his shoe, a sign from Stengel that he would be starting Game Five.

In perhaps the best game story lead ever, the *Daily News* reported on Larsen's start by saying, "The imperfect man pitched a perfect game yesterday."

After drinking himself out of Baltimore and continuing to imbibe nearly up until game time, Larsen turned in the best pitching performance in World Series history, retiring all 27 Dodgers he faced. It still stands today as the only perfect game ever thrown in the Fall Classic.

No pitcher in MLB had thrown a perfect game since 1922, but, for one day, Larsen was up to the task. He threw just 97 pitches and didn't go to 3 balls on anyone until the final batter of the game.

"Don, an affable nerveless man who laughs his way through life, doesn't know how to worry," the *Daily News* wrote.

After Larsen fanned pinch hitter Dale Mitchell on a full count to end the game, Hall of Fame catcher Yogi Berra ran to the mound and leaped into Larsen's arms. The photo of the pitcher cradling Berra is one of the defining moments of World Series history.

The rest of the players acquired by the Yankees had far lesser impacts than the two pitchers. Shortstop Billy Hunter, who was supposed to replace the aging Phil Rizzuto, hit .227, 32 points lower than Rizzuto, who wasn't easing into retirement.

"I thought I'd be taking over at shortstop for Rizzuto," Hunter recalled. "Then, in August, we just got back from a western road trip where I had 14 hits in 28 at bats, and Casey took me out for a pinch hitter in the sixth inning. . . . He took me straight back through the runway into the clubhouse and said, 'I'm sending you to [Triple-A] Denver.'"

New York had acquired Hall of Fame outfielder Enos Slaughter, and only two Yankees had options left—meaning they could be sent to the minor leagues without having to pass through waivers. Hunter was one, and backup catcher Elston Howard was the other.

Hunter reported to Denver and promptly broke his ankle. "I still have a screw in my ankle from that thing," he said.

Hunter played in just 37 games in 1956 and was on the roster, but didn't play in any of the games in the 1956 World Series. "I sat there on the bench the day that Larsen pitched his perfect game," he recalled. "But you know how we athletes are—sitting on the bench doesn't do it."

Hunter was later dealt away in another significant multiplayer trade—a twelve-player swap with New York's "farm team" in the majors, the Kansas City A's. The Yankees and A's participated in a long string of lopsided trades in the 1950s that all seemed to benefit the Yankees.

The twelve-player trade in June 1957 again sent veterans no longer needed by New York to the A's in exchange for up-and-coming players or role players that fit a need on the Yankees roster. Among them was Clete Boyer, who would start at third base for New York until the mid-1960s, and pitcher Bobby Shantz, who would help bolster the team's starting rotation.

Two years later, Larsen was also sent to Kansas City, after his usefulness in New York had diminished. That seven-player trade also included an aging Hank Bauer, the man who had made Gene Woodling expendable. In return, the Yankees received a young slugger who would join the outfield alongside Mickey Mantle: Roger Maris. The trade was one of the most lopsided in history. Maris would go on to win back-to-back MVPs and set the single-season home run record in 1961.

On the same day in October 1956 that sports sections were filled with multiple accounts of Larsen's perfect game, a smaller baseball item was tucked on an inside page in most papers:

Baltimore, Oct. 8—All was confusion here today, in the wake of a New York report that the Baltimore Orioles are considering hiring a baseball office manager as relief for Paul Richards . . . An Associated Press writer reported at the World Series that the "Orioles are shopping for a new general manager." Richards said that was so, but that he would still have the final word on everything connected with players. "There's no truth at all to such a statement." James Keelty Jr., Orioles president said. "We expect to keep things running the same way through the third year of Paul's contract in 1957."

Despite the rumors, Richards remained in his dual role with the Orioles until 1959, when he surrendered GM duties to Lee MacPhail and focused on managing. While many of his deals didn't work out, Richards realized there was strength in numbers, and two pieces acquired during his early work as GM—Triandos and Robinson—helped forge the Orioles' identity for years to come.

Richards was never able to pull off the entire roster exchange he'd attempted on multiple occasions. Reportedly, he was close in 1956, and the Kansas City Athletics were a willing participant. Before the trade could be finalized, however, the A's asked that two players from each side be kept out of the deal. Richards refused, and the deal fell apart. For their part, the A's wanted to hold on to Clete Boyer and Roger Maris.

During the 2011 Winter Meetings, 57 years after his team made the sport's biggest trade, current Yankees' general manager Brian Cashman was frustrated with his inability to swing a deal. Everyone was just too sober.

"I just feel like it's harder now than ever. You don't see those old school seven-to-eleven player deals," Cashman said. "This isn't the old, seat-of-your-pants, get-drunk-in-the-lobby, write-the-names-on-a-napkin type deal. People don't conduct business that way anymore."

WAR COMPARISON

Bob Turley and Don Larsen had bigger names and went on to World Series glory, but, according to WAR, the most valuable player in the seventeen-man trade was Orioles catcher Gus Triandos.

The change of scenery didn't do much to help the other fourteen players involved in the trade. They had averaged just 1.1 wins above replacement before the trade (almost all of them attributable to Gene Woodling's time as a Yankee outfielder) and produced negative 0.1 wins after the deal.

ORIOLES RECEIVED	WAR PRE-TRADE	WAR POST-TRADE
Harry Byrd	0.9	0.6
Willy Miranda	0.2	-0.6
Hal Smith	0.0	0.6
Gus Triandos	-0.3	13.0
Gene Woodling	16.0	-0.2
Jim McDonald	0.3	-1.3
Bill Miller	-0.7	-0.3
Kal Segrist	-0.3	0.1
Don Leppert	0.0	-1.0
Theodore Del Guercio	0.0	0.0
YANKEES RECEIVED	WAR PRE-TRADE	WAR POST-TRADE
Don Larsen	3.8	4.5
Bob Turley	4.9	9.2
Billy Hunter	-1.4	1.0
Mike Blyzka	-1.2	0.0
Darrell Johnson	0.0	-0.2
Jim Fridley	-0.4	0.0
Dick Kryhoski	1.3	0.0

CHAPTER 19

— THE NO-SHOWS —

THE STORY BEHIND THE CURT FLOOD TRADE

A trade that helped reshape the face of baseball.

In 1969, the St. Louis Cardinals traded Tim McCarver to the Philadelphia Phillies, where he would eventually become Steve Carlton's personal catcher. Dick Allen was sent to the Cardinals. The big story of the trade, however, was the inclusion of Curt Flood, who challenged baseball's reserve clause by refusing to report to his new team, the Phillies. The contested trade helped to bring about the age of free agency, although it occurred too late for Flood to be a part of it.

In the 1960s, an African American baseball player was sent somewhere he didn't want to play. So he decided he wouldn't. He'd quit baseball instead. Then he called his mom.

Dick Allen was a Phillies minor leaguer in 1963, when the team assigned him to its Triple-A affiliate, located, at the time, in Little Rock, Arkansas.

That April, Allen reported to the Arkansas Travelers. If going to play in the Deep South wasn't enough of a challenge for the 21-year-old, Allen was to be the first black player ever to suit up for the team.

A capacity crowd of 7,000 showed up for opening day, not all of them there to celebrate the historic moment. A group of white citizens held a protest after Allen arrived in town, and someone painted "(N-word) go home" on his car. Anti-Allen signs, including one reading, "Don't Negro-ize Baseball," were waved outside the ballpark.

Governor Orval Faubus was on hand to throw out the first pitch. Six years earlier, he had tried to block the integration of Little Rock's Central High School.

Allen had seen enough. He was ready to head home. He called his mother—collect—and gave her the news.

"Put that phone up to your ear," she said. "Can you hear me?"

When Allen confirmed he was listening, she said, "God's given you a talent and a place to show it. If you don't use it, you're not being disobedient to me. You're being disobedient to God."

She concluded the call with another piece of advice: "Don't let them drive you out."

Allen took his mother's advice to heart. "If I'm going to die, why not die doing what God gave me a gift to do?" he said. "I'll die right there in that batter's box without any fear."

For the next six years, Allen showed no fear—not to the Dixie fans in Arkansas, and not to Philadelphia's infamous boo birds. He won over the Arkansas crowds, snagging the team's most-popular player award during his one season with the Travelers.

The Philly fans were a tougher sell. Allen endured them for as long as he could, showing his talent and never letting them drive him out. After satisfying God, mother and himself, Allen finally got his ticket out of town. In October 1969, the Phillies completed a deal with the Cardinals that would send Allen to St. Louis, as part of a major seven-player swap.

That's when another African American player decided he didn't want to play in Philadelphia and took the matter to the Supreme Court.

Twelve years before that transaction, at the winter meetings following the 1957 season, Cardinals general manager Bing Devine was busy negotiating his first-ever trade. Devine had been the assistant to St. Louis GM Frank Lane, who was always active in the trade market. Now, with Lane in Cleveland, the newly promoted Devine was ready for his first deal as the man in charge. He met with Reds GM Gabe Paul to discuss options.

"There was not one player we were specifically seeking," Devine recalled in his memoir. "Then this deal developed that we thought we could make. After Gabe and I first talked about it, I remember leaving the meeting with second thoughts. Both of us did. We said, 'Let's think about it and get back to each other in 24 hours.'"

Paul and the Reds were sending 19-year-old third baseman Curt Flood and 30-year-old outfielder Joe Taylor to Devine and the Cardinals. In return, Devine had to give up two right-handed pitchers, Willard Schmidt and Ted Wieand, as well as minor league right-hander Marty Kutyna.

Devine met with manager Fred Hutchinson and expressed his concern that the players the Cardinals were getting, specifically Flood, were unproven.

"I certainly had some fear and trepidation," he recalled. "This was my first big-league deal. It wasn't a blockbuster by any means. But it was one thing to watch Frank Lane making all kinds of trades for two years. Now it was me doing it. Darn right it's different."

The Cardinals were set at third base, with Ken Boyer. There didn't seem to be room for Flood.

Hutchinson gave his worried young GM a vote of confidence. "Make the deal," he said. "We'll fit him in somewhere. We think he can hit. We know he can run. Maybe he can play center field for us."

For the next twelve years, Flood would play center field for the Cardinals—one of the best in the league at the position—and Devine could always look back with pride on his first acquisition.

"A lot people refer to the fact that undoubtedly the best trade I ever made was for Lou Brock because he's in the Hall of Fame, and that's certainly true," Devine said years later. "But in my mind, the Curt Flood trade was probably equal to that, because of it being my first deal. If that hadn't worked out, I probably wouldn't have lasted as long as I did."

Flood found out he'd been traded by the Reds when he received a telegram from the Cardinals.

While Flood was winning World Series titles with St. Louis (in 1964 and 1967), Dick Allen was putting up All-Star numbers with the Phillies. He was also becoming a magnet for the fans' frustrations.

Allen led the league with 125 runs and 13 triples in 1964, securing him the National League Rookie of the Year Award. He hit 40 home runs and drove in 110 runs in 1966, earning the second of three straight All-Star selections.

"All I can tell you is that Dick Allen was the greatest offensive player to ever wear a Phillies uniform," longtime Philadelphia radio host Bill Werndl said in 2014, "and that includes Mike Schmidt."

While Schmidt had a love–hate relationship with the Philadelphia fans two decades later, Allen saw very little love coming his way. Despite being in a northern city, Allen heard racial catcalls from the crowd. He said he learned to keep his head down, because when you looked up, you'd never be able to find the white face that was yelling.

Things got worse after July 3, 1965. Phillies outfielder Frank Thomas got upset during batting practice when he thought Allen was mocking his fielding. "It was really [Johnny] Callison," Allen said, "but Thomas made a racial remark to me."

Thomas actually tangled with two of his African American teammates in the incident. After calling Johnny Briggs "boy," Thomas said that Allen was like "Muhammad Clay." Allen took offense and had words with Thomas. The exchange became physical, and the two players went at it next to the batting cage. Thomas hit Allen in the shoulder with his bat.

Fans took Thomas' side in the dispute, partly because manager Gene Mauch prohibited Allen from speaking to the press about the cause of the altercation. Allen later claimed that Mauch threatened to fine him one third of his yearly salary if he broke the gag order.

As the fans began piling on, Allen went to general manager John Quinn to see if the team could help get the truth out, so the abuse would stop.

"The club knew what happened," Allen said, "but they didn't want to say anything, because they were selling more tickets—People were coming to the park just to boo me."

The home crowd threw things at Allen as he played first base. Later on, when fans switched from throwing garbage and fruit to throwing batteries, he began wearing a batting helmet in the field.

Allen refused to let them drive him out, though. In fact, while playing his position at first base, Allen would drag his feet through the infield dirt, etching out the word "BOO" in giant letters. The fans were happy to comply.

By 1968, Allen had finally had enough. He began flouting his disregard for team rules, hoping to provoke the team into trading him.

"That's what I was trying to do," he admitted. "I was wanting out of there. At the time, a baseball contract said that it was negotiated solely between the uniformed player and the parent club. And, well, they held my contract."

Quoting a soft-spoken version of himself, Allen related his exchange with the club. "Well, geez. I'm hearing all the booing, and they dislike me so bad in the city. Why can't I get out of here?"

He began to drink before games and showed up later and later, piling up fines. He missed team flights. There was an alleged bar fight.

In May 1969, he was fined $1,000 for showing up after the game had started. When he did it a second time, he was suspended 28 days.

As the season ended, Allen demanded a trade, threatening to retire if the team didn't get rid of him. "I'd rather work on a farm and earn $100 a week than play for the Phillies," he told the press.

Allen acknowledged that his approach was different than that employed by Jackie Robinson, the baseball pioneer who played his career, and his retirement, with dignity and restraint.

"I might have been the modern-day Jackie Robinson," Allen said. "Everything he went through, I went through, only I did it in modern times. Jackie probably would have handled things differently. I couldn't do that. God didn't give me the gift of words."

As the Phillies tried to negotiate a way to get Allen out of town, the man who would soon become a baseball pioneer in his own right was having trouble in St. Louis.

From 1963 to 1969, Curt Flood won seven straight Gold Gloves, as the best-fielding center fielder in the National League. From September 2, 1965, through the entire 1966 season, and on until June 4, 1967, Flood didn't make a single error, going 226 games with a 1.000 fielding percentage. That's a National League record, and the 568 consecutive fly balls and line drives that he fielded successfully is a major league record. In 21 World Series games, Curt Flood never made an error. At least, that's what the box scores said.

After winning the Series in 1964 and 1967, St. Louis was looking to win its third championship in five years, against the Tigers in 1968. The Cardinals took a three-games-to-one lead in the series, but the Tigers battled back from the brink of elimination to win Games Five and Six. As they had in their two previous World Series appearances, the Cardinals went to Game Seven.

Mickey Lolich started on two days' rest for the Tigers. Future Hall of Famer Bob Gibson started on three for the Cardinals. Neither would require a reliever.

For six innings, neither team could do anything against the opposing starter. Then, after retiring the first two batters in the seventh inning, Gibson allowed singles to Norm Cash and Willie Horton.

Jim Northrup then hit a line drive to center field. It wouldn't be an easy catch, but it was a ball Flood could definitely get to, and, as he'd shown over the previous seven years, if he could get to a ball, he would catch it.

As the ball left the bat, however, Flood took an uncertain step back and then appeared to take the wrong angle to the ball. After a few steps, he lost his footing and pinwheeled his arms as he tried to keep upright.

He remained on his feet and then turned his back to the plate to try to reach the ball as it sailed at him. Even with all the trouble he'd had, Flood came within about two steps of reaching the ball and ending the inning. Instead, it landed safely and rolled all the way to the wall.

Northrup ended up with a triple, driving in two runs. The Tigers went on to win the game by a 4–1 score, clinching the championship.

"A lot of people say that Curt misjudged the ball," Lolich said. "I don't think he did. He did take a step back, because the ball was hit hard. Then the ball started to slice. He took a step back to get a perspective on the line drive. And then he slipped. But I don't think it's fair to say that's why we won."

Flood wasn't sure he'd have reached the ball in time to catch it, even without the stumble.

"I didn't see the ball because of the sun," he said. "Plus, it had rained the morning of the game. A lot of things weren't right for that game. The time of day; late afternoon; the wet field. I slipped just enough to get a late jump on the ball. If it had been at another time, or game, it would have been just another base hit."

"The most regrettable aspect of the fact that Flood is still held accountable by many people for what happened in the seventh game lies in the reality that Curt Flood was more than my best friend on the ballclub," Bob Gibson wrote, years later. "To me, he personified what the Cardinals were all about. As a man and teammate, he was smart, funny, sensitive and, most of all, unique. As a ballplayer, he was resourceful, dedicated and very, very good. Hell, the little guy was us, through and through."

Flood was blamed by many both inside and outside of the Cardinals organization for costing the team the Series. "I'm sure he could have caught it, if he hadn't charged in on it," manager Red Schoendienst said after the game.

In the offseason, perhaps smarting from the loss, the Cardinals offered him a contract for $77,500—a mere $5,000 raise from what he earned in 1968. Flood turned them down and demanded $90,000.

Flood took his contract concerns to the press, which created further tension with ownership. Flood's rough spring continued when his brother Carl, who had trouble with the law his entire life, was involved in a police chase that was televised live. The Cardinals also removed Flood as team captain during spring training.

If it wasn't clear by then that Flood wasn't long for the team, events during the season removed any doubt. Flood got fined for missing a community event where he was supposed to represent the team; he had suffered an injury in the previous night's game and decided to take the time to rest.

Late in the season, Flood complained to the press, as an unnamed source, that the front office forced the manager to play young players, costing them a shot at the postseason. At one point in September, Flood said to himself, "Brother Flood, you are going to be traded."

Devine knew that Flood was one of the veteran players leaking the allegations to the press, and, a few days after the season ended, he dealt him to the Phillies for Allen.

Along with Allen, the Cardinals would receive Cookie Rojas, a light-hitting veteran infielder who had been an All-Star in 1965, and pitcher Jerry Johnson, who had 10 wins and one save in two seasons with the Phillies.

Allen was thrilled to find out he'd been traded from Philadelphia.

"Six years in this town is enough for anybody," he told the Associated Press. "I'm glad to be away from Quinn and all of them. They treat you like cattle."

Cardinals manager Red Schoendienst was confident that he'd be able to handle the mercurial Allen. "I don't know Allen. I've never spoken to him," he said. "I know his reputation, of course, but I don't know any of the background of what went on in Philadelphia. . . . I usually don't have trouble in handling anybody. The big thing is they have to handle themselves. He will start here with a clean slate."

Schoendienst was busy planning out how he'd use his new players. Rojas would be a utility man. "He's a tough little guy with a bat," the manager said.

Allen would be put in left field, with future Hall of Famer Lou Brock moving to right. The Cardinals' 1969 right fielder, Vada Pinson, would replace Flood in center. To replace Tim McCarver, first baseman Joe Torre would move to catcher. Prospect Joe Hague would fill in at first base.

In addition to Flood, the Phillies were acquiring McCarver, pitcher Joe Hoerner and outfielder Byron Browne. McCarver was a two-time All-Star and had been runner-up for the National League MVP in 1967 with the Cardinals. He also led the league in triples, with 13 in 1966, a virtually unheard-of accomplishment for a catcher.

Hoerner was a free-spirited left-hander who loved a good time. He once threw a live lizard in a teammate's soup. He also once took the team bus on a joyride, hitting an exit sign.

Browne played just 22 games with the Cardinals in 1969. As a rookie with the Cubs in 1966, he had struck out a league-high 143 times.

"We wanted a catcher and a relief pitcher," Phillies GM John Quinn said, "and when Flood's name came into it, you have to believe that any ball club would be happy to have a Curt Flood."

Flood received a call on October 7 from assistant general manager Jim Toomey, who told him he'd been traded to Philadelphia.

Toomey would work in the Cardinals front office for 38 years, in a variety of roles. He served as the team's director of public relations for decades. When he retired, the press box at St. Louis' Busch Stadium was named after him.

However, Flood was offended that Devine himself hadn't called. Instead, he got word from "a middle-echelon coffee drinker."

Flood had expected the trade, but he was still crushed by the news and the way it was delivered.

"If I had been a foot-shuffling porter, they might have at least given me a pocket watch," he said. "One miserable telephone call released the poison of self-pity. The hard-boiled realist who answered the phone was a weeping child when he set the receiver down. The lightning had struck. The dream lay shattered. It was a bad scene."

When Flood finally got to speak to Devine, he asked, "Why did you do this? I may not go."

"Why did I do that?" Devine wrote in his memoir. "To get Richie Allen."

When the deal was announced, he told the press the Cardinals were looking for a power hitter. "Richie Allen was the best available hitter of this type, perhaps the only available hitter of this type," he said. Flood decided to announce his retirement from baseball.

"If I were younger, I would certainly enjoy playing for Philadelphia. But under the circumstances, I have decided to retire from organized baseball, effective today," he said in a statement released on October 8.

Later that day, Flood added that his reaction to the trade was "surprise and personal disappointment."

"When you spend twelve years with one club, you develop strong ties with your teammates and the fans who have supported your efforts over a period of years," he said.

Flood said he planned to make a living in the arts. "I've had to think of my own and my children's future," he said. "Consequently, I've felt that I should give more time to the Curt Flood photo studio franchise business, as well as a large backlog of oil painting commissions."

Flood ultimately changed his mind. On Christmas Eve, he wrote to Commissioner Bowie Kuhn informing him that "it is my desire to play baseball in 1970," but that he would not be going to the Phillies.

"After twelve years in the major leagues," he wrote, "I do not feel that I am a piece of property to be bought and sold irrespective of my wishes. I believe that any system which produces that result violates my basic rights as a citizen and is inconsistent with the laws of the United States."

He requested that Kuhn let it be known to all clubs that he would be available for the upcoming season. Kuhn rejected Flood's assertion of his right to be a free agent, citing baseball's long-established reserve clause.

Essentially, the reserve clause—a standard element of every player's contract since the nineteenth century—said that a team owned a player's rights until the team decided to get rid of him, either by sale, trade or outright release. Other than retiring, a player could do nothing to get out of a contract.

Flood decided to sue Major League Baseball. His case went all the way to the U.S. Supreme Court.

Flood was ostracized within baseball. Although the players' association had voted to support Flood, no current MLB players were willing to testify on his behalf. None of his former Cardinals teammates bothered to come to court.

Flood became a controversial figure in mainstream America as well.

He earned criticism when he told Howard Cosell that MLB players had "a master and slave relationship" with their teams.

Cosell challenged him, saying, "A man that makes $90,000 a year isn't exactly slave wages."

"A well-paid slave is nevertheless a slave," Flood said.

In another interview, he said, "Me, as a black man, I'm probably a lot more sensitive to the rights of other people, because I have been denied these rights."

"What I really want out of this thing is for every ballplayer to have the chance to be a human being and to take advantage of the fact that we live in a free and democratic society," he added.

While Flood was fighting for his freedom at the highest levels of the justice system, Devine and Quinn had some outstanding business to finish.

"It took six months to complete the deal," Devine wrote, "because we kept thinking Flood would change his mind. Finally, in April of '70, we sent Willie Montañez, a first baseman, and a right-handed pitcher named Bob Browning to Philadelphia to complete the deal."

Allen played for the Cardinals in 1970 and provided the power Devine had sought. He had 34 homers in 1970, the most by a Cardinal since Stan Musial in 1954. No one else would match his total until 1987.

"I didn't get to stay too long, but I enjoyed it," Allen recalled. "The Cardinals are a class organization. Red Schoendienst was great to play for. He didn't bother you. It was a refreshing change from Gene Mauch. Red understood what the game was about, because he played."

After the 1970 season, Allen checked into a hospital to have a hamstring injury treated. At seven in the morning, Devine called him. Allen told him he was doing well after the procedure.

"That's not why I called," Devine responded. "I just called to tell you your contract has been sold to the Los Angeles Dodgers."

With Flood never reporting to Philadelphia, the Phillies had just catcher Tim McCarver to show for the Allen deal.

McCarver wasn't particularly happy about the trade. He didn't want to go to the perennial bottom-dwellers in Philly. "I don't like to lose," he said. "We are paid to win ball games. If I can help them do that, then that is my aim and desire."

In the short term, McCarver didn't get to participate in many Phillies wins, but he laid the groundwork for a return to the team at the end of the decade. McCarver had come up with the Cardinals at the same time as pitching prospect Steve Carlton, an introverted lefthander who clashed with St. Louis management over money.

The Cardinals dealt him to Philadelphia in 1972, reuniting him with McCarver.

Carlton went on to win the Cy Young Award with the last-place Phillies, winning 27 games for a team that managed just 59 wins on the year.

McCarver left during the 1972 season, but he would return three years later, to serve as Carlton's personal catcher. McCarver seemed to be the one person who could reach the mercurial Carlton, and he joked that he'd be buried 60 feet 6 inches from the pitcher when the two of them died.

Back in 1972, McCarver was surprised to find out he'd been traded to Montreal. He'd just put $1,100 down on an apartment in Philly when the deal occurred. Phillies GM Paul Owens never called him to let him know he'd been traded.

"Being traded is something I'm acclimated to," McCarver said, "but it would be easier to accept if the people being traded and their families were treated with respect."

Flood's quest to accomplish exactly that treatment for players ultimately failed, when the Supreme Court ruled against him in June 1972. As the case was making its way through the courts, Flood returned to the majors briefly in 1971, playing 13 games with the Washington Senators, but then he left the team, and the country. He battled alcoholism and depression for years before finally putting his life back together.

"It's sad," former teammate Lou Brock said after Flood's death, on Martin Luther King Day 1997. "Most of the pioneers wind up with an arrow in their backs. And he certainly was one of those who had an arrow in his back. As a pioneer, he never got his just due. God will amend that."

Flood's loss in court helped set the stage for future battles. While the owners won the battle, it resulted in a public relations disaster, as fans began to question the idea of the reserve clause. It also helped to unite the players, eventually making the Players' Association one of the most powerful bargaining forces in the country.

Perhaps sensing the shift in public perception, the National Labor Relations Board ruled that it had jurisdiction over labor disputes in baseball. Two years later, after pitchers Andy Messersmith and Dave McNally played a year following the expiration of their contracts with their respective teams, the NLRB ruled that they were free agents, able to sign with the highest bidder. It was a turning point for baseball and, indeed, all of sports. It led to skyrocketing salaries and the massive offseason player turnover that is now commonplace in every major sports league.

Dick Allen lasted a year in Los Angeles before he was traded to the White Sox. He won the MVP Award with Chicago in 1972—leading the league with 37 homers and 113 RBI and finishing third with a .308 average—but he was traded again, to Atlanta, after the 1974 season. The Braves kept him for a month of the 1975 season before trading him back to Philadelphia.

"That's happened throughout my career, where I carried an image of a bad guy," Allen said of the frequency with which he was traded. "I wanted to start fresh. But that image kept going and going and going and didn't stop."

Allen finished his career with Oakland, where he signed after earning free agency in 1976. He was one of the first players to benefit from the freedom that pioneers following in Flood's footsteps were finally able to obtain for all MLB players.

At some point, reflecting back on his time in Philadelphia, Dick Allen decided that maybe he wasn't that much like Jackie Robinson after all.

"I know Jackie made footprints for every black man to come and play baseball," he said, "but I couldn't be like Jackie. I had to hit that man in the mouth. It was over when I hit him, but if he would have said the same thing again, I would have hit that son-of-a-buck in the mouth again. I'm a man of my own convictions."

WAR COMPARISON

The most significant player in the trade had a WAR of 0.0. Curt Flood's refusal to report to his new team made a run-of-the-mill trade of three aging All-Stars (Allen, Flood and McCarver) into one for the history books.

Only Willie Montañez, added to the trade as compensation for Flood's retirement, was able to produce more after the trade than before it.

CARDINALS RECEIVED	WAR PRE-TRADE	WAR POST-TRADE
Dick Allen	35.2	2.3
Cookie Rojas	3.7	-0.7
Jerry Johnson	1.6	0.3
PHILLIES RECEIVED	WAR PRE-TRADE	WAR POST-TRADE
Curt Flood	42.2	0.0
Tim McCarver	20.4	2.8
Byron Browne	0.5	-0.6
Joe Hoerner	6.4	6.1
Willie Montañez	0.0	3.4
Jim Browning	0.0	0.0

CHAPTER 20

— THE BLOCKBUSTER —

THE STORY BEHIND THE ROBERTO ALOMAR TRADE

A good old-fashioned baseball trade.

In winter, 1990, the San Diego Padres and Toronto Blue Jays got together for one of the highest-profile trades that could have been made at the time: Roberto Alomar and Joe Carter for Fred McGriff and Tony Fernández. The four players, all in their primes, combined for 27 All-Star Games, 13 years finishing in the top 10 for MVP voting, three postseason and All-Star MVP awards, 14 Gold Gloves and nine Silver Sluggers.

After completing a trade, a general manager has to make several phone calls. Many of them are uncomfortable ones. He may have to tell a manager that a key player on the team is leaving, or inform a player who had been with the team for years that he has to start over with a new organization.

On December 5, 1990, Toronto GM Pat Gillick had to make one of those calls. He checked out of the O'Hare Hyatt in Chicago and headed to the airport. Before boarding his flight, he called home from an airport phone.

His wife, Doris, answered, and Pat led with the good news: the winter meetings were over and he would be back home in a few hours.

Then came the bad news. He'd traded first baseman Fred McGriff—a Blue Jay since 1986, a top-10 MVP candidate each of the last two years, the 1989 home run champion and the favorite player of one Doris Gillick.

There was an uncomfortable pause, and then Doris spoke.

"Would you come home before you screw up the team any further?" she said.

Gillick had traded for McGriff eight years earlier in a deal he called his best as a general manager. The Yankees were looking to acquire Dale Murray, a 32-year-old reliever who had saved 11 games for the Blue Jays in 1982.

Gillick agreed to take Dave Collins, a switch-hitting outfielder the Yankees signed a year earlier after future Hall of Fame slugger Reggie Jackson departed as a free agent. The Yankees hoped to change from a power hitting team to a National League–style team built on speed.

Collins hit just .253, however, and stole just 13 bases as a Yankee in 1982. He got caught stealing eight times.

The Yankees also gave up starting pitcher Mike Morgan, who went 7–11 in 1982.

All the Jays needed was a throw-in. Gillick suggested several minor leaguers, none of whom Yankees GM Bill Bergesch was willing to give up. Gillick remembered a game earlier that season between the Toronto and New York affiliates in the Florida Rookie League. A slim Yankees first baseman prospect hit a home run that traveled 430 feet and hit the roof of the Blue Jays' clubhouse down the right-field line.

"In the fall, talking to Bergesch, I'm thinking of that ball landing on the roof," Gillick recalled.

Talks dragged on into the winter meetings, when Yankees owner George Steinbrenner got sick of waiting.

"Finally, Steinbrenner wants to know what's the holdup and I say we're hasslin' over a third player and George turns to Bergesch and says, 'Look, we got Jim Spencer playing first base and this kid Mattingly at Columbus is about ready, so let him have McGriff,'" Gillick recalled.

"Let me think about it," Gillick replied.

After walking around the block to kill time, so he didn't appear too anxious, Gillick called back and finished the trade.

Over the next eight years, McGriff developed into a power hitter and one of the top first basemen in the American League. And Gillick didn't do much to give his acquisition of McGriff much competition for the title of career-best trade.

Gillick arrived in Toronto as assistant GM in 1977, the first year of existence for the expansion franchise. He was promoted to general manager the following year and had a role in building the team from the ground up.

"It takes a while to build an organization," he said, after ten years with the Jays. "This organization announced on day one what the game plan was and never wavered."

Preaching patience, Gillick was always reluctant to swing a trade, earning him the nickname "Stand Pat."

At the winter meetings, when team executives sequestered themselves in a hotel for a week to make deals, Gillick left without making a trade in seven out of nine seasons. In fact, in 1985, 1987 and 1988, he made no trades at all during the offseason, from October to April.

That's not to say that Gillick never made an effort to improve his team. In 1985, when the Blue Jays won their first divisional title, Gillick picked up DH Cliff Johnson at the trade deadline. In 1987, when they finished two games behind the Tigers, he added Phil Niekro and Mike Flanagan. In 1989, he picked up outfielder Mookie Wilson at the deadline, and in 1990, he dealt for pitcher John Candelaria.

On September 22, 1987, Gillick made a shrewd late-season deal, sending infielder Mike Sharperson to the Dodgers for pitcher Juan Guzmán, who would become an All-Star and ERA leader for the Jays.

Gillick's next trade came when he dealt minor leaguer Cliff Young to the Angels for reliever DeWayne Buice. That was on March 9, 1989, a span of 534 days since his previous trade.

"We've become more selective as the team got better," Gillick said. "No, I don't think I'm tough to deal with, not at all. No, I'm not in love with the guys in our own farm system. It's just that you get to a certain point where realistically you don't know if you can improve a position and you feel comfortable with what you've got."

Still, the Jays managed just two divisional titles through the franchise's first fourteen seasons, and Gillick was criticized by the media and fans for his failure to aggressively pursue trades.

A May 20, 1988, column in the *Toronto Star* ripped Gillick:

Why is everyone so afraid to point the finger at the one man most responsible for the fact that the Blue Jays rank 12th out of 14 teams in the American League this morning? . . . The man who has been batting .000 for this club in 1988. The man who is zero for 30 or 40 trips, and several hundred phone calls, in his attempts to strengthen this team at the major league level. The man who has done absolutely nothing in the last six months to help this team get better.

Of course, time would prove Gillick correct in turning down some of the offers.

Pitcher Dave Stieb went 16–8 in 1988, 17–8 in 1989 and 18–6 with a no-hitter in 1990. Gillick could have dealt him to the Cubs for catcher Jody Davis. Instead, Davis went to the Braves, where he hit .161 over the next three years.

In December 1988, the Phillies complained publicly about Gillick's foot dragging on a Stieb trade calling it "dilly dallying."

"I don't think we have much chance of doing anything with Toronto anymore," an unnamed Phillie executive said at the Winter Meetings. "We've talked with them on and off since the World Series and we just haven't been able to get anywhere. We've pretty well given up on them."

In exchange for Stieb, Philadelphia was offering pitcher Don Carman, who would go 5–15 in 1989 and would post a 4.92 ERA over the final four years of his career, and outfielder Phil Bradley, who would play just two more seasons in the majors.

Prudent decisions or not, the label "Stand Pat" stuck. The Toronto papers counted the days since the last trade, making a point of announcing when the streak had lasted longer than the American hostages had been held in Iran a decade earlier.

The *Toronto Star* ran stories titled "Is Pat Gillick Afraid to Make a Trade?" "Gillick's the Source of Jay Troubles," "Verdict on Gillick: He's Batting .000," "Will 'Stand Pat' Gillick Make a Move? Jays Boss is Long Overdue for a Deal" and "Come on Pat Gillick! It's Time to Get Serious."

While Pat Gillick was getting ripped for not making a trade, Joe McIlvaine moved across the country to try to live down a trade he regretted.

Like Gillick, McIlvaine was a failed minor league pitcher. Gillick pitched for five years in the Pirates and Orioles systems, topping out at Triple-A. McIlvaine left the seminary for the Tigers' Rookie League team, but he never made it out of A ball, going 16–16 in five years in the Tigers' system.

Longtime MLB manager Jim Leyland, who was McIlvaine's manager in Clinton, Iowa recalled sitting down with the young pitcher following year five. McIlvaine suggested it might be time to retire.

"That might have been his first scouting decision," Leyland said. "I think he hit it on the head."

After hanging up the spikes, McIlvaine scouted for close to a decade before becoming the scouting director for the Mets. In 1985, he was promoted to assistant general manager and vice president of baseball operations.

As a member of the Mets front office, McIlvaine had a major role in building the 1986 World Champions. In 1982, the Mets made an unpopular trade, sending everyone's favorite Met, Lee Mazzilli, to Texas for two minor league pitchers. One was Ron Darling, who would win 12 or more games for six straight years. The other was Walt Terrell, who developed into a MLB starter and was traded two years later for third baseman Howard Johnson, a future 30/30 player.

The Mets traded for pitcher Sid Fernandez and Keith Hernandez in 1983, giving up Neil Allen, Rick Ownbey, Bob Bailor and Carlos Diaz. In 1984, they picked up Gary Carter. In 1985, they traded for Bob Ojeda.

After the title, New York added Kevin McReynolds and David Cone in two other trades. In both of those deals, the Mets gave up prospects and young major leaguers. They got the better of the trading partners each time.

The McReynolds trade helped set up McIlvaine's subsequent fateful trade. The promising young outfielder was inserted into left field for the Mets, which took away a spot from Mookie Wilson. The popular Mets outfielder had been the batter on the famous ground ball that Bill Buckner misplayed in the 1986 series, capping an improbable Mets comeback. Wilson played 78 games in left field in 1986 and 65 in center, splitting center field duties with Lenny Dykstra.

After acquiring McReynolds in the 1986 offseason, Wilson moved into a center-field platoon with Dykstra, seriously reducing the playing time for both of them. Dykstra had just 74 at bats against left-handed pitchers in 1987, compared to 357 against righties.

Dykstra began complaining about the arrangement, at one point demanding that the Mets trade Wilson.

"It's a situation the Mets need to deal with, but I don't know when they're going to do it," Dykstra said. "I don't want to be traded. I want to play in New York, and I stress the word play. I definitely feel one of us needs to play, but the other one shouldn't be sitting."

For the next two seasons, the center-field tandem was referred to by fans and media as Mookstra, combining the two names in the same way that celebrity couples are now nicknamed in the Internet age.

"That's great—for them," Dykstra said in early 1989. "Not for us, though."

"Although both players don't like to admit it and won't admit it, they are a good tandem and have complemented each other well," McIlvaine responded.

Dykstra eventually went to the Mets front office and asked to be traded. His manager, Davey Johnson, had also been pushing for the Mets to deal Dykstra. Johnson clashed with the outfielder on playing time and on the 160-pounder's desire to hit more home runs, which often resulted in big swings and misses during crucial times.

"Our manager was pleading with me for two years to get rid of him," McIlvaine said. "We had two center fielders, and it was like he wanted us to solve his problems."

On June 16, McIlvaine swung a deal that took care of the problem. He dealt Dykstra and relief pitcher Roger McDowell to the Phillies for Juan Samuel, a two-time All-Star at second base. The Mets would move Samuel to center field and bench Wilson.

Both Dykstra and McDowell were popular members of the '86 Mets, and the trade, along with an earlier deal that sent away second baseman Wally Backman, were seen as McIlvaine dismantling the team.

"Time doesn't stand still," McIlvaine argued. "You have to renew the team. As much as we would like to be nostalgic, time goes on."

Johnson said he was surprised by the trade and called it "bittersweet." But he was excited about the potential of adding Samuel to the lineup. "Juan Samuel is an impact player. Whenever I thought about the Phillies the last four or five years, I thought about Juan Samuel. He reminds me of Bobby Bonds. People don't realize what kind of impact player he is."

The trade couldn't have gone much worse for the Mets. Samuel hit just .228 for the rest of the year, and the Mets traded him to the Dodgers in December.

Meanwhile, McDowell saved 19 games over the final three and a half months of the season and posted a 1.11 ERA for the Phillies.

Dykstra took a shot at his former team on his way out of town. "For me, this isn't that sad," he said. "This is the time for me to make a move. I'm 26 and I've been here nearly five years. Maybe it's time to show I can hit those left-handed pitchers."

He did exactly that. Dykstra would lead the NL in hits (twice), runs, walks and on base percentage during his eight years with the Phillies. He'd make the All-Star team three times and finish runner-up for MVP in 1993, when the Phillies made the World Series and the Mets finished last.

McIlvaine was ripped by fans and media after the trade. One columnist referred to McIlvaine's nine months in the seminary, calling him "Father Joe" repeatedly and talking about his decision to "give up God for baseball."

"That was the first time I had seen Joe truly angry," his wife, Marty, said.

"The criticism was not only harsh, but it was cruel," Mets VP Al Harazin said. "Joe took it hard. I think the '86 championship team had become mythical in a way, and trading someone off that team—and not being able to repeat again—there was a lot of frustration."

After the Padres fired GM Jack McKeon in late 1990, the team reached out to the Mets about McIlvaine. The Mets offered him a three-year contract extension and renewed their longtime promise to him that he would replace Frank Cashen as GM.

McIlvaine told the team he wanted to interview with the Padres. He ended up accepting a five-year, $2.5 million deal with San Diego.

McKeon, the man the Padres fired before hiring McIlvaine, was nicknamed "Trader Jack"—the polar opposite of Toronto's Gillick. McIlvaine quickly picked up his own nickname as he started his term with the Padres.

Between late September and late February, 31 Padres front-office employees, scouts and coaches were replaced, earning McIlvaine the name "Hatchet Man." Many of the individuals were actually fired before McIlvaine started, but he took the blame.

"I empathize for the people I had to let go," he said. "You're often affecting people's lives. But we had to have a new attitude and be free of the sins of the past."

Heading into his first winter meetings as a GM, McIlvaine said he wasn't looking to make an impact trade. "Jack McKeon was the show," he said. "I don't want to be the show. In New York, you can't help being the center of attention all the time. In San Diego, people come to see the players. I'll operate in a much quieter way."

McIlvaine also responded to criticism from Mets manager Davey Johnson. "When you have a team that good," Johnson had said, "you don't have to take it apart. Joe McIlvaine, when he finally got the authority to run the club, was trying to hit a home run, trading all those guys in a short time.

"I wasn't trying to hit a home run," he said. "New York's a star town. You try to get stars. They want names. In San Diego, you don't have that same pressure. But some of the best trades I made for the Mets didn't involve big names. Who knew David Cone before we got him? Who knew Sid Fernandez? They weren't marquee stars."

In the early days of the 1990 winter meetings, there were no trades to be had, home runs or singles. The meetings, once dominated by hot-stove trade talk, had become a free-agent shopping mall. Teams devoted their time and attention to negotiating with players and their representatives.

More than $100 million worth of free-agent contracts were negotiated at the winter meetings, and all the headlines coming out of Chicago were devoted to player signings.

The 1990 National League batting champion Willie McGee signed a four-year, $13 million deal with the Giants. Third baseman Terry Pendleton signed with the Braves for four years, $9.8 million. Pitcher Dennis Martínez signed with the Expos for three years and $9.25 million.

Pitcher Kevin Gross went to the Dodgers, Bill Gullickson to the Tigers and longtime Royals outfielder Willie Wilson to the A's.

"The meetings have become perverted—a showcase for the free agents," Twins GM Andy MacPhail said. "I think we've lost a feeling of community that we used to experience at these meetings, and that's regrettable. It used to be a chance to sit down with your peers. Now I'm always sequestered in my room with an agent."

"I've talked to three or four clubs every day for several weeks and can't get anything going," Phillies General Manager Lee Thomas said. "Everyone wants to wait and see what develops with the free agents."

The free-agent frenzy was fueled by baseball's previous attempt to restrain the market. Three years earlier, owners got together and agreed to keep salaries low, freezing out the top free agents on the market in 1987.

After the players union protested, two arbitrators found the owners guilty of collusion. They had to pay a $280 million fine, and sixteen players from the 1987 class were given a second chance at free agency.

One of those sixteen was Padres first baseman Jack Clark. The moody Clark had been a major leaguer since 1975, when he was nineteen. After starring with the Giants and Cardinals, he signed a free-agent contract with the Yankees after the 1987 season, getting $1.5 million. "They were my only offer, and the way the free agent market was going I felt lucky I got one offer," he said.

By 1990, when the arbitrators ruled that he should have received more offers, Clark was with the Padres. As was the case throughout his career, Clark wasn't happy. He had an early season run in with Padres star Tony Gwynn, calling the beloved outfielder "a selfish SOB." A team meeting was called, which Clark punctuated by throwing a cup of root beer at a teammate.

Heading into his first offseason as a GM, McIlvaine faced the prospect of losing his first baseman and the team's leading home run hitter, with 25. McIlvaine offered Clark $2.5 million for one year, but Clark wanted to test the market.

McIlvaine was also trying to move the Padres' second-leading home run hitter. Outfielder Joe Carter had been acquired from the Indians a year earlier in a blockbuster trade arranged by Trader Jack McKeon in his last winter meetings with San Diego. McKeon traded catcher Sandy Alomar Jr., infielder Carlos Baerga and outfielder Chris James to Cleveland for Carter.

Carter responded by hitting a career-low .232. His 24 homers were second on the team, but they were also his lowest total since 1985.

McIlvaine began talking to other teams to gauge interest in his outfielder. He talked to Gillick about a trade to Toronto at the 1990 World Series in October. "I dismissed it at the time," McIlvaine said.

At the general managers' meetings in November, the two GMs talked again. "He told me no," Gillick said.

A month later, at the winter Meetings, Carter was being shopped more aggressively. McIlvaine talked to the Royals about a trade for outfielder Danny Tartabull and a pitching prospect. The Red Sox were also involved in talks, offering outfielder Mike Greenwell.

Gillick made another run at acquiring Carter as well. His plan was to bring in Carter to help shore up his own fractured clubhouse chemistry. Acquiring him would make George Bell expendable. The 1987 MVP, Bell's production had fallen off, along with his attitude, which was never great to begin with. He threw tantrums at spring training in 1988, when he was moved to designated hitter, and he was known to be surly and mean-spirited in the clubhouse.

Bell was a free agent after the 1990 season, and the Blue Jays were ready to let him go. Bell never received a contract offer from the team.

McIlvaine's first offer at the winter meetings was a blockbuster that would resolve both teams' chemistry problems and allow them to watch their surly free agents leave. In exchange for Carter, the Padres would receive 27-year-old first baseman Fred McGriff, the key acquisition in Gillick's self-proclaimed best trade ever.

McGriff had hit 30 home runs each of the last three seasons. San Diego's team leaders in homers over those same three years had hit just 18, 26 and 25. The Blue Jays had DH John Olerud, who had finished fourth in Rookie of the Year voting in 1990, ready to move to first base to replace McGriff.

"We had a natural match there," McIlvaine said, "and really, we could have left it, one for one."

Both GMs were on board with the core of the deal, but McGriff was three years younger than Carter. To make up for the age difference, the Padres would have to throw in another player.

Both teams also had middle infielders that added to the negative chemistry in their respective clubhouses.

Blue Jays shortstop Tony Fernández wasn't a vocal critic, like Bell, but he frequently sulked and begged out of the lineup with what management suspected were phantom injuries and illnesses when he wasn't happy with his spot in the batting order.

"I kind of thought Fernández—he didn't have the attitude I kind of like," Gillick said years later. "I thought it might be time to get him out of there."

In San Diego, 22-year-old second baseman Roberto Alomar, perhaps upset that the team had traded away his brother Sandy Jr. for Carter the previous offseason, clashed with Padres manager Greg Riddoch.

Alomar made the All-Star team in 1990, but he suffered through a midseason slump in the field and at the plate. Veterans also questioned his attitude, calling him selfish and complaining about his work habits.

When the Padres tried to move him from second base to shortstop, to replace aging veteran Garry Templeton, Alomar sulked and drifted through the motions.

After a July game in Chicago, Riddoch and Alomar missed the team bus back to the hotel, staying in the manager's office for a 35-minute closed-door meeting.

"I hadn't liked what I've seen, not at all," Riddoch said. "I just don't know what's going on. I talked to him, gave him some of my observations, and now I'm going to sit him down for a few days and see what happens."

Alomar's father, Sandy Sr., had been one of the coaches that the Hatchet Man, McIlvaine, had dismissed following the season.

Gillick knew that it would be tough for the Padres to bring back the temperamental infielder. He requested that McIlvaine include Alomar in the Carter–McGriff trade.

The Padres had 25-year-old Joey Cora, who hit .270 in 51 games as a reserve in 1990, and Bip Roberts, who hit .309 with 44 stolen bases as the team's left fielder. McIlvaine was comfortable that the pair could handle the second-base job.

He wasn't as comfortable trading two star players for one in return. Alomar was more than a throw-in to even up the age difference. So McIlvaine expanded the deal further. He requested Fernández, which would allow the Padres to replace Templeton at short.

Through the 1990 season, the four players involved in the trade had combined to play nineteen full seasons in the major leagues. They'd received MVP votes in eleven of them and combined for four All-Star appearances, four Gold Gloves, a Silver Slugger, an RBI title and a home run crown.

"The whole negotiations probably took about three or four hours," Gillick said.

Now that the two sides had agreed, what was next?

"That's when we just looked at each other and laughed," McIlvaine said. "I don't think either of us could believe it."

"I like to do big deals," McIlvaine told Gillick. "Let's sleep on it."

"That didn't do a whole lot of good," McIlvaine recalled later. "I didn't get much sleep at all."

On the Blue Jays' side, Gillick met with his inner circle.

"You know, when Pat brought the idea back to us," scout Gordon Lakey said, "there was just total disbelief. These players have been such an integral part of our team, we didn't think about trading them. But the longer we thought about it, the more it made sense."

The two GMs spoke on the phone the next morning. Everyone was still on board. They agreed to meet at 2:00 p.m. to go over the deal one last time and announce it an hour later.

"We didn't even run a press release," Gillick recalled. "I think we wanted it to come out as a surprise, maybe catch everybody a little bit off guard."

McIlvaine stepped up to the podium at the TWA-Northwest room of the O'Hare Hyatt Regency hotel. The assembled media had no idea what was being announced.

"We figured you were sick of hearing about free-agent signings, so we thought we'd give you a good old-fashioned baseball trade, value for value," he said. He listed the four players involved, and he was shocked by the reaction from the people covering the announcement.

"You announce a trade like that to the media at the winter meetings, you are doing so in a room full of cynics," McIlvaine said. "I still remember that as each name was announced, you could hear a little gasp. When the whole thing had been laid out, there were actually guys applauding—reporters! Boy was that fun."

Among those applauding were baseball men standing in the back of the room, including Rangers manager Bobby Valentine; Frank Robinson, manager of the Blue Jays' divisional rival Orioles; and Dodgers manager Tommy Lasorda, a divisional rival of the Padres.

The managers weren't the only people negatively affected by the trade who still praised it.

"I applaud Joe McIlvaine for making one of the most aggressive trades in recent memories," said Jack Clark's agent, Tom Reich, even as he began searching for a new home for his client. "It's a gutsy move. They gave up a lot and got a lot. A lot of people have been writing the Padres off. Mark Twain would be proud of what happened today."

"My first reaction was 'wow,'" Orioles GM Roland Hemond said. "This is what we used to be accustomed to at the winter meetings. It's a good message to everybody that you shouldn't come here thinking you can't make a deal like that."

Toronto fans and media began searching for a new nickname for Stand Pat.

"We've had success," Gillick said. "Not divisions, but we've won a lot of games. Only some people don't think we had much to show for it. Trades are difficult, but this was the time to shake things up."

San Diego fans, by contrast, were outraged at the trade. "I don't think I'll be running for mayor any time soon," McIlvaine said.

Carter heard of the trade while enjoying some R&R during a break in the players' association meeting in Orlando, Florida. "I was just coming in off the golf course when the guy who handles the bags asked if we'd heard of the big trade," Carter said. "We hadn't, so he tells us, and it's at that moment the guy happens to notice my name on the bag. He stopped, looked like he didn't know what to do, then said: 'Well, gee, it involves you.'"

Carter spoke highly of the opportunity to play in Toronto, but he was still reeling from the news.

"I thought I was in pretty good shape in San Diego, especially after giving up my free-agent year to go there [as part of waiving a no-trade the previous winter]. Just the other day, I was saying, boy, I'm glad I'm not having to go through what all these other [free-agent] guys are. I'd just got a house, just got it all furnished and, boom, I'm back on the road again."

Alomar had also just bought a house, on the ocean in Del Mar. Just three years into his MLB career and leaving the only organization he'd played for, he took it tougher than his teammate.

"I didn't know what I did wrong," he said.

The trade looks lopsided in retrospect.

"I enjoyed making that deal, because it was a baseball deal," McIlvaine said, "nothing else. People don't make pure baseball deals anymore. These days, deals are made based on who is going to be a free agent, who is trying to dump a salary, who has arbitration coming up. It almost never has to do with baseball. That trade was talent for talent, value for value. We each thought we were making our club better. Period."

McGriff did exactly what the Padres had hoped. He hit 31 home runs in 1991 and a NL leading 35 in 1992. He had more than 100 RBI both years and was an All-Star, two-time MVP candidate and Silver Slugger.

Fernández had back-to-back 20-steal seasons and was a 1992 All-Star.

The Padres were a surprise contender in 1992. They were tied for first in early June and were as close as five games out in late July. McIlvaine went to the team's ownership group to request a budget increase to add another starting pitcher at the trade deadline. Instead, the team told him he had to reduce budget by trading away salary.

McIlvaine traded Craig Lefferts, who had already won 13 games as the team's third starter. He got a prospect and a player to be named from the Orioles. The Padres finished 16 games out of first.

The next year, ownership told McIlvaine to cut salary again. He was ordered to trade McGriff and All-Star outfielder Gary Sheffield.

"That's where I drew my line in the sand," McIlvaine said. "I said, 'I'm the caretaker of this team, and this is not for the benefit of the team or the fans of San Diego.'"

He resigned instead. McGriff was traded to the Braves, where he became a major component of their string of playoff teams during the 1990s. He would play eleven more seasons and finish with 493 career home runs.

Fernández was traded to the Mets and would play eight more years in MLB for a number of teams—including for the 1993 World Champion Toronto Blue Jays, who acquired him from the Mets in midseason.

Two and a half years after the blockbuster trade that sent away Joe Carter and Roberto Alomar, the Padres had Vince Moore, Donnie Elliott, Melvin Nieves, DJ Dozier, Wally Whitehurst and Raúl Casanova to show for it.

Alomar and Carter went on to form the core of the Blue Jays' back-to-back World Series champions in 1992 and 1993. Alomar would be an All-Star the next eleven seasons and a Gold Glover in ten of them. He was the MVP of the 1992 ALCS and hit .480 in the 1993 World Series.

After five years in Toronto, he joined Gillick in Baltimore. The two were inducted into the Hall of Fame together in 2011.

Carter hit 25 or more home runs in each of the next six seasons, topping 30 homers four times. He topped 100 RBI in six of his seven seasons in Toronto, made five All-Star teams and was in the top 10 for MVP voting three times.

Carter also hit one of the most famous home runs in World Series history, a season-ending walk-off in Game Six to give the Blue Jays the 1993 title. He had 4 home runs in 12 career World Series games.

It turned out the trade bug stuck with Stand Pat. He also picked up future star outfielder Devon White at the 1990 meetings. During the 1991 season, he added outfielders Cory Snyder and Candy Maldonado prior to the trade deadline.

But it was in 1992 and 1993 that Gillick sent critics looking to delete all their Stand Pat stories.

With the Jays contending at the 1992 trade deadline, Gillick traded for reliever Mark Eichhorn on July 30, and he acquired ace starting pitcher David Cone a month later.

In 1993, Gillick picked up future Hall of Famer Rickey Henderson at the trade deadline. In another deadline deal that brought things full circle, Gillick picked up Tony Fernández as a reserve for the stretch run. Fernández hit .333 and drove in a team-high 9 runs in the World Series.

In a minor offseason trade following the 1992 championship, Gillick sent longtime third baseman Kelly Gruber to the Angels for infielder Luis Sojo.

Like everyone else who witnessed the two-for-two trade that helped build the Blue Jays, Gruber spoke highly of his former GM and the deal, years later.

"That kind of caliber of trade takes big balls as we would say in Texas, and certainly Pat had them," said the Houston native. "You're either going to look great or you're not and if you give away two proven players, especially players people liked, not only did they do well here but they were liked, you're climbing uphill. But Pat knew what he was doing."

It all started at the 1990 winter meetings. Just as it seemed that sports pages would need to hire accountants to help make sense of all the free agent deals, two old-school general managers got together to make a swap for baseball reasons.

"You can debate that one for hours and hours, who got the better of it," McIlvaine told the *New York Times* after Alomar was selected for the Hall of Fame. "It might be as big a baseball trade as there's been, in retrospect, when you think about trading four All-Stars."

"It was a trade for the ages," McGriff said.

WAR COMPARISON

Joe Carter looks like the odd man out, posting a negative WAR following one off season in San Diego. Prior to that, however, he'd posted 14.3 wins above replacement in six years with Cleveland, firmly establishing himself as an All-Star on par with the other three.

Following the trade, Alomar, who built himself a Hall of Fame career in Toronto, clearly gave the Blue Jays the advantage in the deal. The Padres certainly should have been happy with the production they received from their two All-Stars, however.

PADRES RECEIVED	WAR PRE-TRADE	WAR POST-TRADE
Fred McGriff	19.3	9.4
Tony Fernández	28.1	3.1
PADRES RECEIVED	WAR PRE-TRADE	WAR POST-TRADE
Roberto Alomar	12.1	22.2
Joe Carter	-1.8	8.3

— CONCLUSION —

As the twenty deals featured in this book make evident, the wild and at-times-unpredictable exchange of players and dollars that characterizes baseball trades is often full of drama, intrigue and surprise. Trades can make or break careers, franchises and fans' spirits. The trading frenzy that takes place during the winter months and in the midst of heated in-season competition is compared to a meat market. But the "meat" being bought and sold is actual human beings.

It's easy to look at a list of prospects offered to a team and get caught up in stats and projections. To teams, however, it's a list of kids. In most cases, a team scouted a prospect in high school, built a relationship with him and drafted or signed him.

The prospect then meets a kindly farm director, like Mitch Lukevics, who helped him transition to pro ball and being away from home, usually far from home, in some strange town, for the first time.

In many cases, just knowing he was on a list presented to another team would crush a player. Many of the kids assumed they'd be with the organization that chose them forever. Often the final lesson a farm director has to teach a player is that it's all just a harsh business.

Looking back for common threads among the worst trades, it's worth noting that many of them took place in the last couple of decades, since free agency was a factor. As the final trade in the book proves, it's become rare and surprising when a trade is made for purely baseball reasons.

As salaries have spiraled out of control, more and more front-office spots are filled by financial people. The Moneyball revolution has filled more of the spots with statistical analysts and economists.

That doesn't necessarily make the game worse, but it does create more room for error when trying to make a trade. Instead of looking at personalities, teams can fall into the trap of making the dollars match up. That leads to the debacle of Mike Piazza's being traded to help secure a cable deal for the team's parent company, then spending all of five games in his new city.

Salary dumps and rent-a-player deals, when done well, can create magic in the middle of a season. Cubs fans who remember Rick Sutcliffe or Tiger fans who were around when Dour Doyle came to town will never forget the stretch run, when one out of every five days, they knew that their team was guaranteed to win. And the epic salary dump the Red Sox pulled off with the Dodgers in 2012, while moving more money than any other midseason deal, was primarily personality driven—baseball people deciding what needed to change.

Of course, it's easy to botch those types of deals as well, as George W. Bush's Rangers and Mark Teixeira's brief time in Atlanta demonstrated.

With all the debate about good and bad trades, and which deals should have been included, it's easy to forget that, first and foremost, this is a book of stories. A story is always better when the audience knows the characters well. They're a lot like baseball trades in that way.

Knowing that Von Hayes might take things a little too seriously could have helped a team with vicious fans think of ways to alter their deal to reduce the pressure.

Knowing that while millionaires were flying cross-country in private jets to join their new team, the men they were traded for were watching the crawl on ESPN, trying to figure out if they needed to pack, helps give faces and voices to financial numbers that can be mind-boggling at times.

Knowing what Larry Bowa and Doyle Alexander were really like helps to explain the details behind their respective trades, just as knowing that Curt Schilling was using a *For Dummies* book to help negotiate while the Red Sox executives were trying to keep from throwing up on their socks inspires fans to love the curse-breaking Boston team just a little bit more.

Jerry Seinfeld, who called out the Yankees for trading Jay Buhner, once complained about the player turnover caused by free agency. "We're basically rooting for laundry," he said.

That's not true. We're rooting for guys. We just know our guys better than the guys in the other laundry. It's why we love them . . . until they change clothes.

— ACKNOWLEDGMENTS —

If this were an awards show, you could go to the kitchen, get a snack and wait for the orchestra to play me off. Since it's not, you'll have to bear with me. I have some people to thank.

To the Rays, Phillies, Yankees, Mariners, Athletics and Diamondbacks organizations, for giving me access to players, coaches and executives and for helping me get in touch with special assistants, scouts and emeritus executives.

To Hayes Permar, for knowing people and getting things done. And for being a friend.

To Melanie McCullough, for knowing people and for reading early drafts of chapters and telling me they were good so I would keep writing.

To Kenny Kramer, inspiration for the *Seinfeld* character of the same (last) name. You're in the acknowledgments. I still owe you a free book.

To my agent, Alec Shane, for investing all that time and effort in me when I was making him no money at all, for promising me it wouldn't always be that way and for sending me a George Jefferson "Movin' on Up" meme when he was proved correct.

To Will Kiester at Page Street Publishing, for his work on the concept of this book and for trusting me to write it. To Josh Leventhal, for keeping my storytelling focused on the trades, even when I uncovered a fun tangent. To Sarah Monroe, for helping Josh edit it into the current readable form you see in front of you. To Sandy Smith, for her patient work in final copyediting. And to everyone else at Page Street Publishing for their hard work behind-the-scenes.

To everyone who took a chance on me when I was just an ex-banker who liked sports, including (but not limited to) Marian Giallombardo, Stan McNeal, Tom Thompson, Aaron Schatz, Matt Aug, John Watson, John Akers and Tony Moss.

To the small group of Delaware writers who inspired and motivated me to follow my dream: Lisa Lutwyche, Nick Lutwyche, Bryan Nance, Pat Meehan and Jacquie Juers.

To my press-box friends in Western New York, who let me crash the party: Lary Bump, Scott Pitoniak, Jim Mandelaro, Bob Matuszak, Chuck "The Truth" Hinkel, John DiTullio, Dave Ricci, Bob Matthews and Brad Thyroff.

To the Triangle media. I can't possibly mention all of you, so we'll stop after Lauren Brownlow.

To all the media relations directors and SIDs who listened to my off-the-wall story ideas, whether you helped me to pursue them or not.

To my sister Courtney, who helped sneak me into university libraries on both coasts to help me track down some of the more elusive sources in my research. To my other sister Wendy, who would have helped sneak me in anyplace I needed, if only I'd asked.

To Mom, for sharing her love of reading and not being too mad when I told her I wasn't going to use the math degree she and Dad paid for.

To Dad, for sharing his love of sports and for pretending not to know that I cheated on all those *Baseball Digest* quizzes.

To Jasmin, Isaiah, Jathan and Mahalya.

To Kayla, Gayle, Lauren, Kimberly and Kristina, for waiting patiently through all the rain delays and pitching changes that kept me away from you for a few more minutes each night. And for all the notes to your teachers that were written on the backs of box scores.

And to the generations of baseball journalists who helped keep a record of these stories, one deadline at a time, while their own people waited patiently at home.

— ABOUT THE AUTHOR —

 Since leaving his job as a bank vice president in 2000, Shawn Krest has covered baseball for dozens of outlets, including MLB.com, MLB Advanced Media, The Sporting News and ESPN.com. His work has appeared in the official game programs for the MLB All-Star Game and League Championship Series, and he's been an official scorer for the International League for more than a decade. Shawn lives in Raleigh, North Carolina, with his daughters and dachshunds.

— INDEX —

Aaron, Hank, 155

Abbot, Kyle, 135

Abbott, Jim, 141, 142

Abbott, Kurt, 24

Abreu, Bobby, 49

Adenhart, Nick, 102, 163, 169

Agee, Tommy, 172

Aguayo, Luis, 88, 89, 94, 131

Albom, Mitch, 67

Alderson, Sandy, 23

Alexander, Doyle, 67–68, 68–70, 71, 74, 221, 222

Allen, Dick, 201–202, 202–204, 207, 208–209

Allen, Neil, 213

Allen, Richie, 206

Almon, Bill, 88

Alomar, Roberto, 216–217, 220

Alomar, Sandy, Jr., 216

Alomar, Sandy, Sr., 217

Alou, Moises, 21, 24, 36

Álvarez, Wilson, 78, 79, 80, 81, 83, 152, 153, 155, 156, 157

Amaro, Rubén, Jr., 84, 135

Amézaga, Alfredo, 96

Anaheim Angels, 48–49, 102, 163–164, 167–168, 169, 183–184, 186

Andersen, Larry, 11

Anderson, Sparky, 69, 138

Andrews, James, 137, 139

Andrus, Elvis, 164, 165, 167, 168

Angell, Roger, 134

Apodaca, Bob, 172

Argyros, George, 60

Árias, Joaquín, 115, 117, 160

Arizona Diamondbacks, 26, 27, 28, 29, 30, 32, 34, 164

Armas, Tony, 38

Arroyo, Bronson, 116

Ash, Gord, 141

Atlanta Braves, 42, 69, 71, 72, 73–74, 158–159, 164–165, 166, 167, 168

Autry, Gene, 183

Avery, Steve, 166

Backman, Wally, 213

Badenhop, Burke, 103, 106

Baerga, Carlos, 216

Bagwell, Jeff, 11

Bailor, Bob, 213

Baines, Harold, 78, 148, 149, 150, 152, 153, 154, 156, 157

Baker, Dan, 135–136

Baker, Dusty, 79

Balabon, Rich, 61

Baller, Jay, 132, 133, 136

Baltimore Orioles, 10, 68, 78, 145, 162–163, 169, 192, 193–194, 195, 196, 197, 199, 200

Banks, Darryl, 122, 126

Banks, Ernie, 155

Barceló, Lorenzo, 79, 82, 83

Barfield, Jesse, 62, 65

Barrios, Manuel, 21, 22, 23

Bauer, Gary, 148

Bauer, Hank, 194, 199

Bavasi, Buzzie, 80

Baylor, Don, 183

Beane, Billy, 179

Beckett, Josh, 46–47, 48, 50, 51, 52, 53, 55, 97

Bedard, Erik, 132, 163, 169

Begala, Paul, 150

Beinfest, Larry, 98

Belle, Albert, 17, 75–76, 77, 80, 81

Bell, George, 157, 216

Beltré, Adrián, 113

Bergesch, Bill, 57, 210, 211

Berra, Yogi, 59, 155, 194, 196, 198

Bibby, Jim, 173

Biddle, Rocky, 43, 45
Billingsley, Chad, 101, 162, 169
Billings, Rich, 173
Bitker, Joe, 154
Blair, Willie, 78
Blake, Casey, 102
Blauser, Jeff, 166
Blum, Geoff, 113
Blyleven, Bert, 10
Blyzka, Mike, 196, 200
Boehringer, Brian, 140
Boggs, Tommy, 89
Bonds, Barry, 13, 112
Bonds, Bobby, 214
Bonilla, Bobby, 14, 20, 22, 23
Boone, Aaron, 108, 109, 112, 113, 116
Boone, Bret, 113
Boras, Scott, 111, 114, 130, 162, 164
Boston Red Sox, 11, 25, 26, 30, 31, 33, 34, 38, 46,
    47, 48, 50, 51, 52, 53, 54, 55, 100, 106,
    108–109, 110–111, 112, 114, 115–116,
    117, 163, 169, 190, 221
Boswell, Thomas, 67
Bowa, Larry, 84, 85–89, 90, 92, 93, 94, 222
Bowden, Jim, 40, 137, 138, 142, 144, 145
Boyer, Clete, 199
Boyer, Ken, 174, 202
Bradley, Phil, 212
Brady, Tom, 156
Brett, George, 120, 173
Brewer, Shonda, 25–26, 29, 30–31, 32, 33
Brickhouse, Jack, 125
Briggs, Johnny, 203
Brock, Lou, 11, 202, 205, 208
Broglio, Ernie, 11
Brooklyn Dodgers, 198
Browne, Byron, 205, 209
Browning, Bob, 207
Browning, Jim, 209
Brown, Kevin, 14–15, 23, 24
Broxton, Jonathan, 102
Brummer, Glenn, 176

Buchholz, Clay, 100, 163, 169
Buckner, Bill, 213
Buhner, Jay, 56–57, 59, 61, 62, 63, 65, 222
Buice, DeWayne, 211
Bundy, Lorenzo, 52
Bunning, Jim, 175
Bunyanesque, Paul, 166
Burba, Dave, 142
Burnett, A. J., 15, 24
Burrell, Pat, 86
Burroughs, Jeff, 173
Busch, August, 174, 175
Bush, Barbara (daughter), 147, 148
Bush, Barbara (mother), 147, 149
Bush, Barney, 147
Bush, George H. W., 147
Bush, George W., 147, 148–149, 150, 155, 156,
    157, 221
Bush, Jenna, 147
Bush, Millie, 147
Byrd, Harry, 196, 200
Byrne, Tommy, 192

Cabrera, Asdrúbal, 100, 106
Cabrera, Melky, 98
Cabrera, Miguel, 95–98, 99–100, 101, 102–103,
    104, 105, 106, 162
Cabrera, Orlando, 38
Cadaret, Greg, 151
Cain, Matt, 100, 101, 106, 163, 169
Cairo, Miguel, 113, 116
Caldwell, Mike, 179
Callison, Johnny, 203
Campaneris, Bert, 183, 185
Campbell, Bill, 121
Campbell, Jim, 72
Candelaria, John, 211
Cano, Robinson, 87–88, 115
Canseco, Jose, 151
Canzler, Russ, 86
Capuano, Chris, 30
Caray, Harry, 185

Carey, Chase, 20

Carlton, Steve, 207–208

Carman, Don, 212

Carpenter, Ruly, 87

Carrasquel, Chico, 193

Carter, Gary, 57, 213

Carter, Joe, 10, 122–123, 124, 126, 216, 218, 220

Caruso, Mike, 79, 82, 83

Casanova, Raúl, 219

Casey, Sean, 103

Cash, Dave, 183

Cashen, Frank, 214

Cashman, Brian, 28, 98–99, 108, 109, 112, 113, 114, 141, 162, 199–200

Cash, Norm, 204

Castillo, Bobby, 119

Castillo, José, 101

Castillo, Luis, 97

Caudill, Bill, 88, 130

Cerv, Bob, 198

Cey, Ron, 93

Chamberlain, Joba, 98, 162

Chambliss, Chris, 183

Chass, Murray, 145

Chech, Charlie, 10

Chernin, Peter, 20

Chiamparino, Scott, 154

Chicago Cubs, 10, 78, 88, 89–90, 90–91, 92, 93, 94, 118, 120, 121–122, 123, 124, 125, 126, 155, 157, 177, 178

Chicago White Sox, 76, 77, 78, 79–80, 81, 82, 83, 88, 99–100, 106, 110, 117, 152, 153, 154, 155, 157, 187, 188, 189, 191, 192, 193

Cincinnati Reds, 10, 137, 138, 139, 142, 143, 144, 145, 146, 183, 202

Cirillo, Jeff, 113

Claiborne, John, 174

Claire, Fred, 16, 19, 20, 21

Clancy, Jim, 176

Clark, Jack, 215, 218

Clark, Roy, 166

Clemens, Roger, 26, 31, 152

Clements, Pat, 65

Cleveland Indians, 10, 39, 40, 41, 42, 45, 75, 76, 77, 100, 106, 118, 120, 122, 123, 124, 125–126, 130, 131, 132, 136, 142, 179, 184

Clifton, Gregg, 27

Clinton, Bill, 14, 15–16, 148

Clyde, David, 173

Colangelo, Jerry, 27, 28

Colletti, Ned, 49–50, 104

Collins, Dave, 210

Colón, Bartolo, 29, 35, 39, 40, 42, 44, 45

Concepción, Dave, 85

Cone, David, 10, 140, 141, 142, 144, 213, 215, 219

Conine, Jeff, 15, 24

Consuegra, Sandy, 193

Cook, Dennis, 24

Cora, Joey, 217

Corrales, Pat, 91, 122, 133, 134

Cosell, Howard, 207

Cotto, Henry, 60, 63

Counsell, Craig, 30

Cowens, Al, 173

Cox, Bobby, 71

Cox, William, 36

Craig, Roger, 180

Crawford, Carl, 48, 50, 51, 52, 53, 55

Crawford, Tyler, 158–159, 166–167, 168

Crede, Joe, 100

Cruz, Julio, 131

Cuza, Fernando, 98

Dalton, Harry, 178, 183

Damon, Johnny, 184

Daniels, Jon, 160–161, 162–163, 167, 168, 169

Darling, Ron, 213

Darwin, Danny, 79, 80, 83

David, Larry, 56, 57, 59, 62–63

Davis, Dick, 88, 94

Davis, Glenn, 25

Davis, Jody, 122, 212

Davis, Rajai, 100

Davis, Storm, 86

DeJesús, Iván, 88, 89, 90, 91, 92, 93, 94, 131

DeJesús, Iván, Jr., 51, 53, 54, 55

De La Cruz, Frankie, 103, 104, 106
De La Rosa, Jorge, 30, 34
De La Rosa, Rubby, 52, 53, 55
Delgado, Carlos, 112
Del Guercio, Theodore, 197, 200
Dempster, Ryan, 54, 55
Dent, Bucky, 182, 185, 188, 189–190, 191
Dernier, Bob, 90, 94, 121, 132, 133, 136
Detroit Tigers, 10, 70, 71–72, 73, 74, 102, 103, 104,
        105, 106, 138, 140, 141, 142, 143, 144,
        162, 171, 173, 204
Devine, Bing, 202, 205, 207
DeWitt, Blake, 102
Diaz, Carlos, 213
Dobson, Pat, 184
Doby, Larry, 186
Dodd, Tom, 58
Dombrowski, Dave, 15, 17, 19–20, 21, 96, 102–103,
        105
Dozier, D. J., 219
Drabek, Doug, 58, 59, 65
Drews, Matt, 141
Drew, Tim, 41, 45
Duncan, Dave, 189
Dunston, Shawon, 85, 86
DuPuy, Bob, 111
Durham, Joe, 195
Durham, Leon, 125, 174, 177, 179, 181
Dykes, Jimmy, 193, 195
Dykstra, Lenny, 213, 214

Eckersley, Dennis, 151
Eckstein, David, 109
Ehlers, Arthur, 193
Eichhorn, Mark, 219
Eisenreich, Jim, 20, 22, 23
Elia, Lee, 135
Elliott, Donnie, 219
Ellis, Dock, 190
Ellsbury, Jacoby, 100, 106, 163, 169
Ellsworth, Steve, 72
Encarnación, Juan, 97
Epstein, Theo, 25, 30, 31, 32, 33, 109, 110, 115

Escobar, Yunel, 164
Espy, Cecil, 151
Estes, Shawn, 78
Ethier, Andre, 49, 162, 169
Etten, Nick, 35
Evans, Darrell, 70
Evans, Terry, 163
Evranian, Charlie, 188

Fassero, Jeff, 36
Faubus, Orval, 201
Feliz, Neftalí, 165, 167, 168
Feliz, Pedro, 100
Felske, John, 127
Fernandez, Alex, 22, 79
Fernandez, Sid, 213, 215
Fernández, Tony, 216, 219, 220
Fetcher, Spot, 147–148
Fetzer, John, 72
Fielder, Cecil, 143
Fields, Josh, 100
Figgins, Chone, 102
Fingers, Rollie, 176, 177, 178, 180, 181
Finley, Charlie O., 172
Finley, Steve, 25
Fischlin, Mike, 130
Fisk, Carlton, 153
Flanagan, Mike, 211
Fletcher, Scott, 148, 150, 152, 153–154, 157
Flood, Carl, 205
Flood, Curt, 202, 204–205, 206, 207, 209
Florida Marlins, 14–15, 16, 19–20, 21–22, 23, 24,
        36, 37–38, 42, 79, 95, 96, 97–98, 99, 100,
        101, 102, 103, 104, 105, 106
Floyd, Cliff, 42–43
Fogerty, John, 149
Foley, Marv, 141
Foli, Tim, 172
Forbes, Steve, 148
Ford, Whitey, 62, 198
Fossum, Casey, 30, 34
Foulke, Keith, 79, 81, 82, 83
Fox, Nellie, 175

Foy, Joe, 172

Francoeur, Jeff, 166

Franco, Julio, 88, 90, 91, 92, 93, 130, 131, 132, 133, 136, 153

Francona, Terry, 46, 47, 103, 110

Frazier, George, 122, 123, 126

Fregosi, Jim, 172

Frey, Jim, 85, 86, 121, 124

Fridley, Jim, 196, 200

Frye, Jeff, 108

Furcal, Rafael, 166

Gagne, Eric, 163, 165, 169

Galarraga, Andrés, 40

Galarraga, Armando, 160

Gamble, Oscar, 184–185, 187, 191

Gammons, Peter, 51, 132, 143

Gant, Ron, 166

Garagiola, Joe, Jr., 27–28, 32

Garcia, Karim, 19

Garciaparra, Nomar, 101, 109, 110, 117

Gardner, Mark, 78

Garland, Jon, 100, 102

Garrett, Wayne, 172

Gaston, Cito, 138

Gehrig, Lou, 59

Gentry, Gary, 172

Geren, Bob, 177, 180

Germán, Esteban, 40

Giambi, Jason, 184

Gibson, Bob, 204, 205

Gibson, Kirk, 70

Giles, Bill, 87, 88, 89, 90, 91, 92, 129, 130, 131, 132

Gillick, Doris, 210–212

Gillick, Pat, 71, 152, 210–212, 214, 220

Girardi, Joe, 99

Giroux, Monique, 38

Glaus, Troy, 88, 99

Glavine, Tom, 41, 73, 166

Goetz, Geoff, 24

Goldsberry, Gordon, 89

Gonzalez, Adrian, 47–48, 50, 51, 52, 55, 160

Gonzalez, Alex, 97

González, Gio, 100, 106

González, Juan, 151, 152, 155, 156

Gooden, Dwight, 57

Gordon, Mike, 142

Gore, Al, 150

Gorman, Tom, 127

Gossage, Rich "Goose," 173, 174, 178

Goss, Mike, 30, 34

Graziano, Bob, 18, 20, 21

Greenberg, Hank, 195

Green, Dallas, 86, 87, 89–90, 121, 122, 123

Green, David, 178, 180

Greenwell, Mike, 216

Grich, Bobby, 183–184

Grieve, Tom, 9, 12, 148, 149–150, 152, 153, 161

Grimes, Burleigh, 10

Grissom, Marquis, 36

Gross, Kevin, 215

Gruber, Kelly, 220

Guante, Cecilio, 65

Guerrero, Vladimir, 38

Guidry, Ron, 177, 186

Guillén, Carlos, 103, 104

Guillén, Ibis, 104

Guillén, Ozzie, 79, 99, 152, 154, 189

Guillen, Rudy, 115

Gullett, Don, 142, 183

Guzmán, Juan, 211

Gwynn, Tony, 215

Hageman, John, 71, 72

Hague, Joe, 205

Hall, Andrew, 158–159, 166–167, 168

Hall, Mel, 10, 121, 122, 124, 126

Hamper, Joe, 193

Hansen, Ron, 197

Harazin, Al, 214

Hargrove, Mike, 131

Harnisch, Pete, 25

Harrah, Toby, 173, 185

Harris, Lenny, 97

Harrison, Matt, 164, 165, 167, 168

Hart, John, 108, 109, 111, 114

Hassey, Ron, 122, 126

Hatch, Orrin, 148

Hayes, Von, 127, 128, 130, 131, 132–134, 135,
    136, 222

Haynes, Nathan, 163

Heilmann, Harry, 134

Hemond, Roland, 88, 175, 189, 218

Henderson, Rickey, 58, 151

Henderson, Steve, 91

Hendrick, George, 174

Hendricks, Elrod, 68

Henry, John, 22, 37–38

Henson, Drew, 113

Hernandez, Keith, 57, 63, 176–177, 213

Hernández, Liván, 20

Hernández, Orlando, 41, 43, 45

Hernández, Roberto, 78, 79, 80, 83

Hernandez, Willie, 70

Herzog, Buck, 171

Herzog, Dorrel Norman Elvert "Whitey," 80,
    170–174, 175, 176–177, 178–179, 180

Hicks, Tom, 107, 108, 109, 111, 112, 114

Hiller, Margaret, 187–188

Hill, Ken, 36, 141, 142

Himes, Larry, 152

Hitchcock, Sterling, 140, 146

Hodges, Gil, 172

Hodges, Ron, 172

Hoerner, Joe, 205, 206, 209

Hoiles, Chris, 71, 74

Holcomb, Scott, 62

Holland, Al, 130

Holman, Brian, 63

Hooten, Burt, 119, 172

Horne, Alan, 99

Hornsby, Rogers, 134

Horton, Willie, 204

Hough, Charlie, 152

Houston Astros, 11, 25, 132, 193

Houston, Tyler, 86

Howard, Elston, 185, 199

Howard, Ryan, 61

Howry, Bobby, 79, 81, 83

Howser, Dick, 185

Hoyer, Jed, 25, 30, 31, 33, 110, 111, 115

Hoyt, LaMarr, 12, 187–189, 191

Hudson, Tim, 164

Hughes, Phil, 98, 162

Hughes, Tommy, 35

Huizenga, Wayne, 15, 20, 23

Humber, Philip, 11

Hunter, Billy, 195, 198, 200

Hutchinson, Fred, 202

Incaviglia, Pete, 151, 152

Inge, Brandon, 103

Jackson, Reggie, 12, 59, 174, 184, 185, 210

Jackson, "Shoeless" Joe, 86

James, Bill, 60

James, Chris, 216

Janzen, Marty, 142

Jarvis, Jason, 142

Jefferson, Stan, 86

Jeter, Derek, 9, 63, 64, 108, 114, 116, 141, 146

Johnson, Charles, 14, 20, 22, 23, 196

Johnson, Cliff, 211

Johnson, Darrell, 194, 200

Johnson, Davey, 143, 213, 214–215

Johnson, Howard, 213

Johnson, Jerry, 205, 209

Johnson, Magic, 49, 52

Johnson, Nick, 29, 34

Johnson, Randy, 26, 130

Johnson, Sandy, 28

John, Tommy, 137

Jones, Adam, 132

Jones, Andruw, 158, 166

Jones, Beau, 165, 168

Jones, Chipper, 165, 166

Jones, Todd, 103

Justice, David, 166

Kamieniecki, Scott, 139

Kansas City Athletics, 193, 199

Kansas City Royals, 173, 174, 216

Kasten, Stan, 49
Keegan, Bob, 193
Keelty, James, Jr., 199
Kelly, Roberto, 61, 65
Kemp, Matt, 53, 101, 106
Kendrick, Howie, 102, 163, 169
Kennedy, Ian, 98, 162
Kennedy, Terry, 176, 177, 181
Kent, Jeff, 93
Kershaw, Clayton, 49, 101, 106, 162, 169
Keyes, Alan, 148
Keyes, Leroy, 128
Key, Jimmy, 139
Kiner, Ralph, 62, 171
Klein, Joe, 143
Klesko, Ryan, 166
Konerko, Paul, 82
Konstanty, Jim, 192
Koosman, Jerry, 172
Kornheiser, Tony, 115, 116
Kotchman, Casey, 163, 167, 169
Koufax, Sandy, 155
Kramer, Kenny, 56, 57, 59, 63
Kranepool, Ed, 172
Kretlow, Lou, 197
Krol, Jack, 174
Kryhoski, Dick, 196, 200
Kuhn, Bowie, 80, 187, 206
Kunkel, Jeff, 154
Kutyna, Marty, 202

Lajoie, Bill, 70, 71, 73–74
Lake, Steve, 122
Lakey, Gordon, 217
Landis, Kenesaw Mountain, 35
Lane, Frank, 192, 193, 202
LaPoint, Dave, 178, 180
LaRoche, Andy, 101
Larsen, Don, 195–196, 197–198, 200
La Russa, Tony, 188–189
Lasorda, Tommy, 16, 19, 67, 119, 120, 218
Lavelle, Gary, 130

League, Brandon, 49
Lee, Cliff, 35, 41, 43, 44, 45, 50
Lee, Derrek, 15, 24, 97
Lefferts, Craig, 219
Leiper, Tim, 38
Leiter, Al, 14, 24, 61, 65
Leno, Jay, 149
Leppert, Don, 197, 200
Lester, Jon, 47, 110, 116, 117
Levine, Randy, 114
Lewis, Fred, 100
Lewis, Mark, 10, 144, 146
Leyland, Jim, 14, 96, 212
Lezcano, Sixto, 178, 180
Lieberthal, Mike, 86
Liefer, Jeff, 43, 45
Lillibridge, Brent, 164
Lincecum, Tim, 100, 101, 106
Lindros, Eric, 129
Littlefield, John, 177, 181
Loaiza, Esteban, 107
Lofton, Kenny, 75
Lolich, Mickey, 204
Loney, James, 51, 52, 53, 54, 55, 101, 162, 169
Lopat, Eddie, 192
Lopes, Davey, 85
Lopez, Albie, 142
López, Javy, 166
Loria, Jeffrey, 22, 36, 38, 98
Los Angeles Dodgers, 16–17, 19, 20, 21, 22–23, 46, 47, 48, 49, 50, 51–52, 53, 54, 55, 67, 101, 102, 106, 118, 119, 124, 144, 162, 169, 198, 214, 215, 221
Lovitto, Joe, 173
Lowell, Mike, 97, 100
Lowry, Noah, 101
Lozano, Dan, 17, 18, 19, 22
Lucchino, Larry, 25, 30, 31, 33, 111, 115
Lucchino, Stacey, 31, 32
Lukevics, Mitch, 9, 66–67, 221
Lyle, Sparky, 90, 94, 173, 174, 186
Lyon, Brandon, 30, 34

MacPhail, Andy, 215

MacPhail, Lee, 199

Maddux, Greg, 41, 81, 166

Madeja, Ken, 72

Magowan, Peter, 16, 81

Mahay, Ron, 165, 168

Mahler, Rick, 71, 74

Maldonado, Candy, 219

Malone, Kevin, 80

Manfred, Rob, 44

Mania, Fernando, 119

Manning, Brian, 79, 82, 83

Manrique, Fred, 153, 154, 157

Mantle, Mickey, 62, 170–171, 196, 198, 199

Marek, Stephen, 167

Marion, Marty, 195

Maris, Roger, 59, 150, 179, 199

Martin, Billy, 173, 185, 190, 196, 198

Martinez, Dave, 141

Martínez, Dennis, 215

Martínez, Pedro, 17, 31, 36, 46, 81

Mathis, Jeff, 102

Matlack, Jon, 172

Matthews, Gary, 121, 124

Mattingly, Don, 49, 52, 59

Matuszek, Len, 89, 131

Mauch, Gene, 203, 207

Maybin, Cameron, 103, 106, 162

Mazzilli, Lee, 213

McCain, John, 148

McCann, Brian, 164

McCarthy, Brandon, 110

McCarver, Tim, 205, 207, 208, 209

McClain, Ron, 38

McCormack, Don, 90, 94

McCourt, Frank, 48

McCourt, Jamie, 48, 49

McDonald, Jim, 196, 200

McDonald, Joe, 72, 73, 74

McDowell, Roger, 63, 213, 214

McGee, Willie, 57–58, 59, 65, 215

McGriff, Fred, 58, 59, 65, 210, 211, 216, 218, 219, 220

McGwire, Mark, 11, 150, 151, 155, 156

McIlvaine, Joe, 212–213, 213–216, 217–218, 219, 220

McIlvaine, Marty, 214

McKeon, Jack, 96, 214, 216

McNabb, Donovan, 129

McNally, Dave, 208

McReynolds, Kevin, 213

Melton, Rube, 35

Mendoza, Mario, 13

Menke, Dennis, 134

Messersmith, Andy, 12, 208

Meulens, Hensley, 61, 65

Michael, Gene, 64, 140, 141–142, 145

Millar, Kevin, 46

Miller, Andrew, 103, 106, 162

Miller, Bill, 197, 200

Miller, Marvin, 77

Miller, Ray, 58

Millwood, Kevin, 41, 161, 166

Milner, John, 172

Milwaukee Brewers, 29, 178

Minaya, Omar, 29, 38, 39–40, 42, 43, 44

Mincher, Don, 62

Minnesota Twins, 37, 73

Minton, Greg, 130

Miranda, Willy, 196, 200

Mitchell, Dale, 198

Molitor, Paul, 178

Montañez, Willie, 207, 209

Montreal Expos, 35, 36, 37–38, 38–39, 40–41, 42–43, 44, 45, 215

Moore, Vince, 219

Morandini, Mickey, 93

Moreland, Keith, 121, 123, 125

Moreno, Arte, 48, 164

Morgan, Joe, 85, 130, 134

Morgan, Mike, 141, 210

Morris, Jack, 70

Mulholland, Terry, 78

Munson, Thurman, 112

Murcer, Bobby, 68

Murdoch, Rupert, 16

Murray, Dale, 58, 65, 210

Musial, Stan, 134, 155, 207

Mussina, Mike, 113

Myers, Greg, 152

Napoli, Mike, 54, 55, 102

Nelson, Davey, 173

Nen, Robb, 14, 24

Nevin, Phil, 62

New York Mets, 14, 22, 23, 24, 44, 62–63, 110, 171–172, 212, 213, 214, 219

New York Yankees, 9, 10, 11, 12, 26, 28, 29, 30, 31–32, 33, 34, 52, 56, 57, 58, 59, 61, 62, 63, 64, 65, 68, 69, 70, 98, 99, 108–109, 112–116, 117, 118, 129–130, 139–141, 142, 144, 145, 146, 151, 162, 167, 170–171, 178, 182, 183, 184, 185, 186, 187, 188, 190, 191, 192, 193, 194, 195, 196–197, 198–199, 200, 210, 211, 215

Niekro, Phil, 71, 211

Nieves, Melvin, 219

Nitkowski, C. J., 10, 142, 143, 144, 146

Northrup, Jim, 204

Nugent, Gerald, 35

Oakland Athletics, 58, 62, 151, 154

O'Connor, Ian, 114

Ohka, Tomo, 38

Ohlendorf, Ross, 99

Ojeda, Bob, 213

Olerud, John, 216

Oliver, Al, 150

Olivo, Frank, 128, 129

Olmsted, Al, 177, 181

Olsen, Scott, 97

O'Malley, Peter, 16

O'Malley, Walter, 16

O'Neill, Paul, 63

Ordóñez, Magglio, 110, 117

Ortiz, David, 47

Orza, Gene, 111

Otis, Amos, 172, 173

Overbay, Lyle, 30

Owens, Paul, 87, 89, 90, 91, 93, 130, 131, 133, 208

Ownbey, Rick, 213

Page, Dave, 47

Pagliarulo, Mike, 59

Palmeiro, Orlando, 82

Palmeiro, Rafael, 153, 156

Palmer, David, 71, 74

Parrish, Larry, 150–151

Patterson, Ken, 157

Paul, Gabe, 122, 130, 185, 187, 188, 202

Pavano, Carl, 97

Peavy, Jake, 54, 55

Peña, Carlos, 40

Pendleton, Terry, 166, 215

Penny, Brad, 97

Perconte, Jack, 130

Perez, Marty, 186, 190

Pérez, Mélido, 140

Perez, Odalis, 29

Pérez, Tony, 96, 183

Perranoski, Ron, 119

Perry, Gaylord, 10, 68

Peters, Hank, 67

Petralli, Geno, 152

Pettitte, Andy, 64, 140, 146

Phelps, Ken, 60–61, 61–62, 63–64, 65

Philadelphia Phillies, 26, 35, 36, 85–86, 87, 88, 89, 90, 91, 92, 93, 94, 121, 127, 128, 129, 130–131, 132–133, 134, 135–136, 178, 179, 202, 203, 205, 206, 207, 208, 209, 212, 213, 214, 215

Phillips, Brandon, 35, 40, 43, 44, 45

Phillips, Mike, 177, 181

Phillips, Steve, 40

Piazza, Mike, 14, 16, 17–21, 22, 23, 24, 221

Piazza, Tommy, 16

Piazza, Vince, 16

Pierce, Billy, 193

Pierre, Juan, 97

Piniella, Lou, 58, 61

Pinson, Vada, 205

Plunk, Eric, 151

Pohlad, Carl, 37

Pole, Dick, 79

Polinsky, Robert, 187, 191

Polonia, Luis, 151

Porter, Darrell, 176

Portugal, Mark, 142

Posada, Jorge, 64, 112, 141, 145, 146

Powell, Colin, 149

Power, Ted, 119

Pugh, Tim, 142

Puig, Yasiel, 49

Pujols, Albert, 49

Punto, Nick, 50–51, 52, 55

Quinn, Bob, 59

Quinn, John, 203, 206, 207

Rabelo, Mike, 103, 104, 106

Ramirez, Hanley, 49

Ramirez, Manny, 46, 109–110, 116, 117

Ramirez, Ramon, 115

Rasmus, Colby, 99

Reagan, Ronald, 148

Reagins, Tony, 102

Reed, Rick, 142

Reichler, Joe, 192

Reich, Tom, 218

Reid, Jason, 18

Reinsdorf, Jerry, 76–77, 80, 81, 82

Reitz, Ken, 93, 177, 181

Rendell, Ed, 129

Rentería, Édgar, 22

Reuss, Jerry, 119

Reyes, Jo-Jo, 165

Reynolds, Allie, 192

Rhoden, Rick, 58, 65

Richards, Ann, 149

Richards, Paul, 193, 194, 196, 199

Riddoch, Greg, 216, 217

Rijo, José, 58, 137–138

Ritz, Kevin, 71, 74

Rivera, Mariano, 9, 10, 64, 140, 141, 144–145, 146

Rivera, Rubén, 141, 146

Rivers, Mickey, 172

Rizzuto, Phil, 193, 195, 198

Robertson, Orlo, 192

Robinson, Brooks, 197, 199

Robinson, Frank, 10, 38, 41–42, 68, 218

Robinson, Jackie, 203, 204

Robinson, Jeff, 70

Rocker, John, 166

Rodriguez, Alex, 98, 99, 107, 108, 109, 110, 111–112, 114, 116–117, 160

Rodríguez, Iván, 97

Rojas, Cookie, 205, 209

Rolen, Scott, 86, 99

Rosenthal, Ken, 101

Rose, Pete, 133, 134

Rueter, Kirk, 78

Russell, Bill, 21

Ruth, Babe, 11, 26, 59, 61

Ruthven, Dick, 122, 131

Ryan, Jack, 10

Ryan, Nolan, 149, 155, 172

Sabathia, C. C., 42, 73

Sabean, Brian, 81, 100

Saberhagen, Bret, 141

Sadlock, Joshua, 44

Sain, Johnny, 192

Saltalamacchia, Jarrod, 164, 168

Samson, David, 98

Samuel, Juan, 130, 132, 133, 136, 213, 214

Sanchez, Alejandro, 131

Sánchez, Humberto, 99

Sanchez, Jesus, 15

Sanchez, Jonathan, 163, 169

Sandberg, Ryne, 51, 84–85, 86, 89, 91, 92, 93, 94

Sanders, Deion, 142

Sanderson, Scott, 122

San Diego Padres, 86, 125, 177, 179, 214, 215, 216, 217, 218, 219, 220

Sands, Jerry, 52–53, 55

San Francisco Giants, 14, 78, 79, 80, 81, 83, 100, 101, 106, 125, 130, 169, 215

Santana, Ervin, 102, 163, 169

Santiago, Benito, 86

Saperstein, Abe, 36

Sardinha, Bronson, 115

Saunders, Joe, 163, 169

Saunders, Tony, 15

Sax, Dave, 72

Sax, Steve, 124

Scheffing, Bob, 172

Schieffer, Tom, 149, 150

Schiller, Derek, 166

Schilling, Curt, 25–26, 28, 29–34, 46, 222

Schmidt, Mike, 92, 129, 133, 134, 203

Schmidt, Willard, 202

Schnaar, Marcia, 38

Schoendienst, Red, 174, 205, 207

Schott, Marge, 138, 139, 144, 145

Schourek, Pete, 138

Schueler, Ron, 78, 79, 81

Schuerholz, John, 165, 166, 168

Schulze, Don, 122, 126

Scioscia, Mike, 102, 164

Scully, Vin, 17

Seaman, Kim, 177, 181

Searcy, Steve, 72, 74

Seattle Mariners, 40, 59–60, 61, 63, 131, 132

Seaver, Tom, 58, 172, 176

Seghi, Phil, 122, 130

Segrist, Kal, 197, 200

Seinfeld, Jerry, 56, 62–63, 222

Selig, Bud, 37, 39, 48, 111

Sexson, Richie, 29

Shantz, Bobby, 199

Shapiro, Mark, 39, 40, 41

Sharperson, Mike, 211

Sheffield, Gary, 14, 17, 20, 21, 22, 23, 81, 219

Shenk, Larry, 90

Shirley, Bob, 177, 180

Short, Bob, 173

Shor, Toots, 198

Showalter, Buck, 109, 140

Sierra, Rubén, 151, 153

Simmons, Ted, 174, 176, 177, 178, 181

Simpson, O. J., 128, 129

Sinatra, Frank, 119

Singleton, Ken, 172

Sizemore, Grady, 35, 41, 43, 44, 45

Slaughter, Enos, 199

Sledge, Terrmel, 160

Smiley, Don, 20, 22

Smiley, John, 138

Smith, Billy, 183

Smith, Hal, 196, 200

Smith, Lee, 90

Smith, Lonnie, 179

Smith, Ozzie, 85, 88, 179

Smoltz, John, 71–72, 74, 166

Snow, J. T., 80

Snyder, Cory, 219

Sojo, Luis, 220

Sorensen, Lary, 170, 176, 178–179, 180

Soriano, Alfonso, 29, 34, 93, 115, 117, 160

Sosa, Sammy, 9, 81, 149–150, 152, 153, 154, 155, 156, 157

Sparks, Joe, 188

Spencer, Jim, 211

Spivey, Junior, 29, 30

Splittorff, Paul, 173

Stanley, Fred, 12, 182–183, 185, 186–187

Stanton, Leroy, 172

Stark, Jayson, 92

St. Claire, Randy, 38

Steinbrenner, George, 26, 27, 28, 29, 34, 56, 57, 58, 59, 61, 63, 64, 68, 139, 140, 145, 182, 183, 184, 185, 186, 187, 190, 191, 211

Steinbrenner, Hank, 99

Stengel, Casey, 171, 173, 192, 195, 197, 198

Stevens, Lee, 40, 45

Stewart, Dave, 151

Stieb, Dave, 130, 176, 212

St. Louis Cardinals, 57, 99, 170, 174–175, 176, 177, 178, 179–180, 180–181, 196, 202, 204, 205, 206, 207, 209

Stoda, Greg, 98

Stone, Jeff, 127, 128

Stoneman, Bill, 163, 164

Stone, Steve, 124

Storm, Hannah, 75, 76
Strange, Doug, 71, 74
Strawberry, Darryl, 57
Sutcliffe, Rick, 10, 84–85, 118–119, 119–121, 122, 123, 124, 125, 126, 221
Sutter, Bruce, 176, 177, 178, 179, 180
Swisher, Steve, 176, 177, 181
Sykes, Bob, 57, 65

Tábata, José, 99
Tampa Bay Devil Rays, 9, 15, 66, 81
Tanana, Frank, 70
Tapani, Kevin, 141
Tartabull, Danny, 216
Tavares, Tony, 38
Taylor, Joe, 202
Teixeira, Mark, 158–160, 161, 162–163, 165, 166, 167–168, 221
Tejada, Miguel, 132
Tekulve, Kent, 176
Templeton, Garry, 88, 175, 179, 217
Tenace, Gene, 177, 180
Terrell, Jerry, 174
Terrell, Walt, 70, 213
Tewksbury, Bob, 58, 70
Texas Rangers, 9, 22, 107–108, 109–110, 111, 112, 114, 115, 116, 117, 147, 148, 149, 150, 151, 152, 153, 154, 155, 156, 157, 159, 160, 161, 163, 164, 165, 167, 168, 172–173, 185, 218, 221
Thomas, Frank, 77, 79, 203
Thomas, Lee, 135, 136, 215
Thrift, Syd, 58
Tidrow, Dick, 82
Toomey, Jim, 206
Torborg, Jeff, 153, 154
Toronto Blue Jays, 68–69, 70, 71, 73, 107–108, 138, 140, 141, 142, 210, 211, 212, 216, 217, 219, 220
Torre, Joe, 205
Torrez, Mike, 190
Trahern, Dallas, 103, 104, 106
Tremendous, Gus, 196

Triandos, Gus, 194, 196, 197, 199, 200
Trillo, Manny, 91, 130, 131, 132, 133, 134, 136
Trotter, Stephanie, 148
Trout, Paul, 70
Trout, Steve, 58, 70
Turley, Bob, 193–195, 198, 200
Tuttle, David, 143, 144, 146

Uggla, Dan, 102
Unser, Del, 90, 94
Urbina, Ugueth, 97
Uribe, Juan, 82
Urrea, John, 177, 181

Valentine, Bobby, 47, 48, 52, 153, 154, 218
Valenzuela, Fernando, 51, 119
Vazquez, Javier, 29, 38
Veeck, Bill, 35–36, 175, 185–186, 187, 188, 191
Ventura, Robin, 79, 81
Victorino, Shane, 49, 54, 55
Vidro, José, 38, 41
Vincent, Fay, 149
Vining, Ken, 79, 82, 83
Visser, Lesley, 76
Vizcaíno, José, 19
Vizquel, Omar, 42, 75, 77
Vosberg, Ed, 24
Vuckovich, Pete, 178, 181
Vukovich, George, 90, 91, 131, 132, 133, 136

Wade, Ed, 28
Walker, Larry, 36
Waller, Ty, 177, 181
Walter, Mark, 49
Warren, Earl, 198
WAR (Wins Above Replacement), 13
 Adrian Gonzalez, 55
 A. J. Burnett, 24
 Alex Rodriguez, 117
 Alfonso Soriano, 34, 117
 Al Leiter, 24, 65
 Allen Webster, 55
 Al Olmsted, 181
 Anaheim Angels, 169

Andre Ethier, 169
Andrew Miller, 106
Andy Pettitte, 146
Arizona Diamondbacks, 34
Ásdrubal Cabrera, 106
Atlanta Braves, 74, 168
Baltimore Orioles, 169, 200
Bartolo Colón, 45
Beau Jones, 168
Bill Miller, 200
Billy Hunter, 200
Bobby Bonilla, 23
Bob Dernier, 94, 136
Bob Geren, 180
Bob Howry, 83
Bob Shirley, 180
Bob Sykes, 65
Bob Turley, 200
Boston Red Sox, 34, 55, 106, 117, 169
Brandon Lyon, 34
Brandon Phillips, 45
Brandon Wood, 169
Brian Manning, 83
Bruce Sutter, 180
Bucky Dent, 191
Burke Badenhop, 106
Byron Browne, 209
Cameron Maybin, 106
Carl Crawford, 55
Casey Fossum, 34
Casey Kotchman, 169
Cecilio Guante, 65
Chad Billingsley, 169
Charles Johnson, 23
Chicago Cubs, 94, 126, 157
Chicago White Sox, 83, 106, 117, 157, 191
Chris Hoiles, 74
Cincinnati Reds, 146
C. J. Nitkowski, 146
Clay Buchholz, 169
Clayton Kershaw, 106, 169
Cleveland Indians, 45, 106, 126, 136
Cliff Lee, 45
Cookie Rojas, 209
Curt Flood, 209
Curt Schilling, 34
Dale Murray, 65
Dallas Trahern, 106

Dan Larsen, 200
Danny Darwin, 83
Darrell Johnson, 200
Darryl Banks, 126
Dave LaPoint, 180
David Green, 180
David Palmer, 74
David Wells, 146
Del Unser, 94
Dennis Cook, 24
Derek Jeter, 146
Derrek Lee, 24
Detroit Tigers, 74, 106, 146
Devon White, 24
Dick Allen, 209
Dick Davis, 94
Dick Kryhoski, 200
Don Leppert, 200
Don McCormack, 94
Don Schulze, 126
Dontrelle Willis, 106
Doug Drabek, 65
Doug Strange, 74
Doyle Alexander, 74
Ed Vosberg, 24
Ed Yarnall, 24
Elvis Andrus, 168
Eric Gagne, 169
Erik Bedard, 169
Ervin Santana, 169
Florida Marlins, 23, 24, 106
Frankie de la Cruz, 106
Fred Manrique, 157
Fred McGriff, 65, 220
Gary Sheffield, 23
Gene Tenace, 180
Gene Woodling, 200
Geoff Goetz, 24
George Bell, 157
George Frazier, 126
George Vukovich, 136
Gio Gonzalez, 106
Grady Sizemore, 45
Gus Triandos, 200
Hal Smith, 200
Harold Baines, 157
Harry Byrd, 200
Hensley Meulens, 65

Howie Kendrick, 169
Ivan De Jesus, 55
Iván DeJesus, 94
Jacoby Ellsbury, 106, 169
Jake Peavy, 55
James Loney, 55, 169
Jarrod Saltalamacchia, 168
Jay Baller, 136
Jay Buhner, 65
Jeff Conine, 24
Jeff Liefer, 45
Jerry Johnson, 209
Jerry Sands, 55
Jerry Willard, 136
Jesse Barfield, 65
Jim Browning, 209
Jim Eisenreich, 23
Jim Fridley, 200
Jim McDonald, 200
Joaquin Árias, 117
Joe Carter, 126, 220
Joe Hoerner, 209
Joe Saunders, 169
John Littlefield, 181
John Smoltz, 74
John Urrea, 181
Jonathan Sanchez, 169
Jon Lester, 117
Jorge De La Rosa, 34
Jorge Posada, 146
Josh Beckett, 55
Juan Samuel, 136
Julio Franco, 136
Kal Segrist, 200
Keith Foulke, 83
Ken Patterson, 157
Ken Phelps, 65
Ken Reitz, 181
Ken Vining, 83
Kevin Brown, 24
Kevin Ritz, 74
Kim Seaman, 181
Kurt Abbott, 24
LaMarr Hoyt, 191
Larry Bowa, 94
Lary Sorensen, 180
Lee Stevens, 45
Leon Durham, 181

Lorenzo Barceló, 83
Los Angeles Dodgers, 23, 55, 106, 169
Luis Aguayo, 94
Magglio Ordóñez, 117
Manny Ramirez, 117
Manny Trillo, 136
Manuel Barrios, 23
Mariano Rivera, 146
Mark Lewis, 146
Mark Teixeira, 168
Matt Cain, 106, 169
Matt Harrison, 168
Matt Kemp, 106
Mel Hall, 126
Miguel Cabrera, 106
Mike Blyzka, 200
Mike Caruso, 83
Mike Goss, 34
Mike Napoli, 55
Mike Phillips, 181
Mike Piazza, 23, 24
Mike Rabelo, 106
Moises Alou, 24
Montreal Expos, 45
Neftalí Feliz, 168
Nick Adenhart, 169
Nick Johnson, 34
Nick Punto, 55
New York Mets, 24
New York Yankees, 34, 65, 117, 146, 191, 200
Nomar Garciaparra, 117
Orlando Hernández, 45
Oscar Gamble, 191
Pat Clements, 65
Pete Vuckovich, 181
Philadelphia Phillies, 94, 136, 209
Reggie Willits, 169
Rick Mahler, 74
Rick Rhoden, 65
Rick Sutcliffe, 126
Robb Nen, 24
Roberto Alomar, 220
Roberto Hernández, 83
Roberto Kelly, 65
Robert Polinsky, 191
Rocky Biddle, 45
Rollie Fingers, 180, 181
Ron Hassey, 126

Ron Mahay, 168
Rubby De La Rosa, 55
Ruben Rivera, 146
Ryan Dempster, 55
Ryne Sandberg, 94
Sammy Sosa, 157
San Diego Padres, 220
San Francisco Giants, 83, 106, 169
Scott Fletcher, 157
Shane Victorino, 55
Sixto Lezcano, 180
Sparky Lyle, 94
Sterling Hitchcock, 146
Steve Searcy, 74
Steve Swisher, 181
St. Louis Cardinals, 180–181, 209
Ted Simmons, 181
Terry Kennedy, 181
Texas Rangers, 117, 157, 168
Theodore Del Guercio, 200
Tim Drew, 45
Tim Lincecum, 106
Tim McCarver, 209
Todd Zeile, 23
Tony Fernández, 220
Ty Waller, 181
Von Hayes, 136
Willie McGee, 65
Willie Montañez, 209
Willy Miranda, 200
Wilson Álvarez, 83, 157

Washington, Claudell, 59
Washington, Ron, 159–160
Wathan, John, 173
Weaver, Earl, 68, 177
Webster, Allen, 51, 53, 54, 55
Weiss, George, 193, 194, 196
Welch, Bob, 119
Wells, David, 10, 26–28, 138–139, 140, 143, 144,
        145, 146
Werndl, Bill, 203
Whitaker, Lou, 70, 144
White, Devon, 24
White, Frank, 173
Whitehurst, Wally, 219
Whitfield, Terry, 186

Whitson, Ed, 129–130
Wickman, Bob, 141
Wieand, Ted, 202
Wilhelm, Hoyt, 10, 197
Wilkerson, Brad, 38, 41, 160
Willard, Jerry, 132, 133, 136
Williams, Bernie, 64
Williams, Brian, 148
Williams, Ted, 134, 135, 172, 173
Willingham, Josh, 104
Willis, Dontrelle, 97, 99, 102, 104, 106
Willits, Reggie, 163, 169
Wills, Bump, 93
Wilson, C. J., 165
Wilson, Enrique, 113
Wilson, Mookie, 211, 213
Wilson, Preston, 24
Wilson, Willie, 215
Winfield, Dave, 57, 59, 64, 139
Winkles, Bobby, 173
Witt, Bobby, 78
Wogan, Adam, 38
Wohlers, Mark, 166
Wood, Brandon, 102, 163, 169
Wood, Kerry, 96
Woodling, Gene, 194, 196, 199, 200
Woods, Gary, 86

Yarnall, Ed, 22, 24
Young, Chris, 160
Young, Cliff, 211
Young, Cy, 10
Young, Michael, 161

Zeile, Todd, 20, 21, 22, 23
Zimmer, Don, 85
Zisk, Richie, 187

e I knew deep in my soul how it could fe
, I got a taste for a ne
any other way feel like
. And you don't want to go back to being y
n. Back before the world got its hands on
i hands on you. And you crave that pump
n a couple decades later, longing once again
the same things that drew me to my journal an
brought me back — a yearning for healing, fa
last year brought this desire into focus. They
y. My forty fourth birthday was just anoth
the first time, that it meant I am nearly
c. I looked around at what I'd built with
ve my life and I love my family, deeply. I
some of the qualities I'd always relied on
ent, always running at high capacity — were b
g years have been a heck of a ride but I t
e. My adrenaline was slowing, revealing in its
e I knew deep in my soul how it could fe
, I got a taste for a new kind of meaning s
any other way feel like wasted time. All t
. And you don't want to go back to being y
n. Back before the world got its hands on
i hands on you. And you crave that pump